Grade 5

Addison-Wesley Mathematics

Robert E. Eicholz
Sharon L. Young

Phares G. O'Daffer
Carne S. Barnett

Randall I. Charles

Stanley R. Clemens
Freddie L. Renfro

Gloria F. Gilmer
Mary M. Thompson

Andy Reeves
Carol A. Thornton

♠ Addison-Wesley Publishing Company

Menlo Park, California ■ Reading, Massachusetts ■ New York
Don Mills, Ontario ■ Wokingham, England ■ Amsterdam ■ Bonn
Sydney ■ Singapore ■ Tokyo ■ Madrid ■ San Juan ■ Paris
Seoul ■ Milan ■ Mexico City ■ Taipei

PROGRAM ADVISORS

John A. Dossey Professor of Mathematics
Illinois State University, Normal, Illinois

Bonnie Armbruster Associate Professor, Center for the Study of Reading
University of Illinois, Champaign, Illinois

Karen L. Ostlund Associate Professor of Science Education
Southwest Texas State University, San Marcos, Texas

Betty C. Lee Assistant Principal
Ferry Elementary School, Detroit, Michigan

William J. Driscoll Chairman, Department of Mathematical Sciences
Central Connecticut State University, New Britain, Connecticut

David C. Brummett Educational Consultant
Palo Alto, California

MULTICULTURAL ADVISORS

Ann Armand-Miller	Bill Bray	Valerna Carter	Moyra Contreras
Gloria Dobbins	Paula Duckett	Barbara Fong	Jeanette Haseyama
James Hopkins	Carol Artiga MacKenzie	Gloria Maldonado	Mattie McCloud
Dolores Mena	Irene Miura	Marsha Muhammad	A. Barretto Ogilvie
Margarita Perez	May-Blossom Wilkinson	Glenna Yee	

CONTRIBUTING WRITERS

Betsy Franco	Mary Heinrich	Penny Holland	Marilyn Jacobson
Ann Muench	Gini Shimabukuro	Marny Sorgen	Connie Thorpe
Sandra Ward	Judith K. Wells		

EXECUTIVE EDITOR

Diane H. Fernández

Cover Photo Credit: Digital Art/West Light

TI-12 Math Explorer™ is a trademark of Texas Instruments.

ISBN: 0-201-86505-X

3 4 5 6 7 8 9 10 11 12 -DO- 98 97 96 95

Contents

3
ADDITION AND SUBTRACTION: WHOLE NUMBERS AND DECIMALS

6

METRIC MEASUREMENT

7

DIVISION: WHOLE NUMBERS AND DECIMALS

8

MORE DIVISION: WHOLE NUMBERS AND DECIMALS

9

UNDERSTANDING FRACTIONS AND MIXED NUMBERS

10

ADDITION AND SUBTRACTION: FRACTIONS AND MIXED NUMBERS

11

CUSTOMARY MEASUREMENT

12

MULTIPLICATION AND DIVISION OF FRACTIONS

13

GEOMETRY

14

RATIO AND PERCENT

Dear Student:

Get ready for an exciting year in mathematics. By the end of the year you'll be a whiz at math! It's going to be fun!

This year, you'll be using what you already know in interesting new ways. For example, you'll be working with huge numbers in the millions and billions — that's a lot of zeros! You'll also learn more about fractions, decimals and calculating averages. You'll become a super problem solver and learn about problems with more than one answer!

Puzzles are fun and some math problems are like puzzles. For example, you'll learn how to figure out the size of the space inside a triangle or a circle.

You'll have opportunities to work in groups and use the Resource Bank in the back of the book which is filled with fascinating facts and ways to help you develop your new math skills.

We know that you will enjoy this exciting year in mathematics.

From your friends at Addison-Wesley.

1

NUMBERS AND OPERATIONS

THEME: WORDS AND SYMBOLS

MATH AND LANGUAGE ARTS

DATA BANK

Use the Language Arts Data Bank on page 468 to answer the questions.

1 If you wanted to do some research on the number system we use, you would be most likely to find the information in books within which group of Dewey Decimal Numbers?

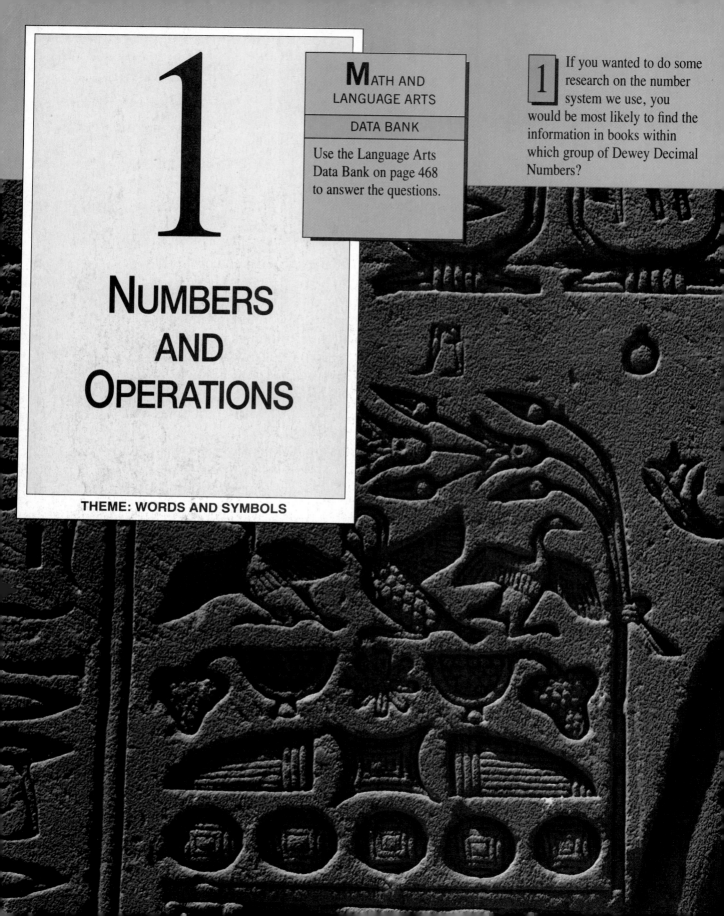

2 In Braille some symbols are used for both numbers and letters. What number in Braille would be written the same as the word "cab"?

3 Write the problem 8 + 12 in Egyptian hieroglyphics. Then write the solution to the problem in Egyptian hieroglyphics.

4 Using Critical Thinking Compare the Egyptian hieroglyphic number symbols with those we use. Describe what you observe to be the main difference between their system and ours.

Picture symbols carved thousands of years ago tell fascinating stories about ancient Egyptians and their culture.

Understanding Numbers

Many math words and symbols appear in newspapers, in magazines, and on television. The language of mathematics is an important part of what you learn in this book.

EXPLORE **Study the Information**

Find at least eight math words and symbols in the article below.

MathMasters Winners Announced

The winner of the 1992 Tri-city MathMasters Contest is eleven-year-old Mai Binh. A fifth grade student at Keller Elementary, Mai correctly solved 49 of the 50 problems on the test for a record score of 98%. Tied for second place with scores of 96% were Ray Parish and Linda Kress of Fairview Elementary.

More than 300 students from the city's twelve elementary schools took part in this year's contest. The average score for all contestants was 80%—another all-time high for this annual contest.

TALK ABOUT IT

1. What are some math words in the article?

2. What are some math symbols in the article?

Numbers can be expressed in different forms. For example, each of the following **numerical expressions** is another name for 24.

Using Symbols	Using Words
3×8	three times eight *or* three multiplied by eight
$15 + 9$	fifteen plus nine *or* nine more than fifteen
$40 - 16$	forty minus sixteen *or* sixteen less than forty

TRY IT OUT

Express the mathematical symbols in words.

1. $7 + 5$ **2.** 8×32 **3.** $48 \div 6$ **4.** $12 - 6$ **5.** $\frac{1}{2}$

Express the mathematical symbols in words.

1. $4 + 34$ **2.** 63×4 **3.** $42 \div 7$ **4.** $16 - 9$ **5.** $\frac{3}{4}$

Choose the correct symbols for the math words. More than one choice may be correct.

6. sixty-five divided by five

 A. $\frac{5}{65}$ **B.** $\frac{65}{5}$ **C.** $65 \div 5$

7. five less than eight

 A. $5 - 8$ **B.** $5 < 8$ **C.** $8 - 5$

8. twenty more than sixty

 A. $20 > 60$ **B.** $60 + 20$ **C.** $20 + 60$

9. one fourth

 A. $\frac{1}{4}$ **B.** 1×4 **C.** $\frac{4}{1}$

Write each numerical expression using symbols.

10. thirty divided by five

11. the product of ten and nine

12. the difference of nine and seven

13. the sum of nine and five

MATH REASONING

Write **true** or **false** for each statement.

14. The numerical expression $\frac{1}{3}$ means both *one third* and *one divided by three.*

15. *Thirty-five divided by seven* has the same meaning as both $35 \div 7$ and $\frac{7}{35}$.

PROBLEM SOLVING

16. This year 21 more students entered the contest than entered last year. Last year 298 entered the contest. Write the numerical expression for the number who entered this year.

17. Language Arts Data Bank How would you write the following numbers using Egyptian hieroglyphic numerals? See page 468.

 A. 13   **B.** 121   **C.** 110,000

▶ **ESTIMATION**

18. Each dot represents one person in a section of the stands in a football stadium. Use the colored lines to help you estimate the total number of people in this section.

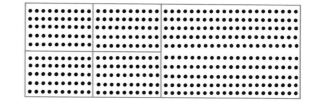

More Practice, page 500, set A

Number Properties

EXPLORE Solve to Understand

Kyle and Dana want to know how many students named neon yellow, rainbow stripes, or apple green as their favorite kind of shoelace. Which child's numerical expression will give the correct total?

Kyle: (5 + 4) + 3
Dana: 5 + (4 + 3)

Do operations inside parentheses ( ) first.

Survey of Students' Favorite Kinds of Shoelaces

color	number of students
neon yellow	5
rainbow stripes	4
apple green	3
candy cane	7

TALK ABOUT IT

1. Does the position of the parentheses in Kyle's and Dana's expressions change the value? Explain.

2. Give a numerical expression whose value changes when the position of the parentheses changes. (Hint: You may have to use two operations.)

These **number properties** help us evaluate expressions.

Commutative (Order) Property
Changing the order of addends or factors does not change the sum or product.

$9 + 3 = 12$

$3 + 9 = 12$

$5 \times 3 = 15$

$3 \times 5 = 15$

Associative (Grouping) Property
Changing the grouping of addends or factors does not change the sum or product.

$3 + (7 + 8) = 18$

$(3 + 7) + 8 = 18$

$5 \times (1 \times 3) = 15$

$(5 \times 1) \times 3 = 15$

Give the property that tells you that both expressions name the same number.

1. $42 + 10 = 10 + 42$

2. $(20 + 8) + 4 = 20 + (8 + 4)$

3. $2 \times (4 \times 6) = (2 \times 4) \times 6$

4. $4 \times 5 = 5 \times 4$

Give the property that tells you that each expression names
the same number.

1. $25 + 12 = 12 + 25$
2. $(6 \times 1) \times 5 = 6 \times (1 \times 5)$
3. $3 + (4 + 6) = (3 + 4) + 6$
4. $16 + (7 + 9) = (16 + 7) + 9$
5. $8 \times 2 = 2 \times 8$
6. $3 \times (4 \times 2) = (3 \times 4) \times 2$
7. $(17 + 11) + 5 = 17 + (11 + 5)$
8. $15 + (5 + 9) = (15 + 5) + 9$

Find the value of each expression.

9. $6 + (8 + 1)$
10. $(36 \div 4) + 5$
11. $(3 + 4) \times 6$
12. $(13 - 7) \times 8$
13. $(7 + 1) + 8$
14. $(6 + 8) - 9$
15. $(24 \div 3) \times 4$
16. $13 - (45 \div 9)$
17. $9 + (4 \times 2)$

APPLY

MATH REASONING

Copy the equations and put in parentheses
to show which operation was done first.

18. $4 \times 2 + 5 = 13$
19. $3 \times 4 - 3 = 9$
20. $8 \times 5 + 2 = 56$

21. $2 \times 4 + 3 = 14$
22. $3 + 4 \times 5 = 35$
23. $24 \div 6 + 2 = 3$

PROBLEM SOLVING

Use the table on page 6.

24. How many students named rainbow
stripes, apple green, or neon yellow
as their favorite?

25. How many more students named
candy cane than named apple green
as their favorite?

MIXED REVIEW

Add, subtract, multiply, or divide.

26. $5 + 8$
27. $6 + 7$
28. $4 + 6$
29. $3 + 9$
30. $6 + 8$

31. $12 - 5$
32. $15 - 9$
33. $11 - 3$
34. $17 - 9$
35. $10 - 6$

36. 8×3
37. 6×6
38. 4×7
39. 5×8
40. 7×2

41. $24 \div 4$
42. $18 \div 6$
43. $15 \div 5$
44. $28 \div 7$
45. $30 \div 6$

More Practice, page 500, set B

Mental Math
Using Compatible Numbers

LEARN ABOUT IT

EXPLORE **Examine the Data**

The Eager Readers Club made a table
to show how many and what kinds of
books the members read during summer
vacation. Ray and Wanda wanted to find
out how many books the members read
in all.

Kind of Book	Number Read
Mystery	90
Adventure	75
Sports	38
Famous People	10
Others	25

Ray used his calculator to solve the problem this way:

$\boxed{\text{ON/AC}}$ $\boxed{90}$ $\boxed{+}$ $\boxed{75}$ $\boxed{+}$ $\boxed{38}$ $\boxed{+}$ $\boxed{10}$ $\boxed{+}$ $\boxed{25}$ $\boxed{=}$?

Wanda used **mental math** to solve the problem this way: $(90 + 10) + (75 + 25) + 38 = ?$

TALK ABOUT IT

1. Do you think that Ray and Wanda got the same answer?

2. What do the parentheses ( ) tell about what Wanda did?

When there are three or more addends or factors in a
problem involving addition or multiplication, look for
compatible numbers. Compatible numbers are numbers
that are easy to compute mentally. Here is how.

Find: $25 + 19 + 75 + 1$ Think: 25 and 75 are easy to add mentally.
                                                     19 and 1 are easy to add mentally.

The commutative and associative properties let you
rearrange and regroup addends.

$(25 + 75) + (19 + 1) = 100 + 20 = 120$

TRY IT OUT

Order and group the addends and factors to make it easy to
compute mentally. Then give the sums and products.

1. $39 + 60 + 17 + 1$ 2. $4 \times 13 \times 25$ 3. $120 + 57 + 80$

4. $50 \times 25 \times 2 \times 4$ 5. $530 + 290 + 70 + 8$ 6. $5 \times 18 \times 20$

Show how you would change the order and grouping. Then solve using mental math.

1. $9 + 23 + 1$ **2.** $5 \times 19 \times 2$ **3.** $75 + 16 + 25$

4. $3 + 40 + 7 + 50$ **5.** $20 \times 37 \times 5$ **6.** $60 + 36 + 40$

7. $50 \times 18 \times 2$ **8.** $25 + 9 + 25$ **9.** $15 + 190 + 2 + 10$

10. $4 \times 8 \times 25$ **11.** $6 + 9 + 94 + 1$ **12.** $87 \times 2 \times 10 \times 5$

13. $95 + 113 + 5$ **14.** $2 \times 160 \times 5$ **15.** $50 + 8 + 3 + 50$

16. $2 \times 31 \times 50$ **17.** $170 + 17 + 30$ **18.** $50 \times 9 \times 2$

19. $125 + 36 + 75$ **20.** $5 \times 4 \times 3 \times 5$

APPLY

MATH REASONING

Name the property (commutative or associative) used to complete steps B and C.

21. A. $25 + (38 + 25)$
B. $25 + (25 + 38)$
C. $(25 + 25) + 38$

22. A. $(14 + 28) + 16$
B. $16 + (14 + 28)$
C. $(16 + 14) + 28$

PROBLEM SOLVING

23. Use the table on page 8. What is the total number of these kinds of books that were read during the summer by the club members: sports, mystery, and famous people?

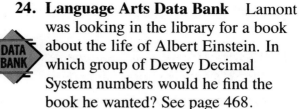

24. Language Arts Data Bank   Lamont was looking in the library for a book about the life of Albert Einstein. In which group of Dewey Decimal System numbers would he find the book he wanted? See page 468.

▶ **MENTAL MATH**

When adding or subtracting a 1, 2, or 3, you can count on or count back to find the sum or difference mentally. For example, to find $49 + 3$, start with 49 and count on: 49.....50, 51, 52. $49 + 3 = 52$

Solve mentally by counting on or counting back.

25. $19 + 2$ **26.** $298 + 3$ **27.** $30 - 1$ **28.** $51 - 2$ **29.** $3 + 679$

Problem Solving
Understanding the Operations

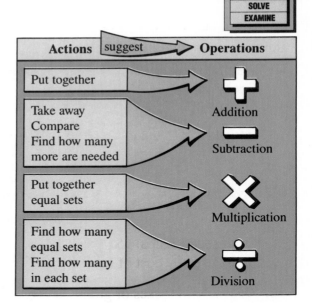

UNDERSTAND			
ANALYZE DATA			
PLAN			
ESTIMATE			
SOLVE			
EXAMINE			

Actions suggest → **Operations**

Put together		$+$ Addition
Take away Compare Find how many more are needed		$-$ Subtraction
Put together equal sets		$\times$ Multiplication
Find how many equal sets Find how many in each set		$\div$ Division

LEARN ABOUT IT

The action in a problem suggests the operation needed to solve the problem. The diagram at the right reviews the actions you learned about in earlier grades.

Sometimes the actions in problems are not easy to recognize. You need to think carefully to decide which of the operations they suggest. Study the examples below.

Tammy had some old coins. She gave 5 of them to Lita and has 4 coins left. How many coins did she have before she gave some away?

Since I want to find how many coins she had to begin with, I need to find the total of the coins she gave away and the coins she still has.

$$4 + 5 = 9$$

Tim had some Presidents buttons. A friend gave him 5 more buttons. Now he has 13. How many buttons did he have before his friend gave him some more?

I want to find how many he already had, so I need to find the difference in the amount he has now and the amount he was given.

$$13 - 5 = 8$$

TRY IT OUT

Name the operation you need to use for each problem. Then solve the problem.

1. Joanna shows 14 different baseball caps in this year's hobby show. Last year she showed only 8. How many more caps did she show this year?

2. Skip has 18 national parks posters. He has 3 from each park he visited. How many parks did he visit?

3. School posters cost $9 each last year. This year they cost $4 more than last year. How much does a school poster cost this year?

4. Brenda bought 3 Save-the-Seals T-shirts. They cost $8 each. How much did Brenda spend for all 3?

Name the operation you need to use. Then solve.

1. Chris had some glass bears. He was given 8 more for his birthday. Now he has 15. How many glass bears did he have before his birthday?

2. Renaldo has 9 famous player baseball cards and 7 famous player football cards. How many famous player cards does he have altogether?

3. Each school T-shirt costs the same amount. Anita paid $15 for 3 T-shirts. What was the cost of each T-shirt?

4. Janis had 12 boxes of greeting cards to sell for a school fund-raising project. She has sold all but 3 boxes of cards. How many boxes has she sold?

5. Anita bought 6 Big Bend National Park arm patches for her friends at home. Each patch costs $3. How much did she spend for the patches?

6. Russ wants to buy a stamp album that costs $18. He has $9. How much more money does he need to buy the album?

7. The Woo family takes a 7-mile bicycle trip together every Saturday in good weather. How far would they ride during 5 trips?

8. Barbara has 48 coins in her coin book. Each page has 8 coins on it. How many pages of her book are filled with coins?

9. Judy now has 9 lava rocks in her rocks box. She did have more, but she gave 8 of them to Ernie yesterday. How many lava rocks did Judy have before she gave some to Ernie?

10. **Write Your Own Problem**   Write a question that you could answer by using the data in this story. Then answer your question.

    In 1987 Kari had 9 full books of stamps. In 1990 she had 14 full books of stamps.

Exploring Algebra
Understanding Variables

Riddle: *What do* MATH *and* READING *have in common?*

To solve the riddle, follow these steps:

- Find the number each letter in the equations stands for. Each letter stands for **0, 1, 2, 3, 4,** or **5** and stands for the same number in each equation.

- Copy the Riddle Answer Key.

- Write each letter above the number it stands for in the equations.

Riddle Answer Key

$$\overline{0}\ \overline{1}\ \overline{2}\ \ \ \overline{3}\ \overline{2}\ \overline{0}\ \ \ \overline{0}\ \overline{2}\ \overline{4}\ \ \ \overline{5}$$

Equations

$$L \times H = L \qquad\qquad E + E = R$$
$$E + T = E \qquad\qquad A - H = R$$

Zero Property of Addition
The sum of a number and zero is that number.

Zero Property of Subtraction
When zero is subtracted from a number, the difference is that number.

One Property of Multiplication
The product of a number and one is that number.

Zero Property of Multiplication
The product of a number and zero is zero.

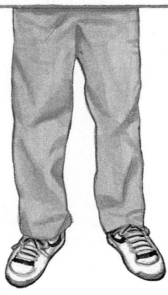

TALK ABOUT IT

1. Which number property did you use to find the number that H stands for in the equation $L \times H = L$?

2. Which number property did you use to find the number that T stands for in the equation $E + T = E$?

This book introduces you to several topics from algebra. One of the most important of these topics is the idea of a **variable.** A variable is a letter that stands for a single number or a range of numbers.

In the boxed equations each variable stands for one of these numbers: 1, 2, 5, 6, or 7. The same variable stands for the same number in each equation. Find the number each variable stands for.

$$C \times C = 36 \qquad H \times T = H$$
$$E + H = 9 \qquad C + E = 8$$
$$H - A = E$$

POWER PRACTICE/QUIZ

Express the math symbols in words.

1. $9 + 11$ **2.** 6×45 **3.** $63 \div 9$ **4.** $22 - 7$ **5.** $\frac{1}{3}$

Choose the correct symbols for the math words. More than one choice may be correct.

6. thirty-five divided by seven

   A. $35 \div 7$ **B.** $\frac{35}{7}$ **C.** $7 \div 35$

7. seven less than fifteen

   A. $7 < 15$ **B.** $15 - 7$ **C.** $7 - 15$

8. the sum of nine and eight

   A. $8 + 9$ **B.** 8×9 **C.** $9 + 8$

9. the product of four and six

   A. $6 \div 4$ **B.** $4 + 6$ **C.** 4×6

Use the properties to help you find the missing numbers.

10. $15 \times 1 = \blacksquare$

11. $4 + (5 + 6) = (\blacksquare + 5) + 6$

12. $12 + 0 = \blacksquare + 12$

13. $8 + \blacksquare = 8$

14. $(3 \times 5) \times 7 = (\blacksquare \times 3) \times 7$

15. $(4 \times 1) \times 5 = \blacksquare \times (\blacksquare \times 5)$

16. $(8 \times 5) \times 2 = (2 \times 5) \times \blacksquare$

17. $\blacksquare + (8 + 4) = (4 + 6) + 8$

Solve using mental math.

18. $5 \times 17 \times 2$

19. $8 + 127 + 2$

20. $12 + 25 + 8$

21. $147 \times 5 \times 2$

22. $60 + 87 + 40$

23. $96 \times 5 \times 20$

24. $16 + 8 + 4 + 19 + 2$

25. $25 \times 7 \times 3 \times 4$

26. $17 + 46 + 23 + 4$

PROBLEM SOLVING

Name the operation that you need to use for each problem. Then solve the problem.

27. Greg has 1 homework assignment for each of the 6 classes he takes. How many homework assignments does he have?

28. Loni plans to read 6 pages in her language arts book and 2 pages in her science book. How many pages does she plan to read?

29. Mary has 2 crossword puzzle books and 5 number puzzle books. How many more number puzzle books than crossword puzzle books does she have?

30. Bill must read 12 pages in his social studies textbook. He will read 4 pages each day. How many days will it take him to finish his reading?

Using Critical Thinking

LEARN ABOUT IT

When Carlos saw his friend Holly, he showed her this record of tips he had made during his first two days of work at the diner. He wondered how much money he would make in tips after six days. "Wow," Carlos exclaimed, "if I can keep this pattern going, I'll have made $126 in tips in my first six days!" "Something's wrong with your calculations," Holly said. "At most you'd make $42 in tips." When they asked Patty to settle the argument, she exclaimed, "Sorry, but you're both wrong! Carlos would make exactly $62 in tips this week."

Who do you think was correct, if anyone?

TALK ABOUT IT

1. What was Carlos trying to do?

2. How did Carlos, Holly, and Patty get their answers?

3. Who, if anyone, is correct—Carlos, Holly, or Patty?

4. Using Carlos' pattern, what would be the total amount of money he would have made in tips at the end of ten days?

5. Can you determine a pattern for certain with just two numbers? with three numbers? Explain.

TIP RECORD	
Day Number	Amount of Tips
1	2
2	4
3	
4	
5	
6	

TRY IT OUT

Look for a pattern. Give the next three numbers.

1. 1, 2, 2, 3, 3, 3, 4, 4, 4, 4, 5, 5, 5, 5, ▦ , ▦ , ▦ , ...

2. 1, 2, 3, 2, 4, 6, 4, 5, 6, 8, 10, 12, 7, 8, 9, ▦ , ▦ , ▦ , ...

14

Look for a pattern in the tables below. Suppose it continues.
Give the next 2 numbers.

Weeks	New Employees		Months	Hamburger Sales (1000s)		Years	Savings ($1000)
1	1		1	2		1	2
2	3		2	5		2	4
3	5		3	8		3	6
3. 4	▓		**5.** 4	▓		**7.** 4	▓
4. 5	▓		**6.** 5	▓		**8.** 5	▓

Give the next three numbers in each pattern.

9. 1, 3, 5, 7, 9, ▓, ▓, ▓, ...

10. 2, 6, 10, 14, 18, ▓, ▓, ▓, ...

11. 1, 2, 4, 7, 11, ▓, ▓, ▓, ...

12. 1, 4, 9, 16, 25, ▓, ▓, ▓, ...

13. 5, 15, 25, 35, ▓, ▓, ▓, ...

14. 50, 43, 36, 29, 22, ▓, ▓, ▓, ..

15. 5, 5, 10, 6, 6, 12, ▓, ▓, ▓, ...

16. 1, 1, 2, 3, 5, 8, ▓, ▓, ▓, ...

17. What patterns do you see in the graph at the right?

18. What would you predict would be the numbers of band members and chorus members in 1990 and 1991?

BAND AND CHORUS MEMBERS

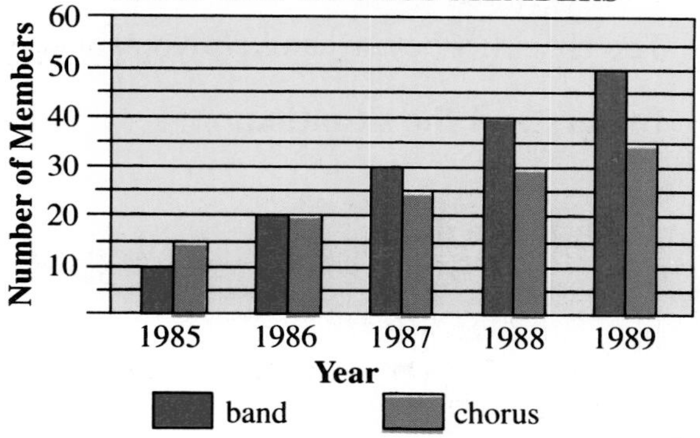

MIXED REVIEW

Give the property that tells you that each expression names the same number.

19. 12 + 15 = 15 + 12

20. 3 + (8 + 6) = (3 + 8) + 6

21. 7 + 0 = 7

22. (1 × 5) × 7 = (5 × 1) × 7

Choose compatible numbers and find the sum or product.

23. 75 + 18 + 25 + 12

24. 4 × 2 × 6 × 50

25. 150 + 17 + 50 + 3

26. 25 × 2 × 2 × 9

27. 4 × 8 × 25 × 2

28. 125 + 27 + 3 + 75

Problem Solving
Introduction

UNDERSTAND
ANALYZE DATA
PLAN
ESTIMATE
SOLVE
EXAMINE

LEARN ABOUT IT

Some problems can be solved by using one of the operations—addition, subtraction, multiplication, or division. These are called **one-step** problems. One-step problems can be solved using the strategy **Choose the Operation**.

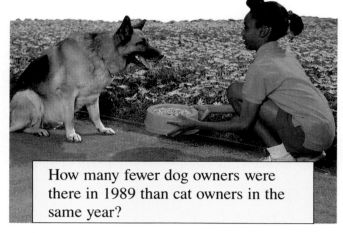

How many fewer dog owners were there in 1989 than cat owners in the same year?

Pets Owned (1,400 people surveyed)		
Pet	1989	1990
Cat	621	560
Dog	582	601
Birds	89	93
Fish	61	52
Other	43	94

The checklist below can help you solve problems.

Understand the situation.

> I want to compare the number of dog owners to the number of cat owners in 1989.

Analyze the data.

> Dogs in 1989: 582   Cats in 1989: 621

Plan what to do.

> Since I want to **compare** the two numbers, I should subtract.

Estimate the answer.

> 582 is about 580. 621 is about 620.
> 620 − 580 = 40   The answer should be about 40.

Solve the problem.

> 621 − 582 = 39   There were 39 fewer dog owners than cat owners in 1989.

Examine the answer.

> 39 is close to the estimate of 40, so 39 is a reasonable answer.

TRY IT OUT

Choose the numerical expression you would use to solve the problem.

1. How many more dog owners were there in 1990 than in 1989?

   A. 582 + 601   **B.** 601 − 582

2. What was the total number of cat owners and dog owners in 1990?

   A. 621 + 582   **B.** 560 + 601

Pick the numerical expression you would use to solve the problem.

1. The number of fish owners in 1991 is expected to be twice as great as it was in 1989. How many fish owners are there expected to be in 1991?

   A. 61 + 2
   B. 2 × 61

2. The number of bird owners in 1990 was three times the number of bird owners in 1980. How many bird owners were there in 1980?

   A. 93 ÷ 3
   B. 93 × 3

3. An average dog eats $250 worth of dog food in a year. How much was spent on dog food by the people surveyed in 1990?

   A. $250 + 601
   B. $250 × 601

4. The people surveyed came from 5 regions of the U.S. Each region had the same number of people. How many were from each region?

   A. 1,400 × 5
   B. 1,400 ÷ 5

Solve.

5. One kind of dry dog food sells for $5 a bag. Each bag lasts a week. How much would it cost to buy this dog food for 1 month (4 weeks)?

6. Ali bought collars for her 4 puppies. The collars cost $16 in all. Each collar cost the same. What was the cost for each collar?

7. Muffin had two litters of kittens. There were 6 kittens in her first litter. There were 5 kittens in her second litter. How many kittens did Muffin have?

8. **Data Hunt** Make a survey of 10 of your friends. Find out how many have dogs or cats as pets. Find how many more there are of one kind of pet than there are of the other.

Write Your Own Problem

Write questions that can be answered using the data given in the table on page 16 and the numerical expressions given below.

9. 93 − 52

10. 560 + 601

11. 601 − 560

More Practice, page 522, set B

17

Problem Solving
Deciding When to Estimate

UNDERSTAND
ANALYZE DATA
PLAN
ESTIMATE
SOLVE
EXAMINE

When you solve problems, you must decide whether you need an **estimate** or an **exact answer:** When you make an estimate, you are finding *about how much* or *about how many.*

Movie Prices	
Student: $2.50	Adult: $4.75
Popcorn	**Drinks**
Large: $1.50	Small (8 oz): $1.25
Small: $0.95	Large (12 oz): $1.95

Suppose you have $5. Do you have enough money for a ticket, a small box of popcorn, and a small drink?

All I need to know is whether I have enough money. I can estimate the total cost.

How much change should a student get from $5 for a ticket and a large box of popcorn?

A clerk must give the exact amount. I need to find the exact answer.

These examples show that the person who needs the answer and the real-world situation help you decide whether an exact answer or an estimate is needed.

TRY IT OUT

Explain whether you should estimate the answer or whether you need an exact answer.

1. You have $2.00. Can you afford to buy a small drink and a large popcorn?

2. What is the total cost of 3 adult tickets?

3. You have a $10 bill. Can you buy a large drink for each of your 4 friends and yourself?

Explain whether you can estimate the answer or whether you need an exact answer.

1. The show will start at 1:56 p.m. It will last 1 hour and 49 minutes. What time should you tell your parents they should meet you outside the theater at the end of the show?

2. Fulton School has 317 girls and 289 boys. If a family friend asks you how many students are in the school, what kind of answer would you give?

3. Fruit drinks cost 75¢ each and apples cost 45¢ each. Jered had $3. Did he have enough money to buy 2 drinks and 1 apple?

4. There are 34 red gym shirts and 28 green gym shirts in a box. How many more shirts are needed for the 100 students who take gym?

5. Suppose you saved $15. How much more money do you need to buy a school jacket that costs $29.95?

6. A school bus can hold 65 students. This morning there were 12 empty seats. How many students were on the bus?

7. Maria bought 12 stamps for the invitations to her birthday party. Each stamp cost 29¢. How much did she pay altogether for the stamps?

8. Karla sold posters for the student council. Each poster sells for $8.95. Will she reach her goal of $100 if she sells 10 posters?

9. The 5th-6th grade band has 35 members. Last year there were 47 members. How many more were in the band last year?

10. Each student will drink about 2 cans of juice at the school picnic. How many cans of juice should be bought if there are 78 students coming to the picnic?

11. **Determining Reasonable Answers**   Tell whether the calculator answer is reasonable. If it is not, explain why not.

    Each section of the bleachers holds 125 students. How many students can sit in 5 sections?

Group Decision Making

UNDERSTAND
ANALYZE DATA
PLAN
ESTIMATE
SOLVE
EXAMINE

Group Skills
Listen to Others
Encourage and Respect Others
Explain and Summarize
Check for Understanding
Disagree in an Agreeable Way

You will be asked to work with other students for many lessons in this book. To make a good team, all members of your group need to feel that their ideas and questions are important. Building a good team spirit is one of the keys to working successfully in cooperative groups.

Suppose someone in your group suggests an idea that the rest of you think will not work. What could you say to the person that would show that you respect his or her opinion even though you disagree with the idea? What might you do or say to make sure that the person will feel free to offer suggestions in the future?

Cooperative Activity

For this activity your group will need 8 blue blocks, 4 yellow blocks, and 4 red blocks and a grid like the one below. Use the rules that follow to place the blocks in the grid.

20

Rule 1   There are at least 2 blues in the first row.

Rule 2   There are no reds in row 2.

Rule 3   There are exactly 2 yellows in either row 2 or row 3, but not in both rows.

Rule 4   Each blue touches at least 1 other blue at corners. No blues are next to each other in a row or column.

Some Questions to Answer

1. How many different ways did you find to arrange the blocks?

2. Have each person in your group talk about whether or not they thought they were able to contribute their fair share of ideas.

3. Was it difficult to do this activity together? Explain why or why not.

Check Your Group Skills

4. Think about how your group worked together. Give two or three examples of how someone gave encouragement or treated another group member with respect.

21

WRAP UP

Vocabulary Match

Match each phrase on the left with the correct word(s) on the right. Some words will not be used.

1. a way of naming a number
2. computing in your head
3. find about how many or how much
4. a property that states that you can change the order of numbers
5. a property that states that you can change the grouping of numbers

A. parentheses
B. mental math
C. associative property
D. commutative property
E. estimate
F. numerical expression

Sometimes, Always, Never

Complete each statement by writing **sometimes, always,** or **never.** Explain your choice.

6. Thirty-six divided by nine is __?__ written in symbols as $36 \div 9$.

7. When you evaluate an expression that includes parentheses ( ), you should __?__ do the operations inside parentheses last.

8. If $B = 3$, $C = 1$, and $D = 4$, then $B + C$ will __?__ equal D and $D - C$ will __?__ equal B.

Project

All whole numbers except 0 can be written as sums of other whole numbers in different ways. For example, $8 = 3 + 5$, $8 = 6 + 2$, $8 = 1 + 3 + 4$, and so on. Some whole numbers can be written as the sum of consecutive numbers. For example, $3 = 0 + 1 + 2$, $6 = 0 + 1 + 2 + 3$, and so on. For each whole number from 1 through 15, find all possible ways to write the number as a sum of consecutive numbers.

POWER PRACTICE/TEST

Part 1 Understanding

Write the numerical expression using symbols.

1. the product of four and six

2. forty-five divided by five

3. one less than nineteen

Give an example of each property.

4. commutative property, addition

5. commutative property, multiplication

6. associative property, addition

7. associative property, multiplication

Part 2 Skills

Find the value of these expressions using mental math.

8. $75 + 87 + 25$

9. $20 \times 47 \times 5$

10. $16 \times 4 \times 25$

11. $60 + 93 + 2 + 40$

Find the value of each variable in the following equations. Each variable stands for one and only one of these numbers: 2, 3, 4, 5, and 7.

12. $M + P = R$ $P + P = T$ $R - T = S$ $P + S = M$

Part 3 Applications

13. Name the operation. Then solve. At the bookstore, paperback books cost $5 and hardback books cost $9. What is the cost of 6 paperbacks?

14. Tell whether you need an exact answer or an estimate. Then solve.
Jim wants to buy a book for $6.95 and a globe for $18.25. He has $22. Does he have enough money?

15. **Challenge.** Carla asked students who had pets to tell her what kind of pets they had. She made a table.

	Kind of pet			
	Dog	Cat	Bird	Fish
Number of Students	5	4	3	7

Four students had 2 kinds of pets each. One student had 3 kinds. All the rest had 1 kind of pet each. How many students had at least 1 kind of pet?

23

ENRICHMENT
Triangular and Square Numbers

Early Greek mathematicians related numbers to shapes. Look at the arrangements of dots shown at right. Can you see why 6 is an example of a triangular number and why 9 is an example of a square number?

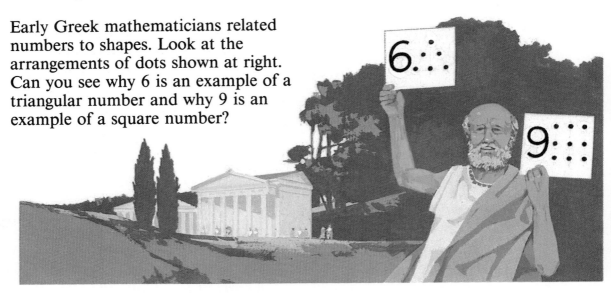

The chart below shows several patterns with triangular numbers.

Dot Arrangement	Triangular Number	Difference	Equation
•	1		1 = 1
		2	
••	3		1 + 2 = 3
		3	
••••	6		1 + 2 + 3 = 6
		4	
•••••	10		1 + 2 + 3 + 4 = 10

1. Describe the pattern you see between triangular numbers and their differences.

2. Describe the pattern you see in the number sentences.

3. There are 15 triangular numbers from 1 through 120. Use the patterns in the chart to find and list them.

4. Make a similar chart for square numbers. The first four square numbers are 1, 4, 9, and 16. What patterns do you find?

CUMULATIVE REVIEW

Add, subtract, multiply, or divide.

1. 7 × 9

   A. 72   B. 54   C. 56   D. 63

2. 80 + 320 + 6

   A. 386 B. 326 C. 406 D. 460

3. 447 − 20

   A. 227 B. 220 C. 427 D. 467

4. 32 ÷ 4

   A. 9   B. 8   C. 7R4 D. 8R2

Name each figure.

5.
A. angle
B. perpendicular lines
C. segment
D. parallel lines

6.
A. circle
B. cube
C. square
D. trapezoid

7.

A. congruent segments
B. perpendicular lines
C. parallel lines
D. skew lines

8. How would you group these factors to find the product of 45 × 4 × 10 × 25 mentally?

  A. (4 × 10) × (25 × 45)
  B. (4 × 25) × (45 × 10)
  C. (45 × 4) × (10 × 25)
  D. (10 × 25) × (45 × 4)

Choose the correct symbols.

9. twenty-four more than eighty-two

  A. 24 × 82   B. 82 ÷ 24
  C. 82 − 24   D. 82 + 24

10. fifty divided by five

  A. $\frac{5}{50}$ B. 5 ÷ 50
  C. 50 − 5   D. $\frac{50}{5}$

Choose the operation or symbol you need to solve each problem.

11. Barbara has invited 6 girls to her birthday party. She wants to give each girl 3 small gifts. How many gifts should she buy?

  A. addition   B. multiplication
  C. subtraction D. division

12. Erik wants to buy a school jacket that costs $24. If he saves $4 a week, how many weeks will it take him to save enough money to buy the jacket?

  A. +   B. ×
  C. −   D. ÷

2

PLACE VALUE: WHOLE NUMBERS AND DECIMALS

THEME: COLONIAL HISTORY

MATH AND SOCIAL STUDIES

DATA BANK

Use the Social Studies Data Bank on page 480 to answer the questions.

1 How many more states entered the Union in 1788 than in 1787? How many states had entered the Union by the end of 1788?

2 How many decades old must a state be before it can celebrate its 100th birthday? before it can celebrate its 200th birthday?

3 How many of the original 13 states had been part of the Union for two centuries by the end of 1987?

4 Using Critical Thinking What will the next century be called? In what year will that century begin? In what year will that century end? Use the data to justify your answers.

Students reach out to touch the Liberty Bell, symbol of our nation's independence for over 200 years.

Place Value Through Thousands

LEARN ABOUT IT

EXPLORE Use Play Money
Work in groups. Imagine that you are
a bank teller. Use play money to show
$1,256 in 3 different ways. Use only
$1,000, $100, $10, and $1 bills.

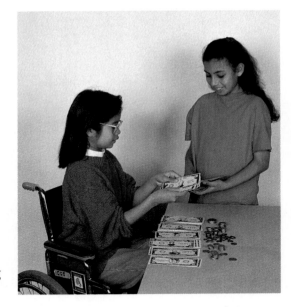

TALK ABOUT IT

1. Can you show $1,256 without using any
   $1,000 bills? Explain.

2. Describe how you can show $1,256 using
   the fewest pieces of play money.

All whole numbers can be written using only the **digits** 0, 1,
2, 3, 4, 5, 6, 7, 8, and 9. Large numbers are separated by
commas into groups with three digits, called **periods.** The
value of a digit is shown by its **place** in a number.

Periods →

Place values →

	Thousands Period			Ones Period		
hundred thousands	ten thousands	thousands	hundreds	tens	ones
2	3	8	4	7	5
200,000	30,000	8,000	400	70	5

We write, in **expanded form:** 200,000 + 30,000 + 8,000 + 400 + 70 + 5
We write, in **standard form:** 238,475
We read: "two hundred thirty-eight thousand, four hundred seventy-five"

TRY IT OUT

Write each in standard form and in expanded form.

1. two thousand, five hundred forty

2. nine hundred sixty-five

3. seven hundred ninety-one thousand, six hundred twenty-one

Read each number. Then use place value to tell what the red digit means.

4. 213,546   5. 19,798   6. 3,725   7. 638,407

Write the number for each amount in standard form.

1.

2 thousands, 3 hundreds, 4 tens, 1 one

2. 4 thousands, 4 hundreds, 4 ones

Use place value to tell what the red digit in each number means.

3. 37,649   4. 213,765   5. 347,821   6. 792,463

Write in standard form.

7. 500,000 + 80,000 + 3,000 + 70 + 2   8. 800,000 + 70,000 + 400 + 60 + 5

9. 400,000 + 3,000 + 70 + 8   10. 90,000 + 10 + 7

Write in standard form and in expanded form.

11. forty-five thousand, six hundred   12. two hundred forty-eight thousand

13. seven hundred twenty-five thousand,   14. seven hundred thirty thousand, one
    sixty

Write each number in words.

15. 39,405   16. 61,824   17. 135,400   18. 794,608

MATH REASONING

The beads on the number frame show the number 314,412.

Draw number frames that show: **19.** 421,304   **20.** 204,213

PROBLEM SOLVING

21. Karla cashed a check for a customer and gave him these
    bills: 6 tens, 2 thousands, 4 ones, and 7 hundreds.
    What was the amount of the check that she cashed?

▶ **USING CRITICAL THINKING   Support Your Conclusion**

22. Mary claimed that the value of each place on a place-
    value chart is 10 times the value of the place to its
    right. Is she correct? Give examples to explain.

More Practice, page 500, set D

Millions and Billions

EXPLORE **Make a Decision**

- 1 thousand tennis balls would fill a box about 1 foot deep and 3 feet on each side.
- 1 million (1,000 thousand or 1,000,000) tennis balls would fill a space the size of a classroom.

Do you think your entire school is big enough to hold 1 billion (1,000 million or 1,000,000,000) tennis balls?

TALK ABOUT IT

1. About how many classrooms would be needed to hold 10 million (10,000,000) tennis balls?
2. About how many classrooms would be needed to hold 100 million (100,000,000) tennis balls?
3. How does thinking of 1 billion as 1,000 million help to think about the number of classrooms needed for 1 billion tennis balls?

The table below shows how the smaller periods relate to the larger periods.

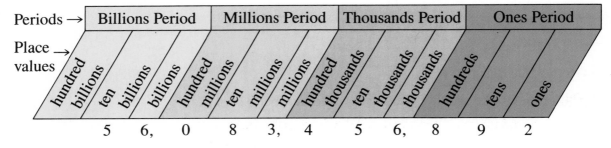

Periods →	Billions Period			Millions Period			Thousands Period			Ones Period		
Place values →	hundred billions	ten billions	billions	hundred millions	ten millions	millions	hundred thousands	ten thousands	thousands	hundreds	tens	ones
	5	6,	0	8	3,	4	5	6,	8	9	2

We read: "fifty-six billion, eighty-three million, four hundred fifty-six thousand, eight hundred ninety-two"

Read each number. Then use place value to tell what the red digit means.

1. 5,937,862
2. 935,467,854
3. 836,975,123,468
4. 9,367,800,672

Use place value to tell what each red digit means.

1. 14,753,000   **2.** 368,571,000,000   **3.** 35,296,417   **4.** 73,550,221

Give the letter for the number in the list in which the digit 4 has a value of

5. 400,000   **6.** 4,000,000,000

7. 4,000,000   **8.** 400,000,000

A 354,782,631,983	B 782,629,480,115
C 356,487,215,009	D 209,364,080,296

Write in standard form.

9. 700,000,000 + 30,000,000 + 2,000,000 + 500,000 + 4,000

10. 800,000,000,000 + 5,000,000,000 + 600,000,000 + 2,000,000

11. three hundred forty-five million, eight hundred two thousand, six hundred

12. fifty-four billion, two hundred fifteen million, one thousand, three hundred

Write each number in words.

13. 510,431,200   **14.** 650,215,400,020

APPLY

MATH REASONING

15. How much greater is A than B?
   A. 718,425,319,250   **B.** 717,425,319,250

PROBLEM SOLVING

16. A company said it made 1,000,000 tennis balls in 1 year. The same year it made 10 times as many table tennis balls as tennis balls. How many table tennis balls was that?

MIXED REVIEW

Use the number properties to help you find the missing numbers.

17. $27 + \blacksquare = 27$ **18.** $8 + \blacksquare = 12 + 8$ **19.** $2 \times (5 \times 7) = (2 \times \blacksquare) \times 7$

20. $32 \times 1 = \blacksquare$ **21.** $\blacksquare \times 17 = 17 \times 23$ **22.** $(6 + 5) + 4 = (\blacksquare + 6) + 5$

More Practice, page 501, set A   **31**

Comparing and Ordering Whole Numbers

LEARN ABOUT IT

EXPLORE Examine the Data

Susan found her state in an alphabetical listing of states by area in square miles. She wanted to make a list of these states in order from smallest to largest.

State	Area (square miles)
Florida	58,560
Georgia	58,876
Hawaii	6,450
Idaho	83,557
Illinois	56,400

TALK ABOUT IT

1. Which number in the list above has the greatest digit in the ten thousands place?
2. Which two numbers in her list have the same digits in the thousands place but different digits in the hundreds place?

Here is one way to **compare** two numbers:
Compare 56,131 and 57,598.
- Line up the numbers by place value.
- Start at the left and find the first place where the digits are different.
- Compare those digits. The numbers compare the same way.

Example: 56,131
          57,598

> The digits in the thousands place are different.

$6 < 7$ so $56,131 < 57,598$
or $57,598 > 56,131$

Here is one way to **order** numbers:
- Compare the numbers two at a time.
- List the numbers from greatest to least or from least to greatest.

Order   23,578   2,354   23,592
$23,578 > 2,354$ and $23,592 > 23,578$
    In order: 23,592 ← greatest
              23,578
              2,354 ← least

TRY IT OUT

Write $>$, $<$, or $=$ for each ▥.

1. 2,135 ▥ 2,136
2. 382 ▥ 467
3. 1,000 tens ▥ 10,000
4. 5,008 ▥ 5,080
5. 543,817 ▥ 540,298
6. 38,417 ▥ 38,409
7. Order these numbers from least to greatest: 543,890   542,760   54,817   535,300
8. Order these numbers from greatest to least: 101,999   99,990   110,000   109,990

Write >, <, or = for each 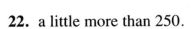.

1. 743 ▧ 758

2. 3,976 ▧ 3,980

3. 9,999 ▧ 10,000

4. 16,878 ▧ 16,783

5. 54,079 ▧ 54,079

6. 786,300 ▧ 786,099

7. 365 thousand ▧ 356,000

8. 979,000,000 ▧ 236 billion

9. 34 thousand ▧ 34,000

10. 49 billion ▧ 490,000,000

Which numbers in the box are

11. greater than 480,823?

12. less than 50,000?

13. between 295,000 and 405,000?

14. greater than 45,000 and less than 68,500?

382,417	416,950	38,245
376,892	405,887	40,590
281,045	683,215	68,322
473,819	517,325	51,735

Write each group of numbers in order from least to greatest.

15. 3,574; 3,618; 358; 3,592

16. 24,327; 25,782; 24,315; 2,579

17. 5,389; 5,840; 589; 5,390

18. 87,400; 78,400; 84,562; 87,399

19. 456,800; 453,400; 45,418; 456,512

20. 1,000,000; 909,000; 1,100,000

APPLY

MATH REASONING

Write three numbers that are

21. a little more than 250,000.

22. a little more than 250.

23. a little less than 250,000.

24. a little less than 250.

PROBLEM SOLVING

25. Which state is smaller, Iowa or Wisconsin?

26. **Social Studies Data Bank**   Which of the original 13 states have areas greater than 50,000 square miles? See page 480.

DATA BANK

State	Area (mi²)
Alabama	51,609
Iowa	56,290
Michigan	58,216
Wisconsin	56,154

▶ **ALGEBRA**

Find the number represented by each variable. Each variable represents one unknown number.

27. $b - a = a$
$b + c = 20$
$a + a = 14$

28. $d + e = f$
$f - d = 6$
$d + d = 10$

Rounding Whole Numbers

GALVESTON

Population: 62,000
Metropolitan area population: 196,000
City charter Date: 1839
Great Hurricane: 1900

LEARN ABOUT IT

EXPLORE **Think About the Situation**

Kristi and Dave made a poster about their city. According to the 1980 census the population was 61,902. They decided that for their poster it would make sense to round that number.

TALK ABOUT IT

1. Explain how this number line can be used to show that 61,902 is closer to 62,000 than to 61,000.

61,000 61,100 61,200 61,300 61,400 61,500 61,600 61,700 61,800 61,900 62,000

2. Why does it make sense to use a rounded number on the poster?

To **round** to any place:

- First underline the digit in the place to which you want to round.

- Look at the digit one place to its right. If the digit is less than 5, round **down.**

- If the digit is 5 or more, round **up.**

Examples: Round 52,434 to the nearest thousand.

5$\underline{2}$,434

5$\underline{2}$,434
52,000

Round 52,534 to the nearest thousand.

5$\underline{2}$,534 → 53,000

Other Examples

A Round to the nearest **ten thousand:** 1$\underline{5}$7,843 → 160,000
B Round to the nearest **hundred thousand:** 1$\underline{5}$0,000 → 200,000
C Round to the nearest **million:** 4$\underline{2}$,300,000 → 42,000,000

TRY IT OUT

Round to the nearest thousand.
Round to the nearest ten thousand.
Round to the nearest million.

1. 4,817
3. 27,294
5. 7,824,315

2. 27,294
4. 380,467
6. 43,500,000

34

Round to the nearest thousand.

1. 12,346   **2.** 74,652   **3.** 35,350   **4.** 10,238   **5.** 98,500

Round to the nearest ten thousand.

6. 174,825   **7.** 356,219   **8.** 473,532   **9.** 789,613   **10.** 999,850

Round each number to the greatest place possible.

11. 845,750   **12.** 98,945   **13.** 283,002   **14.** 9,543,918

15. 4,723,800   **16.** 30,345,604   **17.** 42,500,750   **18.** 99,635,400

When rounded to the nearest hundred thousand, which populations

19. round to 100,000?
20. round to 200,000?
21. round to 300,000?

City Populations	
Abilene, TX	96,573
Akron, OH	239,229
Birmingham, AL	280, 413
Gary, IN	156,056
Greensboro, NC	163,493
Louisville, KY	317,503
Orlando, FL	120,181
Tulsa, OK	328,684

MATH REASONING

22. Give the greatest number and the smallest number that round to 20,000 when rounded to the nearest thousand.

23. Give the greatest number and the smallest number that round to 1,000 when rounded to the nearest thousand.

PROBLEM SOLVING

24. A newspaper article said that the Mountain City airport took in about $4,000,000 in parking fees. What year was the article most likely discussing?

25. The average attendance at Mountain College football games last year was 37,845. What rounded number would a newspaper be apt to use to report this data?

Airport Parking Earnings	
1989	$3,384,217
1990	$4,228,350
1991	$4,965,272

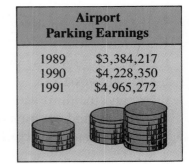

▶ **USING CRITICAL THINKING   Give a Counterexample**

Decide whether the statement below is correct or incorrect. If you think it is incorrect, give an example to show why.

26. A three-digit number rounded to the nearest hundred will always have exactly two zeros.

More Practice, page 501, set C

Problem Solving
Draw a Picture

UNDERSTAND
ANALYZE DATA
PLAN
ESTIMATE
SOLVE
EXAMINE

You can use a problem-solving strategy called **Draw a Picture** to help you solve many problems.

To get ready for the Flying Disc Games, George started mowing at one end of the football field. He mowed up to the 30 yard line. Rosa started at the other end of the field. She mowed up to the 40 yard line. The football field is 100 yards long. How many yards were not yet mowed?

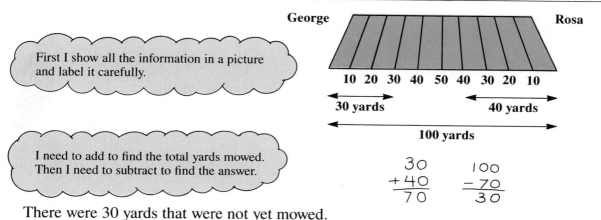

First I show all the information in a picture and label it carefully.

I need to add to find the total yards mowed. Then I need to subtract to find the answer.

$$\begin{array}{r} 30 \\ +40 \\ \hline 70 \end{array} \qquad \begin{array}{r} 100 \\ -70 \\ \hline 30 \end{array}$$

There were 30 yards that were not yet mowed.

TRY IT OUT

In the distance throwing event at the Flying Disc Games, Katie made four throws. Each of her throws was longer than the one before it. The distance between the first throw and the fourth was 15 feet. The distance between the second throw and the third was 2 feet. The distance between the third throw and the fourth was 7 feet. How much longer was the second throw than the first?

- Which throws were the longest and the shortest?
- How far apart were the first throw and the fourth throw?
- How far apart were the third throw and the fourth throw?
- Copy and complete the drawing below to solve the problem.

First throw   Fourth throw

|———————————— 15 ft ————————————|

36

Draw a picture to help you solve the following problems.

1. Jim and Ingrid were throwing flying discs directly toward each other. They were 18 yards apart. Jim threw his disc 5 yards between his legs. Ingrid threw hers 4 yards using a behind-the-back throw. How far apart were the two flying discs after they landed on the ground?

2. On the way to the Flying Disc Games, Ozzie will pass 4 towns. Kingston is between Montclare and Bedford. Kingston is 3 miles from Montclare. Bedford is between Kingston and Dublin. Bedford and Dublin are 6 miles apart. The distance from Montclare to Dublin is 17 miles. How far is it from Kingston to Bedford?

Solve. Choose a strategy from the list or use other strategies that you know.

3. Darla has a large flying disc that is 13 inches across the middle. She also has a small disc that measures 6 inches across the middle. How much wider across the middle is the larger disc?

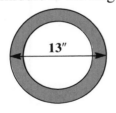

13″

Some Strategies
Act Out
Use Objects
Choose an Operation
Draw a Picture

6. Larry and Dave were 16 yards apart. They threw their flying discs toward each other with their left hands. Each threw his disc 9 yards. How far apart were the discs when they landed on the ground?

7. James divided 28 campers into 4 teams to play flying disc football. There were the same number of campers on each team. How many were there on each team?

4. At camp, a rectangular field was marked off for a flying disc competition. Starting at one of the corners, a cone marker was set up at every 5 yards around the field. The field is 40 yards long and 20 yards wide. How many cones were needed?

8. Small flying discs were on sale for $4 each. How much would 6 discs cost?

5. The first day Flora tried to spin the disc on her fingertip, she could do it for only 5 seconds. The next day, she could do it for 9 seconds longer. How long could she do it the second day?

Exploring Algebra
Variables and Expressions

LEARN ABOUT IT

You learned in Chapter 1 that a numerical expression is a name for a number. You also learned that a variable can be used to stand for a single number. In this lesson you will explore how variables are used in expressions like $n + 8$.

EXPLORE Think About the Situation

Todd's teacher drew these figures on the chalkboard and asked, "What numerical expression could you write to show the length of the whole board?" When a student responded "$8 + 4$," the teacher said, "Very good! Now, suppose you know the length of only the first part of the board? What expression could you write to give the total length?"

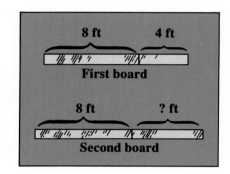

TALK ABOUT IT

1. What is the value of the expression $8 + 4$?
2. Which of these expressions could you write to show the total length of the second board?
   A. $8 + n$ **B.** $8 - n$ **C.** $8 + y$ **D.** $8 \times y$

An expression like $n + 8$ that contains a variable is called an **algebraic expression.**

To evaluate an algebraic expression, you replace the variable with a number and perform the operation. Here is how to do it.

Evaluate $n + 8$ when $n = 9$.

Replace n with 9 and add. $9 + 8 = 17$

Evaluate $18 \div y$ when $y = 6$.

Replace y with 6 and divide. $18 \div 6 = 3$

TRY IT OUT

Find the value of each expression.

1. $y - 7$ when $y = 15$
2. $8 + m$ when $m = 6$
3. $7 \times t$ when $t = 3$
4. $n \div 8$ when $n = 32$
5. $13 - g$ when $g = 5$
6. $h \times 9$ when $h = 5$

38

POWER PRACTICE/QUIZ

Use the number in the box. Give the digit that is in the
place named.

1. hundreds
3. ten thousands

2. billions
4. hundred millions

358,140,239,607

Give the digits that are in the **period** named.

5. thousands   **6.** billions   **7.** ones   **8.** millions

Write the number from the box in which
the digit 7 has the given value.

9. 7,000
11. 700,000

10. 7,000,000,000
12. 70,000,000,000

5,723,019	175,222,951
43,837,636	247,186,665,290
304,239,931	25,938,463
429,694,531,684	472,145,954,266

Write the number in standard form.

13. 6 thousands, 5 ones, 7 tens, and 2 hundreds
14. 40,000,000 + 3,000,000 + 9,000 + 800 + 6
15. ten thousand, forty-one
16. five hundred million, sixty-seven thousand, four hundred eight

Write >, <, or = for each ▓.

17. 2,375 ▓ 2,368   **18.** 59,075 ▓ 58,986   **19.** 10 thousand ▓ 100 hundred
20. Order from least to greatest: 101,900   109,100   101,899   101,690

Round to the **nearest thousand:**   **21.** 89,560   **22.** 8,050   **23.** 116,495

Round to the **nearest million:**   **24.** 15,495,999   **25.** 9,501,001

PROBLEM SOLVING

26. Della wants to make a rectangular fence in her
backyard. She needs to use 6 posts on each long side
and 4 posts on each short side of the fence. How many
posts does she need to use in all?

27. Five girls ran in the 12-mile marathon. Alicia came in
last. Barbara finished ahead of Cindy. If Cindy was
ahead of Debra and JoAnn was just behind Debra, who
came in third?

28. Tom made 2 stops during his 50-mile bike trip. He first
stopped after 20 miles. His second stop was 15 miles
before the end of the trip. How many miles did he
travel between his first and second stops?

Decimal Place Value
Tenths and Hundredths

ones   tenths   hundredths

LEARN ABOUT IT

EXPLORE Use Place Value Blocks

Work in groups. You need blocks for ones, tenths, and hundredths. Use at least one but no more than two blocks of each value. How many decimal numbers can you make using some or all of those blocks? Make a table like this to show the numbers. One possibility is shown for you.

ones	tenths	hundredths
1	2	1

TALK ABOUT IT

1. How many numbers can you show using exactly 2 ones and 1 or 2 of each of the other pieces?
2. How many different numbers could you show without using any hundredths pieces?
3. How many different numbers did you find altogether? Do you think you found them all? Explain.

Here is how you can show, write, and read decimals.

We see:

We think:

hundreds	tens	ones	tenths	hundredths
		2	6	5

We write: 2.65

We read: "two and sixty-five hundredths"

> 6 tenths is the same as 60 hundredths.

TRY IT OUT

Use place value materials. Show, write, and read each number.

1. 1 one, 5 tenths, 6 hundredths
2. 0 ones, 7 tenths
3. 3 ones, 5 hundredths
4. 2 ones, 3 tenths, 1 hundredth
5. 4 ones, 1 tenth
6. 5 ones, 2 hundredths

Write the decimal for each picture.

1. 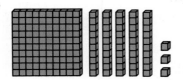   **2.**   **3.**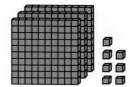

Write all the numbers from the box

4. where the digit 6 has a value of 60.
5. where the digit 7 has a value of 7.
6. where the digit 2 has a value of 0.2.
7. where the digit 9 has a value of 0.09.

76.92	96.72	27.96
68.19	29.67	76.27
79.27	27.62	62.79

Match each food item to the decimal word name.

8. twelve hundredths kg (kilogram)
9. one and two hundredths kg
10. one and two tenths kg

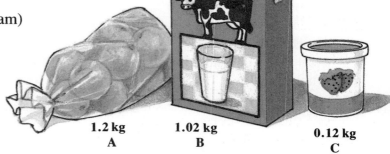

1.2 kg
A

1.02 kg
B

0.12 kg
C

MATH REASONING

Which expression does not belong in each group? Tell why.

11. 2.4; 2 + 0.40; 2.40; two and four hundredths
12. 8.09; 8 + 0.90; eight and nine hundredths

PROBLEM SOLVING

13. Talk About Your Solution   Solve the problem below.
Then compare your solution with that of a classmate.
   What is the smallest number of thumbtacks needed
to attach 4 rectangular pieces of paper to a board? Each
corner of each piece of paper must be tacked.

▶ **CALCULATOR**

Count by hundredths on your calculator using this key code:
[ON/AC] [+] 0.01 [=] [=] [=]. Stop when the display
shows each of the numbers below. How many times would
you have to press [=] to show each number?

14. 0.09   **15.** 0.29   **16.** 0.1   **17.** 0.15

Thousandths

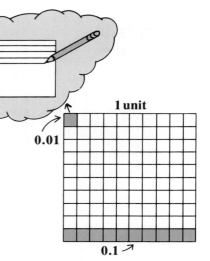

1 unit

0.01

0.1 ↗

EXPLORE Use Models Cut out a ten-by-ten square from graph paper. Label the whole square 1 unit. Lightly shade one row of the small squares. Label the row 0.1. Lightly shade just one of the small squares and label it 0.01.

If you could divide the small square into ten parts, each of these parts would be one thousandth. How would you label one of these parts?

TALK ABOUT IT

1. If 0.1 is "one tenth" and 0.01 is "one hundredth," what is "one thousandth"?
2. Which has a greater value, one hundredth or one thousandth? Explain.
3. How many thousandths are in one hundredth? in the whole unit?

Here is how to write and read decimals with thousandths.

We see:

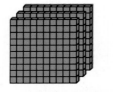

We think:

ones	tenths	hundredths	thousandths
3	1	2	5

We write: 3.125

We read: "three and one hundred twenty-five thousandths"

TRY IT OUT

Write the decimal and the word name for each.

1.   2 ones
3 tenths
0 hundredths
4 thousandths

2.   0 ones
0 tenths
4 hundredths
2 thousandths

42

Write the decimal and the word name for each.

1.   3 ones
                                      2 tenths
                                      4 hundredths
                                      5 thousandths

2.   0 ones
                                      6 tenths
                                      5 hundredths
                                      3 thousandths

Give the numbers from the box in which the digit 8
has a value of

0.876	75.482	238.056
1.84	43.82	250.132
2.378	78.334	4.328

3. 0.08   **4.** 0.8

5. 0.008   **6.** 8

Write in standard form.

7. eleven and thirty-four hundredths   **8.** forty and four thousandths
9. two and three hundred seventy-one thousandths
10. seven hundred twenty-one and thirty-nine thousandths

Write the word name for each decimal.

11. 3.254   **12.** 42.305   **13.** 0.248   **14.** 6.004

MATH REASONING

Use mental math and place value to find how much less A is than B.

15. A. 0.372   **16. A.** 3.857   **17. A.** 29.379   **18. A.** 0.9
     B. 0.373   **B.** 3.867   **B.** 29.380   **B.** 0.91

PROBLEM SOLVING

19. Carla's time for the bicycle race was 45.538 seconds.
The winning time was 45.528 seconds. By how many
seconds did Carla lose the race?

20. Benji needs to weigh 40.4 kg to wrestle in the grade 5
wrestling meet. He weighs 40 kg. How much weight
does he need to gain?

▶ **ESTIMATION**

Match each decimal with its point on the number line.

21. 0.45   **22.** 0.719   **23.** 0.204   **24.** 0.102   **25.** 0.77   **26.** 0.29

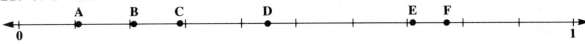

More Practice, page 501, set E

Comparing and Ordering Decimals

EXPLORE Examine the Data

Kerry found his state on a list of state populations per square mile. He looked at other states on the list and said, "It's easy to see that Nebraska has the fewest people per square mile."

State	Population per square mile
Colorado	29.2
Kansas	29.27
Nebraska	20.54
Oregon	27.31
Arizona	25.11

TALK ABOUT IT

1. At what place in the numbers did Kerry look to make the statement he made?

2. Which state on the list has the greatest number of people per square mile? How did you decide?

The steps you use to **compare** decimals are like those for whole numbers.

Compare 0.845 and 0.85.

- Line up the numbers by place value.

- Start at the left and find the first place where the digits are different.

- Compare those digits. The numbers compare the same way.

Example: 0.845
         0.85

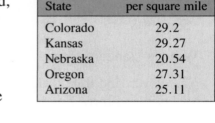

The digits in the hundredths place are different.

$4 < 5$ so $0.845 < 0.85$ or $0.85 > 0.845$

Here is one way to **order** decimals:

- Compare the numbers two at a time.

- List them from greatest to least or least to greatest.

Order 2.143, 0.214, and 2.14.
$2.143 > 2.14$ and $2.14 > 0.214$
In order: 2.143 ← greatest
2.14
0.214 ← least

TRY IT OUT

Write $>$, $<$, or $=$ for each ▥.

1. 4.35 ▥ 4.36   2. 0.82 ▥ 0.67   3. 0.27 ▥ 0.270   4. 1.099 ▥ 1.99

5. Order these numbers from smallest to largest: 6.73   6.783   0.673   6.7

44

Write $>$, $<$, or $=$ for each .

1. 7.30 ⦀ 7.03

2. 12.6 ⦀ 12.60

3. 0.95 ⦀ 0.89

4. 14.8 ⦀ 14.48

5. 0.069 ⦀ 0.690

6. 39.6 ⦀ 36.9

7. 3.47 ⦀ 3.49

8. 27.15 ⦀ 27.150

9. 1.295 ⦀ 12.96

10. 4.510 ⦀ 4.49

11. 0.790 ⦀ 0.791

12. 50.19 ⦀ 50.2

Use the number list to answer these questions.

Which numbers are

13. greater than 1.5?

14. less than 0.075

15. between 0.5 and 1?

1.438	0.75	0.07
0.567	0.055	1.63
1.003	1.501	0.078
0.3	0.47	1.295

APPLY

MATH REASONING

Copy the numbers. Place a decimal point in the middle number so that the numbers are in order from least to greatest.

16. 3   345   4

17. 0.3   573   1

18. 0.34   406   0.43

PROBLEM SOLVING

19. Use all three of the digits 0, 3, and 5 to make decimals less than 1. In each decimal use each digit only once. (Do not count the zero left of the decimal point.) How many can you write? Arrange the ones you write in order from least to greatest.

20. Social Studies Data Bank   Which state had the most people per square mile in 1980? See page 480.

▶ MENTAL MATH

You can count on by tenths, hundredths, or thousandths to mentally add or subtract some decimal numbers.

Examples $4.25 + 0.3$ $\rightarrow$ Think: 4.25, 4.35, 4.45, 4.55
$0.718 + 0.003$ $\rightarrow$ Think: 0.718, 0.719, 0.720, 0.721

Count on to find these sums mentally.

21. $2.38 + 0.3$

22. $3.465 + 0.002$

23. $0.667 + 0.04$

Rounding Decimals

> ANIMAL BIRTH WEIGHTS
> AT THE CITY ZOO
>
> Gorilla....2.134 kg
> Panda.... 0.096 Kg
> Lion..... 1.262 Kg

LEARN ABOUT IT

You can apply what you know about rounding whole numbers to help you round decimals.

EXPLORE Examine the Data

Rosita rounded the birth weights when she wrote this part of her report about baby animals.

> The gorilla weighed about 2 kg at birth, but the lion weighed only about 1 kg.

TALK ABOUT IT

1. Use this number line to explain why the gorilla's weight was closer to 2 kg than to 3 kg.

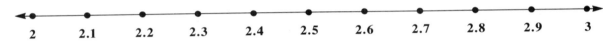

| 2 | 2.1 | 2.2 | 2.3 | 2.4 | 2.5 | 2.6 | 2.7 | 2.8 | 2.9 | 3 |

2. Would it make sense to round the panda's weight to the nearest kilogram? Explain.

You round decimal numbers using steps similar to those you use for whole numbers.

- First underline the digit in the place to which you want to round.
- Look at the digit one place to its right.
- If the digit is less than 5, round **down.**
- If the digit is 5 or more, round **up.**

Round 4.324 to the nearest tenth.

4.3̲24

4.3̲24
4.3

Round 4.364 to the nearest tenth.
4.3̲64 → 4.4

Other Examples

Round to the nearest hundredth.   0.45̲63 → 0.46
Round to the nearest whole number.   2̲.539 → 3

TRY IT OUT

Round each number to the place of the underlined digit. For example: 2.15̲8 (round to the nearest hundredth) → 2.16

1. 5.2̲3   **2.** 2̲.51   **3.** 78.34̲5   **4.** 0.8̲27   **5.** 14.09̲9   **6.** 20̲.45

Round each number to the place of the underlined digit.

1. 8.4̲3
2. 15.7̲6
3. 66.0̲6
4. 49̲.55
5. 52̲.63
6. 21.7̲5
7. 0̲.58
8. 1.4̲2
9. 56.2̲9
10. 0.7̲4
11. 1.28̲8
12. 7.05̲2
13. 0.9̲34
14. 1.5̲37
15. 9.6̲73
16. 8̲.624
17. 39̲.851
18. 21.38̲1
19. 1.9̲64
20. 99.99̲1

Give the names of the animals whose weights

21. round to 1 kg.
22. round to 2 kg.
23. round to 3 kg.

Weights of Young Animals in Zoo Hospitals	
anteater	1.945 kg
ostrich	1.468 kg
wild turkey	2.3 kg
kangaroo	2.86 kg
python	1.497 kg
turtle	2.5 kg

MATH REASONING

24. Give two different decimal numbers with digits in the thousandths place that round to 5.2 when the numbers are rounded to the nearest tenth.

PROBLEM SOLVING

25. A report said Hillston spent $4.25 million on feeding and caring for animals in the zoo last year. Hillston spent $13.8 million on road repairs. Round each number to the nearest million. Then find about how much more money was spent on road repairs.

26. **Data Hunt** Look through some newspapers and find 2 examples where numbers have been rounded. Explain why you think the numbers are rounded rather than exact.

Add or subtract.

27. $12 - 12$
28. $18 + 0$
29. $11 - 4$
30. $2 + 108$
31. $10 - 7$
32. $2 + 3 + 5$

Multiply or divide.

33. 10×4
34. $36 \div 6$
35. $12 \div 4$
36. 124×0
37. $24 \div 8$
38. 6×7
39. 9×3
40. 7×8
41. $45 \div 9$
42. 25×4
43. $21 \div 21$
44. $5 \times 2 \times 0$

More Practice, page 502, set B

Problem Solving
Understanding the Question

| UNDERSTAND |
| ANALYZE DATA |
| PLAN |
| ESTIMATE |
| SOLVE |
| EXAMINE |

LEARN ABOUT IT

One of the first things you should do when you solve a problem is to make sure you understand the question. Sometimes it helps to put the question in your own words.

> The distance traveled in one early gas balloon race was 673 miles. The distance in another race was 1,315 miles. How much greater was the distance traveled in the second race?

First I'll read the question.

How much greater was the distance traveled in the second race?

Then I'll ask the question in a different way.

What is the difference in the distances traveled in the races?

TRY IT OUT

Read each problem. Which question asks the same thing?

1. The Big Sky Ballooning Company gave 25 hot-air balloon rides last week. There were 5 people aboard for each ride. How many people went on rides?

   A. What was the total number of people who went on rides?

   B. How many people were aboard each balloon?

2. The weight of a balloon is 335 pounds. The people aboard the balloon weigh 481 pounds altogether. What is the total weight?

   A. How much more do the people weigh than the balloon?

   B. How much do the people and the balloon weigh together?

Write a question for each statement. Then solve the problem.

3. To become a private ballooning pilot, you need 10 hours of training. Jan has 6 hours of training already.

4. One balloon can hold 6 people. There are 4 balloons in all.

5. There are 30 ground crew workers at the balloon race. Each balloon has 6 ground crew workers.

6. One gas balloon race lasted 17 hours. Another race lasted 8 hours less.

Solve. Use any problem solving strategy.

1. Joey is 4 years old. When he is 4 times as old as he is now, he can get a license to be a ballooning pilot. How old will he be when he can get the license?

2. The balloon has 36 pounds of propane gas left. Each gallon of gas weighs 4 pounds. How many gallons are left?

3. Two balloons were 17 miles apart. The red balloon flew 6 miles toward the blue one. The blue balloon flew 3 miles toward the red one. How many miles apart were they then?

Use the Balloon Race table for problems 4–8.

Gordon Bennett Balloon Race (Gas Balloons)			
Date	Number of Participants	Launch Site and Destination	Winner
1906	16	France to England	U.S.A.
1907	9	Missouri to New Jersey	Germany
1908	23	Germany to Norway	Switzerland
1909	17	Switzerland to Poland	U.S.A.
1910	10	Missouri to Quebec, Canada	U.S.A.
1911	7	Missouri to Wisconsin	Germany
1912	22	Germany to U.S.S.R.	France
1913	18	France to England	U.S.A.

4. Which of the races listed in the table had twice as many participants as the race in 1907?

5. How many more participants did the race in 1906 have than the race in 1911?

6. The U.S.A. won two times as many races as which other country?

7. Which race had 8 fewer participants than the race in 1909?

8. Order the numbers of participants in the races from least to greatest.

9. **Suppose** A class of 32 students signed up to go ballooning. There is 1 balloon and it holds up to 8 students at a time. How many balloon rides are needed?

Suppose the facts were changed. Which of these facts would change the solution to the problem?
A. The balloon holds only 6 students.
B. The trip cost $75 for the class.
C. 2 students are absent on the day of the trip.
D. 8 students are absent on the day of the trip.

Data Collection and Analysis
Group Decision Making

UNDERSTAND
ANALYZE DATA
PLAN
ESTIMATE
SOLVE
EXAMINE

Doing a Survey
Group Skill:
Listen to Others

The numbers of elephants, rhinos, gorillas, and many other kinds of animals have grown much smaller over recent years. Many animals are on the endangered species list. Do you and other people know which animals are or are not classified as endangered? Conduct a survey to find out.

Collecting Data

1. Look in an almanac or other reference book to find some lists of endangered animals. Look under *animals* in the index.

2. Work with your group to make a list of 5 animals that are endangered and 5 animals that are not endangered. Mix the listings so that the endangered and not endangered are not grouped together.

3. Show the list to 20 people. Ask them to tell whether they think that each animal on the list is or is not endangered. Make tallies on your list to record the answers of the people you survey, as in the example below.

Do you think each of the following animals is or is not an endangered species?

	Yes	No
1. Gorilla		
2. Giraffe		
3. Panda		
4.		

4. Make a bar graph to show the data collected in your survey. For each endangered animal, draw a bar to show how many of those surveyed knew that it is endangered. Be sure to choose a scale for your graph that will give you enough space to record the greatest number of tallies for any endangered animal on your list.

Here is how you might start your graph.

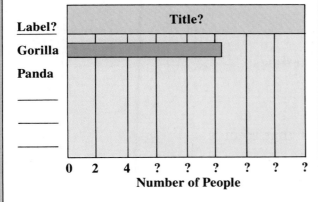

5. Check your graph. Did you give it a title and appropriate labels?

Presenting Your Analysis

6. Write a paragraph to tell what your group found out. Which endangered animal was correctly identified as endangered by the greatest number of the people you surveyed? Were you surprised by the results?

Wrap Up

Place Value Words

Choose the word from the box that completes each sentence correctly. Not all words will be used.

ones	hundredth	billions	place
millions	thousand	hundreds	periods

1. The number 460,254,178 has three __?__ .

2. To find the value of a digit, look at its __?__ in a number.

3. There are ten thousandths in one __?__ .

4. A number in the __?__ has four periods.

5. Ten __?__ is the same as one thousand.

Sometimes, Always, Never

Complete each statement by writing **sometimes, always,** or **never.** Explain your choice.

6. 54.821 __?__ rounds to 55.

7. 349 is __?__ the greatest whole number that rounds down to 300.

8. The value of a place in a number is __?__ greater than the value of any place to its left.

Project

Estimate the number of days it would take you to count by ones to 1 million. Assume that you count for 8 hours a day. Begin by estimating how many numbers per second or per minute you can count.

HINT: Start at 1. Count for 10 seconds. How many numbers did you count? Do it again, starting at 325. Do it again, starting at 124,578. How many numbers did you count in all? How many seconds did you count in all? About how many numbers per second is that?

POWER PRACTICE/TEST

Part 1   Understanding

Write each number in words.

1. 4,329,607   **2.** 7,000,158,000   **3.** 3.05   **4.** 12.071

5. Give the greatest whole number and the smallest whole number that round to 10,000 when rounded to the nearest thousand.

6. Give the greatest two-place decimal number and the smallest two-place decimal number that round to 7 when rounded to the nearest tenth.

Part 2   Skills

Find the value of each expression.

7. $x + 7$ when $x = 12$

8. $13 - y$ when $y = 11$

Write $>$, $<$, or $=$ for each ▥ .

9. 28,374 ▥ 28,376

10. 150,420 ▥ 150,320

11. 8.116 ▥ 8.126

Round to the place value of the underlined digit.

12. 8,4<u>7</u>6,325   **13.** 50<u>6</u>,328   **14.** 4.<u>1</u>25   **15.** <u>6</u>.832

Part 3   Applications

16. Write a question for the statements. Then solve the problem.
Bruce has filled 8 pages of his photo album. Each page of the album holds 4 photos.

17. Rita and Mark live 18 miles from each other. They plan to meet halfway between their homes, in Midtown. Rita has gone 7 miles toward Midtown. Mark has gone 6 miles toward Midtown. How far apart are Rita and Mark?

18. Challenge. Write as a number in standard form: fifteen thousand, fifteen hundred fifteen and fifteen hundredths.

ENRICHMENT
Roman Numerals

The Ancient Romans developed a numeral system that was used throughout most of Europe until Arabic numerals came into popular use in the sixteenth century. The Romans wrote their numbers using these letters or symbols.

I	V	X	L	C	D	M
1	5	10	50	100	500	1,000

The Romans combined these symbols to write other numerals. Roman numerals do not have place value. Instead, the Romans added the value of a symbol when they wrote it to the right of a symbol that was of equal or greater value.

II means 1 + 1, or 2.	CLV means 100 + 50 + 5, or 155.
XXI means 10 + 10 + 1, or 21.	MDC means 1,000 + 500 + 100, or 1,600.

When the Romans wrote I, X, or C to the left of a symbol of greater value, they subtracted.

IV means 5 − 1, or 4.	XC means 100 − 10, or 90.
XL means 50 − 10, or 40.	CM means 1,000 − 100, or 900.

Write the standard number for these Roman numerals.

1. VII   **2.** XIII   **3.** LV   **4.** CLX   **5.** LIX   **6.** MCMLXXI   **7.** DCIV

Write the Roman numerals for these standard numbers.

8. 25   **9.** 8   **10.** 109   **11.** 54   **12.** 19   **13.** 1,550   **14.** 206

CUMULATIVE REVIEW

1. Subtract.

$\begin{array}{r} 504 \\ -\ 276 \end{array}$

A. 372   B. 880
C. 238   D. 228

2. Multiply.

327×4

A. 1,288   B. 1,308
C. 1,228   D. 1,302

Identify each figure.

3.

A. cone
B. cylinder
C. sphere
D. pyramid

4.

A. equilateral triangle
B. right triangle
C. scalene triangle
D. obtuse triangle

5. In the equation $G \times H = G$, G is a whole number greater than 0. What number does the H stand for?

A. 0   B. 1   C. 2   D. 3

6. In the equation $L - M = L$, what number does the M stand for?

A. 0   B. 1   C. 2   D. 3

7. Which three digits are in the millions period in the number 475,680,321,419?

A. 475   B. 680   C. 321   D. 419

8. If N, P, and Q stand for numbers, which property tells you that $(N + P) + Q = N + (P + Q)$?

A. zero property of addition
B. commutative property of addition
C. zero property of multiplication
D. associative property of addition

9. Choose the next three numbers in the pattern.

5, 11, 17, 23, 29, ___, ___, ___

A. 31, 37, 41   B. 33, 35, 37
C. 25, 21, 17   D. 35, 41, 47

10. Use mental math. How would you group the numbers to find $36 + 240 + 2 + 60$?

A. $(36 + 60) + 240 + 2$
B. $(36 + 60) + 240 + 2$
C. $(240 + 60) + 36 + 2$
D. $(60 + 2 + 36) + 240$

11. Trisha and her father are building a fence around a rectangular area 20 feet wide and 30 feet long. They want to put a post every 5 feet. How many posts will they need?

A. 24   B. 22   C. 20   D. 18

3

ADDITION AND SUBTRACTION: WHOLE NUMBERS AND DECIMALS

THEME: KEEPING FIT

MATH AND HEALTH AND FITNESS

DATA BANK

Use the Health and Fitness Data Bank on page 474 to answer the questions.

1 What is the minimum number of hours of sleep per day needed by the 10-year-old? How many more hours is this than the minimum needed by the average person over 60?

2 How much greater is the maximum number of hours of sleep needed by the average 4-year-old than the maximum number needed by the average person over 60?

3 Would you get more iron from eating one serving of cooked beef or from eating two slices of roast pork and a cup of raw carrots?

4 **Using Critical Thinking** Find a pattern in the data about hours of sleep needed by humans. Give some reasons that you think may explain why the pattern occurs.

People of widely varying abilities can enjoy the challenges and rewards of athletic competition.

Estimation
Using Rounding

LEARN ABOUT IT

You can use what you know about rounding
to estimate sums and differences.

EXPLORE Examine the Data

A newspaper reported that about 1,000 people
attended the Madison Middle School's Fitness
Fair. Use the data in the graph to decide whether
you think the newspaper's report was justified.

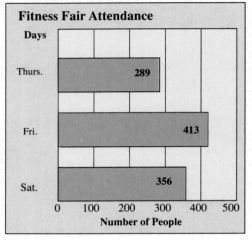

Fitness Fair Attendance

TALK ABOUT IT

1. Is the Thursday attendance closer to 200 or
   to 300 when it is rounded?
2. Is the Friday attendance closer to 400 or
   to 500?
3. What is the Saturday attendance rounded to
   the nearest hundred?

One way to estimate is to round numbers and use mental
math to find the sum or difference. We can do this with
decimals as well as with whole numbers. Here is how.

Find the sums.

nearest hundred

$$219 \rightarrow 200$$
$$298 \rightarrow 300$$
$$+389 \rightarrow 400$$
$$\overline{900}$$

nearest dollar

$$\$3.19 \rightarrow 3$$
$$+ 5.72 \rightarrow 6$$
$$\overline{\$9}$$

Find the differences.

nearest hundred

$$1,679 \rightarrow 1,700$$
$$-1,226 \rightarrow 1,200$$
$$\overline{500}$$

nearest whole number

$$14.8 \rightarrow 15$$
$$- 7.2 \rightarrow 7$$
$$\overline{8}$$

We can also round to other places when appropriate, such
as tens, tenths, and thousands.

TRY IT OUT

Estimate by rounding. Round so that you can use mental math.

1.	2.	3.	4.	5.
368	1,295	8.26	$8.79	3,984
+529	− 887	−4.93	+9.07	+9,156

Estimate by rounding. Round so you can use mental math.

1. 92 +28	**2.** 73 +68	**3.** 123 − 57	**4.** 16.6 − 7.8	**5.** 617 +376	

6. 3.4 +5.9	**7.** 1,486 − 626	**8.** 6.81 −3.2	**9.** 3,456 +6,790	**10.** 15,987 − 8,584

11. $5.89 + 6.13	**12.** $9.89 −2.19	**13.** $8.56 + 4.65	**14.** $6.75 + 3.49	**15.** $4.58 − 1.90

APPLY

MATH REASONING

16. Use estimation. Pick two numbers that have a difference close to 500. Try 5 pairs of numbers. Then find the actual differences. Which is closest to 500?

257	1,275	749
798	698	1,203
136	1,657	612
1,098	1,409	1,894
897	937	384
419	1,386	1,562
1,805	809	1,184

PROBLEM SOLVING

17. Thursday 117 people had their blood pressure checked. Friday 192 people had their blood pressure checked. Estimate how many people in all had their blood pressure checked on Thursday and Friday.

18. Health and Fitness Data Bank The average cat sleeps about 16 hours per day. How many hours more per day does the cat sleep than a 10 year-old human who sleeps the minimum number of hours for that age? See page 474.

DATA BANK

MIXED REVIEW

Write each numerical expression using words.

19. 56 ÷ 8   **20.** 36 − 6   **21.** 9 × 9   **22.** $\frac{2}{3}$

Write each numerical expression using symbols.

23. fifteen divided by three   **24.** one fifth   **25.** seventy-two less nine

More Practice, page 502, set C

Reviewing Whole Number Addition and Subtraction

The examples below will help you review adding and subtracting whole numbers.

A

$$\begin{array}{r} {\scriptstyle 1} \\ 637 \\ +835 \\ \hline 1,472 \end{array}$$

12 ones = 1 ten and 2 ones

B 69 + 108 + 125 + 6

Line up addends so digits with the same place value are in the same column.

$$\begin{array}{r} {\scriptstyle 1\ 2} \\ 69 \\ 125 \\ +6 \\ \hline 200 \end{array}$$

C

$$\begin{array}{r} {\scriptstyle 6\ 13} \\ 7\cancel{3}8 \\ -275 \\ \hline 463 \end{array}$$

1 less hundred gives 10 more tens.

D

$$\begin{array}{r} {\scriptstyle 5\ 9\ 14} \\ 6\cancel{0}\cancel{4} \\ -286 \\ \hline 318 \end{array}$$

60 tens = 59 tens and 10 ones

Add or subtract.

1. $\begin{array}{r} 506 \\ +853 \\ \hline \end{array}$
2. $\begin{array}{r} 527 \\ -454 \\ \hline \end{array}$
3. $\begin{array}{r} 385 \\ +207 \\ \hline \end{array}$
4. $\begin{array}{r} 7,645 \\ +8,397 \\ \hline \end{array}$
5. $\begin{array}{r} 853 \\ -317 \\ \hline \end{array}$

6. $\begin{array}{r} 704 \\ -628 \\ \hline \end{array}$
7. $\begin{array}{r} 4,263 \\ -1,896 \\ \hline \end{array}$
8. $\begin{array}{r} 9,156 \\ +8,375 \\ \hline \end{array}$
9. $\begin{array}{r} 57,364 \\ +18,906 \\ \hline \end{array}$
10. $\begin{array}{r} 54,375 \\ -17,682 \\ \hline \end{array}$

11. 175 − 84

12. 305 − 196

13. 274 + 3,866 + 95

14. 1,519 − 915

15. 2,176 + 897

16. 328 + 97 + 205 + 88

Add or subtract.

1. 69 +46	**2.** 247 −136	**3.** 495 +230	**4.** 1,578 − 391	**5.** 5,038 +2,847
6. 467 +548	**7.** 5,289 + 76	**8.** 4,364 − 867	**9.** 6,034 −2,993	**10.** 51,764 +27,896
11. 45 58 +75	**12.** 594 385 +257	**13.** 65 93 +451	**14.** 6,576 937 +8,142	**15.** 47,836 4,927 + 398

16. 74 + 85   **17.** 365 + 278   **18.** 186 − 27   **19.** 9,634 − 5,798

20. Subtract 376 from 704.   **21.** Find the sum of 78, 156, and 732.

MATH REASONING Without calculating, tell which sum is greater.

22. 724 + 88 + 165 OR 524 + 488 + 165

23. 453 + 325 + 210 OR 385 + 299 + 195

PROBLEM SOLVING

24. Jack started driving in Bloomington. Now he is between Milford and Rockford and is 45 miles from Rockford. How far is he from Bloomington?

Bloomington to Milford	85 mi
Milford to Rockford	196 mi

25. Verna flew 2,500 miles on Sunday, 485 miles on Monday, and 1,265 miles on Tuesday. How many miles altogether did she fly in three days?

▶ **ESTIMATION**

Choose numbers from the cards to make subtraction problems.

26.
393

27.
231

28.
663

529
417
712

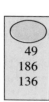
49
186
136

More Practice, page 502, set D

Front-End Estimation

LEARN ABOUT IT

You can use mental math to estimate sums.

EXPLORE Solve to Understand

- How many pairs of numbers can you find on the bulletin board that have a sum within 10 of the target number 100?

- List the target pairs and tell whether each sum is more or less than 100.

TALK ABOUT IT

1. How would you find a number that forms a target pair with 32?

2. How can you see that 55 and 59 do not form a target pair?

3. Can you look only at the tens digits to find target pairs? Explain.

Front-end estimation is a method of estimation where we add the digits with the greatest place value (the front-end digits) to get a rough estimate. Then we use the rest of the digits to adjust the estimate.

Add the front-end digits. → Adjust using the other digits.

$$
\begin{array}{r}
3\,9\,6 \\
2\,6\,3 \\
+\,5\,3\,7 \\
\end{array}
\qquad 1{,}000\ +
$$

$$
\begin{array}{r}
3\,9\,6 \\
2\,6\,3 \\
+\,5\,3\,7 \\
\end{array}
\qquad
\text{about } 200 \text{ more}
$$

Estimate: 1,200

TRY IT OUT

Use the front-end digits to estimate. Tell whether the exact sum or difference is more than or less than your estimate.

1.	475	2.	934	3.	508	4.	820
	+420		−306		−259		470
							+381

Use front-end digits to estimate. Tell whether the exact sum or difference is more than or less than your estimate.

1. 449
    +246

2. 978
    −536

3. 987
    +875

4. 862
    −358

5. 629
    +308

6. 384
    625
    +824

7. 486
    589
    +795

8. 678
    329
    +598

9. 456
    749
    +804

10. 987
    243
    +548

APPLY

MATH REASONING

Estimate to find the best missing number for each ▦ .

11. $46 +$ ▦ is close to 80

12. $29 +$ ▦ is close to 50

13. $67 -$ ▦ is close to 30

Missing Numbers   24 48
                   35 27

PROBLEM SOLVING

14. Pedro earned $256 one week and $369 the next. Then he spent $417 dollars for a television set. Estimate the amount of money he then had left to put in the bank.

15. **Determining Reasonable Answers**   In a telephone poll, Ted made 398 calls the first week and 476 the second. Use estimation to decide whether or not Ted's computed total is reasonable. If it is not reasonable, find the correct answer.

Ted
Total calls: 974

▶ **USING CRITICAL THINKING**   Support Your Conclusions

Study the examples shown. Make up some other examples. Then complete these statements with the word **odd** or **even.**

16. The sum of any two odd numbers is always ___?___ .

17. The sum of an odd and an even number is always ___?___ .

18. The sum of any two even numbers is always ___?___ .

$0 + 1 = 1$
$1 + 1 = 2$
$2 + 1 = 3$
$2 + 2 = 4$
$2 + 3 = 5$

More Practice, page 503, set E

Problem Solving
Guess and Check

UNDERSTAND
ANALYZE DATA
PLAN
ESTIMATE
SOLVE
EXAMINE

LEARN ABOUT IT

To solve some problems you need to do
more than just choose an operation. You
can often use a problem solving strategy
called **Guess and Check.**

> Vic's school had a yearly food drive. Vic won a movie
> pass for bringing in a total of 56 cans of food in two days.
> He brought in 12 more cans the second day than the first.
> How many cans did he bring in each day?

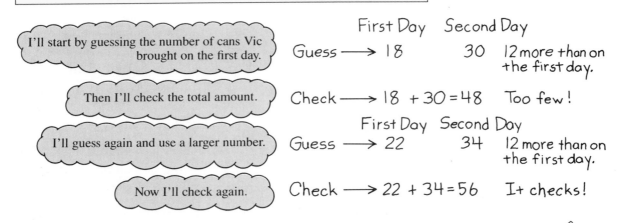

I'll start by guessing the number of cans Vic brought on the first day.

	First Day	Second Day	
Guess ⟶	18	30	12 more than on the first day.

Then I'll check the total amount.

Check ⟶ 18 + 30 = 48   Too few!

I'll guess again and use a larger number.

	First Day	Second Day	
Guess ⟶	22	34	12 more than on the first day.

Now I'll check again.

Check ⟶ 22 + 34 = 56   It checks!

Vic brought in 22 cans the first day and 34 the second day.

TRY IT OUT

Judith helped pack up the games and
stuffed animals collected for the Toys for
Children Project. She packed 97 toys in
all. There were 23 fewer stuffed animals
than games. How many stuffed animals
were there?

	Animals	**Games**
Guess 1	25	48
Check	25 + 48 = 73	
Guess 2		
Check		
Guess 3		
Check		

- What was the total number of toys Judith packed?
- How many fewer stuffed animals were there than games?
- Copy and complete the table to solve the problem.

64

Use the strategy Guess and Check to help you solve each problem.

1. Eban and Clint Lemon each have a box of cans to donate to the food drive. Eban said, "If you give me 4 cans, we'll each have the same number." Together they have 32 cans. How many cans does Eban have?

2. Sandy and Rosa together gave a total of 88 hours of service at the Senior Retirement Home last year. Rosa gave 24 fewer hours than Sandy. How many hours of service did each girl give?

MIXED PRACTICE

Choose a strategy from the strategies list or use other strategies you know to solve these problems.

Some Strategies	
Act Out	Choose an Operation
Use Objects	Draw a Picture
Guess and Check	

3. Judith could fit 6 games in each box for the Toys for Children Project. She packed 6 boxes. How many games did she pack?

4. Mrs. Grand, the principal, said she would jump into a pool with her clothes on if the students at Lincoln collected 350 cans of food for charity. How many cans more than that did they collect?

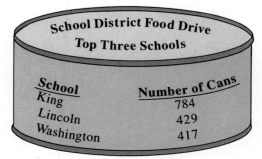

School District Food Drive
Top Three Schools

School	Number of Cans
King	784
Lincoln	429
Washington	417

5. About how many cans did the top three schools bring in for the food drive?

6. Altogether, 7,679 cans were brought in for the food drive. How many cans were donated by all the schools not counting those from King School?

7. George rode in a bike-a-thon to raise money to fight heart disease. He collected a total of $40 from 8 different people. Each person gave the same amount of money. How much did each person give?

8. Naomi saved $79. She gave $11 less to charity than she kept. How much did she give to charity?

9. The newspaper in Bo's town gave $5,676 to charity last year. A bank gave $8,598. How much did the two give altogether?

10. A truck delivered cans from the food drive to 4 different towns. The trip is 1,012 miles long, starting in Bay and ending in Dodge. The towns between Bay and Dodge are Ross and then Statton. The distance between Bay and Ross is 347 miles. The distance between Ross and Statton is 126 miles. How far is it between Ross and Dodge?

More Practice, page 522, set E

Adding Decimals
Making the Connection

The picture at the right shows how we can use place-value blocks to show decimals.

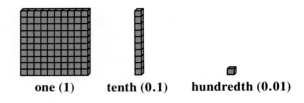

one (1)   tenth (0.1)   hundredth (0.01)

EXPLORE **Use Place Value Blocks**

Work with a partner.

- Spin a spinner three times to get a number of hundredths, tenths, and ones. Record the numbers in a table like the one at the right. Use blocks to show how many.

- Repeat this for a second number.

- Push the two groups of blocks together. Make all possible trades. Make a table to record how many blocks in all.

- Repeat this activity two times.

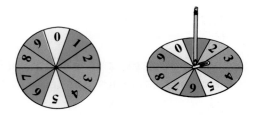

ones	tenths	hundredths

TALK ABOUT IT

1. Describe any trades you made in the activity above.

2. Why is it possible that you did not make any trades?

3. What is the greatest number of trades that you could have to make?

You have used blocks to find how many in all when you add two decimal numbers. The example below shows that recording this is like recording what you do when adding whole numbers, except for lining up the decimal points. Here is how you find the sum 2.35 + 3.28.

What You Do

What You Record

1. Are there enough hundredths to make a trade?

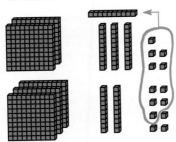

Put together and trade.

Line up the decimal points to add.

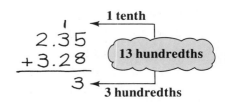

2. Are there enough tenths to make a trade?

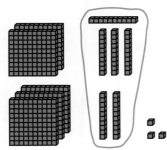

Put together.
No trade

$$
\begin{array}{r}
\overset{1}{}2.35 \\
+3.28 \\
\hline
63
\end{array}
$$

3. How many ones are there?

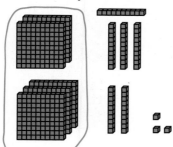

Put together.
No trade

$$
\begin{array}{r}
2.35 \\
+3.28 \\
\hline
5.63
\end{array}
$$

Be sure to place the decimal point.

TRY IT OUT

Use place value blocks to add. Record your work.

1. $\begin{array}{r} 0.45 \\ +0.34 \\ \hline \end{array}$
2. $\begin{array}{r} 1.06 \\ +2.32 \\ \hline \end{array}$
3. $\begin{array}{r} 0.78 \\ +0.46 \\ \hline \end{array}$
4. $\begin{array}{r} 2.54 \\ +1.08 \\ \hline \end{array}$

Adding Decimals

EXPLORE   Analyze the Process

Suppose you chose chicken, a sliced tomato, and corn for a meal. How many milligrams (mg) of vitamin C would they provide?

To solve this problem add 8.75, 28.39 and 12.7.

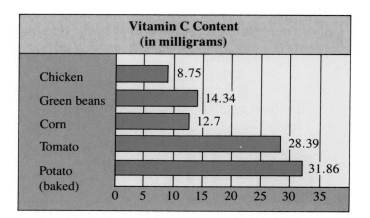

Vitamin C Content (in milligrams)

Chicken	8.75
Green beans	14.34
Corn	12.7
Tomato	28.39
Potato (baked)	31.86

Line up the decimal points.	Add the hundredths. Trade if necessary.	Add the tenths. Trade if necessary.	Add the whole numbers. Write the decimal point.
8.75 28.39 +12.7	8.75 38.39 +12.7 ——— 4	8.75 28.39 +12.7 ——— 84	8.75 28.39 +12.7 ——— 49.84

TALK ABOUT IT

1. Why do we line up decimal points?

2. Use estimation to show that the answer is reasonable.

3. Give the answer to the Explore problem in a complete sentence.

Other Examples

A
$$\begin{array}{r} \$7.80 \\ +\ 9.65 \\ \hline \$17.45 \end{array}$$

B
$$\begin{array}{r} 9.576 \\ +0.489 \\ \hline 10.065 \end{array}$$

C
$$\begin{array}{r} 0.763 \\ 4.69 \\ +1.8 \\ \hline 7.253 \end{array}$$

Add.

1.
$$\begin{array}{r} \$0.76 \\ +\ 1.34 \end{array}$$

2.
$$\begin{array}{r} 1.746 \\ +0.205 \end{array}$$

3.
$$\begin{array}{r} 1.6 \\ +0.753 \end{array}$$

4.
$$\begin{array}{r} 7.864 \\ +0.189 \end{array}$$

5.
$$\begin{array}{r} 6.478 \\ 0.7 \\ +2.85 \end{array}$$

Add.

1. 46.8 +59.7	**2.** 37.8 + 9.6	**3.** 6.27 +2.88	**4.** 0.85 +4.36	**5.** 3.7 +2.46
6. 7.386 +0.049	**7.** 36.35 +19.2	**8.** 4.180 +3.675	**9.** $5.63 + 2.48	**10.** 8.985 +4.69
11. 36.8 19.3 +26.4	**12.** 128.7 36.480 + 9.867	**13.** 1.869 2.088 +3.548	**14.** 0.687 0.975 0.836 +0.548	**15.** $124.73 642.80 376.57 +290.17

16. 26.6 + 42.9   **17.** $16.37 + $17.96   **18.** 6.478 + 0.7 + 2.85

Estimate each sum to the place value of the underlined digit.

19. 0.3̲4 + 0.6̲7   **20.** 7̲.6 + 6̲.9   **21.** 43̲.62 + 9̲.47   **22.** 21̲.97 + 37̲.41

MATH REASONING

Without adding, tell whether each sum is greater than or less than 2.

23. 0.875 + 1.105   **24.** 1.086 + 0.92   **25.** 1.006 + 0.999

PROBLEM SOLVING

26. Ian had 46.2 mg of vitamin C. Which two items from the chart did he have?

27. Loran had beans, corn, and a tomato. How much vitamin C did she get?

28. Health and Fitness Data Bank Find the number of milligrams of vitamin C in three things you like to eat What is the total amount of vitamin C you would get from one serving of each? See page 474.

► **CALCULATOR**

Use a calculator to change the first number into the second number. Use the addition or subtraction key only once for each problem.

29. first: 6.78 → second: 6.38   **30.** first: 43.5 → second: 73.5

31. first: 0.545 → second: 0.245   **32.** first: 2.37 → second: 2.49

Using Critical Thinking

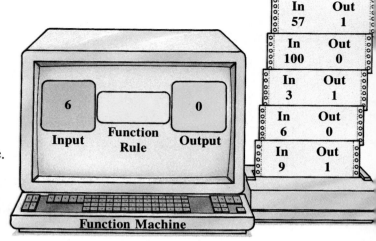

Function Machine

LEARN ABOUT IT

Dr. Awesome was showing Nathan and Stephanie the function machine he made. When he put an input number in the machine, it used a rule and produced an output number. Then it printed an input-output card to show the results.

Nathan said, "I see. If my input number was 6 and my rule was add 3, my output number would be 9." "Right!" said Dr. Awesome.

Stephanie turned on the machine and put in different input numbers. The machine used another rule to print the cards shown above. "I think the machine is broken," said the doctor. "I'm not so sure," said Nathan. "I think I know the rule."

TALK ABOUT IT

1. What does the function machine do?
2. Why do you think Dr. Awesome thought the machine was broken?
3. Do you think the machine is broken? If not, what is the rule?
4. What would the output be for these inputs: 5, 10, 17?

TRY IT OUT

Suppose each set of cards was produced by a function machine. Give the function rule for each. Then give 3 more pairs that the rule might produce.

1.

In	Out
1	1
2	4
3	9
4	16
5	25

2.

In	Out
1	3
2	5
3	7
4	9
5	11

3.

In	Out
1	6
2	11
3	16
4	21
5	26

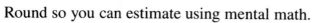

POWER PRACTICE/QUIZ

Round so you can estimate using mental math.

1.	27 + 46	**2.**	89 − 33	**3.**	621 − 82	**4.**	418 + 168	**5.**	$19.57 − 3.98

Add or subtract.

6.	$127.24 + 83.27	**7.**	43,188 + 86,832	**8.**	462 − 385	**9.**	23,040 + 37,625	**10.**	7,207 − 4,308

Estimate the sum or difference.

11.	378 + 455	**12.**	3,149 + 465	**13.**	317 − 222	**14.**	527 − 350	**15.**	285 464 + 677

Tell which expressions give the same answer as the first.
More than one may be correct.

16. 87 + 24
   A. 80 + 20 + 11   **B.** 87 + 20 + 4   **C.** 87 + 20 + 11

17. 153 − 86
   A. (150 − 80) + (6 − 3)   **B.** (140 − 80) + (13 − 6)   **C.** (100 − 80) + (53 − 6)

Add.

18.	$6.29 + 5.07	**19.**	23.4 + 61.6	**20.**	3.005 + 2.12	**21.**	0.036 1.208 + 29.1	**22.**	$316.07 412.10 + 628.86

23. 0.994 + 0.123   **24.** 1.1 + 0.3 + 6.06   **25.** 12.3 + 104.027 + 6.1354

PROBLEM SOLVING

Solve by guessing and checking.

26. Emilia is two years older than Nicholas. The sum of their ages is 20. How old is each child?

27. Ryan has 5 coins that total 65¢. What coins does he have?

28. Tracey collected 21 shells in 3 days. Each day she collected 4 more shells than she collected the day before. How many shells did she collect each of the 3 days?

29. Ms. Chou has twice as many children in her class as Mr. James has in his. There are a total of 48 children in the two classes. How many children are in each class?

Problem Solving
Choosing a Calculation Method

UNDERSTAND
ANALYZE DATA
PLAN
ESTIMATE
SOLVE
EXAMINE

LEARN ABOUT IT

One of the decisions you must make when you solve problems is which calculation method you should use.

Calculation Methods
- Paper and Pencil
- Mental Math
- Calculator

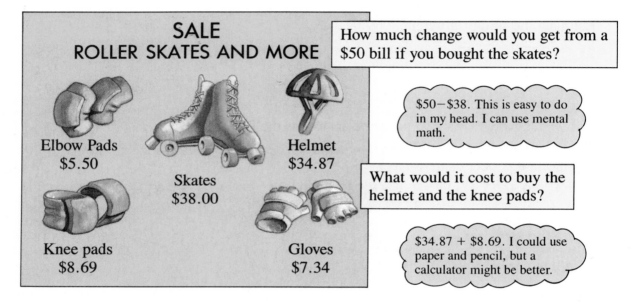

SALE
ROLLER SKATES AND MORE

Elbow Pads
$5.50

Skates
$38.00

Helmet
$34.87

Knee pads
$8.69

Gloves
$7.34

How much change would you get from a $50 bill if you bought the skates?

$50−$38. This is easy to do in my head. I can use mental math.

What would it cost to buy the helmet and the knee pads?

$34.87 + $8.69. I could use paper and pencil, but a calculator might be better.

When you have to choose a calculation method, you may find it helpful to:
- *First try mental math.* Look for numbers that can be computed easily in your head.
- *If mental math would be difficult, choose between paper and pencil and a calculator.* Problems that require many steps and trades are often more quickly solved using a calculator.

TRY IT OUT

Choose an appropriate calculation method and tell why.
Then solve.

1. $365 - 43$

2. 28×20

3. 134×24

4. $1075 - 289$

5. $\$40.50 \times 2$

6. $150 \div 25$

7. $30 \times 40 \times 5$

8. $\$95.85 - \$14.75$

Choose an appropriate calculation method and tell why.
Then solve.

1. $28.74 + $24.95

2. 5 × 127

3. 41 + 12 + 19

4. 49 + 19 + 32 + 166

5. $75 − $62.50

6. $320 × 20

7. 4 × 3 × 30

8. 3,000 − 299

9. 700 − 438

10. 400 ÷ 20

11. $35 − $12.75

12. $8.75 × 8 × 12

Solve. Choose the calculation method that seems best for
you. Use data on page 72 when needed.

13. The cost of two books about roller
skating is $11.50. One costs $2.50
more than the other. What is the cost
of each book?

14. Some new skates and other items you
want cost $55 including tax. You have
saved $33.45. How much more
money do you need to buy the things
you want?

15. How much less do the gloves cost
than the helmet?

16. About how much would it cost to
buy all of the equipment that is
on sale?

17. The entry fee for a skating contest is
$15. For entering, you get a free
T-shirt worth $8.95. How much more
is the entry fee than the amount the
T-shirt is worth?

18. A subscription to a skating magazine
costs $27 a year. There are 9 issues a
year. What is the cost of each issue?

19. How much difference is there in the special prices
between the most expensive and the least expensive
skating shirt?

Great Shirts for Skating
Regular prices $13.79 to $21.95
Special prices $8.89 to $15.89

▶ **COMMUNICATION**   **Writing to Learn**

20. Suppose you have a friend who said, "I always use my
calculator to do computations." Write a letter to this
friend giving some examples that would show that it is
sometimes better not to use a calculator.

Subtracting Decimals
Making the Connection

You have used place value blocks to add decimals. You can also use them to show how to subtract decimals.

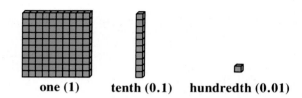

one (1)   tenth (0.1)   hundredth (0.01)

EXPLORE Use Place Value Blocks
Work with a partner.

- Spin a spinner three times to get a number of hundredths, tenths, and ones. Record the number in a table, and use blocks to show how many.

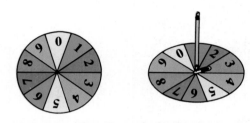

- Repeat the spins until you get a number smaller than your first number. Record the number in your table.

ones	tenths	hundredths

- Take away this number from the blocks that show your first number. Trade when you need to. Record how many blocks are left.

- Repeat this activity two times.

TALK ABOUT IT

1. Describe any trades that you made in the activity above.
2. What is the smallest number of trades you might have to make? the greatest number?
3. How does the number for the blocks that were left compare to the number for the blocks in the first group?

You have used blocks to find how many are left when you take away a decimal number. The example below shows that recording this is like recording what you do when subtracting whole numbers, except for lining up decimal points. Here is how you subtract 1.25 from 3.62.

What You Do

What You Record

1. Can you take away 5 hundredths without trading? How many tenths and hundredths are there after the trade?

 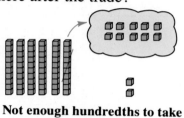

Not enough hundredths to take away 5. Regroup.

Line up the decimal points to subtract.

$$\begin{array}{r} \overset{5\ \ 12}{3.\cancel{6}\cancel{2}} \\ -1.25 \\ \hline \end{array}$$

2. How many hundredths are left after you take away 5 hundredths?

$$\begin{array}{r} \overset{5\ \ 12}{3.\cancel{6}\cancel{2}} \\ -1.25 \\ \hline 7 \end{array}$$

3. How many tenths do you take away? how many ones?

Be sure to place the decimal point.

$$\begin{array}{r} \overset{5\ \ 12}{3.\cancel{6}\cancel{2}} \\ -1.25 \\ \hline 2.37 \end{array}$$

TRY IT OUT

Use place-value blocks to subtract. Record your work.

1.   0.65
   −0.24

2.   1.24
   −0.17

3.   3.08
   −0.46

4.   3.14
   −1.38

Subtracting Decimals

EXPLORE Analyze the Process

The width of the rectangular swimming pool is 5.94 m (meter) less than the length. What is the width of the swimming pool?

Since you are taking away a certain amount from another, use subtraction.

16.31 m

To solve this problem, subtract 5.94 from 16.31.

Line up the decimal points.	Subtract the hundredths. Trade if necessary.	Subtract the tenths. Trade if necessary.	Subtract the whole numbers. Place the decimal point.
16.31 − 5.94	2 11 16.3̸1̸ − 5.94 ——— 7	5 12 11 1̸6̸.3̸1̸ − 5.94 ——— 37	5 12 11 1̸6̸.3̸1̸ − 5.94 ——— 10 37

TALK ABOUT IT

1. Where did the 11 above the 1 in the second step come from?
2. Why did you have to trade from ones to tenths?
3. Give an estimate for 16.31 − 5.94.
4. Give an answer to the Explore problem in a complete sentence.

Other Examples

A
```
  3 16
$4̸.6̸0
− 1.80
——————
$2.80
```

B
```
  8 9 14
0.9̸0̸4̸
−0.478
——————
0.426
```

C
```
  856.7
−534.16
```
Write 856.7 as 856.70.
→
```
    6 10
856.7̸0̸
−534.16
———————
 322.54
```

1.	2.	3.	4.	5.
0.803 −0.369	$47.60 − 24.15	58.3 −23.76	6.75 −3.84	50.18 −30.09

Subtract.

1. $\begin{array}{r} 8.4 \\ -3.6 \end{array}$	**2.** $\begin{array}{r} 8.34 \\ -4.65 \end{array}$	**3.** $\begin{array}{r} 57.82 \\ -18.97 \end{array}$	**4.** $\begin{array}{r} 304.26 \\ -\ 96.56 \end{array}$	**5.** $\begin{array}{r} 7.064 \\ -1.244 \end{array}$
6. $\begin{array}{r} 596.74 \\ -258.68 \end{array}$	**7.** $\begin{array}{r} 9{,}743 \\ -\ 862.6 \end{array}$	**8.** $\begin{array}{r} \$89.42 \\ -\ 64.86 \end{array}$	**9.** $\begin{array}{r} \$102.51 \\ -\ 84.38 \end{array}$	**10.** $\begin{array}{r} \$547.23 \\ -\ 268.59 \end{array}$

11. $4.3 - 0.9$ **12.** $3.85 - 1.596$ **13.** $\$547.34 - \$98.67$ **14.** $81.05 - 4.3$

Use rounding to estimate each difference to the place value of the underlined digit.

15. 8̲.78 − 1̲.92   **16.** 5̲.3 − 2̲.7   **17.** 18̲9.75 − 3̲2.26   **18.** 37̲.2 − 26̲.8

MATH REASONING

19. Use each of the given digits one time. Write a problem with a difference greater than 3 and less than 3.5. Can you find more than one problem?

1   2   3

4   5   6

PROBLEM SOLVING

20. The distance around a triangular exercise field is 34.25 m. Each of two of the sides is 13.6 m long. What is the length of the third side?

21. The distance around a rectangular playground is 54.31 m. The total length of three of the sides is 36.01 m. What is the length of the other side?

▶ ESTIMATION

Estimate each sum or difference using one of the estimation techniques you have learned.

Estimation Techniques
■ Front-end
■ Rounding
■ Compatible Numbers

22. $390 - 94$ **23.** $1{,}395 - 215$

24. $4.9 + 5.02$ **25.** $13.82 - 9.4$

26. $926 - 387$ **27.** $3.92 + 4.09$

Mental Math
Using Compensation

EXPLORE Solve to Understand

Can you think of a mental shortcut to find the total number of pictures students had paid for by the end of Wednesday?

Student Payments for Class Pictures		
Day	Number Paid	Total Number Paid
Mon.	135	135
Tues.	212	347
Wed.	198	?

TALK ABOUT IT

1. What numbers were added to get the total for Tuesday?

2. What numbers would you add to find the total for Wednesday?

3. Suppose you added 200 + 347. Would this sum be greater than or less than 198 + 347? How much more or less?

Compensation is a mental math technique we can use to help us add or subtract. When one of the numbers involved in a problem is close to another number that is easier to work with mentally, we use the easier number to find an answer. Then we adjust that answer by adding to it or subtracting from it.

■ Find 347 + 198.

> Add 2 too much and find 347 + 200.   Subtract 2 from 547.

$347 + 200 = 547; 547 - 2 = 545$

■ Find 463 − 198.

> Subtract 2 too much and find 463 − 200.   Add 2 to 263.

$463 - 200 = 263; 263 + 2 = 265$

In the first example, when 2 was added to 198 to make the addition easier, we had to **compensate** by subtracting 2. In the second example, when 200 rather than 198 was subtracted, 2 had to be added to **compensate.**

Use compensation to find the sum or difference.

1. 97 + 538 **2.** 253 − 99 **3.** 101 + 657 **4.** 403 − 95

78

Find the sums or differences mentally. Use compensation.

1. $29 + 37$ **2.** $48 + 27$ **3.** $99 + 17$ **4.** $483 + 298$ **5.** $397 + 456$

6. $43 - 9$ **7.** $51 - 9$ **8.** $62 - 8$ **9.** $684 - 196$ **10.** $571 - 295$

11. $4{,}588 + 298$ **12.** $685 - 396$ **13.** $567 + 297$ **14.** $2{,}778 - 98$ **15.** $3{,}998 + 547$

APPLY

MATH REASONING

Complete each statement.

16. Adding 8 is like adding 10 and then subtracting __?__ .

17. Subtracting 9 is like subtracting 10 and then __?__ (adding or subtracting) 1.

18. Adding 9 is like adding 10 and then subtracting __?__ .

PROBLEM SOLVING

19. Cynthia collected $197 for yearbooks and $79 for class pennants. How much did she collect in all?

20. Missing Data   Make up reasonable data so you can find the answer mentally.
Problem: Daniel bought 3 T-shirts and an $8 yearbook. How much change should he receive from a $50 bill?

 MIXED REVIEW

Find the value of each expression.

21. $(9 + 15) - 6$ **22.** $(36 \div 6) \times 5$ **23.** $22 - (33 \div 3)$ **24.** $(4 \times 8) - 12$

Write in standard form.

25. $7{,}000{,}000{,}000 + 500{,}000{,}000 + 2{,}000{,}000 + 800{,}000 + 40{,}000 + 1{,}000 + 500 + 90 + 6$

26. seventy-two billion, one hundred fifty-seven million, eight hundred sixty-three thousand, two

27. sixty-five million, seventy thousand, fifty-eight

More Practice, page 503, set C

79

Problem Solving
Using a Calculator

UNDERSTAND
ANALYZE DATA
PLAN
ESTIMATE
SOLVE
EXAMINE

LEARN ABOUT IT

When you want to add the same amount to, or subtract the same amount from, many different numbers, it is helpful to use the addition and subtraction **constants** on your calculator.

The Special package is $879 more than the Basic package for each tour. What will be the total cost for each Special tour?

	ECONOMY	BASIC	SPECIAL	DELUXE
Tour A: South to Brazil		$3476.—		
Tour B: Experience the Orient		$2875.—		
Tour C: Touring the Congo		$2498.—		
Tour D: Australia down under		$3319.—		

There is no special key on your calculator for the addition and subtraction constants. It is a hidden calculator feature. The second number is held in the calculator memory and can be added or subtracted again and again. This key code will give the amounts for the four Special tours.

[ON/AC] 3476 [+] 879 [=] ↓   2875 [=] ↓   2498 [=] ↓   3319 [=] ↓

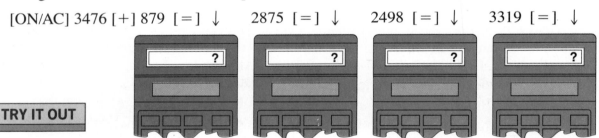

TRY IT OUT

Use the constant feature on your calculator to complete the following.

1. Copy the table above. Use the key code given above and write in the amounts for each Special tour.

2. Each Economy tour is $468 less than a Basic tour. Find the total cost for each Economy tour. Write each amount in your table. (The subtraction constant is like the addition constant, but uses the [−] key instead of the [+] key.)

3. The cost of a Deluxe tour is $1,329 more than a Basic tour. Find the total cost for each Deluxe tour and write it in your table.

4. Next year the cost of all Basic tours will increase by $178. How much will each Basic tour cost next year?

Solve. Use any problem solving strategy.

1. Sam is flying from San Francisco to Tokyo. The distance from San Francisco to Honolulu is 2,398 miles in the air. The distance from Honolulu to Tokyo is 3,859 miles. How far will Sam fly?

2. When Miko's tour group arrived in India, their suitcases were in 7 piles. There were the same number of suitcases in each pile. The group had a total of 49 suitcases. How many suitcases were in each pile?

3. Nick and his dad paid a total of $96 for their train fare to Boston. Nick's fare was $32 less than his dad's. How much was his dad's fare?

4. The River Rhine tour costs $2,797 for one person and $4,129 for two people traveling together. How much more does it cost for two people?

5. Before packing any items for his China trip, Ray weighed them on a scale. Each pair of socks weighed 6 ounces. How many ounces would 7 pairs of socks weigh?

Use the table below for problems 6 and 7.

Safari Prices			
	Rough-It	Basic	Luxury
One week		$2,345	
Two weeks		$3,195	
Three weeks		$3,976	

6. The Rough-It Safari package costs $547 less than the Basic package. How much does each Rough-It package cost? Copy the table and write in the amount for each Rough-It package.

7. The Luxury Safari package costs $926 more than the Basic package. What is the cost of each Luxury package? Write the amounts in the table.

8. **Talk About Your Solution**   Solve the problem below. Then explain your solution to a classmate. Compare your solutions.

In Tokyo, Jan ordered an American breakfast on Monday and a Japanese breakfast on Tuesday. The total cost of the breakfasts was $46. The American breakfast was $22 more than the Japanese breakfast. How much was the American breakfast?

Applied Problem Solving
Group Decision Making

UNDERSTAND
ANALYZE DATA
PLAN
ESTIMATE
SOLVE
EXAMINE

Group Skill:
Check for Understanding

You and your mother are hiking through the Bitteroot Mountains with a donkey carrying your gear. One night you tie the donkey too loosely, and it strays away. It may take you as long as 3 days to reach help. Since you need to carry your own supplies now, you cannot take all you have with you. What will you leave behind?

Facts to Consider

■ The temperatures have been as low as 34 degrees at night and as high as 75 degrees during the day.

■ It has rained one night out of four.

■ You and your mother are both wearing hiking boots, jeans, and a short-sleeved shirt.

■ You will probably be able to go back later to get the things you leave behind.

■ You and your mother each can carry 5 more kilograms of items from the lists that follow:

Equipment (for both)	
cooking stove	1.0 kg
sleeping bags	1.6 kg
foam pad for sleeping bag	0.3 kg
tube tent	0.6 kg
camera	0.7 kg
tripod to hold camera	1.4 kg
radio (for weather information)	0.2 kg
flashlight	0.6 kg
TOTAL	**6.4 kg**

Clothing (for each)	
rainsuit	0.5 kg
heavy sweater	0.3 kg
down jacket	0.8 kg
warm shirt	0.6 kg
wool pants	0.6 kg
jeans	1.0 kg
shorts	0.5 kg
TOTAL	**4.3 kg**

Food	
4 liter bottles of water	4.0 kg
20 granola bars	0.5 kg
peanut butter and jelly in a tube	0.2 kg
6 packages instant cocoa powder	0.1 kg
crackers and hard bread	0.1 kg
two big hunks of cheese	1.8 kg
bag of dried fruit	0.2 kg
6 candy bars	0.1 kg
2 cans tuna	0.5 kg
4 cans chicken	1.0 kg
TOTAL	**8.5 kg**

Some Questions to Answer

1. What is the total weight of the items on the lists?

2. Which three items of equipment are the heaviest?

3. If you left behind the radio and tripod, how many kilograms is that altogether? How many more kilograms would you need to get rid of?

4. Would a calculator be helpful for answering questions 1–3? Explain why.

What Is Your Decision?

Make a list showing which items you are going to take with you and a list showing which you will leave behind. Include the total weight on each list. Give reasons for your decision.

83

WRAP UP

Matching Descriptions and Examples

Match the mental math and estimation techniques with the examples.

1. counting back

2. using compatible numbers

3. using compensation

4. estimating by rounding

5. front-end estimating

A. $82 - 4$ 81, 80, 79, 78

B. $517 - 98 = (517 - 100) + 2$

C. $90 + 37 + 10 + 13 = 100 + 50$

D.
$$
\begin{array}{rr}
378 & 400 \\
+\ 234 & +\ 200 \\
\hline
& 600
\end{array}
$$

E.
$$
\begin{array}{rr}
756 & 700 \\
-\ 439 & -\ 400 \\
\hline
& 300
\end{array}
$$

Sometimes, Always, Never

Complete each statement by writing **sometimes**, **always**, or **never**. Explain your choice.

6. The sum of two odd numbers is __?__ an even number.

7. The sum of an even number and an odd number is __?__ an even number.

8. When you add a 3-digit whole number and a 2-digit whole number you __?__ get a 4-digit whole number.

9. When you add hundredths to hundredths, you __?__ get thousandths.

Project

Do an estimation experiment. Fill a jar with small objects of different colors (colored chips, play coins, colored paper clips, or mixed dry beans). One person estimates the number of each color or type of object and another estimates the number of other objects. Then estimate the total number of objects in the jar.

Discuss the ways you estimated. Decide which you think may be most accurate. Check your estimates.

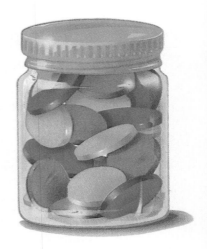

POWER PRACTICE/TEST

Part 1   Understanding

For each problem, tell the places in which you would need to trade.

1.   2,480
   + 3,075

2.   4,516
   − 2,345

3.   5.76
   + 2.93

4.   7.96
   − 5.78

Would you choose calculator, paper and pencil, or mental math to do each? Why?

5. $14.24 × 3 × 15

6. 5 × 4 × 20

Part 2   Skills

Add or subtract.

7.   38,023
   + 9,148

8.   6,016
   − 2,948

9.   5.973
   + 4.82

10. $304.26
   −   87.39

Use rounding to estimate.

11.   326
   + 459

12.   5,077
   −   959

Use front-end estimation and adjust.

13.   541
   + 869

14.   574
   − 136

Use compensation and mental math for each.

15. 142 + 298

16. 349 + 120

17. 74 − 25

18. 560 − 199

Part 3   Applications

19. Mr. Peary met his daughter in Troy. It took him 48 minutes longer to drive there than it took his daughter. If the total driving time for both together was 120 minutes, how long did each drive?

20. Challenge.   Scott's class entered a charity race. Mr. Riley said he would pay $1.25 for each mile the class ran. Mrs. Sanchez said she would pay twice as much for each mile run. Scott's class collected $93.75 from them. How much did each pay?

ENRICHMENT
Finding and Using Patterns

The sum of the numbers in each row, column, and diagonal of a **magic square** is the same. According to a Chinese myth, the first magic square appeared over 4,000 years ago. It was on the shell of a turtle.

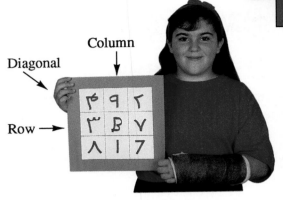

Diagonal

Column

Row →

The magic square shown in this picture uses East Arabic numbers. It was found in a book written by a Muslim African mathematician.

The following steps will help you make your own magic square. The magic sum is 15.

1. Draw a 3-by-3 square like the one in the picture (but without the numerals).

2. List the 8 ways you can name 15 by using three different addends from the numbers 1 through 9. One way is $1 + 5 + 9$ (with the addends in any order).

3. Use the list you made for step 2 to complete a table like this one.

Number	1	2	3	4	5	6	7	8	9
How many times number appears in list of addends	2								

4. Find how many times the number in the magic square's center box will be used to get the magic sum of 15. (Hint: 1 column, 1 row, 2 diagonals) Find the number in the table that appears that many times in your list. Write that number in your magic square's center box.

5. Find how many times a number in your square's corner boxes will be used to get the magic sum. Find how many times a center number in each outside row or column will be used to get the magic sum. Now complete your magic square!

Use the digits 0 through 8 to make another 3-by-3 magic square. This time the magic sum is 12.

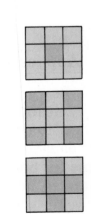

CUMULATIVE REVIEW

Add.

1. 326 + 84 + 125

   A. 425   B. 535   C. 445   D. 545

2. 27 + 44 + 13 + 86

   A. 170   B. 169   C. 150   D. 179

3. 125 + 49 + 175

   A. 249   B. 339   C. 349   D. 319

4. Which number has six fewer hundredths than tenths?

   A. 1.46   B. 5.84   C. 4.93   D. 6.39

5. Which is another way to say 58 − 24?

   A. fifty-eight plus twenty-four

   B. twenty-four less than fifty-eight

   C. fifty-eight divided by twenty-four

   D. twenty-four more than fifty-eight

6. Which operation would you use? Paula counted 16 red cars on her way to school and 14 red cars on her way home. How many more red cars did she see on her way to school?

   A. addition   B. multiplication

   C. subtraction   D. division

7. Use place value to tell what the 4 means in 1,654,671,583.

   A. 4 hundreds   B. 4 millions

   C. 4 thousands   D. 4 billions

Use front-end estimation to estimate the sum.

8.
```
   527
   853
 + 721
```
   A. 2,000   B. 1,900

   C. 2,100   D. 2,200

9.
```
   945
   258
 + 799
```
   A. 1,800   B. 2,100

   C. 1,900   D. 2,000

Add.

10. 6.214 + 5.87 + 6.49

   A. 7.450   B. 17.474

   C. 12.733   D. 18.574

11.
```
  $345.16
   894.78
 + 776.27
```
   A. $1,805.01   B. $2,016.21

   C. $2,016.00   D. $1,805.21

12. Sean drove 321 miles in two days. He drove 57 miles more on the first day than on the second day. How many miles did he drive on the second day?

   A. 167   B. 189   C. 128   D. 132

13. Which calculation method might you use to solve this problem? Terri bought 20 memo books at 49¢ each. Can she pay for them with a ten dollar bill?

   A. mental math   B. calculator

   C. estimation   D. paper and pencil

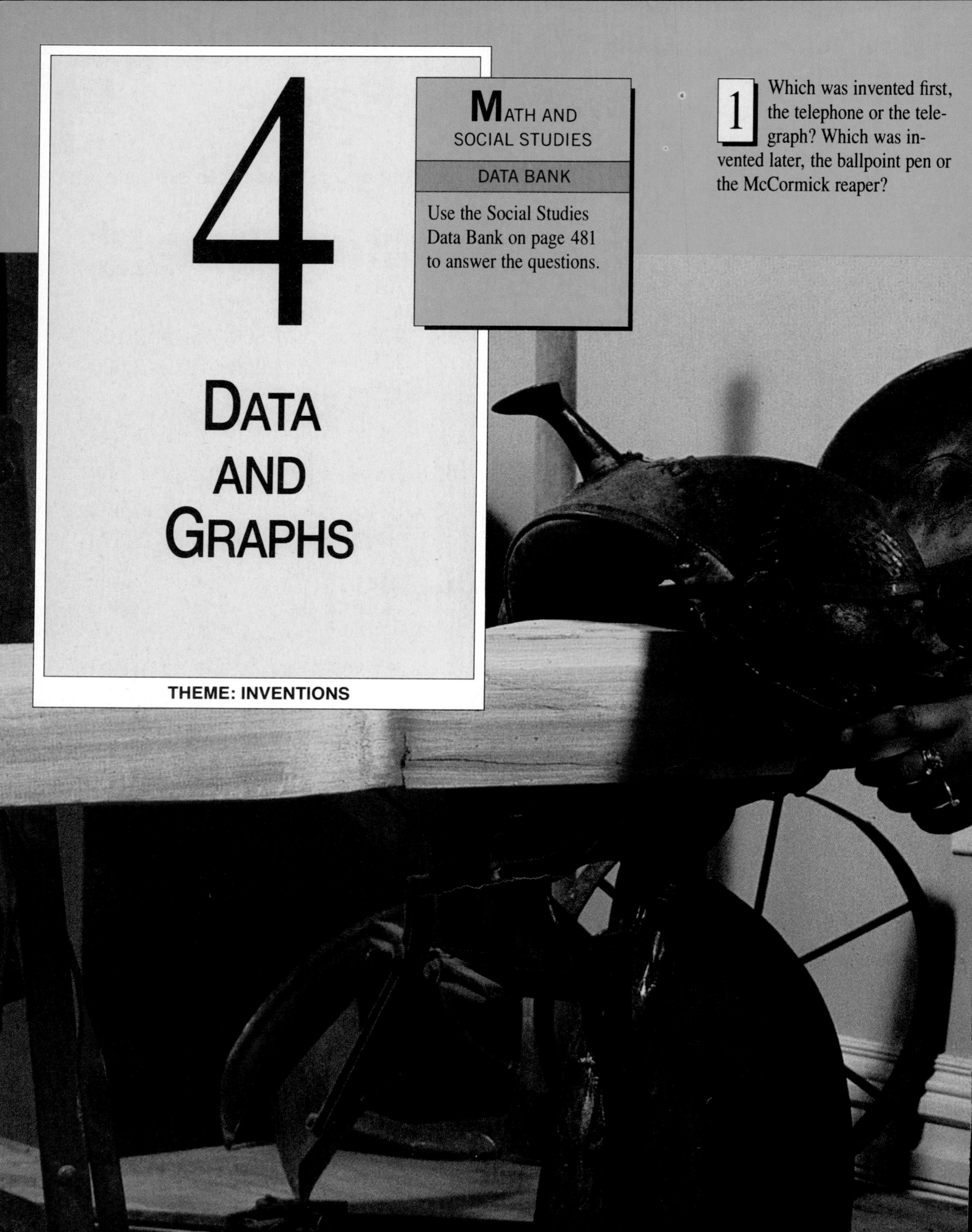

4

DATA
AND
GRAPHS

THEME: INVENTIONS

MATH AND
SOCIAL STUDIES

DATA BANK

Use the Social Studies
Data Bank on page 481
to answer the questions.

1 Which was invented first,
the telephone or the telegraph? Which was in-
vented later, the ballpoint pen or
the McCormick reaper?

2 List the years of the following inventions in order, from most recent to oldest: steamboat, telegraph, telephone, electric washer, typewriter.

3 Benjamin Franklin invented the lightning rod 124 years before Alexander Graham Bell invented the telephone. When did Franklin invent the lightning rod?

4 **Using Critical Thinking** Connie made a list of the years these items were invented: steamboat, telegraph, typewriter, car starter. Then she added one more year to the list. What do you think it was? Why?

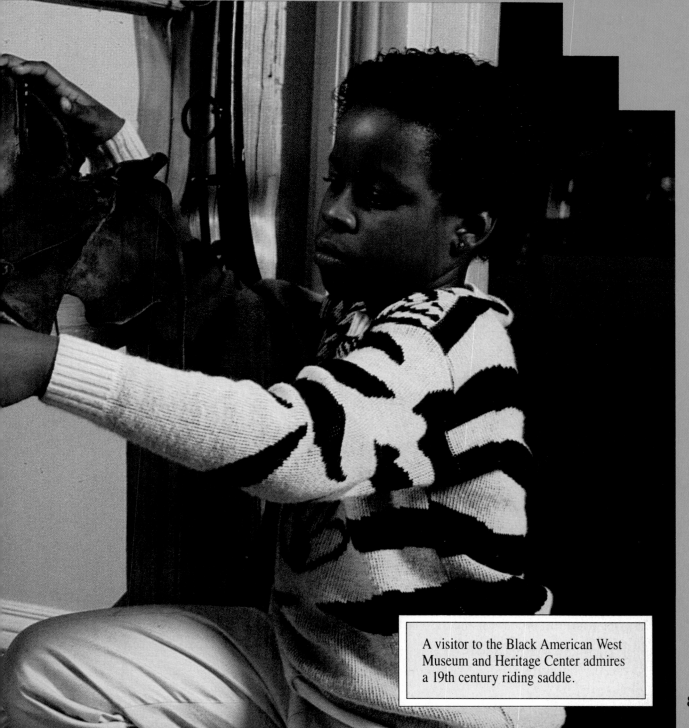

A visitor to the Black American West Museum and Heritage Center admires a 19th century riding saddle.

89

Thinking About Graphs

EXPLORE Analyze a Graph

Study the bar graph, line graph, and pictograph.

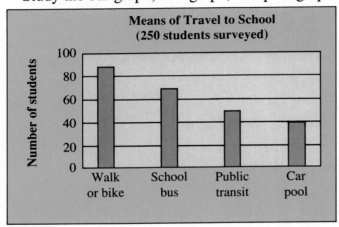

Means of Travel to School
(250 students surveyed)

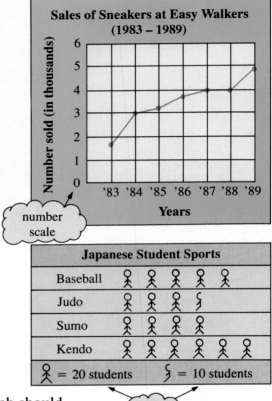

Sales of Sneakers at Easy Walkers
(1983 – 1989)

number scale

TALK ABOUT IT

1. How do the greatest number of students get to school?

2. In what year were the sales of sneakers the greatest? the least? How did you decide?

3. Which Japanese sport has the greatest number of student participants? Explain.

Japanese Student Sports	
Baseball	🧍 🧍 🧍 🧍 🧍
Judo	🧍 🧍 🧍 🧍
Sumo	🧍 🧍 🧍 🧍
Kendo	🧍 🧍 🧍 🧍 🧍 🧍

🧍 = 20 students   🧍 = 10 students

key

All graphs should have a **title,** each part of a graph should have a **label,** and bar and line graphs should have a **number scale.** A pictograph should have a **key** that tells what number each symbol represents.

Use the graphs above to answer these questions.

1. What is the title of each graph?

2. What are the labels for the sides of the bar graph?

3. How many students does each half picture represent in the pictograph?

Languages Spoken in India (2,000 people surveyed)	
Hindi	𝕩 𝕩 𝕩 𝕩 𝕩 𝕩
Oriya	𝕩 𝕩 𝕩 𝕤
Telugu	𝕩 𝕩 𝕩 𝕩 𝕩
English	𝕩 𝕩 𝕩 𝕩 𝕩 𝕩

𝕩 = 100 people   𝕤 = 50 people

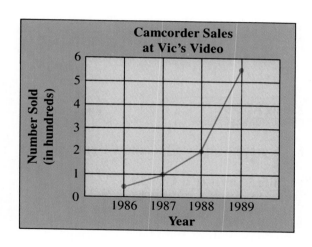

1. Give the title of the pictograph.

2. Give the title of the line graph.

3. What do the numbers 1, 2, 3, 4, 5, and 6 represent in the line graph?

4. What is the key for the pictograph?

MATH REASONING

5. Can you tell from the pictograph above whether Hindi and English are spoken by *exactly* the same number of people who were surveyed?

6. Between which two years was the growth in Camcorder sales the greatest? How did you decide?

PROBLEM SOLVING

Use the data in the graphs on page 90 to solve.

7. About how many more students walk or bike to school than go by car pool?

8. By about how much did sneaker sales increase from 1983 to 1989?

▶ **ESTIMATION**

9. Predict the number of aerobics classes there will be in the year 2000.

10. About how many aerobics classes will there be in the year 2020 if the rate of increase in classes continues?

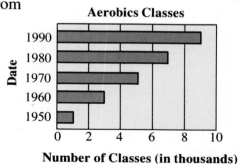

Reading and Interpreting Line Graphs

LEARN ABOUT IT

Line graphs are used to show trends in data.

EXPLORE Analyze a Graph

When do you usually buy a swimsuit? The graph at the right shows swimsuit sales at a particular store for March through August.

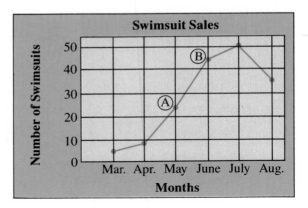

TALK ABOUT IT

1. As you go up the vertical number scale, each mark represents how many swimsuits?
2. Point A on the graph lies on the line for what month?
3. Which month had the highest sales? How did you decide?

- The horizontal and vertical number scales on a line graph are sometimes called the **horizontal axis** and **vertical axis.**
- The **slope** of the line tells whether there is an increase, a decrease, or no change.
- Each point on a line graph stands for two values. Point B on the graph above stands for June on the horizontal scale and for about 45 on the vertical scale. About 45 swimsuits were sold in June.

TRY IT OUT

Use the temperature graph at the right.

1. For which hours during the day did the students collect data?

2. What was the high temperature of the day according to the graph?

3. Do you predict the temperature at 5 p.m. will be higher or lower than 16° C?

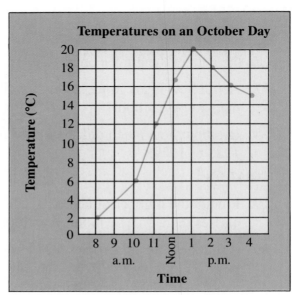

Use the sports graph.

1. As you go up the vertical number scale, each mark represents how many students?

2. What year had the smallest number of men participants? women?

3. In which years did the number of male participants drop from the previous year?

4. About how many more women were participating in 1990 than in 1983?

5. Are the two lines about the same distance apart for each year?

6. Did the number of women participants increase more or less than the number of men participants from 1983 to 1990?

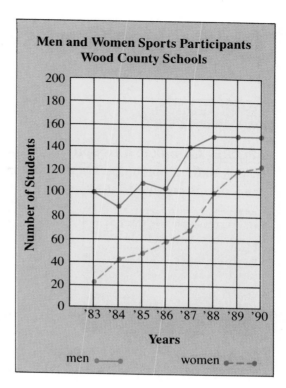

Men and Women Sports Participants
Wood County Schools

APPLY

MATH REASONING

7. Make a prediction based on the sports graph above. How many men and women participants do you predict there will be in 1991? in 1995?

PROBLEM SOLVING

8. Estimate how many more men were participating in sports in 1990 than in 1983. Then do this for the women. By how much more did the number of women increase?

▶ **USING CRITICAL THINKING**   Interpret a Graph

Tanya rides her bicycle to school. It takes her 20 minutes. Here is a graph showing the time she travels and her speed on her bike. Write an explanation of why her speeds change during her trip.

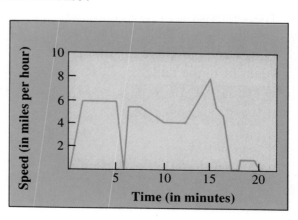

93

Making Line Graphs

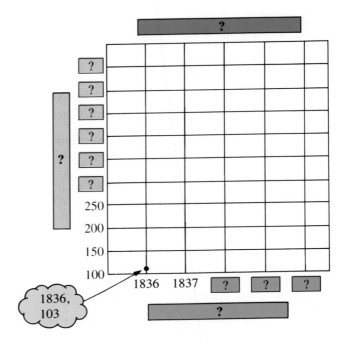

LEARN ABOUT IT

EXPLORE Complete a Graph

Copy and complete the graph about
inventions patented.

Year	Number of Inventions Patented in the U.S.
1836	103
1837	426
1838	514
1839	404
1840	458

TALK ABOUT IT

1. What is the largest number you need for the vertical
   axis? the horizontal axis? How did you decide?
2. Why would an interval of 100 rather than 50 not be as
   good a choice for the vertical number scale?
3. Did the number of inventions patented increase each
   year? Explain.

To make a line graph:

- Draw each axis. Select a scale for each.
- Label the parts of the graph. Title the graph.
- Plot the points for the data. Connect the
  points with line segments.

TRY IT OUT

Copy and complete the line graph. Use
data from the table.

Year	Population per square mile
1790	4.5
1800	6.1
1810	4.3
1820	5.5
1830	7.4

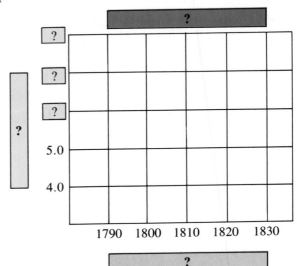

94

Use the given data to make line graphs.

1.

Day of the Week	Number of Minutes of Homework
Day 1	20
Day 2	45
Day 3	20
Day 4	60
Day 5	45

2.

Year	Number of Vans Sold by One Dealer
1985	8
1986	12
1987	18
1988	28
1989	35

APPLY

MATH REASONING

3. Decide whether the data below would best be graphed using a bar graph, a line graph, or a pictograph. Explain why.

Kilowatt Hours of Electricity Used by Five Families in One Year					
Family	Davis	Lee	Conrad	Jacobs	Grasso
Kwh	27,000	46,000	49,000	24,000	35,000

PROBLEM SOLVING

4. Use the table on page 94. Estimate how many more inventions were patented in 1838 than in 1836.

5. Social Studies Data Bank   Make a line graph that shows how many patents on inventions were requested in the years 1836−1840. See page 481.

MIXED REVIEW

Write $<$, $>$, or $=$ for each ▒.

6. 8.04 ▒ 8.40   **7.** 2.362 ▒ 2.326   **8.** 6.41 ▒ 4.41   **9.** 20.01 ▒ 20.010

Find the sums.

10. 41.92 + 67.98   **11.** 0.009 + 0.009   **12.** 7.8 + 9.098

Double Bar Graphs

A double bar graph compares two sets of data using the same units.

EXPLORE **Analyze a Graph**
This graph compares the costs of renting and buying a masquerade costume. What parts of the costume would you consider buying and what parts would you rent?

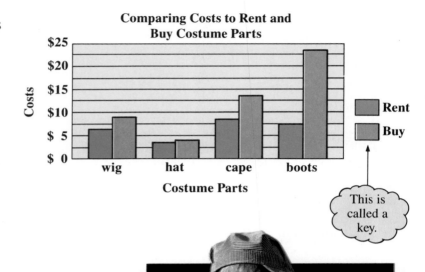

Comparing Costs to Rent and Buy Costume Parts

Costs / Costume Parts

Key: Rent, Buy

This is called a key.

TALK ABOUT IT

1. What do the orange bars represent?
2. Which item costs almost as much to rent as to buy?
3. If you were to rent only one item, which would you rent and why?

To make a double bar graph:
- Select a scale that fits the data.
- Make a key for the graph.
- Draw the axes and label the parts of the graph.
- Draw the bars.
- Title the graph.

TRY IT OUT

Use the graph above to answer these questions.

1. About how much does it cost to rent a cape?
2. Estimate the cost of buying a wig.
3. Estimate the cost of buying boots.
4. About how much more does it cost to buy boots than to rent boots?

1. Copy and complete the double bar graph.
   Survey Question and Results
   Which one of these people would you
   most like to have known?

	Adults	Children
Susan B. Anthony	16	12
Albert Einstein	22	18
Martin Luther King	24	31
Helen Keller	9	15

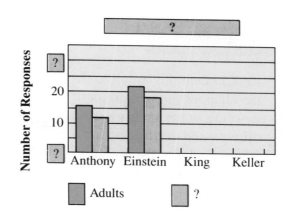

MATH REASONING

Could each set of data be graphed using a double bar
graph? Write **yes** or **no.**

2.
Plant Height	
2 days	1 cm
4 days	1.5 cm
6 days	21.5 cm

3.
Scores:	Game 1	Game 2
Wildcats	57	64
Tigers	34	45
Bears	56	40

4.
	Fall City	Twin Peaks
Rainfall	13 in.	9 in.
Temp.	72°	53°
Altitude	1,200 ft	3,200 ft

PROBLEM SOLVING

5. **Data Hunt**   Make a double bar graph to show the daily
   high and low temperatures for your city for one week.

▶ **USING CRITICAL THINKING   Comparing Graphs**

Some graphs can be misleading. Study these graphs.

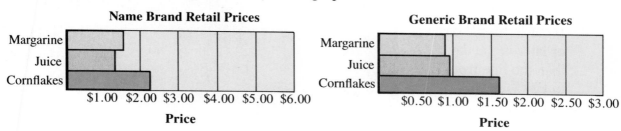

6. What is the interval on the scale at the left? on the scale
   at the right?
7. If you did not look at the horizontal scales, which prices
   would you think are higher, name brand or generic? Explain.

Using Critical Thinking

Keiko made this graph to show the changes in the amount of gasoline in her family's car as time passed during one Saturday. When Carl saw the graph, he said, "That graph has no numbers. It doesn't tell me a thing!" Berti smiled, and said, "It tells me just what happened to the car during that day!" What story does the graph tell you about what happened to the car on Saturday?

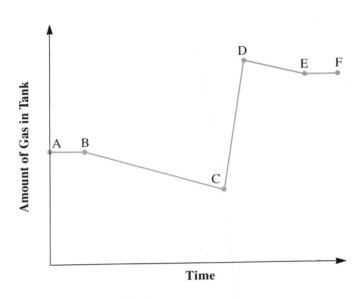

TALK ABOUT IT

1. What could a downward sloping line mean on the graph? an upward sloping line?

2. How would the line on the graph look if the car was parked in the garage for a couple of hours?

3. Is the line from A to B earlier in the day or later in the day than the line from E to F?

4. Tell a story about what happened. Compare your story with the stories of other students.

98

Burnett's Family Vacation

Miles Driven: 600, 500, 400, 300, 200, 100, 0

Time: Begin Day 1, End Day 1, End Day 2, End Day 3, End Day 4, End Day 5 (Noon)

Use the graph at the right for exercises 1–3.

1. On which day did the Burnetts do the most driving?

2. They stayed at their grandmother's house one day and did not drive at all. What day did they stay at their grandmother's?

3. Give an explanation for what could have happened during day 5.

Use the graph at the right for exercises 4–6.

Pat's Test Scores

Test Scores: 100, 90, 80, 70, 60, 50

Marking Periods: Sept., Nov., Jan., Mar., May

4. Were Pat's scores at the end of the school year better or worse than at the beginning of the year?

5. For which marking periods were the scores the same?

6. Did this student's scores ever drop? If so, when?

7. Draw a graph like the ones above. Make the graph tell a story about someone's pulse rate while doing some kind of an activity (for example, riding a bike). Write a short story that goes with your graph.

Running Totals with a Calculator

LEARN ABOUT IT

EXPLORE Examine the Data

The students at Carver School had a drive to collect used toys and games. The goal was for each grade to collect a total of 100 toys and games in 5 weeks. The results for each week are shown in the table.

Here is how Peggy used a calculator to find out if the third grade class reached the goal.

Toys and Games Collected			
	Grade 3	Grade 4	Grade 5
Week 1	18	32	39
Week 2	34	29	18
Week 3	27	25	44
Week 4	26	19	23
Week 5	17	31	19

Keys	Display	
[ON/AC] 18 [+] 34 [+]	<u>52</u>	Not enough. Add week 3.
27 [+]	<u>79</u>	Still not enough. Add week 4.
26 [+]	<u>105</u>	That's enough!

TALK ABOUT IT

1. Why did Peggy stop and look at the total display each time?

2. Peggy did not press the [=] key. Why?

TRY IT OUT

Use your calculator to solve each problem.

1. Which grade reached the collection goal first?

2. Suppose the goal had been 60 toys and games rather than 100. Which grade would have reached that goal first?

3. Which grade collected the most toys and games altogether?

POWER PRACTICE/QUIZ

For items 1–4, use the graph at the right.

1. What is this kind of graph called?

2. What is the title of the graph?

3. What do the numbers on the vertical axis show?

4. Between what two hours did the greatest temperature change occur?

5. What kinds of graphs could you use to compare two sets of data using the same units?

6. What number of units are shown by the portion of the pictograph at the right?

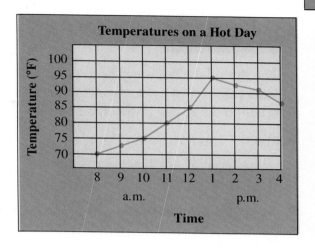

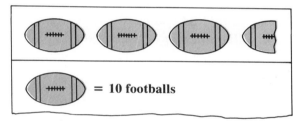

= 10 footballs

PROBLEM SOLVING

The table at the right shows the results of a newspaper collection drive that two fifth grade classes took part in. Use the data for items 7–10.

Pounds of Newspapers Collected				
	Week 1	Week 2	Week 3	Week 4
Class A	30	26	17	15
Class B	40	42	55	60

7. Make a line graph to show the data for Class B. Use a scale with 5-pound intervals to show the amount collected each week.

8. Make a double bar graph to show the data for both classes. Choose a scale with some interval other than 5 pounds to show the amounts collected each week.

9. Which class showed an increase in amount collected each week?
   Which class showed a decrease?

10. Suppose Bobby Brownlee was the top collector in his class and then he moved to the other class. Which class do you think he left? When do you think he left?

Range, Mean, Median, and Mode

LEARN ABOUT IT

The difference between the greatest and
least numbers in a set of numerical data
is called the **range** of the data.

EXPLORE Analyze Some Data

Find the range for the ages at which the
presidents listed in the table took office.

TALK ABOUT IT

Presidents' Ages When Inaugurated	
George Washington	57
William Henry Harrison	68
John Tyler	51
Franklin Pierce	48
James Buchanan	65
Abraham Lincoln	52
William Howard Taft	51

1. How did you find the range for the ages?
2. Suppose Lincoln's age had been 50 rather than 52.
   Would that change the range? Explain.
3. What number between 48 and 68 is about in the middle
   of the list of ages? How did you decide?

The **mean** or **average** of a set of numbers can be found by
finding the sum of all of the numbers and then dividing by
the number of addends. Here is how to find the mean of the
presidents' ages.

Mean $= (57 + 68 + 51 + 48 + 65 + 52 + 51) \div 7$

$\qquad = 392 \div 7 = 56$ $\quad$ (392 ÷ 7 $\boxed{56}$)

The **median** is the middle number when the data are
arranged in order. If there are two middle numbers, the
median is the mean of the two middle numbers.

48 $\quad$ 51 $\quad$ 51 $\quad$ 52 $\quad$ 57 $\quad$ 65 $\quad$ 68
$\qquad\qquad\qquad$ ↑
$\qquad\qquad\qquad$ Median

The **mode** is the number that appears most often in a set of
data. For the presidents' ages the mode is 51. Sometimes
no one number appears more often than any others. In such
cases there is no mode.

TRY IT OUT

Find the range, mean, median, and mode for each set.

1. 45, 76, 88, 99, 104, 56 $\qquad\qquad$ 2. 78, 88, 85, 90, 78, 71, 63

Find the range, mean, median, and mode for each set of data.

1. 17, 24, 24, 30, 20   **2.** 17, 24, 34, 27, 18   **3.** 43, 29, 29, 38, 26, 15

4. 103, 113, 97, 89, 98   **5.** 125, 146, 140, 159, 140   **6.** 215, 219, 202, 219, 225

7. $3.75, $8.25, $5.50, $3.75, $4.00   **8.** $20, $12, $28, $12, $35, $91

APPLY

MATH REASONING

9. Change one number in the following data so that the range is 20. 7, 5, 18, 21, 6, 24, 17

10. Change one number in the following data so that the mode is 12. 15, 13, 18, 12, 16, 25

11. Without computing, tell which set of data has the greater mean.
A. 46, 56, 82, 91, 75, 81   **B.** 56, 82, 91, 46, 120, 81

PROBLEM SOLVING

12. When becoming President of the U.S., Millard Fillmore was 50 years old, Theodore Roosevelt was 42, Woodrow Wilson was 56, and Harry Truman was 60. What is the mean for the ages at which these men became President?

13. Social Studies Data Bank   What is the range for the set of ages at which Presidents Washington through Harrison were inaugurated? What is the mode? What is the median? See page 481.

MIXED REVIEW

Write the word name for each decimal number.

14. 0.09   **15.** 1.002   **16.** 0.32   **17.** 2.061

Subtract.

18.   37.88   **19.**   2.543   **20.**   34.6   **21.**   7.803
       − 21.46   − 0.697   − 16.7   − 4.637

More Practice, page 503, set D

103

Making a Questionnaire

Pottery made by a skilled artist of Acoma Pueblo, New Mexico

LEARN ABOUT IT

EXPLORE   Complete a Questionnaire

Work in groups. Write your answers to the questionnaire.

> 1. Your grade? _____
> 2. What item or items could you bring to be shown at your school's Small World Arts and Crafts Fair? _____
> 3. How would you rate the following kinds of entertainment for the fair? (**1** means "would enjoy very much" and **5** means "would not enjoy at all.")
>
> **A.** Native costumes parade   1   2   3   4   5
> **B.** "Guess the Culture" contest   1   2   3   4   5
> **C.** Dances of many lands   1   2   3   4   5
> **D.** "How to . . ." demonstrations   1   2   3   4   5
>   (origami, weaving, beadwork, . . .

Hand-decorated gourd from Kenya, eastern Africa

TALK ABOUT IT

1. Is each question clear? Do you think everyone would interpret each question the same way?
2. Do you think every student would clearly understand what each activity is?

To make a questionnaire:
- Decide on the subject you want information about.
- Brainstorm ideas you want to cover in the questionnaire.
- Write questions for the questionnaire.
- Give your questionnaire to a few people to find out whether all questions are clearly stated.
- Revise the questionnaire if necessary.

TRY IT OUT

Suppose you have been asked to decide what games and food booths to have at a school carnival.

1. Brainstorm ideas you might put on your questionnaire.
2. Give reasons why it might or might not make sense to have a student's name on the questionnaire.
3. Write four questions you might include on your questionnaire.

Statue of a Chinese Imperial Palace guard (Han Dynasty)

1. Copy and complete the questionnaire.

Name_____	
A. What grade are you in? Circle one. K–2 2–4 4–6 6–8	**C.** Circle the price you would be most willing to pay for a ticket to the fair. $0.50 $1.00 $2.00 $3.00
B. Which of these foods is your favorite? Circle it. Spinach Eggs Carrots	**D.** Circle the number of brothers and sisters you have. 1 2 3 4

Use the questionnaire above for exercises 2–7.

2. Why would a fourth-grader have difficulty answering item A?

3. Rewrite question A so that the grade levels do not overlap.

4. What is wrong with item B?

5. What is wrong with Question C?

6. Rewrite item C so that you can find out the most someone would pay.

7. Rewrite item D so that everyone can answer.

MATH REASONING

8. How could you fairly select 25 students in your school to be given a questionnaire about choosing a new name for your school?

PROBLEM SOLVING

9. Lanny gave out a questionnaire to 9 girls and 7 boys. He got back completed questionnaires from 6 girls and 5 boys. How many completed questionnaires has he not yet gotten back?

▶ **ESTIMATION**

10. Cut out some 1 ft² paper "tiles." Use them to estimate the area of your classroom floor. Explain how you made your estimate.

105

Problem Solving
Make a Table

UNDERSTAND
ANALYZE DATA
PLAN
ESTIMATE
SOLVE
EXAMINE

LEARN ABOUT IT

To solve some problems you may find it helpful to use the given data and a strategy called **Make a Table.**

Helga's after school service club set up an assembly line to make stuffed brown bears. The furry fabric needed to make 3 bears cost $11. How much does the fabric for 18 bears cost?

I'll make a table using the data in the problem.

Now I'll complete the table to find the solution.

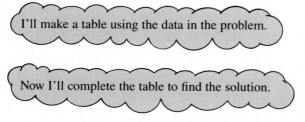

This data was given in the problem.						
bears	3					
fabric	$11					

		2×3	3×3	4×3	5×3	6×3
bears	3	6	9	12	15	18
fabric	$11	$22	$33	$44	$55	$66
		2×11	3×11	4×11	5×11	6×11

The fabric for 18 bears costs $66.

TRY IT OUT

Jim and Juan are the quality control inspectors at the end of the assembly line. Out of every 5 completed bears, 4 bears pass their inspection. The class has completed 25 bears. How many of them would you expect to pass the inspection by Jim and Juan?

- Out of 5 completed bears, how many usually pass inspection?

- How many bears has the class completed?

- Copy and complete the table below to solve the problem.

Completed bears	5	10	15	20	25
Bears that pass	4				

106

Make a table to help you solve each problem.

1. The class needs 10 ounces of stuffing for every 4 bears. How much stuffing does the class need in order to make 20 bears?

stuffing				
bears				

2. The first week, the class made bears at a rate of 3 every 20 minutes. How many did they make in 120 minutes (2 hours)?

bears				
minutes				

MIXED PRACTICE

Choose a strategy from the strategies list or use other strategies you know to solve these problems.

Some Strategies	
Act Out	Draw a Picture
Use Objects	Guess and Check
Choose an Operation	Make a Table

3. The bear's eyes cost 9¢ each. How much would 8 eyes cost?

4. During the week that the bear-mascots were on sale, the class also made and sold lemonade. They used 5 lemons for every 8 cups of lemonade. How many lemons did they need for 48 cups of lemonade? Make a table like the one below to help you.

lemons					
cups					

Use this graph for problems 7 and 8.

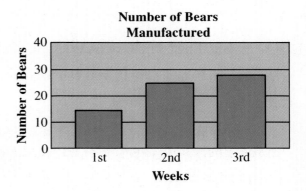

5. It cost the class $146.75 to make all the bears. They made a total of $191.54 in sales. How much profit did they make?

6. The class sold 98 bears. 12 more students from the upper grades bought a bear than students from the lower grades. How many customers were from the upper grades?

7. The class worked 5 days the second week of the assembly line. They made the same number of bears each day. How many bears did they make each day?

8. About how many bears did the class make altogether in the second and third weeks?

Estimation
Substituting Compatible Numbers

LEARN ABOUT IT

EXPLORE Make Some Estimates

The costs of the items Patty bought for a picnic are shown below. Estimate the total cost of Patty's items. Replace numbers in the list with compatible numbers.

Picnic Items and Costs			
paper cups	$1.59	buns	$3.49
paper plates	$2.19	ketchup	$1.19
cheese slices	$2.64	pickles	$1.67
soft drinks	$7.54	mustard	$0.98
charcoal	$2.58	ice	$1.63
ground beef	$8.70	chips	$2.59

Compatible Numbers	
$0.25 or 25	$1.25 or 125
$0.50 or 50	$1.50 or 150
$0.75 or 75	$2.50 or 250
$1.00 or 100	$5.00 or 500

TALK ABOUT IT

1. Suppose you rounded amounts for the cups and cheese to the nearest dollar. Do you get the same estimate?
2. Does this way of estimating always give the same answer as rounding? Think of an example to show why or why not.

To estimate Patty's total, you can use a technique called **substituting compatible numbers.** Replace some or all of the numbers with numbers that are easy to compute with mentally. Then add or subtract.

Here are some examples of how to estimate by substituting compatible numbers.

29.4 + 72.6	$3.89 + $4.58	553 − 229
Estimate: 25 + 75 = 100	Estimate: $4.00 + $4.58 = $8.58	Estimate: 550 − 225 = 325

TRY IT OUT

Substitute compatible numbers to estimate each cost.

1. paper plates and charcoal

2. soft drinks and ground beef

3. mustard and ice

4. buns and ketchup

Substitute compatible numbers to estimate each sum or difference.

1. 143 − 54   **2.** 79 + 123   **3.** 193 + 261   **4.** 874 − 196

5. 597 + 324   **6.** 158 − 78   **7.** 989 − 496   **8.** 354 + 78

9. $6.06 − $3.95   **10.** $2.49 + $6.03   **11.** $248.99 + $97.88   **12.** $553 − $103.49

13. $174 + $245 + $25 + $150   **14.** $429 + $128 + $564 + $459 + $79 + $298

APPLY

MATH REASONING

Use estimation to find the approximate value of the variable.

15. $227 + x$ is about 475.   **16.** $y + 668$ is about 1,000.

PROBLEM SOLVING

Use the data list about camping gear.

17. Zina is going on a fishing trip with her best friend. She needs a sleeping bag and a fishing pole. Estimate the cost for these items.

18. Terry's family is going on a camping trip this summer. They bought 4 items whose total cost was a little less than $300. What could they have bought?

19. Sandy bought a sleeping bag and paid for it with a hundred dollar bill. About how much change did she get back?

Camping Gear Costs	
Back pack	$229.99
Tent	$179.97
Fishing pole	$ 29.95
Pots and pans	$ 22.99
Sleeping bag	$ 76.95
First aid kit	$ 27.50
Camp stove	$135.75
Raft	$ 55.95

▶ MENTAL MATH

You can break apart a decimal and use mental math to add a whole number to it. For example, 3.4 + 2 is 3 + 2 + 0.4, or 5.4.

Use mental math to find these sums.

20. 8 + 9.4   **21.** 12.8 + 4   **22.** 2.5 + 7   **23.** 7 + 6.8

24. 7.9 + 3   **25.** 8 + 12.5   **26.** 10.8 + 9   **27.** 13 + 2.7

More Practice, page 504, set A

Problem Solving
Extra Data

UNDERSTAND
ANALYZE DATA
PLAN
ESTIMATE
SOLVE
EXAMINE

LEARN ABOUT IT

Some problems have extra data that is not
needed to solve the problem. You may
have to sort through the data to find the
facts you need.

During September 155 doves, 3 owls, and
49 sparrows were brought to the Wildlife Shelter
with injuries. How many more doves than
sparrows were brought to the shelter?

I'll find only the data I need to
solve the problem.

I'm ready to use the data to solve
the problem.

Doves   Sparrows
155   49

$$\begin{array}{r} 155 \\ -\ 49 \\ \hline 106 \end{array}$$

106 more doves than sparrows were brought in with injuries.

TRY IT OUT

Solve.

1. In May 725 animals were cared for at
the shelter. In June 446 were cared for.
In December only 57 were cared for.
How many more animals were cared
for in May than in December?

2. Maria checked in 8 crows at the
shelter. She checked in 8 times as
many sparrows as crows and 7 times
as many mockingbirds as crows. How
many mockingbirds were checked in?

3. Jan kept records of animals at the
shelter. There were almost 13 times as
many birds as mammals in one year.
There were 676 birds and 49 mammals.
What was the total number of animals
Jan kept a record of?

4. Of the 676 birds Jan recorded, 152
were released in good health within 6
weeks. Of the 49 mammals, 23 were
released within 6 weeks. How many
animals were released within 6 weeks?

110

Solve. Use any problem solving strategy.

1. Last month 7 times as many squirrels as owls were brought to the shelter. Five owls were brought in. How many squirrels were brought in?

2. Approximately 2 out of every 8 animals cared for at the shelter are released in good health. How many animals would you expect to be released out of 40 animals cared for?

Animals cared for			
Animals released			

3. Three years ago, when Jess was 13, she volunteered 54 hours in 6 months at the Wildlife Shelter. She worked the same number of hours each month. How many hours did she volunteer each month?

4. In the 4 years from 1987 through 1990, how many animals have been cared for at the shelter?

Year	Animals Cared For
1987	2,886
1988	2,853
1989	3,350
1990	3,137

5. In 1990, 369 of the animals cared for at the shelter were mammals and the rest were birds. In 1991, 398 of the animals were mammals and 3,137 were birds. How many animals were cared for in 1991?

6. The shelter's cost for food for the animals was $1,280 for July. That cost was $268 less than the cost for June. What was the cost for June?

7. The animal shelter is open to visitors for 6 hours a day every day except Sunday and Monday. How many hours a week is the shelter open to visitors?

8. **Thinking About Your Solution**
The shelter cared for 88 more sea birds than sea mammals one month. The same month the shelter cared for 72 more land birds than sea mammals. Explain how you can tell without computing whether the shelter cared for more sea birds or more land birds that month.

Data Collection and Analysis
Group Decision Making

UNDERSTAND
ANALYZE DATA
PLAN
ESTIMATE
SOLVE
EXAMINE

Doing a Simulation
Group Skill:
Encourage and Respect Others

Herman is a little odd. He only wears red socks or blue socks. He bought 2 blue pairs and 4 red pairs on sale and stuffed them all in a dresser drawer. Each morning when he wakes up, he sleepily digs around in his drawer and pulls out the first two socks he finds without turning on the lights. Do you think he will get a blue pair, a red pair, or a mismatched pair more often? A **simulation,** in which you act out the situation to see what is likely to happen, will help you answer this question.

Collecting Data

1. Work with your group to cut out 6 pairs of sock shapes. Color 2 pairs blue and 4 pairs red. The socks should all be the same size and shape.

2. Put all of the socks in a paper bag and mix them. Take turns drawing out two socks. Record each "pair" in a table like the one shown. Then put the socks back into the bag. Do this 50 times.

	Number of "Pairs"	Total
Red Pairs	ЖТ ΙΙ	
Blue Pairs	ЖТ ΙΙΙΙ	
Mismatched Pairs	ΙΙΙ	

3. Count the number of red pairs, blue pairs, and mismatched pairs you drew. Write the totals in your table.

4. Make a bar graph using the data in the table. Make the scale longer or shorter to suit the data in your table.

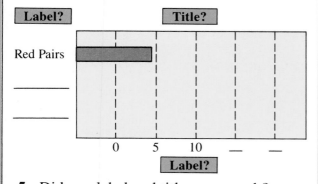

Label?

Title?

Red Pairs

0   5   10   __   __

Label?

5. Did you label and title your graph?

6. Did your predictions about whether Herman would draw more red pairs, blue pairs or mismatched pairs come close to the results of your simulation?

7. Write three or four sentences to tell what happened in your simulation. Why do you think you got the results you did?

Wrap Up

Word Scavenger Hunt

Each word described below can be found in this chapter. Write the word.

1. a 5-letter word for the vertical and horizontal number lines on graphs

2. a 13-letter word for an instrument to collect data

3. an 8-letter word for the distance between two numbers on a scale

4. a 3-letter word that shows what number a picture represents on a pictograph

Sometimes, Always, Never

Complete each statement by writing **sometimes**, **always**, or **never**. Explain your choice.

5. In a pictograph, you __?__ need a key to tell you what quantity each picture represents.

6. The numbers used in graphs are __?__ estimates.

7. Graphs are __?__ used to predict future events.

8. You can __?__ draw bar graphs for the same data that look different by changing the scale.

Project

Survey your classmates about a topic of special interest to you. For example, you might ask, "For a vacation, would you rather go camping, go to an amusement park, go to the beach, or visit historic places?" Organize your responses in a table. Show the results of your survey in a bar graph.

POWER PRACTICE/TEST

Part 1 Understanding

1. What does each picture represent in the pictograph?

2. How many trees were planted in 1988?

3. Make a line graph that shows someone's test scores for 5 math quizzes. Write a story about your graph.

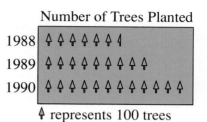

Number of Trees Planted

1988	⚐ ⚐ ⚐ ⚐ ⚐ ⚐ ⚐
1989	⚐ ⚐ ⚐ ⚐ ⚐ ⚐ ⚐ ⚐
1990	⚐ ⚐ ⚐ ⚐ ⚐ ⚐ ⚐ ⚐ ⚐ ⚐

⚐ represents 100 trees

Part 2 Skills

4. Draw a double bar graph for the data in this chart.

Magazines Sold

Week	Grade 5	Grade 6
1	145	152
2	160	163
3	157	158

5. How many more magazines did Grade 6 sell than Grade 5?

6. How many magazines were sold in all during Week 1?

Find each of the following for this set of data:
151, 210, 176, 185, 164, 164, 175

7. mean   8. mode   9. median   10. range

Use compatible numbers to estimate each sum or difference.

11. $856 − $305.24   12. 341 + 53 + 98   13. 77 + 123 + 198

Part 3 Applications

14. A charter bus can carry 50 people. The music club has 80 members who will need to ride on the bus. Tickets cost $4 each. How many buses are needed?

15. **Challenge** The Odd Folks Library lets you take out 3 books on each visit, but you must give one back immediately. How many visits will it take you to have 10 books?

115

ENRICHMENT
Organizing Data to Make Comparisons

A table can be used to organize data so that you can compare. How you make the table depends on what you want to compare.

Look at this set of data.

Make a table that you can use to compare the number of people who like each game show. Use your table to answer these questions.

Name	Grade	Male/Female	Favorite Game Show
Melinda	5	F	Target Wheel
Joe	4	M	Turn Around
Paul	5	M	Roll Again
Mimi	5	F	Turn Around
Ursula	4	F	Roll Again
Erin	4	F	Buzz
Elsie	5	F	Turn Around
Judy	4	F	Turn Around
Jimenez	5	M	Roll Again
Pablo	5	M	Roll Again
Amanda	4	F	Target Wheel
Alisa	5	F	Turn Around
Jamal	5	M	Roll Again
Pam	4	F	Turn Around
Jolene	4	F	Target Wheel
Jane	4	F	Turn Around
Gerald	5	M	Buzz
Toby	5	F	Roll Again
Mason	5	M	Turn Around
Harold	4	M	Target Wheel

1. How many people were surveyed?

2. What are the names of the shows in order from the most liked to the least liked?

3. How many more people chose *Roll Again* than chose *Target Wheel*?

Make a table that you can use to compare the fourth graders' favorite shows with the fifth graders' favorite shows. Use your table to answer these questions.

4. How many in each grade were surveyed?

5. What is each grade's favorite show?

6. Which grade liked *Target Wheel* more? By how many more students was it chosen in that grade than in the other?

Make a table that you can use to compare the girls' favorite shows with the boys' favorite shows. Use the table to answer these questions.

7. How many girls were surveyed? how many boys?

8. Which show did the greatest number of girls like best? the greatest number of boys?

116

CUMULATIVE REVIEW

1. What is 8,426,744 rounded to the nearest thousand?

    A. 8,400,000   B. 8,430,000
    c. 8,000,000   D. 8,427,000

2. Which number is between 7.321 and 7.330?

    A. 7.327   B. 7.320
    c. 7.331   D. 7.319

3. What is the standard form of 700,000 + 3,000 + 40 + 6?

    A. 7.346   B. 70,346
    c. 703,046   D. 73,046

4. Which number is less than 385,271?

    A. 385,283   B. 385,309
    c. 385,268   D. 386,004

5. Which number rounds to 4?

    A. 4.7   B. 3.98   c. 3.49   D. 4.6

Add or subtract.

6. 3.56 + 1.56

    A. 5.18   B. 5.12   c. 6.22   D. 6.18

7. 3.22 − 1.15

    A. 2.07   B. 1.02   c. 2.17   D. 3.37

8. Leah and Owen have 24 goldfish in all. Leah has 4 more than Owen. How many goldfish does she have?

    A. 12   B. 14   c. 16   D. 20

9. How would you group the numbers to find
$4 \times 10 \times 25 \times 87$ mentally?

    A. $(4 \times 10) \times 25 \times 87$
    B. $(4 \times 25) \times 87 \times 10$
    c. $(10 \times 87) \times 25 \times 4$
    D. $(10 \times 25) \times 87 \times 4$

10. To find 8,516 + 394 using compensation:

    A. Add 400 to 8,516, then subtract 4.
    B. Add 400 to 8,516, then subtract 6.
    c. Add 4 to 8,516, then subtract 394.
    D. Subtract 6 from 8,516, then add 6 to 394

11. After solving a problem you should:

    A. Plan what to do
    B. Understand the situation
    c. Analyze the data
    D. Examine the answer

12. Which question can be asked about the following data? Seth has $12. Team shirts cost $5 each.

    A. How much change did he receive?
    B. How much are three ties?
    c. Can he buy two shirts?
    D. Can he buy a new hat?

5

MULTIPLICATION: WHOLE NUMBERS AND DECIMALS

THEME: ENERGY SOURCES

MATH AND SCIENCE

DATA BANK

Use the Science Data Bank on page 470 to answer the questions.

1 Which of the listed household electrical appliances costs the most to use per hour? Which of the listed appliances costs the least to use per hour?

2 Find out how much power a Wind Wizard windmill produces at optimum wind speed. At that speed, how much power will 2 Wind Wizards produce? How much power will 3 produce?

3 Which is greater, the cost of using an electric iron for 3 hours or the cost of using the color television set for 6 hours? How great is the difference in the two costs?

4 Using Critical Thinking Jay studied the list of electricity costs and said, "The clothes dryer costs more to use each month than any other appliance." Do you agree with Jay? Explain.

A supervisor carefully records data registered on meters in the control room of a large utilities plant.

119

Mental Math
Special Products

EXPLORE Discover a Pattern

A small Elektro windmill produces 50 watts of power. Windmills are often placed in groups in windy places. Copy and complete the table to show how much power is produced by the larger groups of windmills.

Number of windmills	Power output in watts
10	500
20	
30	
40	
50	
60	

TALK ABOUT IT

1. What multiplication was needed to find the amount of power produced by 10 windmills? by 20 windmills? by 60 windmills?
2. A single Eagle III windmill can produce 3 kilowatts of power, so 2 of these windmills could produce 6 kilowatts of power. How can you use this fact to find the amount of power that 20 of these windmills could produce?

To multiply two multiples of 10 or 100, multiply the front digits in each factor. Attach as many zeros as there are in both factors.

■ **Here is how to do it.**

Problem:	90×40
Multiply the front digits.	9×4
Write the product.	36
Attach the zeros.	3,600

■ **Here is why it works.**

$90 \times 40 = (9 \times 10) \times (4 \times 10)$
$(9 \times 4) \times (10 \times 10) \leftarrow$ Using the
36×100 commutative
$3,600$ and the
              associative
              properties.

Other Examples $80 \times 50 = 4,000$ $40 \times 600 = 24,000$ $200 \times 500 = 100,000$

Use mental math to find the products.

1. 30×40 **2.** 60×50 **3.** 30×700 **4.** 80×500 **5.** 900×800

1. 30×90 2. 80×60 3. 40×800 4. 80×500 5. 60×200

6. 70×100 7. 400×900 8. 70×600 9. 60×40 10. 70×80

11. 50×60 12. 30×900 13. 50×600 14. 60×900 15. 40×700

16. 80×100 17. 50×90 18. 70×10 19. 90×700 20. 300×400

21. $20 \times 30 \times 20$ 22. $10 \times 400 \times 20$ 23. $60 \times 200 \times 10$

24. $100 \times 20 \times 50$ 25. $40 \times 10 \times 10 \times 60$ 26. $300 \times 20 \times 200$

APPLY

MATH REASONING

27. Show as many different ways as you can to write multiples of 10 or 100 in place of the variables to complete the equation.
$a \times b = 2{,}400$

PROBLEM SOLVING

28. Each farmer in a group of 20 farmers is thinking of buying 10 windmills that can be used to pump water. If the cost of each windmill is $500, what would be the cost for all the windmills the farmers are thinking of buying?

29. **Science Data Bank** How many watts of power would a group of 20 Wind Titan windmills produce when they are running at optimum wind speed? See page 470.

30. **Missing Data** Tell what other data you need to solve this problem. Each Wind Wizard windmill can produce 600 watts of power. How many watts of power can be produced by the Wind Wizards located at the Galestorm Gap windmill farm?

► **COMMUNICATION**   **Writing to Learn**

31. Write a statement explaining how you can use the product in equation A to find the product in equation B.

    A. $47 \times 5 = 235$ **B.** $47 \times 50 = $ ▥

More Practice, page 504, set B

Estimating Products Using Rounding

LEARN ABOUT IT

EXPLORE Solve to Understand

Use the data about Murtle the Dolphin's food to answer these questions:

- About how many pounds of fish does Murtle eat in a year?

- What is Murtle's approximate weight?

MURTLE THE DOLPHIN
Food Data

1. Murtle eats about 19 pounds (lb) of fish each day.
2. Murtle's weight stays at about 20 times the weight of the food she eats daily.
3. Murtle likes fish. Her favorite fish cost 35¢ per pound. There are about 7 of the fish in a pound.
4. Murtle will jump 20 ft out of the water to get her food. She eats 4 times a day.

TALK ABOUT IT

1. Explain how you found estimates for the questions above.

2. Make up another question using data about Murtle that can be answered by estimating.

One way to estimate products is to round the factors to their highest place and use mental math to find the product. Here is how to do it.

Round each factor to its highest place. ⟶ | Round to the nearest 10. | | Round to the nearest 100. |

$$19 \times 365$$
$$\downarrow \qquad \downarrow$$
Use mental math to multiply. ⟶ $20 \times 400 = 8,000$

Other Examples

Round both factors to the nearest 10. ⟶ 146×12
$$\downarrow \qquad \downarrow$$
$$150 \times 10 = 1,500$$

Round only the greater factor. ⟶ 9×398
$$\downarrow$$
$$9 \times 400 = 3,600$$

TRY IT OUT

Use rounding and mental math to estimate the products.

1. 78×37 **2.** 11×155 **3.** 93×89 **4.** 287×9 **5.** 42×517

Estimate by rounding.

1. 72 × 8   **2.** 55 × 8   **3.** 49 × 7   **4.** 28 × 75   **5.** 17 × 36

6. 84 × 47   **7.** 486 × 28   **8.** 678 × 45   **9.** 216 × 90   **10.** 986 × 9

11. 219 × 6   **12.** 370 × 10   **13.** 495 × 316   **14.** 21 × 58   **15.** 67 × 415

APPLY

MATH REASONING

16. Use estimation to pick two numbers from the list whose product is close to 3,200. Then use a calculator to find the actual products. Which two factors give a product closest to 3,200?

Number List		
7	5	39
98	69	27
36	65	812
4	43	24
89	370	54
41	86	615
6	729	18

PROBLEM SOLVING

17. Feed for dolphins costs only 5¢ for 2 bags. What would 12 bags cost? Copy and complete the table below to find out.

18. A college student earned $8.75 an hour helping at Murtle's sea animal show. About how much will she earn in 32 hours?

bags	2	4	6	8	10	12
cost						

MIXED REVIEW

Round each number to the place of the underlined digit.

19. 2̲85   **20.** 98̲7   **21.** 1,1̲18   **22.** 20.0̲7   **23.** 7̲32   **24.** 4̲,810

Write each number in words.

25. 84.21   **26.** 948,571   **27.** 7.981

Use place value to tell what the digit **6** in each number means.

28. 6,897,112,020   **29.** 877.006   **30.** 4,367,870

More Practice, page 504, set C

Reviewing Whole Number Multiplication

LEARN ABOUT IT

The examples below will help you review whole number multiplication.

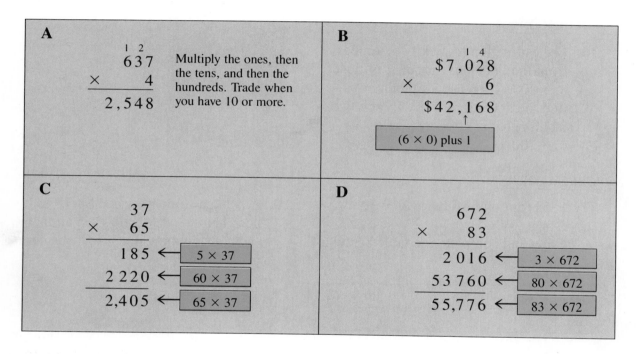

A

$$\begin{array}{r} {\scriptstyle 1\ 2} \\ 637 \\ \times \quad 4 \\ \hline 2{,}548 \end{array}$$

Multiply the ones, then the tens, and then the hundreds. Trade when you have 10 or more.

B

$$\begin{array}{r} {\scriptstyle 1\ 4} \\ \$7{,}028 \\ \times \quad\quad 6 \\ \hline \$42{,}168 \end{array}$$

$\uparrow$

(6×0) plus 1

C

$$\begin{array}{r} 37 \\ \times \quad 65 \\ \hline 185 \\ 2220 \\ \hline 2{,}405 \end{array}$$

185 ← 5×37
2220 ← 60×37
2,405 ← 65×37

D

$$\begin{array}{r} 672 \\ \times \quad 83 \\ \hline 2016 \\ 53760 \\ \hline 55{,}776 \end{array}$$

2016 ← 3×672
53760 ← 80×672
55,776 ← 83×672

TRY IT OUT

Multiply.

1. $\begin{array}{r} 33 \\ \times\ 8 \\ \hline \end{array}$
2. $\begin{array}{r} 486 \\ \times\ \ 3 \\ \hline \end{array}$
3. $\begin{array}{r} 590 \\ \times\ \ 9 \\ \hline \end{array}$
4. $\begin{array}{r} 1{,}962 \\ \times\ \ \ 6 \\ \hline \end{array}$
5. $\begin{array}{r} 3{,}480 \\ \times\ \ \ 4 \\ \hline \end{array}$

6. $\begin{array}{r} 56 \\ \times 23 \\ \hline \end{array}$
7. $\begin{array}{r} 49 \\ \times 48 \\ \hline \end{array}$
8. $\begin{array}{r} 89 \\ \times 56 \\ \hline \end{array}$
9. $\begin{array}{r} 96 \\ \times 24 \\ \hline \end{array}$
10. $\begin{array}{r} 27 \\ \times 79 \\ \hline \end{array}$

11. $\begin{array}{r} 302 \\ \times\ 94 \\ \hline \end{array}$
12. $\begin{array}{r} 567 \\ \times\ 32 \\ \hline \end{array}$
13. $\begin{array}{r} 489 \\ \times\ 86 \\ \hline \end{array}$
14. $\begin{array}{r} 638 \\ \times\ 55 \\ \hline \end{array}$
15. $\begin{array}{r} 972 \\ \times\ 73 \\ \hline \end{array}$

Multiply.

1. 79
    × 5

2. 436
    × 8

3. 207
    × 9

4. 3,509
    × 7

5. 6,327
    × 6

6. 96
    × 54

7. 38
    × 77

8. 83
    × 69

9. 90
    × 80

10. 75
    × 75

11. 176
    × 24

12. 263
    × 57

13. 926
    × 43

14. 869
    × 78

15. 375
    × 66

16. Find the product of 75 and 25.

17. Five times $126 is what amount?

Estimate each product.

18. 4 × 89

19. 3 × 298

20. 51 × 65

21. 42 × 79

APPLY

MATH REASONING

For the exercises below, estimate whether the exact product is less than or greater than the given number. Find the exact answer to check.

22. 134 × 23   Less than or greater than 2,000?
23. 68 × 78   Less than or greater than 5,000?

PROBLEM SOLVING

24. In 1990, a small theater presented 12 performances of a play called *You Can't Take It with You.* If 145 people attended each of the performances, what was the total number who saw the show?

25. **Extra Data**   Tell which data is not needed. Then solve. Barry worked 7 hours Monday, 8 Tuesday, 6 Wednesday, and 8 Thursday. He earns $6 per hour. What were his total earnings for the first three days?

▶ MENTAL MATH

Choose a mental math technique to solve each problem.

Mental Math Techniques
Counting On/Back
Choosing Compatible Numbers
Using Compensation

26. 3 × 50

27. 68 + 3

28. 40 × 80

29. 24 + 71 + 26

30. 724 + 199

31. 5.25 + 4.75

Problem Solving
Multiple-Step Problems

UNDERSTAND
ANALYZE DATA
PLAN
ESTIMATE
SOLVE
EXAMINE

LEARN ABOUT IT

Some problems can be solved using two or more of the operations **addition, subtraction, multiplication,** and **division.** These problems are called **multiple-step problems.**

Nikki works part time at a clothing store. She put price tags on 15 pairs of jeans that cost $32 each. She put price tags on 16 pairs that cost $24 each. What was the total value of the jeans Nikki tagged?

First I'll find the value of the first set of jeans.

$15 \times \$32 = \$480$

Then I'll find the value of the second set of jeans.

$16 \times \$24 = \$384$

To find the total value, I'll add the value of both sets.

$\$480 + \$384 = \$864$

The total value of the jeans Nikki tagged was $864.

TRY IT OUT

1. Julia had $32.79 left in her clothing budget. She saw a sweatshirt for $16.98 and a pair of jeans for $23.75. How much more money does she need to buy both items?

2. Kai bought one pair of jeans for $21.95 and another pair that had been priced at $23.89 but were on sale at $4.78 off. How much did he pay in all?

3. When some new jeans arrived, Rudi filled 12 shelves with 25 pairs of jeans on each shelf. He filled 6 racks with 45 pairs of jeans on each rack. How many jeans did he put on shelves and racks?

4. Geri bought 2 pairs of jeans for $23.99 each. She used the $16.98 in cash she got back from returning a shirt. She also had a $50 bill with her. How much of the $50 bill did she spend?

Solve. Use any problem solving strategy.

1. Rico's great grandfather was 22 years old when he panned for gold in 1853. That was the year that the first jeans were made. By 1990 how many years had passed since jeans were first made?

2. Bergland's Department Store received a new shipment of 60 jeans. Each pair had a value of $30. What was the value of the whole shipment?

3. Ralph put back on shelves the jeans people had left in 8 different dressing rooms. The same number of jeans had been left in each room. He put back 32 jeans in all. How many jeans were in each room?

4. At Roy's school 2 out of 5 students usually wear jeans. How many students would you expect to wear jeans in a class of 30 students?

jeans	2	4	6	8	10	12
students	5					

Use the table below for problems 5–7.

Results of Rub Test for Jeans		
Material	Weight	Number of rubs before material tore
A cotton	12 oz	596
B cotton	14 oz	2,558
C cotton polyester	14 oz	2,863
D cotton polyester nylon	12 oz	2,873

5. Which material lasted for 174 more rubs than 4 times the number of rubs on material A?

6. How many more rubs did the strongest material allow than the weakest?

7. How many fewer rubs were there before material B tore than before material D tore?

8. **Write Your Own Problem** Write a problem about jeans that can be solved by using multiplication.

Problem Solving
Solve a Simpler Problem

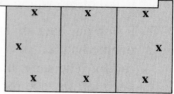

UNDERSTAND
ANALYZE DATA
PLAN
ESTIMATE
SOLVE
EXAMINE

LEARN ABOUT IT

Sometimes you can find the answer to a problem by solving a problem that is like it but has smaller numbers. This problem solving strategy is called **Solve a Simpler Problem.**

Roger is helping to set up 20 small tables for an exhibit of Eskimo sculpture at his school. Each table can have one sculpture on each side. If Roger pushes all the tables together to make one long table, how many sculptures can he display?

Instead of drawing 20 tables, I'll solve a simpler problem using 2, 3, and 4 tables. That may help me solve the more difficult problem.

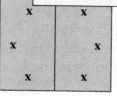

I see! Two sculptures can be displayed at each of the 20 tables. Then 2 more sculptures can be placed at each end.

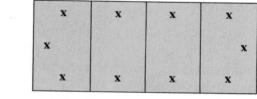

$$2 \times 20 = 40 \qquad 40 + 2 = 42$$

42 sculptures can be displayed.

TRY IT OUT

Thelma was in charge of planning a dinner for visiting students from Anchorage, Alaska. She made a large square table from 25 small square tables. Each small table can seat one person on a side. How many students can sit at the large table? (Hint: Try 4 small tables. Then try 9.)

- How many students can sit on each side of a small square table?

- What shape does Thelma want the large table to be?

- Copy and complete the drawings to solve the problem.

Solve a simpler problem to help you solve each problem.

1. Bobby Lee told Thelma to put the 25 tables in one long row instead of in a square. How many seats would there be using Bobby Lee's idea?

2. At the dinner, Tana made 15 cuts in the same direction across each meat loaf. How many pieces did she get from each loaf?

MIXED PRACTICE

Choose a strategy from the strategies list or use other strategies you know to solve these problems.

Some Strategies	
Act Out	Guess and Check
Use Objects	Make a Table
Choose an Operation	Solve a Simpler
Draw a Picture	Problem

3. At the dinner for Alaskan students, Pete wanted to cut a long loaf of bread into 36 slices. How many cuts did he need to make?

4. How many miles is the shortest route from Fairbanks to Anchorage?

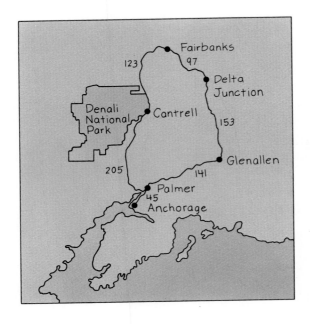

5. Barb bought patches as souvenir gifts from her trip to Alaska. The cost of the patches was $4 for 5. How many patches could she buy with $16?

6. Jeff and his family are driving on the Alaskan Highway to Dawson Creek, British Columbia. They have driven about 600 miles. The entire drive will be about 900 miles. About how far do they still have to go?

7. Mrs. Vasquez saw an advertisement for a trip called "Sailing the Inside Passage." The cost is $148 a day. How much would a 12-day trip cost altogether?

8. The Alaskan oil pipeline is buried for 345 miles. The whole pipeline is 109 miles longer than twice the number of miles that are buried. How long is the whole pipeline?

Mental Math
Breaking Apart Numbers

This lesson introduces another number property that can help you use mental math to solve problems.

EXPLORE Solve to Understand

Find each product in column A. Find the value of each expression in column B.

A	B
2×32	$(2 \times 30) + (2 \times 2)$
5×21	$(5 \times 20) + (5 \times 1)$
4×42	$(4 \times 40) + (4 \times 2)$

TALK ABOUT IT

1. What did you discover about the values in each row?
2. $30 + 2$ is another way of writing what 2-digit number?
3. In the last row, how was 42 broken apart into two numbers?

The **distributive property** can help you mentally multiply a 2-digit number by a 1-digit number, such as 4×23. This property involves both multiplication and addition.

- **Here is how to do it.**
  Problem: **4×23**
  Break apart 23: 20 and 3
  Multiply: $4 \times 20 = 80$
  $4 \times 3 = 12$
  Add: $80 + 12 = 92$
  $4 \times 23 = 92$

- **Here is why it works.**

$$\begin{array}{r} 23 \\ \times\ 4 \\ \hline \end{array} \qquad \begin{array}{r} 20 + 3 \\ \times\qquad 4 \\ \hline 80 + 12 = 92 \end{array}$$

20×4 3×4

TRY IT OUT

Use the distributive property and mental math to find the products.

1. 2×12
2. 3×13
3. 2×14
4. 4×12
5. 3×23
6. 2×34
7. 3×42
8. 4×23
9. 2×16
10. 4×24
11. 2×23
12. 3×43
13. 16×4
14. 53×2
15. 6×32

More Practice, page 504, set E

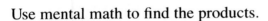

Power Practice/Quiz

Use mental math to find the products.

1. 20×70 **2.** 60×50 **3.** 800×90 **4.** 900×40 **5.** 300×700

6. 500×200 **7.** $30 \times 6{,}000$ **8.** 80×70 **9.** 40×80 **10.** $70 \times 7{,}000$

11. $20 \times 30 \times 600$ **12.** $90 \times 90 \times 10$ **13.** $50 \times 10 \times 200 \times 10$

Round so you can estimate using mental math.

14.	**15.**	**16.**	**17.**	**18.**
64	47	279	841	625
$\times\ 9$	$\times 18$	$\times\ 85$	$\times\ 37$	$\times\ 73$

Multiply.

19.	**20.**	**21.**	**22.**	**23.**
103	68	630	496	567
$\times\ 7$	$\times 25$	$\times\ 8$	$\times\ 39$	$\times\ 79$

24.	**25.**	**26.**	**27.**	**28.**
54	2,605	907	146	4,352
$\times 45$	$\times\ 6$	$\times\ 88$	$\times\ 24$	$\times\ 7$

PROBLEM SOLVING

29. Andrew has 6 quarters, 8 nickels, and 5 dimes. How much money does Andrew have?

30. Luanna has 80 pictures to put in her photo album. The album holds 4 photos on each page. There are 18 pages. How many pictures will be left over?

31. Carole is pasting pictures in her scrapbook. Six of the pages will each hold 6 pictures and 8 of the pages will each hold 4 larger pictures. How many pictures can she fit in the scrapbook?

32. Julia wants to cut a 36-inch submarine sandwich into 20 pieces. How many cuts will she make if she makes all cuts in the same direction?

33. Vito has a display of 5 Great American Women stamps on each page of a 48-page album. How many stamps does he have in his album:

34. Guy bought fifteen 25¢ postage stamps. He gave the clerk a $10 bill. How much change should the clerk give Guy?

131

Multiplying Decimals
Making the Connection

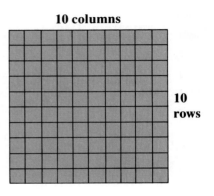

10 columns

10 rows

Each row is 0.1 of the square.
Each column is also
0.1 of the square.

LEARN ABOUT IT

We can use graph paper to show some
decimal products.

EXPLORE **Use a Graph Paper Model**
Work with a partner.

- Use 10 by 10 sections of graph paper.

- One partner shades one or more (but not *all*) of the rows
  using a crayon or a colored pencil. Name the decimal
  that tells what part of the square is shaded.

- The other partner then shades one or more (but not *all*)
  of the columns using a crayon or pencil of a different
  color. Again, name the decimal that tells what part of
  the square is shaded.

- Decide together what decimal names the part of the
  square that is shaded with both colors.

- Repeat this activity several times.

TALK ABOUT IT

1. Suppose you shaded 6 rows
   and 4 columns. What
   decimals would you write to
   record the parts of the square
   that you shaded?

2. Suppose you shaded 3 rows and 5 columns. What decimal
   would you write to record the part of the square that was
   shaded with both colors?

3. Suppose one student shades 3 rows with no space between
   them. Another student also shades 3 rows but leaves space
   between the rows. Both students then shade 4 columns
   with no space between columns. Would the decimal that
   the students record to tell what part of the square is
   shaded twice be the same for each student? Use graph
   paper to explain.

You have shaded rows and columns on graph paper and named the decimals for the parts that were shaded. You also gave the decimal for the parts that were shaded twice. Now you will learn how to record what you have done. This will help you understand how to find the product of two decimals such as 0.7 and 0.6.

What You Do   **What You Record**

Show 7 tenths by shading 7 columns. 0.7

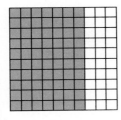

Show 6 tenths of 7 tenths by shading 6 rows. $0.6 \text{ of } 0.7$
                                                or 0.6×0.7

How many small squares are shaded twice? $0.6 \times 0.7 = 0.42$

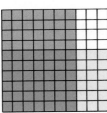

42 out of 100 squares are shaded twice.

0.42 of the large square is shaded twice.

The product of 0.7 and 0.6 is 0.42.

TRY IT OUT

Use 10 by 10 sections of graph paper to show each product. Record your work using symbols.

1. 0.4×0.8 **2.** 0.5×0.7 **3.** 0.1×0.1 **4.** 0.9×1

Multiplying Decimals

EXPLORE Solve to Understand

A potato is an underground stem of a potato plant. Each potato is about 0.8 water. How many pounds of water are in a potato that weighs 0.7 pounds (lb)?

To solve this problem multiply 0.8 and 0.7.

Multiply as with whole numbers.	Write the product so that it has as many decimal places as the sum of the decimal places in the factors.
$$\begin{array}{r} 0.7 \\ \times\,0.8 \\ \hline 56 \end{array}$$	$$\begin{array}{rl} 0.7 & \leftarrow \text{1 decimal place} \\ \times\,0.8 & \leftarrow \text{1 decimal place} \\ \hline 0.56 & \leftarrow \text{2 decimal places} \end{array}$$

TALK ABOUT IT

1. In the second step why was the decimal point placed in front of the 5?
2. Is it reasonable that the product is less than 1? Why?
3. Give the answer to the Explore problem in a complete sentence.

Other Examples

A
$$\begin{array}{rl} 0.83 & \leftarrow \text{2 decimal places} \\ \times\,0.4 & \leftarrow \text{1 decimal place} \\ \hline 0.332 & \leftarrow \text{3 decimal places} \end{array}$$

B
$$\begin{array}{r} 5.3 \\ \times\,1.4 \\ \hline 212 \\ 53 \\ \hline 7.42 \end{array}$$

C
$$\begin{array}{r} 0.073 \\ \times\qquad 8 \\ \hline 0.584 \end{array}$$

Multiply.

1. $\begin{array}{r} 0.8 \\ \times\,0.7 \\ \hline \end{array}$

2. $\begin{array}{r} 5.8 \\ \times\,0.4 \\ \hline \end{array}$

3. $\begin{array}{r} 0.046 \\ \times\qquad 7 \\ \hline \end{array}$

4. $\begin{array}{r} 9.67 \\ \times\,1.8 \\ \hline \end{array}$

5. $\begin{array}{r} 0.75 \\ \times\,9.3 \\ \hline \end{array}$

Multiply.

1. $\begin{array}{r} 3.2 \\ \times\,0.3 \\ \hline \end{array}$	**2.** $\begin{array}{r} 5.03 \\ \times\;\;0.7 \\ \hline \end{array}$	**3.** $\begin{array}{r} 5.02 \\ \times\;\;0.1 \\ \hline \end{array}$	**4.** $\begin{array}{r} 24 \\ \times\,0.2 \\ \hline \end{array}$	**5.** $\begin{array}{r} 0.509 \\ \times\;\;\;\;\;6 \\ \hline \end{array}$
6. $\begin{array}{r} 1.2 \\ \times\,0.6 \\ \hline \end{array}$	**7.** $\begin{array}{r} 7.4 \\ \times\,0.05 \\ \hline \end{array}$	**8.** $\begin{array}{r} 0.94 \\ \times\;\;0.2 \\ \hline \end{array}$	**9.** $\begin{array}{r} 4.02 \\ \times\;\;0.4 \\ \hline \end{array}$	**10.** $\begin{array}{r} 4.5 \\ \times\,2.7 \\ \hline \end{array}$
11. $\begin{array}{r} 424 \\ \times\,7.2 \\ \hline \end{array}$	**12.** $\begin{array}{r} 0.67 \\ \times\;\;\;\;6 \\ \hline \end{array}$	**13.** $\begin{array}{r} 40 \\ \times\,2.3 \\ \hline \end{array}$	**14.** $\begin{array}{r} 1.9 \\ \times\;\;7 \\ \hline \end{array}$	**15.** $\begin{array}{r} 12.8 \\ \times\,0.01 \\ \hline \end{array}$

16. 0.2×1.74 **17.** 5.5×0.3 **18.** 0.011×90 **19.** 300×0.001

Copy the product. Write the decimal point in the correct place.

20. $\begin{array}{r} 24.6 \\ \times\;\;3.5 \\ \hline 8610 \end{array}$	**21.** $\begin{array}{r} 11.3 \\ \times\,0.3 \\ \hline 339 \end{array}$	**22.** $\begin{array}{r} 7.5 \\ \times\,0.3 \\ \hline 225 \end{array}$	**23.** $\begin{array}{r} 1.5 \\ \times\,0.4 \\ \hline 060 \end{array}$	**24.** $\begin{array}{r} 12 \\ \times\,0.06 \\ \hline 072 \end{array}$

25. Find the product of 6.9 and 0.64.

26. If the factors are 0.8 and 7.6, what is the product?

MATH REASONING

27. Write two numbers whose product is 0.48.

28. Write two numbers whose product is 2.4.

PROBLEM SOLVING

29. If a potato is 0.8 water, what is the weight of the water in a giant potato that weighs 2.87 lb?

30. If each potato is 0.8 water, how much more water is there in a 0.8 lb potato than there is in a 0.6 lb potato?

USING CRITICAL THINKING   Analyze the Evidence

31. Who am I??????
   - I am a multiple of 5 and a multiple of 7.
   - I am not an odd number.
   - I am less than 100.

32. If you double me and add 12, you get 44. Who am I?

33. 8 more than 4 times me is 112. Who am I?

More Practice, page 505, set A

Estimating with Decimals

EXPLORE Evaluate an Answer
It takes 8.79 hours (h) of work to make 1 minute
(min) of music on a compact disk. How many hours
of work would it take to make a 26.5 min disc?
Ava's answer is shown on the calculator at the right.

TALK ABOUT IT

1. Is the calculator answer reasonable? Explain.
2. How would you round the decimals to estimate
   the answer?
3. Can you think of another way to estimate the product?

- Sometimes you can replace the given numbers with
  compatible numbers to estimate products. For example:

Problem: 24.3 × 4.78
Replace the factors with
compatible numbers.   → 24.3 × 4.78
                           ↓   ↓
                          25 × 4 = 100   24.3 × 4.78 is about 100.

- Sometimes sums can be estimated using **clustering.** We
  can use this technique when each addend is close to (or
  "clusters around") a number that is easy to compute
  with mentally. For example:

Problem: Estimate 24.6 + 26.6 + 25 + 24.85.
Replace each addend with 25.   25 + 25 + 25 + 25 = 4 × 25 = 100
24.6 + 26.6 + 25 + 24.85 is about 100.

Round or substitute compatible numbers to estimate each product.

1. 46.3 × 57.9   2. 23.4 × 58.78   3. 35.62 × 54.89   4. 67.76 × 83.45

Estimate each sum. Use clustering.

5. 9.75 + 10.3 + 11.1   6. 81.3 + 78.96 + 80.05 + 82   7. 905 + 908 + 897

Estimate each product. Use any estimation technique you choose.

1. 3.87×4.19 **2.** 4.23×8.76 **3.** 872×614 **4.** 0.968×6.45

5. 12.7×3.216 **6.** 15.386×1.89 **7.** 43.28×3.14 **8.** 9.013×6.872

Estimate each sum. Use clustering.

9. $9.82 + 10.04 + 10.1 + 9.79$ **10.** $304 + 297 + 308 + 287$

11. $0.94 + 1.05 + 1.1 + 0.9$ **12.** $2,020 + 1,988 + 2,016$

APPLY

MATH REASONING

Use **estimation** to find the missing factor. In each case, the product must be not less than 40 or greater than 50.

13. $0.8 \times$ ▦ $=$ __?__   **14.** $1.5 \times$ ▦ $=$ __?__   **15.** $2.06 \times$ ▦ $=$ __?__

16. $0.06 \times$ ▦ $=$ __?__   **17.** $0.2 \times$ ▦ $=$ __?__   **18.** $8.04 \times$ ▦ $=$ __?__

PROBLEM SOLVING

19. Darel worked 18.5 h at the recording studio last week. He earns $5.75 an hour. About how much did he earn last week working at the recording studio?

20. The record store is having a sale on old 45 rpm records. The records cost $0.25 each, but for every three a customer buys, the store gives 1 free record. Justine spent $1.50 on these records. How many did she get?

▶ **CALCULATOR**

Tell which of the key codes below will give the correct answer to the problem. Find the incorrect key code and tell why it will not give the correct answer.
Problem: Ben had $73 in the bank. Then he earned $6 a day for 24 days. How much money does he now have altogether?

21. [ON/AC] 73 [M+] 6 [X] 24 [M+] [MR]

22. [ON/AC] 73 [+] 6 [X] 24 [=]

23. [ON/AC] 6 [X] 24 [+] 73 [=]

More Practice, page 505, set B

More About Multiplying Decimals

EXPLORE Analyze the Process

Deena and her mother used a new recipe
for sweet potato pie. It had to bake for
45 minutes. Electricity for the oven costs
$0.0018 per minute. What was the cost
of the electricity used to bake the pie?

To solve the problem, multiply $0.0018 by 45.
Here is how to do it.

Multiply as with whole numbers.	Write the product so that it has as many decimal places as the sum of the decimal places in the factors.
$\begin{array}{r} \$0.0018 \\ \times \quad 45 \\ \hline 90 \\ 72 \\ \hline 810 \end{array}$	$\begin{array}{r} \$0\ 0018 \\ \times \quad 45 \\ \hline 90 \\ 72 \\ \hline \$0\ 0810 \end{array}$

Sometimes you need to write zeros in the product.

TALK ABOUT IT

1. What would be the product if both factors were whole numbers?
2. Why was a zero added to the right of the decimal point in the final product?

Other Examples

A	**B**	**C**	**D**
$\begin{array}{r} 0.09 \\ \times\ 0.6 \\ \hline 0.054 \end{array}$	$\begin{array}{r} 0.2 \\ \times 0.04 \\ \hline 0.008 \end{array}$	$\begin{array}{r} 0.003 \\ \times \quad 2 \\ \hline 0.006 \end{array}$	$\begin{array}{r} 37 \\ \times 0.002 \\ \hline 0.074 \end{array}$

Multiply. Write in zeros when necessary.

1.	2.	3.	4.	5.
$\begin{array}{r} 0.4 \\ 0.3 \\ \hline \end{array}$	$\begin{array}{r} 5.03 \\ \times\ 0.7 \\ \hline \end{array}$	$\begin{array}{r} 0.009 \\ \times \quad 8 \\ \hline \end{array}$	$\begin{array}{r} 0.05 \\ \times\ 0.3 \\ \hline \end{array}$	$\begin{array}{r} 6.2 \\ \times 0.01 \\ \hline \end{array}$

Multiply. Write in zeros when necessary.

1. $\begin{array}{r} 0.006 \\ \times \quad 3 \\ \hline \end{array}$

2. $\begin{array}{r} 0.008 \\ \times \quad 6 \\ \hline \end{array}$

3. $\begin{array}{r} 0.09 \\ \times \ 0.6 \\ \hline \end{array}$

4. $\begin{array}{r} 0.2 \\ \times 0.04 \\ \hline \end{array}$

5. $\begin{array}{r} 0.06 \\ \times \ 0.8 \\ \hline \end{array}$

6. $\begin{array}{r} 2.6 \\ \times 0.04 \\ \hline \end{array}$

7. $\begin{array}{r} 0.9 \\ \times 0.06 \\ \hline \end{array}$

8. $\begin{array}{r} 0.18 \\ \times \ 0.5 \\ \hline \end{array}$

9. $\begin{array}{r} 1.2 \\ \times 0.06 \\ \hline \end{array}$

10. $\begin{array}{r} 7.4 \\ \times 0.05 \\ \hline \end{array}$

11. $\begin{array}{r} 0.94 \\ \times \ 0.2 \\ \hline \end{array}$

12. $\begin{array}{r} 0.02 \\ \times \ 0.4 \\ \hline \end{array}$

13. 4.1×0.003

14. 0.05×0.3

15. 0.4×0.02

MATH REASONING

Use **estimation** to decide in which box each decimal product belongs.

16. 0.5×0.062

17. 16×0.15

18. 0.03×0.042

19. 0.024×0.060

20. 0.81×1.17

21. 0.07×0.42

A
0.001–0.010

B
0.020–0.20

C
0.30–3.00

DATA BANK

PROBLEM SOLVING

22. A clothes dryer uses \$0.006 worth of electricity each minute it is running. What would be the cost of running the dryer for 15 minutes?

23. **Science Data Bank** What would be the cost of the electricity for a color television set turned on for 5 hours a day every day of one week? See page 470.

MIXED REVIEW

Add.

24. $\begin{array}{r} 8.92 \\ +9.87 \\ \hline \end{array}$

25. $\begin{array}{r} 9.53 \\ +5.80 \\ \hline \end{array}$

26. $\begin{array}{r} 55.94 \\ +67.09 \\ \hline \end{array}$

27. $\begin{array}{r} \$12.58 \\ + \quad 8.65 \\ \hline \end{array}$

28. $\begin{array}{r} \$155.50 \\ + \quad 75.88 \\ \hline \end{array}$

Multiply.

29. 792×8

30. 84×17

31. 346×24

32. 866×70

Problem Solving
Using a Calculator

UNDERSTAND
ANALYZE DATA
PLAN
ESTIMATE
SOLVE
EXAMINE

LEARN ABOUT IT

When you use a calculator to solve multiple-step problems, it is helpful to use **memory** keys.

Tony and his mother want to buy 3 sleeping bags, 2 lanterns, and a camp stove at sale prices. Tony's mother has saved $250 to buy these items. Tony wants to know how much money they will have left.

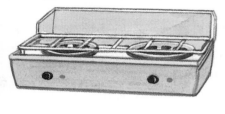

SALE

	Regular	Sale
sleeping bag	$49.95	$39.99
camp stove	$34.95	$29.99
80-quart cooler	$69.95	$55.99
lantern	$37.95	$32.99
backpack	$28.95	$23.99

This is how Tony used the memory keys to solve the problem.

[ON/AC] 250 [M+] 3 [×] 39.99 [=] [M−] 2 [×] 32.99 [=] [M−] 29.99 [M−] [MR]

| Added to memory | Subtracted from memory | Subtracted from memory | Subtracted from memory |

Tony and his mother will have $34.06 left after buying the items.

Memory Key	
[ON/AC] clears the memory.	[M−] subtracts from the total in memory.
[M+] adds to the total in memory.	[MR] recalls the total in memory.

TRY IT OUT

1. How much would 4 sleeping bags and 3 lanterns cost at the sale price?

2. Mr. Peterson is buying 2 coolers, 3 backpacks, and 1 lantern on sale. He has three $100 bills. How many of the bills will he need to give the clerk?

3. Martha's father gave the clerk $150 for 2 sleeping bags and a cooler at the sale price. How much change did he get?

4. If Jeff's aunt buys 3 sleeping bags, 2 backpacks, and a stove at sale prices, how much will she spend?

Solve. Use any problem solving strategy.

1. Each camper at Firebird Camp had to pay $25 for the overnight campout. If there were 64 campers, how much money did they pay in all?

2. The 64 campers were split up into 8 different campsites. If each campsite had the same number of campers, how many were at each campsite?

3. A 3-person tent costs $77.98, a 5-person costs $105.89, and an 8-person costs $205.89. How much more does the largest tent cost than the smallest?

4. For firewood on the camping trip, Kia chopped a fallen tree trunk into 25 pieces. All chops were straight across the trunk. How many cuts did she make?

Use this table for problems 5-7.

Sale price		
parka	$31.98	(regularly $39.50)
woolen shirt	$24.98	(regularly $26.50)
winter vest	$42.98	(regularly $45.50)
hiking boots	$36.98	(regularly $42.50)

5. Fara Asad's father bought the family some clothing for winter camping. How much would he pay for a woolen shirt and a pair of hiking boots if he buys them on sale?

6. Mr. Asad has $225. How much will he have left if he buys 4 woolen shirts and 3 pairs of hiking boots on sale?

7. How much less would Mr. Asad pay for 4 pairs of hiking boots at the sale price than at the regular price?

135.97

8. **Missing Data** This problem has missing data. Tell what data is needed to solve the problem. Mrs. Kato bought backpacks for Michiko and her brothers. The backpacks cost $39.99 each. How much did she pay?

Mental Math
Multiplying Decimals by 10, 100, and 1,000

EXPLORE Find a Pattern

Use a calculator. Copy and complete the table. Then select four other decimals. Show the products when each decimal is multiplied first by 10, then by 100 and then by 1,000.

Decimal	3.142				
× 10					
× 100					
× 1000					

TALK ABOUT IT

Look for patterns in your table. Complete the following statements.

1. To multiply a decimal by **10**, "move" the decimal point __?__ places to the __?__ .
2. To multiply a decimal by **100**, "move" the decimal point __?__ places to the __?__ .
3. To multiply a decimal by **1,000**, "move" the decimal point __?__ places to the __?__ .
4. Suppose you multiply 4.5 by 100. Explain how you find and write the product.

When you multiply by 10, 100, or 1,000, the number of zeros tells you how many places to move the decimal point. To see why this works, think about 10×2.45. This is the same as the sum of ten addends of 2.45.

$10 \times 2.45 = 2.45 + 2.45 + 2.45 + 2.45 + 2.45 + 2.45 + 2.45 + 2.45 + 2.45 + 2.45 = 24.5.$

The decimal point in the factor 2.45 is one place to the right in the product 24.5.

TRY IT OUT

Use mental math to find these products.

1. 10×3.678
2. 100×16.89
3. $1,000 \times 4.629$
4. 6.782×100

5. 10×73.2
6. 100×5.43
7. $1,000 \times 0.545$
8. 10×0.378

Use mental math to solve these equations.

1. 3.4×10 2. 5.23×100 3. $1{,}000 \times 0.132$ 4. 100×2.856

5. 10×0.56 6. $1{,}000 \times 0.2$ 7. 3.175×100 8. 0.531×10

9. $4.23 \times 1{,}000$ 10. 100×5.68 11. 0.713×10 12. 100×1.1

13. 6.82×10 14. 2.19×100 15. $7.9 \times 1{,}000$ 16. 10×0.053

APPLY

MATH REASONING

In each problem below, the same shape stands for the same number. Tell what numbers should be placed in each shape to keep the scales in balance.

17.   **18.**

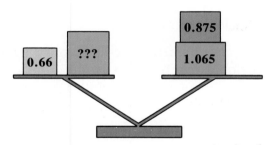

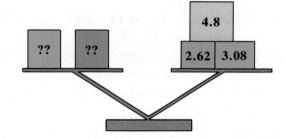

PROBLEM SOLVING

19. Dana has two types of coin collector wrappers for pennies. One holds 10 pennies and the other holds 100 pennies. She has 4 of the smaller packages and 6 of the larger ones full of pennies. How many pennies does she have in these wrappers?

▶ **CALCULATOR**

20. Choose a 3 place decimal. Use the constant multiplier on your calculator to multiply the decimal by 10. Keep using the constant key to multiply by 10. How many times must you multiply by 10 to produce the same result as multiplying by 100? by 1,000?

Applied Problem Solving
Group Decision Making

UNDERSTAND
ANALYZE DATA
PLAN
ESTIMATE
SOLVE
EXAMINE

Group Skill:
Listen to Others

Next month is National Peanut Month. Your class is in charge of setting up a peanut butter snack bar for one lunch during the month. What kinds of peanut butter snacks will you offer? How many of each kind will you prepare?

Facts to Consider

- Your class conducted a survey to help you in your planning. The survey results are shown below.

  Survey Question: *What is your favorite peanut butter snack?*

Peanut butter on crackers	卌 卌 卌
Peanut butter on apple slices	卌 II
Peanut butter balls rolled in sesame seeds	卌
Peanut butter on celery sticks	卌 卌 卌 II
Peanut butter and honey on crackers	IIII
Peanut butter on banana	卌 II

- You have 1 small, 1 medium, and 2 large jars of peanut butter to use.
- Each kind of snack you will prepare uses 2 tablespoons of peanut butter per serving.

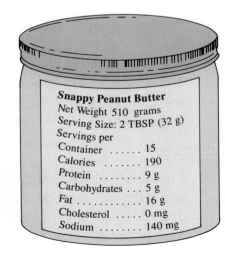

Snappy Peanut Butter
Net Weight 510 grams
Serving Size: 2 TBSP (32 g)
Servings per
Container 15
Calories 190
Protein .... 9 g
Carbohydrates ... 5 g
Fat .... 16 g
Cholesterol ..... 0 mg
Sodium .... 140 mg

144

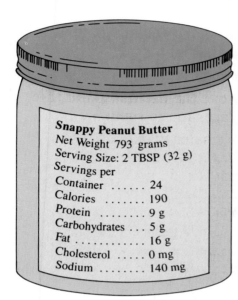

Snappy Peanut Butter
Net Weight 793 grams
Serving Size: 2 TBSP (32 g)
Servings per
Container 24
Calories 190
Protein .... 9 g
Carbohydrates ... 5 g
Fat .... 16 g
Cholesterol ..... 0 mg
Sodium .... 140 mg

Snappy Peanut Butter
Net Weight 1,133 grams
Serving Size: 2 TBSP (32 g)
Servings per
Container 35
Calories 190
Protein .... 9 g
Carbohydrates ... 5 g
Fat .... 16 g
Cholesterol ..... 0 mg
Sodium .... 140 mg

Some Questions to Answer

1. How many students in the survey chose each snack?

2. Which data on the labels could help you figure out how many snacks could be made from the amount of peanut butter available? How many snacks can be made in all?

3. How could you make use of the survey to decide how many of each snack to prepare?

What Is Your Decision?

Make a table for the students who will be preparing the snacks. Show how many of each snack they should make. Explain how you decided on these quantities?

145

WRAP UP

Sentence Completion

Complete each sentence by matching Part I and Part II.

Part I	Part II
1. To multiply 4.627 by 1,000,	**A.** move the decimal point one place to the right.
2. The product of 8.47 and 0.8	**B.** is less than 8.
3. The product of 4.12 and 2.03	**C.** move the decimal point three places to the right.
4. To multiply 0.143 by 10,	**D.** is greater than 8.

Sometimes, Always, Never

Complete each statement by writing **sometimes**, **always**, or **never**. Explain your choice.

5. When you multiply hundredths by tenths, the product is __?__ hundredths.

6. When you multiply a whole number by 100, the product __?__ will have exactly two zeros.

7. To multiply a decimal by 10, __?__ move the decimal point one place to the left.

Project

You can use **lattice multiplication** to find products such as 25 × 34. Start with a blank lattice like this one. Place the factors as shown. Use one factor for columns and the other for rows.

Multiply the column and row values for each box.

Start at the right. Find the sum for each diagonal. Regroup to the next diagonal when necessary.
25 × 34 = 850

Find these products using the lattice. Tell how many boxes you will need.

1. 237 × 42   **2.** 45 × 482   **3.** 139 × 476

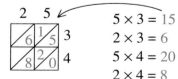

2, 5, 3, 4
4 digits →
4 boxes

$5 \times 3 = 15$
$2 \times 3 = 6$
$5 \times 4 = 20$
$2 \times 4 = 8$

$5 + 2 + 8 = 15$

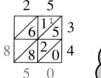

Write 5.
Regroup 1.

146

POWER PRACTICE/TEST

Part 1 Understanding

1. Which one uses rounding to estimate 42 × 672?

   A. 50 × 700 = 35,000
   B. 50 × 600 = 30,000
   C. 40 × 600 = 24,000
   D. 40 × 700 = 28,000

2. Which one uses clustering to estimate
   83.2 + 76.8 + 81.04 + 79?

   A. 83 + 77 + 81 + 79 = 320
   B. (83 + 81) + (77 + 79) = 320
   C. 4 × 80 = 320
   D. (80 + 75) + (80 + 75) = 320

3. If you use mental math to find 83 × 77, you would probably break the factor 83 into

   A. 60 + 23   B. 80 + 3
   C. 70 + 13   D. 90 − 7

4. Which one uses compatible numbers to estimate 23.04 × 4.27?

   A. 25 × 4 = 100   B. 23 × 4 = 92
   C. 23 × 5 = 115   D. 25 × 5 = 125

Part 2 Skills

Use mental math to find each product.

5. 700 × 40
6. 800 × 600
7. 6 × 48

Multiply.

8. 1,075
    × 6

9.   148
    × 54

10.   6.7
    × 3.4

11.   3.71
    × 0.52

12.   0.03
    × 2.4

Part 3 Applications

13. Tina returned an art book and got a $15.47 credit. Then she bought a music book for $12.86 and a dictionary for $36.89. How much change does she get from $40?

14. 8 friends love to talk on the phone. One night, each friend talked to each of the others once. How many phone calls did the friends make in all?

15. **Challenge.** Use the digits 2, 3, 4, and 5 to give the number for each ▓.
    ▓ × ▓ × ▓ + ▓ = 34

147

ENRICHMENT
Exponents

When a number is used as a factor several times, we can write it using an **exponent**. The exponent tells how many times the number, called the **base**, is used as a factor.

$$2 \times 2 \times 2 \times 2 = 2^4 \xleftarrow{\text{exponent}} \text{base}$$

2^4 is read "two to the fourth power."

Exponents are very helpful for writing powers (products of multiplying the number by itself) of 10.

Look at this chart.

Powers of Ten

10^1	10	= 10
10^2	10×10	= 100
10^3	$10 \times 10 \times 10$	= 1,000
10^4	$10 \times 10 \times 10 \times 10$	= 10,000
10^5	$10 \times 10 \times 10 \times 10 \times 10$	= 100,000

1. Do you notice a pattern involving the exponent and the number of zeros in the product?

Astronomers and other scientists use powers of 10 to write very large numbers.

The planet Neptune is about 3,000,000,000 miles from Earth. To make it easier to work with such a large number, astronomers write 3×10^9.

$$3{,}000{,}000{,}000 = 3 \times 1{,}000{,}000{,}000 = 3 \times 10^9$$

Write these numbers the way an astronomer would.

2. 5,000,000   3. 20,000   4. 800 million

5. You can write 59,237 in expanded form using powers of 10. Write each term using powers of 10. For example, $50{,}000 = (5 \times 10^4)$.

$$59{,}237 = (5 \times 10^4) + (9 \times 10^3) + (2 \times 10^2) + (3 \times 10^1) + 7$$

Write these numbers in expanded form using powers of 10.

6. 3,457   7. 146,230   8. 43,625,700

148

CUMULATIVE REVIEW

Add or subtract.

1. $324.16
   − 99.58

A. $375.42
B. $224.58
C. $215.58
D. $324.58

2. 854 + 563 + 27 + 106

A. 1,550
B. 1,793
C. 1,530
D. 1,451

3. 4.2 + 18.75 + 21.04 + 1.006

A. 91.85
B. 60.27
C. 59.17
D. 44.996

Use this graph for questions 4 and 5.

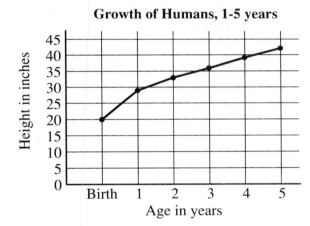

Growth of Humans, 1-5 years

4. Between what two ages does the most growth occur?

A. 3 and 4
B. birth and 1
C. 1 and 2
D. 2 and 3

5. Predict the average height for age 6.

A. 43 in.
B. 48 in.
C. 45 in.
D. 50 in.

6. Harry has a part-time job stuffing envelopes. He can stuff 65 in 5 minutes. How many can he stuff in an hour? Make a table.

A. 780
B. 520
C. 450
D. 585

7. Which number has a 6 in the hundredths place?

A. 604.12
B. 163.45
C. 506.87
D. 806.06

8. Which number is between 27.045 and 30.047?

A. 27.04
B. 30.05
C. 27.1
D. 30.048

Use these numbers for items 9–11:
14, 26, 35, 19, 22, 26, 24.

9. The range of the numbers is

A. 12
B. 35
C. 21
D. 26

10. The median is

A. 26
B. 24
C. 23.6
D. 21

11. The mode is

A. 26
B. 24
C. 21
D. 23.6

12. In 1513, Juan Ponce de Leon explored the coast of Florida. Francis Drake landed in California 66 years later, and 28 years after that, Captain John Smith started the first English colony at Jamestown. In what year was Jamestown settled?

A. 1541
B. 1579
C. 1592
D. 1607

6

METRIC MEASUREMENT

THEME: COMPETITIVE SPORTS

MATH AND
HEALTH AND FITNESS

DATA BANK

Use the Health and
Fitness Data Bank on
page 475 to answer
the questions.

1 In which of the listed
years was the fastest time
recorded for the Olympic
women's 800-meter race? In
which year was the slowest time
recorded for that race?

2 In 1984 Kim Gallagher won the silver medal for the Olympic women's 800-meter run with a time of 1 minute, 58.63 seconds. How much slower than the winning time was she?

3 In 1984 the bronze medal winner (third-place finish) was 1.23 seconds slower than the gold medal winner. How long did it take the bronze medal winner to run the race?

4 **Using Critical Thinking** Compare the times for the women's 800-meter winners in the 1960s with those in the 1980s. Can you make a general statement about what you observe?

The Olympic Games offer female and male athletes from many nations the chance to meet in friendly competiton.

Estimating Length

You can use what you
know about **meters (m)**,
decimeters (dm), and
centimeters (cm) to
estimate lengths.

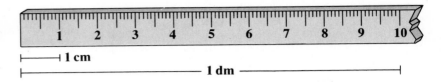

1 m = 10 dm = 100 cm
1 dm = 10 cm

EXPLORE Analyze the Process

Estimate in centimeters the width of your
open math book.

TALK ABOUT IT

1. How does thinking about the width of one page help you
   think about the total width of both pages?
2. If you knew the width of half a page, how could you find
   the width of your open book?

Unitizing is a method of estimating by dividing an object
into smaller equal parts and then using the estimated length
of one part to estimate the total length of the object. For
example, you can estimate the length of a chalkboard by
visually dividing it into smaller parts.

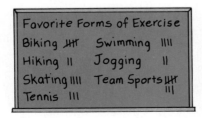

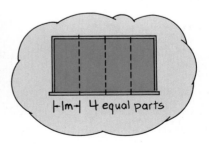

Use the unitizing method to make the estimates described
below.

1. the length of your pencil in centimeters
2. the width of your desk top in decimeters
3. the length of a chalkboard in meters

Use the unitizing method to make each estimate. Then measure to check your estimates. Record in a table as shown.

Object	Estimate	Actual
1. notebook width	_____	_____

1. **A.** notebook width in centimeters
   B. notebook length in centimeters

2. **A.** shoe width in centimeters
   B. shoe length in centimeters

3. **A.** door width in decimeters
   B. door height in decimeters

4. **A.** bulletin board width in decimeters
   B. bulletin board height in decimeters

APPLY

MATH REASONING

Write **reasonable** or **not reasonable** for each statement.

5. The width of my little finger is about 1 cm. So the width of my hand is about 10 dm.
6. The width of a piece of notebook paper is about 23 cm. So the length is about 28 cm.

PROBLEM SOLVING

7. Devra's bedroom is a rectangle with a width of about 3 m and a length of about 4.5 m. About how many meters is the perimeter of her room?
8. A carpenter makes 3-legged stools and 4-legged stools. This week she made a total of 35 stools and she used a total of 125 legs. How many of each type did she make?

► USING CRITICAL THINKING   Analyze the Situation

9. In the story about David and the giant Goliath, Goliath's height was given as "6 cubits and a span." How could you find the length of a string as close to Goliath's actual height as possible?

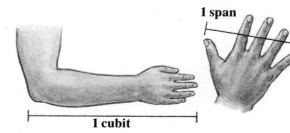

More Practice, page 506, Set A

Meters and Centimeters

LEARN ABOUT IT

EXPLORE   Use a Meter Stick

Work in groups. List some objects whose
length, width, height, or perimeter you
estimate to be between 1 m and 2 m.
Measure the objects to the nearest
centimeter to check. Record your
measurements in centimeters.

TALK ABOUT IT

1. Should any of your measurements be less than 100 cm
   or more than 200 cm? Explain why or why not.
2. Use both meters and centimeters to express each
   measurement.
3. Do you think a table 1.5 m long would be more than or
   less than 100 cm long? more than or less than 200 cm?

Measurements with meters and centimeters can be written
using meters and centimeters (3 m 58 cm), using only
centimeters (358 cm), or using only meters (3.58 m—
1 cm = 0.01 m, so 58 cm = 0.58 m).

- To change from centimeters to meters,
  think of the number of hundreds. Each
  100 cm is 1 m.

  247 cm = ? m

  2 m 47 cm (200 cm = 2 m)
  247 cm = 2.47 m

- To change from meters to centimeters,
  first think how many centimeters are in
  the whole number part and then how
  many are in the decimal part.

  4.08 m = ? cm

  4 m 8 cm (4 m = 400 cm)
  4.08 m = 408 cm

TRY IT OUT

Write each measurement two ways, in centimeters and in meters.

1. 2 m 83 cm   2. 6 m 50 cm   3. 1 m 6 cm   4. 3 m 8 cm   5. 1 m 94 cm

Give the missing numbers.

6. 435 cm = ▦ m   7. 826 cm = ▦ m   8. 7.84 m = ▦ cm

Change each measure to meters.

1. table length
2. table width
3. table height

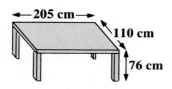

←—205 cm—→
110 cm
76 cm

4. door height
5. door width
6. door thickness

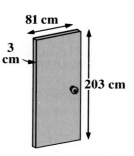

81 cm
3 cm
203 cm

Change each measure to centimeters.

7. bed length
8. bed width
9. bed height

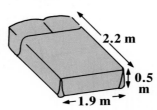

2.2 m
0.5 m
←1.9 m→

10. bookcase height
11. bookcase width
12. bookcase depth

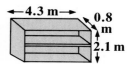

←4.3 m→
0.8 m
2.1 m

APPLY

MATH REASONING

Look for patterns in the table. Complete statements 13 and 14.

324.0 cm .... 3.24 m	5.43 m .... 543.0 cm
120.0 cm .... 1.20 m	7.08 m .... 708.0 cm
75.0 cm .... 0.75 m	0.54 m .... 54.0 cm

13. To change centimeters to meters, move the decimal point __?__ .
14. To change meters to centimeters, move the decimal point __?__ .

PROBLEM SOLVING

15. Robert Seagren's Olympic gold medal winning pole vault in 1968 was 5.40 m. Would a vault of 550 cm be higher or lower than Seagren's jump?

16. **Health and Fitness Data Bank** In the 1984 Olympics how much higher would Mike Tully have had to jump in order to have tied the jump made by the gold medal winner? See page 475.

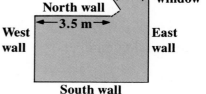

DATA BANK

ESTIMATION

Give the best estimate for each length.

17. South wall   **A.** 4 m **B.** 5 m **C.** 7 m
18. West wall   **A.** 1 m **B.** 2 m **C.** 3 m
19. East wall   **A.** 3 m **B.** 4 m **C.** 5 m

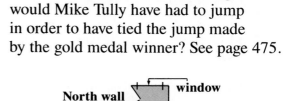

window
North wall
←3.5 m→
West wall
East wall
South wall

Centimeters and Millimeters

Decimals can be used to record **millimeters** (mm) as parts of a centimeter.

$$1 \text{ cm} = 10 \text{ mm}$$
$$1 \text{ mm} = 0.1 \text{ cm}$$

EXPLORE **Examine the Data**

During a storm, Josh read his homemade rain gauge every hour to see how much rain had fallen since the storm started. He recorded the amounts using millimeters only.

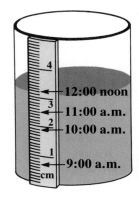

TALK ABOUT IT

1. Why would 7 mm be a more accurate measurement than 1 cm for the 9:00 a.m. reading?
2. How do you think Josh decided that the reading for 11:00 a.m. was 25 mm?
3. If Josh had used decimals for the noon reading, would 3.2 cm be a reasonable amount to record? Explain your reasoning.

To change from millimeters to centimeters, think of tens. Each ten millimeters is 1 centimeter.

$$24 \text{ mm} = ? \text{ cm}$$

2 cm 4 mm (20 mm = 2 cm)

24 mm = 2.4 cm

To change from centimeters to millimeters, think how many millimeters are in the whole number part and then how many are in the decimal part.

$$4.8 \text{ cm} = ? \text{ mm}$$

4 cm 8 mm (4 cm = 40 mm)

4.8 cm = 48 mm

Write each measurement two ways. First use only centimeters. Then use only millimeters.

1. 5 cm 7 mm
2. 3 cm 9 mm
3. 4 cm 0 mm
4. 6 cm 4 mm

Give the missing numbers.

5. 24 mm = ▨ cm
6. 7.8 cm = ▨ mm
7. 9 mm = ▨ cm

Give each rainfall amount in millimeters.

1. 8:00 a.m.
2. 9:00 a.m.
3. 10:00 a.m.
4. 11:00 a.m.
5. 12:00 noon

Give each rainfall amount in centimeters using decimals.

6. 4:00 p.m.
7. 5:00 p.m.
8. 6:00 p.m.
9. 7:00 p.m.
10. 8:00 p.m.

MATH REASONING

Select the best unit (m, cm, or mm) for each measure.

11. tree height: 3.8 __?__
12. ruler thickness: 2 __?__
13. photograph height: 15.4 __?__
14. drawer depth: 10 __?__

PROBLEM SOLVING

15. Last Monday, Josh made this graph to show rainfall during a storm. Was the total rainfall more or less than 4 cm?

16. About how many millimeters of rain fell from 10:00 a.m. to 2:00 p.m.?

17. **Extra Data** About 3 mm of rain fell between noon and 1 p.m. The greatest amount fell between 10:00 a.m. and 11:00 a.m. About how much fell during that hour?

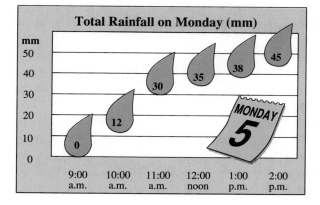

Find these products mentally.

18. 50×60
19. 20×80
20. 30×400
21. 70×30
22. 9×600

Multiply.

23. $\begin{array}{r} 7.5 \\ \times\,0.3 \\ \hline \end{array}$

24. $\begin{array}{r} 0.77 \\ \times\ 6.5 \\ \hline \end{array}$

25. $\begin{array}{r} 7.45 \\ \times 3.11 \\ \hline \end{array}$

Estimate by rounding.

26. $\begin{array}{r} 223 \\ \times\ 89 \\ \hline \end{array}$

27. $\begin{array}{r} 881 \\ \times\ 91 \\ \hline \end{array}$

Area of a Rectangle

The **area** of a figure is the number of **square units** that cover it exactly. In the figure shown, the square unit is 1 square centimeter (cm²). The area of the larger square is 4 square centimeters (4 cm²).

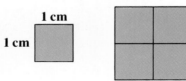

1 square centimeter (cm²)

1 cm

1 cm

EXPLORE **Look for a Pattern**
Draw some rectangles of different sizes on centimeter graph paper. Make a table and record the length, width, and area of each rectangle. Look for a pattern in the table.

rectangle	length	width	area
A	6 cm	4 cm	24 cm²
B			
C			
D			

TALK ABOUT IT

1. What method did you use to find the area of each rectangle?
2. If you had only the length and width measurements written in the table, how could you find the area of each rectangle?

One way to find the area of a rectangle is to use a **formula.**

$$\begin{array}{ccc} \text{Area} & \text{length} & \text{width} \\ \text{A} = & \text{l} \times & \text{w} \end{array}$$

Example

$A = 13 \times 8 = 104$

The area of the rectangle is 104 cm².

The formula for the area of a square is **side** × **side**.
$A = s \times s$

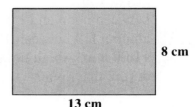

8 cm

13 cm

Use the formula to find the area of each rectangular figure.

1.

42.8 cm

65.3 cm

2.

14 m

12 m

3.

35 cm

54 cm

Use the area formula to find each area.

1. Table top area in square meters (m²)

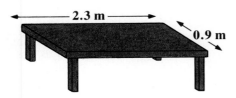

2.3 m
0.9 m

2. Window area in square centimeters (cm²)

104 cm
63 cm

3. Mirror area in square centimeters

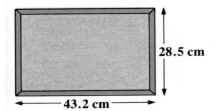

28.5 cm
43.2 cm

4. Area of the top of the counter in square meters

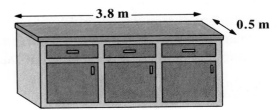

3.8 m
0.5 m

MATH REASONING

Guess and check to find the missing length or width for each rectangle.

5. Area = 156 cm²
length = 13 cm
width = ?

6. Area = 225 cm²
length = 15 cm
width = ?

7. Area = 1,200 m²
length = ?
width = 30m

PROBLEM SOLVING

8. Marjo needs to know the area of her bedroom floor so that she can order a new carpet. The room is rectangular. The width is 3.4 m and the length is 4.7 m. What is the area in square meters?

9. Data Hunt Measure the length and width of each object to the nearest centimeter. Then find each area in square centimeters.
A. front cover of your math book
B. piece of notebook paper
C. the top of your desk

▶ **USING CRITICAL THINKING   Give an Example**

10. Draw a picture and give the dimensions of a rectangle with an area of 24 square units. Give another example of a rectangle with the same area but a different perimeter.

More Practice, page 506, Set D

Kilometers

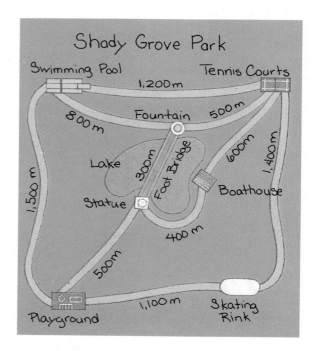

LEARN ABOUT IT

You can use what you know about meters to help you think about a longer unit of length, the **kilometer** (km).

> **1 km = 1,000 m**
> **1 m = 0.001 km**

EXPLORE Solve to Understand

Imagine you are planning a 5-km race through Shady Grove Park. Find at least one route that would be 5 km long. Trace the map and show the route.

TALK ABOUT IT

1. What distances written on the map are greater than 1 km?
2. If 100 m can be written as 0.1 km, how would you write 200 m as a kilometer measure?

TRY IT OUT

For items 1–4, express each distance in kilometers. Use decimals as needed.

1. from the swimming pool to the tennis courts
2. from the playground to the swimming pool
3. from the statue to the boathouse
4. from the fountain across the footbridge to the statue
5. Which places in the park are 0.5 km from each other?
6. Which places in the park are 1 km from each other?

Are these distances more than, less than, or the same as 2.5 km?

7. from the swimming pool to the tennis courts to the skating rink
8. from the boathouse to the statue to the fountain to the swimming pool

160

POWER PRACTICE/QUIZ

Estimate using the unitizing method. Then measure to check.

1. height of a doorknob in decimeters

2. length of a book page in centimeters

Copy and complete the table below to show each measurement three ways.

Dining Room Table				
		m and cm	cm	m
3.	height		75 cm	
4.	width			1.2 m
5.	length	2 m 5 cm		

A plant's height was measured each day for one week.

6. Write the plant's height each day in millimeters.

7. Write the plant's height each day in centimeters, using decimals.

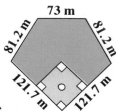

Find the area of each surface.

8. desk top

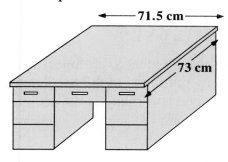

9. kitchen floor

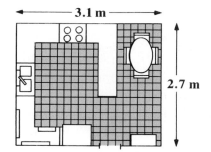

PROBLEM SOLVING

10. As a warm up, the players on the baseball team jog around the entire field twice. How far does each player jog?

11. When Shana walks fast, she travels about 3 m with every 4 steps. She counted 36 fast steps from her house to the end of the block. About how many meters is that?

161

Capacity and Volume

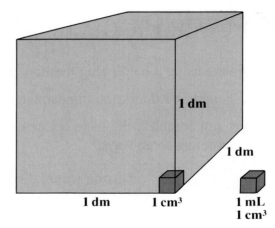

1 dm

1 dm

1 dm   1 cm³   1 mL
1 cm³

Decimals can be used to record amounts
of capacity with the **liter** (L) and
milliliter (mL). These units are closely
related to the cubic decimeter (dm³) and
cubic centimeter (cm³) units of volume.

1 L of water will exactly fill a box that has a volume of 1 dm³.
1 mL of water will exactly fill a box that has a volume of 1 cm³.

$$1 \text{ L} = 1,000 \text{ mL} \qquad 1 \text{ mL} = 0.001 \text{ L}$$

EXPLORE Make a Liter Model

Work in groups. Select a container that you think holds
more than 1 L. Then pour 100 mL of water into the
container. Mark that water level. Next, find a way to mark
the 1L water level on the container.

TALK ABOUT IT

1. How does knowing the number of milliliters in a liter
   help you make your own liter container?

2. Where on your container would you mark the level for 0.5 L?

- To change milliliters to liters, think
  of the number of thousands. Each
  1,000 mL is 1 L.

    3,285 mL = ? L

    3 L 285 mL   3,000 mL = 3 L

    3,285 mL = 3.285 L

- To change liters to milliliters, think how
  many milliliters in the whole number
  part and how many in the decimal part.

    4.75 L = ? mL

    4 L 750 mL   4 L = 4,000 mL

    4.75 L = 4,750 mL

Give the missing numbers.

1. 500 mL = ▦ L   **2.** 2,064 mL = ▦ L **3.** 6,280 mL = ▦ L **4.** 1.5 L = ▦ mL

Change each measure to liters.

1. mustard

2. mayonnaise

3. salad dressing

mustard
1,360 mL

mayonnaise
950 mL

Salad dressing
237 mL

Change each measure to milliliters.

4. fruit punch

5. apple juice

6. tomato juice

fruit punch
0.946 L

apple juice
3.78 L

tomato juice
1.892 L

APPLY

MATH REASONING

Tell whether each statement is **true** or **false**.

7. $250 \text{ mL} = 250 \text{ cm}^3$

8. $500 \text{ mL} = 50 \text{ cm}^3$

9. $15 \text{ L} = 15 \text{ dm}^3$

PROBLEM SOLVING

10. Your recipe for fruit punch calls for 750 mL of orange juice. If you buy a bottle of juice labeled 0.65 L, will you have enough? If not, how much more will you need?

11. How could you pour from one container into another so that each would have 0.25 L of liquid?

A   B   C

400 mL   50 mL   300 mL

12. You want to make 4 loaves of bread. For each loaf you need 350 mL of milk. You have 1.5 L of milk. Will that be enough?

MIXED REVIEW

Multiply.

13. $\begin{array}{r} 0.008 \\ \times \quad 2 \\ \hline \end{array}$

14. $\begin{array}{r} 0.005 \\ \times \quad 9 \\ \hline \end{array}$

15. $\begin{array}{r} 0.007 \\ \times \quad 2.8 \\ \hline \end{array}$

16. $\begin{array}{r} 0.003 \\ \times \quad 3.87 \\ \hline \end{array}$

17. $\begin{array}{r} 0.004 \\ \times \quad 2.07 \\ \hline \end{array}$

Solve using mental math.

18. $704 - 5$

19. $34 \times 2 \times 5$

20. $37 + 14 + 3$

21. $42 \times 5 \times 2$

More Practice, page 507, set A

Kilograms and Grams

You can use what you know about thousands and thousandths to help you record masses in **grams** (g) and **kilograms** (kg).

about 1 kg

1 kg = 1,000 g

about 1 g

1 g = 0.001 kg

EXPLORE **Use a Metric Scale**

Work in groups. Estimate in grams the masses of different amounts of water. Try some amounts more than 1 L and some less than 1 L. Check your estimates by finding each amount in grams. Record in a table.

Amount of water in mL	Estimated mass	Actual mass

TALK ABOUT IT

1. Did the amounts of water more than 1 L have masses greater than 1 kg? Did the amounts less than 1 L have masses less than 1 kg?

2. In the metric system, 1 L of water has a mass of 1 kg and 1 mL of water has a mass of 1 g. What do you think the mass of 1.5 L of water should be?

To change grams to kilograms, think of the number of thousands. Each 1,000 g is 1 kg.

$$2,400 \text{ g} = ? \text{ kg}$$

2 kg 400 g ⟨2,000 g = 2 kg⟩

$$2,400 \text{ g} = 2.4 \text{ kg}$$

To change kilograms to grams, think how many grams are in the whole number part and how many are in the decimal part.

$$3.75 \text{ kg} = ? \text{ g}$$

3 kg 750 g ⟨3 kg = 3,000 g⟩

$$3.75 \text{ kg} = 3,750 \text{ g}$$

Give the missing numbers.

1. 500 g = ▦ kg

2. 1,764 g = ▦ kg

3. 2,810 g = ▦ kg

4. 1.5 kg = ▦ g

5. 7.514 kg = ▦ g

6. 0.25 kg = ▦ g

Change each measure to kilograms.

1. cheese
2. bread
3. olives
4. sliced turkey

cheese
950 g

bread
900 g

olives
595 g

sliced turkey
72 g

Change each measure to grams.

5. ham
6. sausage
7. sliced beef
8. chicken

ham
2.534 kg

sausage
0.45 kg

sliced beef
1.3 kg

chicken
1.08 kg

APPLY

MATH REASONING

Copy and complete the table.

	amount of water	mass in g	mass in kg
9.	250 mL	___ g	___ kg
10.	___ mL	500 g	___ kg
11.	___ mL	___ g	0.75 kg

PROBLEM SOLVING

12. Rhonda bought 50 g of sliced cheese and 50 g of sliced ham. If she needs 0.5 kg of each, did she get enough?

13. Vann wants to make 4 meat loaves. The recipe calls for 750 g of ground beef and 250 g of ground pork for each loaf. How many kg of ground beef should he buy?

▶ COMMUNICATION   Writing to Learn

14. Kathy said there had to be a mistake on these box weights because boxes that hold the same amount also have to weigh the same amount. Write several sentences explaining why you agree or disagree with Kathy's statement.

rice
2.481 kg

detergent
1.452 kg

cereal
0.875 kg

More Practice, page 507, set B

Problem Solving
Make an Organized List

UNDERSTAND
ANALYZE DATA
PLAN
ESTIMATE
SOLVE
EXAMINE

LEARN ABOUT IT

To solve some problems, you may need to write down all the possibilities in a planned way. This problem solving strategy is called **Make an Organized List.**

At swimming practice, Art, Bob, Carlos, David, and Egon raced against each other 2 at a time. How many races were there if everyone raced everyone else?

> First I'll list all the races that Art was in. I'll use initials for the boys' names.

A-B
A-C
A-D
A-E

> Then I'll write the races that Bob, Carlos, David, and Egon were in. I'll cross out any repeats. B-A is the same as A-B, C-A is the same as A-C, and so on.

A-B	B̶-̶A̶	C̶-̶A̶	D̶-̶A̶	E̶-̶A̶
A-C	B-C	C̶-̶B̶	D̶-̶B̶	E̶-̶B̶
A-D	B-D	C-D	D̶-̶C̶	E̶-̶C̶
A-E	B-E	C-E	D-E	E̶-̶D̶

There were 10 races in all.

TRY IT OUT

At the swim meet, Jenna will be swimming in one freestyle race. She can swim in the 50 m, 100 m, or 200 m freestyle. She will be swimming in Heat 1, Heat 2, or Heat 3 for her freestyle event. How many different races could her coach assign her to?

- What are the different freestyle races Jenna could swim in?
- What are the different heats she could swim in?
- Copy and complete the organized list below to help solve the problem.

50 m—Heat 1
50 m—Heat 2
50 m—Heat 3

166

Make an organized list to help solve each problem.

1. Jamie can swim in lanes 1 through 4. She can do the breaststroke, butterfly, backstroke, or freestyle. How many possible choices does she have?

2. In the spring, Mark is busy with both swim team and baseball. The baseball jackets for his team each have 2 digits on them. Each digit is a 1, 2, 3, or 4. What are all the possible numbers for Mark's jacket?

MIXED PRACTICE

Choose a strategy from the strategies list or other strategies you know to solve these problems.

Some Strategies	
Act Out	Guess and Check
Use Objects	Make a Table
Choose an Operation	Solve a Simpler Problem
Draw a Picture	Make an Organized List

3. In the 1984 Olympic finals, Gaines swam the 100 m freestyle in 49.80 seconds (s). In the finals of the 1988 Olympics, Biondi swam the same event in 48.63 s. This was 0.21 s slower than Biondi's world record in the event. How much faster was Biondi than Gaines in the Olympic finals?

4. Maya practices 25 days each month. Each day she swims freestyle for 850 m and backstroke for 625 m. How many meters does she swim per month?

5. For the swim team awards dinner, 30 square tables were pushed into one long table. One person can be seated on each side of a square table. How many people can be seated at the long table?

6. Yoshio's long armspan of 1.52 m helps him swim faster in school meets. Matt Biondi's armspan is 1.4 times as long as Yoshio's. What is Biondi's armspan?

7. Tina needs to decorate the sports shop window with one of the new swimsuits and swimcaps for competition. There are black, blue, red, and purple suits. There are gold, silver, white, gray, and green caps. How many different combinations can she choose from?

8. In the 1988 Olympics, Janet Evans weighed 47.73 kg. One of her opponents was 34.09 kg heavier. How much did the heavier swimmer weigh?

Time

LEARN ABOUT IT

Many Olympics and other sports records are measures of the best time recorded for a given event.

EXPLORE Use a Calculator

Work with a partner and use a calculator to estimate how long 1 minute (min) is. Press [ON/AC] and [+] 1 on your calculator. Have your partner use a watch or timer. When your partner says "Start" begin to press = on your calculator and press once for each second you think has passed. Stop when your calculator shows 60. Was your estimated minute longer or shorter than 1 minute on the watch?

TALK ABOUT IT

1. How many seconds long was your estimate of 1 minute?

2. Was your estimate too short, too long, or just right?

Lengths of time can be recorded using only one unit or using two or more units.

Units of Time
1 day (d) = 24 hours (h)
1 hour = 60 minutes (min)
1 minute = 60 seconds (s)

1 unit: 83 s   2 units: 1 min 23 s

You can change a measurement from one time unit to another.

200 s → 3 min 20s
200 − 60 = 140
  − 60 = 80
  − 60 = 20

You can subtract 3 groups of 60 from 200 with 20 remaining.

4 h 8 min → 248 min
Find the number of minutes in 4 h. Then add minutes.
  4 × 60 = 240
and 8 more make 248.

TRY IT OUT

Give the missing numbers.

1. 110 s = ▦ min ▦ s

2. 304 s = ▦ min ▦ s

3. 25 h = ▦ d ▦ h

4. 5 min 9 s = ▦ s

5. 2 h 30 min = ▦ min

6. 2 d 12 h = ▦ h

Give time in seconds only.

River Road Race

	Name	Time
1.	Enders	2 min 23 s
2.	Fong	1 min 54 s
3.	Gates	3 min 18 s
4.	Hastings	4 min 2 s

Give time in minutes and seconds.

Lucky Lake Race

	Name	Time
5.	Andrews	118 s
6.	Brown	135 s
7.	Conway	152 s
8.	Diaz	184 s

Give time in hours and minutes.

Fun Run

	Name	Time
9.	Ito	115 min
10.	Jacobs	183 min
11.	Klein	139 min
12.	Lopez	242 min

Give time in minutes only.

Run in the Sun

	Name	Time
13.	Moore	3 h 14 min
14.	Nawaz	2 h 37 min
15.	Olson	4 h 1 min
16.	Paris	1 h 59 min

APPLY

MATH REASONING

Which of these amounts of time—1 day, 2 days, or 3 days—is the best approximation for these numbers of hours?

17. 50 hours   **18.** 27 hours   **19.** 40 hours   **20.** 75 hours

PROBLEM SOLVING

21. Gregory's time in last year's cross country race was 123 min. This year his time for the race was 1 h 59 min. Did he beat his old time?

22. Health and Fitness Data Bank In what years were the winning Olympic times less than 120 s in the women's 800 m run? See page 475.

▶ MENTAL MATH

Use mental math to find the amount of **elapsed time.**

23. While training for a marathon race, Peggy ran from 8:35 a.m. until 11:50 a.m. How long did she run in hours and minutes?

24. Peggy stayed with her grandparents from 11:10 a.m. to 5:30 p.m. How long was she there?

Problem Solving
Using Data from a Thermometer

UNDERSTAND
ANALYZE DATA
PLAN
ESTIMATE
SOLVE
EXAMINE

LEARN ABOUT IT

Scientists use degrees Celsius (0°C) to record temperatures above and below zero. The temperature 15°C is read "fifteen degrees Celsius above zero." The temperature −11°C is read "eleven degrees Celsius below zero."

Scientists in very cold places often use thermometers with ethyl alcohol in them instead of mercury. Ethyl alcohol freezes at −150°C. How do you read and write the temperature at which mercury freezes?

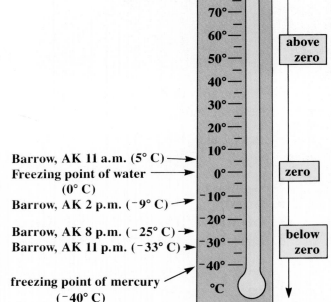

boiling point of water (100° C)

above zero

Barrow, AK 11 a.m. (5° C)
Freezing point of water (0° C)

zero

Barrow, AK 2 p.m. (⁻9° C)

Barrow, AK 8 p.m. (⁻25° C)
Barrow, AK 11 p.m. (⁻33° C)

below zero

freezing point of mercury (⁻40° C)

°C

First I'll find zero on the thermometer.

Zero is the freezing point.

Then I'll find how many degrees above or below zero.

Mercury freezes at forty degrees Celsius below zero. I can write ⁻40°C.

Mercury freezes at −40°C.

TRY IT OUT

1. Lorraine recorded the temperatures in one day in Barrow, Alaska. Some of her measurements are shown on the thermometer above. What was the temperature at 2 p.m.?

2. What was the temperature in Barrow at 8 p.m.?

3. What temperature did Lorraine record at 11 p.m.?

4. What was the highest temperature Lorraine recorded? When did she record it?

Solve. Use any problem solving strategy.

1. Nitrogen gas becomes a liquid at about −147°C. To study liquid nitrogen, Mr. Dodge divided his class of 35 students into 7 groups. There were the same number of students in each group. How many students were in each group?

2. One day in January, the temperature in Singapore was 3.3 degrees hotter than 10 times the temperature in Moscow. The temperature in Moscow was 2.75°C. What was the temperature in Singapore?

3. Geri made ice cubes of different colors and shapes for her party. She froze blue, green, red, yellow, and purple ice cubes. The shapes were square, hearts, and spheres. How many choices of different ice cubes did she have?

4. The thermometer shows the average summer temperature in Florida. This is 3 times higher than the average summer temperature in Iceland. What is the average summer temperature in Iceland?

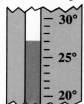

5. One freezing weekend, Jeremy skied at two different ski areas. The first area had mountains as high as 1,981 m. The second had mountains 976 m higher. About what was the height of the mountains at the second ski area?

6. The Garcia family's medical thermometer measures temperatures as high as 41°C. Their scientific thermometer can measure temperatures about 9.75 times as high. About how many degrees can the scientific thermometer measure?

7. Jong lives in Dallas, Texas. He kept track of the high temperature for the first day of the month for 4 months. How many degrees difference was there between the high temperatures August 1 and November 1?

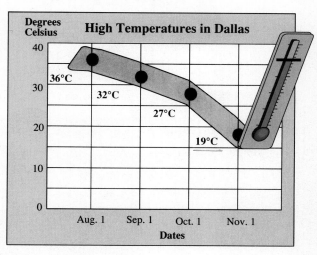

8. Thinking About Your Solution The temperature at 6:00 a.m. was 10°C. It rose 32 degrees by noon. It rose another 17 degrees by 2 p.m. It dropped 59 degrees by 8 p.m. What was the temperature at 8 p.m.?

   A. Solve.
   B. Write your answer in a complete sentence.
   C. Write a description of how you solved the problem.
   D. Name the strategy or strategies you used to solve it.

Data Collection and Analysis
Group Decision Making

UNDERSTAND
ANALYZE DATA
PLAN
ESTIMATE
SOLVE
EXAMINE

Doing an Investigation
Group Skill:
Explain and Summarize

Investigation

Can you predict how high a ball will bounce if it is dropped from 1 meter or 3 meters? You can do an **investigation** to find out if there is a relationship between how far a ball is dropped and how high it bounces.

Collecting Data

1. You are going to drop a ball from different heights and measure how high it bounces. Your group will need a ball and a measuring tape or stick. Discuss with your group how you will measure the height the ball is dropped and the height of the bounce.

2. Drop the ball from at least six different heights and measure how high it bounces. You may want to find the average of two bounces from each height and round to the nearest whole unit. Record the data in a table like the one below.

Height Dropped	Height Bounced (average of two tries)
50 cm	12 cm
100 cm	28 cm
150 cm	37 cm

Organizing Data

3. You and your group make a line graph using the data in your table. Adjust the scales on the graph so that the largest and smallest measurements in your table fit on the graph. Show a point on your graph for each pair of measurements in your table.

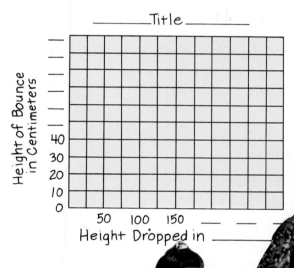

_____Title_____

Height of Bounce in Centimeters

40
30
20
10
0

50 100 150 ___ ___ ___

Height Dropped in _____

Presenting Your Analysis

4. Write a summary of your investigation procedures and your results. Include a description of any pattern you observed. How did you make your measurements? What do you notice about your graph?

5. Make some predictions. Do you think there is a maximum height the ball will bounce? How high do you think the ball would bounce if you dropped it 10 m? Be prepared to tell how you made your predictions.

WRAP UP

Choosing Metric Units

Choose answers from the list at the right.

1. Write three units that measure length in order from least to greatest.

2. Write two units that measure volume.

3. Write two units that measure area.

4. Write two units that measure mass.

square meter
centimeter
cubic meter
kilogram
meter
cubic centimeter
gram
kilometer
square centimeter

Sometimes, Always, Never

Complete each statement by writing **sometimes, always,** or **never.** Explain your choice.

5. When you change from a smaller metric unit to a larger one, the number of units __?__ increases.

6. If two rectangles have the same perimeter, they __?__ have the same area.

7. To change a larger unit of time to a smaller unit, you __?__ multiply twice.

Project

Choose a model that you think represents a volume of about 1 cm^3. Then find an object that is about ten times greater in length, width, and height. What is its approximate volume? Find and list some objects that you estimate to have this volume.

Try to find some larger objects that are about ten times greater than this in length, width, and height. What is their approximate volume? Find and list some objects that you estimate to have this volume.

POWER PRACTICE/TEST

Part 1 Understanding

Select the most appropriate unit for each measure.
mm, cm, m, km, mL, L, g, kg

1. Mass of a turkey: 7 __?__

2. Amount of ink in a pen: 2 __?__

3. Width of tip of shoelace: 2 __?__

4. Height of a giraffe: 6.4 __?__

5. Length of 12 city blocks: 1 __?__

6. Mass of a nickel: 5 __?__

7. Width of index finger: 1 __?__

8. Amount of water a sink will hold: 10 __?__

About how many hours is:

9. 135 min?

10. 350 min?

Part 2 Skills

Give the missing numbers.

11. 324 cm = ▥ m

12. 42.6 cm = ▥ mm

13. 500 m = ▥ km

14. 6.7 L = ▥ mL

15. 3.6 kg = ▥ g

16. 164 s = ▥ min ▥ s

17. 468 mL = ▥ L

18. 3,125 g = ▥ kg

19. 4 m 28 cm = ▥ cm

20. 387 min = ▥ h ▥ min

Part 3 Applications

21. Greg asked Marilyn for change for a half dollar. How many different coin combinations are possible? Do not use pennies.

22. **Challenge.** The highest temperature ever recorded was in North Africa. The temperature was 1°C hotter than 2 times the temperature on an average summer day. The temperature on an average summer day is 28.4°C. What was the highest recorded temperature?

ENRICHMENT
Time Zones

Because the earth rotates on its axis, the sun is overhead at different times for different parts of the earth. The earth has been divided into 24 different standard time zones, since there are 24 hours in a day. The time in each zone is one hour more or one hour less than the time in the next time zone.

This map shows the six time zones of the United States. Use the map to answer the questions below.

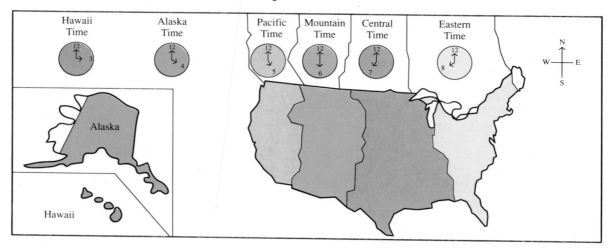

1. What happens to time as you travel east across the time zones?

2. What happens to time as you travel west across time zones?

Suppose it is noon Alaska Time.

3. What is the Central Time?

4. What is the Mountain Time?

5. What is the Pacific Time?

6. What is the Hawaii Time?

Suppose it is 3:30 p.m. Mountain Time.

7. What is the Eastern Time?

8. What is the Alaska Time?

9. What is the Pacific Time?

10. What is the Central Time?

11. A plane left Washington, D.C., at 11 a.m. Eastern Time and arrived in Los Angeles at 1 p.m. Pacific Time. How long did the flight take?

12. A flight from New Orleans to Honolulu takes 7 hours. If the plane leaves at 10 a.m. Central Time, what would be the time in Hawaii when it arrives?

CUMULATIVE REVIEW

Use rounding to estimate.

1. 5,827 − 1,216

    A. 5,000 − 1,000 = 4,000
    B. 6,000 − 2,000 = 4,000
    C. 5,000 − 2,000 = 3,000
    D. 6,000 − 1,000 = 5,000

2. 1.247 + 6.8 + 15.91

    A. 1 + 7 + 16 = 24
    B. 1 + 6 + 15 = 22
    C. 2 + 6 + 16 = 24
    D. 1 + 7 + 15 = 23

Use this graph for questions 3–4.

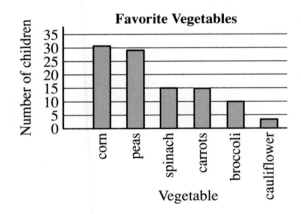

3. Which two vegetables are liked the most?

    A. spinach and carrots
    B. corn and peas
    C. peas and spinach
    D. carrots and broccoli

4. About how many children were questioned?

    A. 50   B. 100   C. 150   D. 200

Multiply.

5. 600 × 500

    A. 3,000   B. 30,000
    C. 300,000   D. 3,000,000

6.
$$\begin{array}{r} 542 \\ \times\quad 4 \\ \hline \end{array}$$

    A. 546
    B. 2,068
    C. 2,168
    D. 20,168

7.
$$\begin{array}{r} 27 \\ \times\ 85 \\ \hline \end{array}$$

    A. 2,295
    B. 351
    C. 112
    D. 2,315

8. Estimate using compatible numbers.
246 + 98 + 51 + 107 + 62 + 41

    A. 400   B. 500   C. 600   D. 700

9. To multiply 476 × 8 using the distributive property and mental math:

    A. multiply the 4 by 8, add 76.
    B. multiply 400, 70, and 6 by 8, then add.
    C. multiply 476 by 10, and subtract 16.
    D. round 476 to 500 and multiply by 8.

10. Each of 8 teams in a volleyball tournament is scheduled to play every other team once. How many games are scheduled?

    A. 64   B. 28   C. 56   D. 15

7

DIVISION: WHOLE NUMBERS AND DECIMALS

THEME: TRANSPORTATION

MATH AND SOCIAL STUDIES

DATA BANK

Use the Social Studies Data Bank on page 482 to answer the questions.

1 What was the total cost of building the National Road from Cumberland, Maryland, to Wheeling, West Virginia?

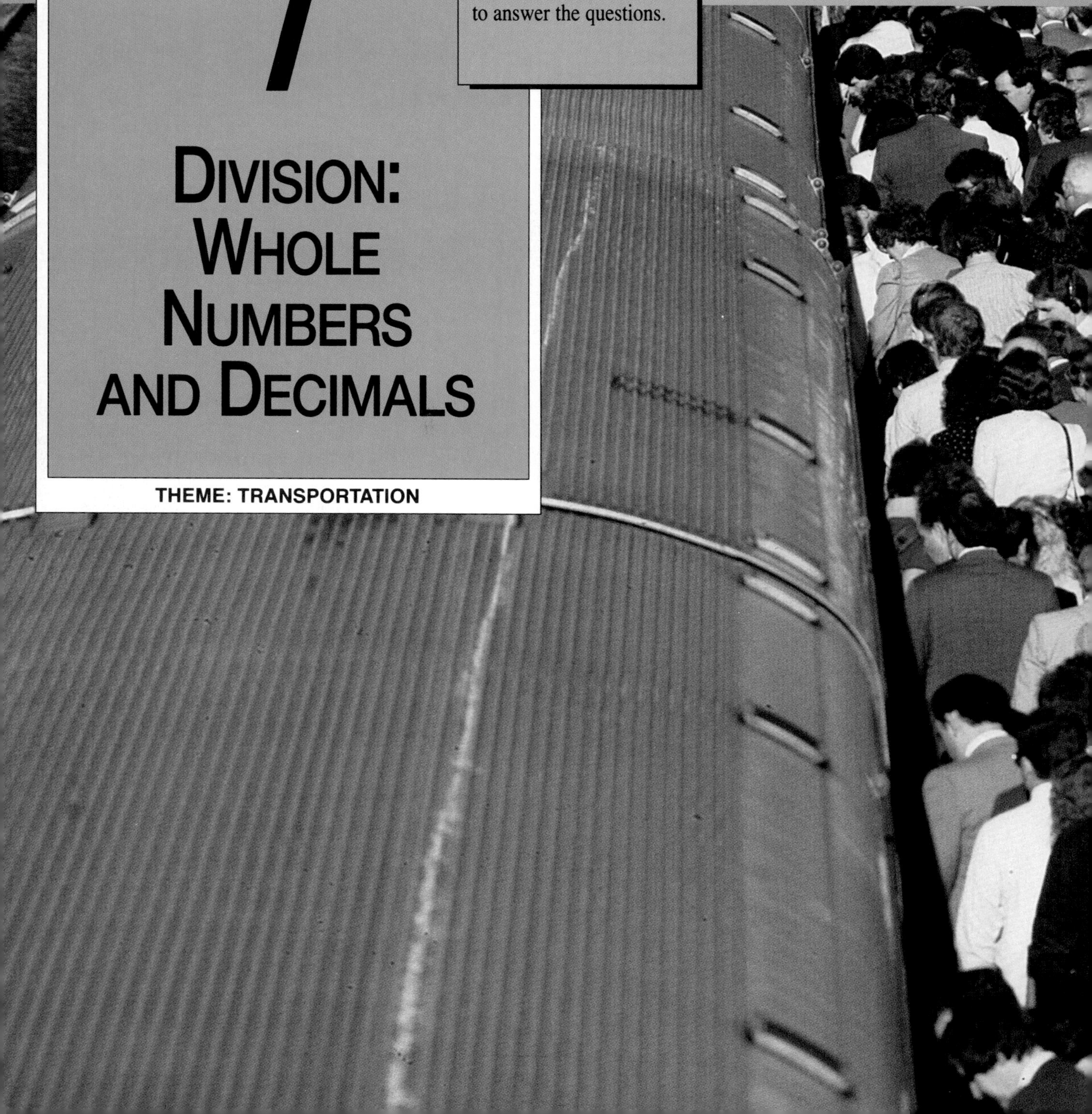

2 About how long would it have taken a stagecoach in 1870 to travel from Cumberland to Wheeling on the National Road?

3 During which 30-year period did the traveling speed of a car increase the most? How much greater was the speed per hour at the end of that period than at the beginning of the period?

4 **Using Critical Thinking** Compare the line graphs showing traveling speeds on railroads and on highways. How are the graphs different for the years after 1960? What may have caused the difference?

M–1

TRACK **1**

Thanks to recent advances in railroad technology, some of today's passenger trains can reach speeds of 170 mph.

Mental Math
Special Quotients

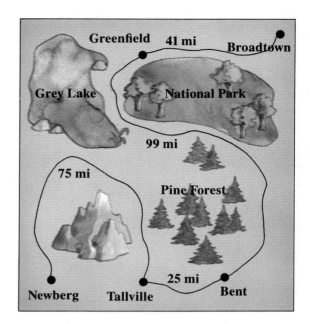

Quotients that involve basic division facts are usually easy to find using mental math.

EXPLORE Solve to Understand

The Pedalpushers Bike Club was planning a 4-day tour from Newberg to Broadtown. How many miles would they have to ride each day to get to Broadtown if they rode the same distance each day?

TALK ABOUT IT

1. How can you use mental math to find the total distance from Newberg to Broadtown?

2. Since the bikers will travel the same distance each day, what operation should be used to find the distance each day?

You can use basic division facts to find larger quotients.

■ **Here is how to do it.**

Problem: $240 \div 4$

Look for a basic fact.	$240 \div 4$
Solve the basic fact.	$24 \div 4 = 6$
Attach the zeros.	60

■ **Here is why it works.**

240 is 24 tens. ("tens" means 1 zero)
24 tens ÷ 4 = 6 tens
6 tens is 60.

You can use multiplication to check. $60 \times 4 = 240$
The club would have to travel 60 miles each day.

Other Examples

$24 \div 4 = 6$
$2,400 \div 4 = 600$

$40 \div 5 = 8$
$4,000 \div 5 = 800$

Use mental math to find these quotients.

1. $420 \div 6$ **2.** $80 \div 2$ **3.** $3,200 \div 8$ **4.** $300 \div 5$ **5.** $7,200 \div 8$

Use mental math to find the quotients.

1. $210 \div 3$ **2.** $540 \div 6$ **3.** $160 \div 8$ **4.** $350 \div 7$

5. $1,200 \div 3$ **6.** $5,400 \div 9$ **7.** $4,200 \div 6$ **8.** $3,000 \div 5$

9. $16,000 \div 4$ **10.** $32,000 \div 8$ **11.** $27,000 \div 9$ **12.** $48,000 \div 8$

13. Find the quotient of 420 and 7.   **14.** What is 6,400 divided by 8?

APPLY

MATH REASONING

Write $>$, $<$, or $=$ for each ▓.

15. $2,800 \div 4$ ▓ 10×70 **16.** 30×20 ▓ $480 \div 6$

17. $8,000 \div 8$ ▓ 800×10 **18.** $3,500 \div 7$ ▓ 100×50

PROBLEM SOLVING

19. The Great Outdoors Bike Club made a 300-mile trip in 6 days. They rode the same number of miles each day. How far did they ride each day?

20. When Leroy, Rick, and Gwen left school one day, each was wearing a bicycle helmet that belonged to one of the others. Each was also wearing a jacket that belonged to someone other than the owner of the helmet. Rick had on Gwen's helmet. Copy and complete the table at the right.

	helmet	jacket
Leroy		
Rick	Gwen's	
Gwen		

▶ **USING CRITICAL THINKING**   Discover a Pattern

21. Look for patterns in Set A. Copy and complete Set B.

Set A: $28 \div 4 = 7$, $280 \div 4 = 70$, $2,800 \div 4 = 700$, $28,000 \div 4 = 7,000$

Set B: $32 \div 8 = 4$, $320 \div 8 = $ ▓, $3,200 \div 8 = $ ▓, $32,000 \div 8 = $ ▓

Look at the number of zeros in the dividend and the number of zeros in the quotient in the examples above. Can you make a **generalization** (a statement that holds true in many cases) about the number of zeros in the dividend and the number of zeros in the quotient? Do you think your generalization works for all cases?

More Practice, page 507, set D

Estimating Quotients
Rounding and Compatible Numbers

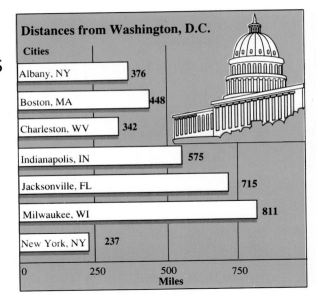

Distances from Washington, D.C.

Cities	Miles
Albany, NY	376
Boston, MA	448
Charleston, WV	342
Indianapolis, IN	575
Jacksonville, FL	715
Milwaukee, WI	811
New York, NY	237

LEARN ABOUT IT

You can substitute compatible numbers to estimate quotients.

EXPLORE Examine the Data

In the early 1800s travelers often rode on stagecoaches. On good roads stagecoaches could travel 8 miles per hour. Think about how many hours it would take a stagecoach to travel from Washington, D.C., to Charleston, W.V.

TALK ABOUT IT

1. What data from the paragraph above and what data from the graph do you need in order to find about how long it would take a stagecoach to travel from Washington to Charleston?

2. Can you easily use rounding and mental math to estimate the number of hours the trip would take?

Rounding 342 to the nearest ten or the nearest hundred would not be very helpful, because $340 \div 8$ and $300 \div 8$ are not easily solved using mental math. You can more easily solve this problem by replacing 342 with a number that can easily be divided by 8.

■ Here is one way to estimate $342 \div 8$.

Substitute a compatible number for 342.

$$\downarrow$$
$$320 \div 8 = 40$$

The trip would take a stagecoach about 40 hours.

TRY IT OUT

Estimate how many hours it would take a stagecoach to travel from Washington to:

1. Albany   2. Boston   3. Indianapolis   4. Jacksonville

Which would be a better choice for estimating the quotient?

1. 138 ÷ 8   **A.** 80 ÷ 8   **B.** 160 ÷ 8

2. 168 ÷ 5   **A.** 150 ÷ 5   **B.** 200 ÷ 5

3. 405 ÷ 7   **A.** 350 ÷ 7   **B.** 420 ÷ 7

Estimate each quotient by substituting compatible numbers.

4. 147 ÷ 3   **5.** 254 ÷ 5   **6.** 556 ÷ 7   **7.** 244 ÷ 6

8. 163 ÷ 2   **9.** 362 ÷ 4   **10.** 636 ÷ 8   **11.** 4,849 ÷ 6

12. 1,243 ÷ 3   **13.** 3,152 ÷ 4   **14.** 7,241 ÷ 9   **15.** 535 ÷ 9

16. 6,279 ÷ 9   **17.** 4,854 ÷ 7   **18.** 4,189 ÷ 7   **19.** 5,598 ÷ 6

APPLY

MATH REASONING

Write > or < to show whether the exact quotient is greater than or less than the given estimate.

20. 3,473 ÷ 5   Estimate: 3,500 ÷ 5 = 700
21. 367 ÷ 7   Estimate: 350 ÷ 7 = 50
22. 6,575 ÷ 8   Estimate: 6,400 ÷ 8 = 800

PROBLEM SOLVING

23. Annie took a train from Washington to New York. The train made a few stops but got to New York in 3 hours. About how many miles per hour did the train travel?

24. Social Studies Data Bank About how many hours would it take to travel the 342 miles from Washington to Charleston in a Model T car of 1930? See page 482.

DATA BANK

MIXED REVIEW

Give the unit—**mm, cm, dm,** or **m**—that is most reasonable.

25. length of an ant: 6 __?__   **26.** height of a tree: 7 __?__   **27.** width of your foot: 6 __?__

Give the number for each ▦ .

28. 265 cm = ▦ m   **29.** 6.95 m = ▦ cm   **30.** 11 mm = ▦ cm

More Practice, page 507, Set E

Dividing Whole Numbers
Making the Connection

We can understand the steps in division
by using place value blocks and thinking
about division as sharing.

EXPLORE Use Place Value Blocks

Work with a partner.

- One partner uses place value blocks
  (tens and ones) to show a two-digit
  number greater than 50.
- The other partner chooses 2, 3, 4, or 5
  as the number of groups into which the
  blocks are to be divided.
- Together the partners divide the blocks
  into the chosen number of groups so
  that each group has the same number.
  Record the number in each group and
  the number left over.
- Repeat this activity several times. Try it
  once using blocks with the value of a
  three-digit number.

TALK ABOUT IT

1. Did you start with the tens or the ones blocks when you
   divided them into groups? Does it make a difference?
   Explain.
2. When did you have to trade? Give an example that
   shows when you have to trade.
3. When you divide blocks into groups, is it possible that
   you may not be able to place all of the blocks you
   started with in one of the groups?

You have divided blocks into groups and recorded the number in each group and the number left over. Now you will learn how to use symbols to record those steps. Here is how to divide 72 into 3 groups.

| **What You Do** | **What You Record** |

Show 72 as 7 tens and 2 ones. Show 3 groups.

$$3\overline{)72}$$

How many tens can be placed in each group?

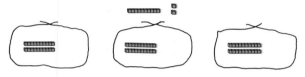

$$\begin{array}{r} 2 \\ 3\overline{)72} \\ 6 \\ \hline 1 \end{array}$$

← 2 tens in each group

← 6 tens shared in all

← 1 ten left

Can you trade 1 ten so that it can be divided into 3 groups?

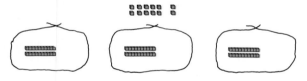

$$\begin{array}{r} 2 \\ 3\overline{)72} \\ 6 \\ \hline 12 \end{array}$$

← Bring down the ones.

How many ones can be placed in each group?

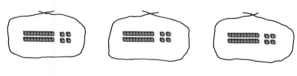

$$\begin{array}{r} 24 \\ 3\overline{)72} \\ 6 \\ \hline 12 \\ 12 \\ \hline 0 \end{array}$$

← 4 ones in each group

← 12 in all groups

← 0 left to be shared

TRY IT OUT

Find each quotient using place value blocks. Record your work using symbols.

1. 24 ÷ 2   **2.** 36 ÷ 2   **3.** 45 ÷ 3   **4.** 24 ÷ 4

Each picture shows the result *after* dividing. Use the multiplication fact to give the original division problem.

5.
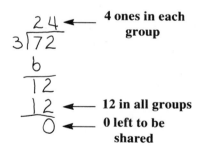
2 × 24 = 48

6.
3 × 12 = 36

Dividing
2- and 3-digit Quotients

Detroit to
Philadelphia
580 mi

EXPLORE **Analyze the Process**

Jamie flew the distance in 4 h. She traveled the same number of miles each hour. How many miles did she travel each hour?

She traveled the same distance each hour, so we divide.

Divide hundreds.	Divide tens.	Divide ones.
$$\begin{array}{r} 1 \\ 4\overline{)580} \\ 4 \\ \hline 1 \end{array}$$ ■ Divide. ■ Multiply. ■ Subtract. ■ Compare.	$$\begin{array}{r} 14 \\ 4\overline{)580} \\ 4\downarrow \\ \hline 18 \\ 16 \\ \hline 2 \end{array}$$ ■ Bring down. ■ Divide. ■ Multiply. ■ Subtract. ■ Compare.	$$\begin{array}{r} 145 \\ 4\overline{)580} \\ 4 \\ \hline 18 \\ 16\downarrow \\ \hline 20 \\ 20 \\ \hline 0 \end{array}$$ ■ Bring down. ■ Divide. ■ Multiply. ■ Subtract. ■ Compare.

TALK ABOUT IT

1. In the first step of the solution, where did the 4, written below the 5, come from?
2. In the second step, what number was divided by 4 to get the 4 in the quotient?

Other Examples

A
$$\begin{array}{r} 16\ \text{R2} \\ 5\overline{)82} \\ 5 \\ \hline 32 \\ 30 \\ \hline 2 \end{array}$$

B
$$\begin{array}{r} 21 \\ 4\overline{)84} \\ 8 \\ \hline 04 \\ 4 \\ \hline 0 \end{array}$$

C
$$\begin{array}{r} 47\ \text{R1} \\ 2\overline{)95} \\ 8 \\ \hline 15 \\ 14 \\ \hline 1 \end{array}$$

TRY IT OUT

Divide.

1. $3\overline{)413}$ 2. $6\overline{)71}$ 3. $3\overline{)827}$ 4. $7\overline{)935}$ 5. $2\overline{)768}$

Divide.

1. 3)$\overline{69}$	**2.** 5)$\overline{55}$	**3.** 2)$\overline{48}$	**4.** 4)$\overline{84}$	**5.** 3)$\overline{93}$
6. 4)$\overline{64}$	**7.** 2)$\overline{93}$	**8.** 6)$\overline{87}$	**9.** 7)$\overline{91}$	**10.** 4)$\overline{87}$
11. 4)$\overline{57}$	**12.** 3)$\overline{53}$	**13.** 8)$\overline{90}$	**14.** 4)$\overline{925}$	**15.** 8)$\overline{976}$
16. 4)$\overline{648}$	**17.** 3)$\overline{639}$	**18.** 3)$\overline{648}$	**19.** 8)$\overline{915}$	**20.** 3)$\overline{711}$

21. Find the quotient when 675 is the dividend and 5 is the divisor.

Use mental math to find each quotient:

22. 2)$\overline{80}$	**23.** 4)$\overline{3,200}$	**24.** 3)$\overline{270}$	**25.** 5)$\overline{3,000}$	**26.** 7)$\overline{490}$

APPLY

MATH REASONING

Without dividing, tell which quotient is greater.

27. 4)$\overline{684}$ or 4)$\overline{864}$ **28.** 4)$\overline{684}$ or 2)$\overline{684}$ **29.** 5)$\overline{810}$ or 6)$\overline{576}$

PROBLEM SOLVING

30. Rosita sailed her boat and swam a total of 12 h. She sailed twice as many hours as she swam. How long did she sail?

31. Renaldo flew 720 miles in 2 days. He flew the same distance each day. How many miles did he fly each day?

▶ **MENTAL MATH**

You can break apart a number to find the quotient. Use the method shown at the right to find these quotients.

$126 \div 3$
Think: $120 \div 3$ plus $6 \div 3$
        ↓   ↓
      40   plus   2 is 42.

32. $155 \div 5$ **33.** $184 \div 2$ **34.** $248 \div 4$ **35.** $189 \div 3$

More Practice, page 508, set A

Dividing
Deciding Where to Start

LEARN ABOUT IT

EXPLORE   Analyze the Process

Sharif and 3 friends took a bus to summer camp. The total cost of the 4 tickets was $392. The price of each ticket was the same. How much did each ticket cost?

Since each ticket costs the same amount, we can divide to find the cost of each. Here is how.

Decide where to start.	Divide the tens.	Divide the ones.
$4\overline{)392}$	$\begin{array}{r} 9 \\ 4\overline{)392} \\ \underline{36} \\ 3 \end{array}$ ■ Divide. ■ Multiply. ■ Subtract. ■ Compare.	$\begin{array}{r} 98 \\ 4\overline{)392} \\ \underline{36}\downarrow \\ 32 \\ \underline{32} \\ 0 \end{array}$ ■ Bring down. ■ Divide. ■ Multiply. ■ Subtract. ■ Compare.
4 > 3 Not enough hundreds 4 < 39 Divide the tens first.		

TALK ABOUT IT

1. If you have three $100 bills, can you divide them into 4 groups without trading?
2. What two numbers can be multiplied to get the 36 in the second step?

Other Examples

A
$$\begin{array}{r} 58\ R4 \\ 8\overline{)468} \\ \underline{40} \\ 68 \\ \underline{64} \\ 4 \end{array}$$

B
$$\begin{array}{r} 13\ R2 \\ 5\overline{)67} \quad ✔ \\ \underline{5} \\ 17 \\ \underline{15} \\ 2 \end{array}$$

Check by multiplying:

$$\begin{array}{r} 13 \\ \times\ 5 \\ \hline 65 \end{array} \qquad \begin{array}{r} 65 \\ +\ 2 \\ \hline 67 \ ✔ \end{array}$$

TRY IT OUT

Divide. Check by multiplying.

1. $8\overline{)168}$ 2. $3\overline{)435}$ 3. $5\overline{)467}$ 4. $6\overline{)296}$

Where do you start dividing? Answer **hundreds** or **tens**.

1. $6\overline{)347}$ **2.** $3\overline{)474}$ **3.** $4\overline{)228}$ **4.** $6\overline{)770}$ **5.** $4\overline{)295}$

Divide. Check by using multiplication.

6. $5\overline{)425}$ **7.** $9\overline{)327}$ **8.** $6\overline{)411}$ **9.** $3\overline{)257}$ **10.** $7\overline{)119}$

11. $6\overline{)176}$ **12.** $5\overline{)184}$ **13.** $3\overline{)179}$ **14.** $4\overline{)476}$ **15.** $8\overline{)296}$

16. $5\overline{)423}$ **17.** $7\overline{)371}$ **18.** $5\overline{)197}$ **19.** $8\overline{)539}$ **20.** $8\overline{)227}$

Use mental math to find each quotient.

21. $7\overline{)147}$ **22.** $5\overline{)520}$ **23.** $3\overline{)927}$ **24.** $8\overline{)324}$ **25.** $6\overline{)234}$

APPLY

MATH REASONING

26. Make up a division problem where the quotient is 75.

27. Make up a division problem where the divisor is 4 and the remainder is 1.

PROBLEM SOLVING

28. Camp supplies for 4 girls cost $272. Each paid the same. What was the cost for each girl?

29. Data Hunt Find the cost of a tent that would hold five people. If the total cost was shared by five people how much would each pay?

30. Unfinished Problem Write a question that you can solve using the data below. Then answer your question. At camp 168 girls were placed in 7 cabins. Each cabin could hold no more than 25 girls.

▶ **ALGEBRA**

We can write **numerical expressions** that name the same number as equations. For example, since $23 + 15$ and $40 - 2$ are both names for 38, we can write $23 + 15 = 40 - 2$. An equation means that both sides of the equal sign name the same number.

Copy and give the number for each ▦.

31. $42 - 12 = 6 \times$ ▦   **32.** $18 \times 3 = 85 -$ ▦   **33.** $36 \div 6 =$ ▦ $\div 8$

More Practice, page 508, Set B

Dividing
Special Cases

LEARN ABOUT IT

EXPLORE **Analyze the Process**

Ramon and his family are planning a trip to Big Bend National Park. They are allowing 6 days to make the 1,248 mile trip. If they travel the same distance each day, how many miles will they travel per day?

Decide where to start.	Divide the hundreds.	Divide the tens.	Divide the ones.

Decide where to start.

$$6\overline{)1,248}$$

> 6 > 1   Not enough thousands
> 6 < 12 Divide the hundreds.

Divide the hundreds.

$$\begin{array}{r} 2 \\ 6\overline{)1,248} \\ \underline{12} \\ 0 \end{array}$$

- Divide.
- Multiply.
- Subtract.
- Compare.

Divide the tens.

$$\begin{array}{r} 20 \\ 6\overline{)1,248} \\ \underline{12}\downarrow \\ 04 \\ \underline{0} \\ 4 \end{array}$$

- Bring down.
- Divide.
- Multiply.
- Subtract.
- Compare.

Divide the ones.

$$\begin{array}{r} 208 \\ 6\overline{)1,248} \\ \underline{12} \\ 04 \\ \underline{0}\downarrow \\ 48 \\ \underline{48} \\ 0 \end{array}$$

- Bring down.
- Divide.
- Multiply.
- Subtract.
- Compare

TALK ABOUT IT

1. Why is the first digit in the quotient above the 2?
2. Use estimation to check the computed quotient.

Other Examples

A
$$\begin{array}{r} 308 \\ 6\overline{)1,848} \\ \underline{18} \\ 04 \\ \underline{0} \\ 48 \\ \underline{48} \\ 0 \end{array}$$

B
$$\begin{array}{r} 316 \\ 7\overline{)2,212} \\ \underline{21} \\ 11 \\ \underline{7} \\ 42 \\ \underline{42} \\ 0 \end{array}$$

C
$$\begin{array}{r} 860\ R5 \\ 9\overline{)7,745} \\ \underline{72} \\ 54 \\ \underline{54} \\ 05 \\ \underline{0} \\ 5 \end{array}$$

TRY IT OUT

Divide.

1. $6\overline{)1,836}$

2. $4\overline{)1,280}$

3. $3\overline{)1,390}$

4. $5\overline{)4,047}$

Divide. Check using multiplication.

1. $3\overline{)618}$ 2. $4\overline{)432}$ 3. $3\overline{)213}$ 4. $5\overline{)205}$ 5. $7\overline{)721}$

6. $4\overline{)363}$ 7. $5\overline{)402}$ 8. $6\overline{)965}$ 9. $9\overline{)920}$ 10. $4\overline{)835}$

11. $7\overline{)2,128}$ 12. $8\overline{)6,456}$ 13. $9\overline{)2,727}$ 14. $7\overline{)2,660}$ 15. $2\overline{)1,004}$

16. 1,632 divided by 4 is what number?

Find each quotient using **mental math.**

17. $150 \div 3$ 18. $540 \div 6$ 19. $2,400 \div 8$ 20. $48,000 \div 6$ 21. $42,000 \div 7$

APPLY

MATH REASONING

Use **estimation** to tell whether the exact quotient is less than or greater than the given number.

22. $6\overline{)1,920}$ <300 or > 300?   23. $5\overline{)2,040}$ < 400 or > 400?

PROBLEM SOLVING

24. Francine traveled with her family to Olympic National Park. The 1,664-mile trip took them 8 days. If they traveled the same distance each day, how many miles did they travel per day?

25. **Social Studies Data Bank**   Casey rode his bike along the original route of the National Road, from Cumberland to Wheeling and back. He was on the road for 5 days. How many miles per day did he ride? See page 482.

DATA BANK

▶ CALCULATOR

On a calculator $3,789 \div 8$ gives 473.625. The remainder is shown as a decimal. Some calculators have a special key that gives the remainder as a whole number. For other calculators you can use this method to find the remainder.

- Multiply the quotient, 473, by the divisor, 8: $473 \times 8 = 3,784$.
- Subtract this product from the dividend, 3,789: $3,789 - 3,784 = 5$. The remainder is 5.

Find the quotient and whole number remainder using a calculator.

26. $6\overline{)4,965}$ 27. $9\overline{)6,721}$ 28. $7\overline{)5,529}$ 29. $8\overline{)2,231}$

More Practice, page 508, set C   **191**

Finding Averages

LEARN ABOUT IT

EXPLORE Use a Paper Model
Work in groups. Cut out four strips of
paper. Use these lengths: 5 in., 5 in., 6 in.,
8 in. Tape all four pieces together end to
end. Fold the long strip in half. Then fold
it in half again. Now open the strip. The
fold lines show four new sections, each
the same length. Measure the length of
one of the new sections.

TALK ABOUT IT

1. What is the length of each new section?

2. Is the length of the new section less than 8 in.? Is the
   length greater than 5 in.?

3. Could the length of a new section be less than 5 in.?
   Explain your answer.

The length of each new section above is the average of the
four numbers. Here is how to find the **average** of a group
of numbers.
Problem: Find the average of 385, 402, and 416.

Add. $\begin{array}{r} 385 \\ 402 \\ +416 \\ \hline 1,203 \end{array}$ →   Divide the sum
by the number
of addends.   → $\begin{array}{r} 401 \\ 3\overline{)1,203} \end{array}$ The quotient is
the average.

TRY IT OUT

Find the average of each set of numbers.

1. 26; 22; 33

2. 456; 275; 382

3. 17; 24; 28; 31; 20

4. 762; 849; 693; 804

5. 2,064; 3,488; 4,656; 7,624

6. 3; 6; 4; 5; 9; 9

7. 39; 58; 76; 43; 67; 77

8. 511; 584; 652; 871; 702

9. 46; 35; 54; 40; 60

10. 535; 410; 613; 512; 485

11. 1,273; 1,477; 975; 833; 1,002

POWER PRACTICE/QUIZ

Divide using mental math.

1. $360 \div 9$ 2. $280 \div 7$ 3. $4,500 \div 5$ 4. $5,600 \div 8$

5. $4,000 \div 8$ 6. $420 \div 6$ 7. $2,400 \div 3$ 8. $490 \div 7$

9. $560 \div 7$ 10. $2,500 \div 5$ 11. $810 \div 9$ 12. $6,400 \div 8$

13. $2,700 \div 9$ 14. $720 \div 8$ 15. $630 \div 7$ 16. $2,000 \div 4$

Estimate each quotient.

17. $465 \div 6$ 18. $217 \div 5$ 19. $199 \div 3$ 20. $739 \div 8$

21. $800 \div 9$ 22. $550 \div 7$ 23. $327 \div 4$ 24. $113 \div 2$

25. $445 \div 5$ 26. $315 \div 8$ 27. $411 \div 7$ 28. $261 \div 9$

Divide. Use multiplication or estimation to check.

29. $2\overline{)86}$ 30. $3\overline{)376}$ 31. $8\overline{)890}$ 32. $4\overline{)324}$ 33. $5\overline{)377}$

34. $8\overline{)108}$ 35. $3\overline{)211}$ 36. $7\overline{)274}$ 37. $5\overline{)615}$ 38. $8\overline{)700}$

39. $6\overline{)624}$ 40. $8\overline{)875}$ 41. $9\overline{)926}$ 42. $7\overline{)85}$ 43. $3\overline{)325}$

PROBLEM SOLVING

44. David used place value blocks to show each of these division problems. For which of the problems did he have to trade tens for ones?

   A. $3\overline{)96}$ B. $7\overline{)42}$
   C. $4\overline{)52}$ D. $3\overline{)84}$

45. How can 32 students be divided into teams so that each team has either 5 or 6 players?

46. Saka and 2 friends washed 12 cars. They earned $5 for each car. If they shared the money equally, how much does each of them receive?

47. Paula's goal is to jog a total of 25 mi each week. She plans to reach her goal by jogging the same number of miles on each of the remaining days of the week. How many miles will she jog on each of those days?

Paula's Jogging Record						
Mon	Tues	Wed	Thu	Fri	Sat	Sun
4	3	3	3	?	?	?

193

Problem Solving
Interpreting Remainders

| UNDERSTAND |
| ANALYZE DATA |
| PLAN |
| ESTIMATE |
| SOLVE |
| EXAMINE |

LEARN ABOUT IT

Sometimes division does not give you the full answer to a problem. You may need to understand the meaning of a remainder. Think about the different ways you must interpret the remainders in the problems below.

There are 125 campers going to River Rafters Camp. They are riding to the camp in vans. Each van holds 9 campers. How many vans are needed?

At the rafting supplies store, Jeff put together some sets of life jackets. He had 119 jackets. He needed 8 jackets for each raft. For how many rafts could he put together a full set of life jackets?

$$\begin{array}{r} 13 \text{ R}8 \\ 9)\overline{125} \\ 9 \\ \hline 35 \\ 27 \\ \hline 8 \end{array}$$

13 full vans are needed, but another is needed for the 8 remaining campers.

14 vans are needed.

$$\begin{array}{r} 14 \text{ R}7 \\ 8)\overline{119} \\ 8 \\ \hline 39 \\ 32 \\ \hline 7 \end{array}$$

The remaining 7 jackets are not enough to make a full set.

He could put together a full set of life jackets for 14 rafts.

TRY IT OUT

1. Joel has $102 to buy rubber patch kits for the rafts. Each patch kit costs $9. How many patch kits can he buy?

2. At camp, no more than 7 rafting students ride with an instructor on each raft. How many rafts are needed for 131 students?

3. Each lunch table seats 14 campers. There were 158 campers for lunch one day. How many tables were needed?

4. The owner of the camp had $692 to spend for T-shirts for the campers. Each shirt cost $6: How many shirts could he buy?

194

Solve. Use any of the strategies.

1. There are 5 sessions at rafting camp. What was the average number of campers per session?

Sessions at Camp	
Session	Attendance
1	128
2	158
3	176
4	180
5	203

2. Mary has saved $80 for a rafting trip that costs $140. How much more money does she need?

3. Grip rope for the sides of a raft costs $4 for 10 ft. How much would 40 feet of grip rope cost?

4. Kerry, one of the campers, used up 12 rolls of film taking pictures of campers during the summer. There are 24 shots in each roll. One roll costs $4.79. How many pictures did she take?

5. In the display case at the rafting store, there are 42 stickers that cost $0.80 each and 28 stickers that cost $1.50 each. What would be the total cost of all of them?

6. One of the instructors bought juice for the rafting students. That day there were 203 students. The drinks came in 6-packs. How many packs did he need to get?

7. The rafting store has 136 sports caps for sale. The store manager wants to display as many as possible on the wall in rows of 9. How many rows of sports caps can there be?

8. **Thinking About Your Solution** Bev needs sneakers and socks. There are 3 colors of each: white, blue, and red. How many possible combinations of sneakers and socks can Bev buy?

   A. Solve.
   B. Write your answer in a complete sentence.
   C. Name the strategy or strategies you used to solve it.

Problem Solving
Work Backward

UNDERSTAND
ANALYZE DATA
PLAN
ESTIMATE
SOLVE
EXAMINE

Some problems can be solved by starting with a given number and reversing the actions in the problem. This problem solving strategy is called **Work Backward.**

It often helps to make a flowchart and a reverse flowchart for the problem.

Bo asked Deena how many inches long Deena's pet iguana is. She said, "If you subtract 10 from its length and then double that difference, you will get 28." How long is the iguana?

> I can use what I know to make a flowchart.

Flowchart

$$\text{Length?} \rightarrow \boxed{-10} \rightarrow \boxed{\times 2} \rightarrow 28$$

> Now I can work backward using a reverse flowchart.

Reverse flowchart

$$\text{Length 24} \leftarrow \boxed{+10} \leftarrow \boxed{\div 2} \leftarrow 28$$

The iguana is 24 in. long.

TRY IT OUT

Gabriela spent half of her money at the zoo's gift shop. She spent half of what she had left on food at the zoo. She had $1.06 left. How much money did she start out with?

- What part of her money did she spend at the zoo's gift shop?

- What part of the money she had left did she spend on food?

- Copy and complete the flowchart and reverse flowchart to help solve the problem.

$$\text{money ?} \rightarrow \boxed{\div 2} \rightarrow \boxed{\div 2} \rightarrow \$1.06$$

$$\text{money ?} \leftarrow \boxed{?} \leftarrow \boxed{?} \leftarrow \$1.06$$

Work backward to solve each problem.

1. Gino asked the woman who fed the puma at the zoo how old the puma was. She said, "If you multiply the puma's age in years by 12 and divide by 3, you get 44." How old is the puma?

2. When Jeremy's white mice had babies, he gave away half of them. Then he sold 6 to the pet store. He had 7 left. How many mice did he have to begin with?

MIXED PRACTICE

Choose a strategy from the strategies list or use other strategies you know to solve these problems.

Some Strategies	
Act Out	Guess and Check
Use Objects	Make a Table
Choose an Operation	Solve a Simpler Problem
Draw a Picture	Make an Organized List
Work Backward	

3. Jake had 4 snakes. What was the average length of his snakes?

Snake	Length (in.)
Boa Constrictor	73
Boa Constrictor	68
Rainbow Boa	37
Python	66

4. An elephant's heart beats 25 times per minute. How many times does it beat in 24 hours?

5. Donna has a total of 30 pet fish and birds. She has 8 more fish than birds. How many birds does she have?

6. If you add the speed of a cheetah to the speed of a wildebeest and then divide by 2, you get 60. What is the speed of a cheetah?

Animal	Speed (mph)
Human	27.89
Coyote	43
Greyhound	39.45
Wildebeest	50

7. How much faster in miles per hour is a greyhound than a human?

8. A rabbit's heart beats about 200 times per minute. It lives for about 5 years. About how many times does its heart beat in an hour?

Dividing Decimals
Making the Connection

LEARN ABOUT IT

You can use play money to show that the steps you use to divide decimals make sense.

EXPLORE **Use Play Money**

- Work with a partner.
- One partner uses play money to show a number greater than $0.50 but less than $25.
- The other partner chooses a number of groups—2, 3, 4, 5, or 6. Together the partners divide the money into the chosen number of groups and then record the number in each group.
- Repeat this activity several times.

TALK ABOUT IT

1. When you divided the play money into groups, did you start with the largest value of money or the smallest? Could you do it either way?

2. When did you have to trade dollars or dimes? Explain how you did it.

3. Did any of your activities end with money left over? Could this happen when you share real money among some friends?

You have divided play money into groups and recorded the amount in each group. You can use symbols to record the steps you followed. The steps are the same as when you divide with whole numbers. Here is how you divide $9.42 into 3 groups.

What You Do	**What You Record**

Show $9.42 as 9 ones, 4 dimes, 2 pennies.
Show 3 groups.

$$3\overline{)\$9.42}$$

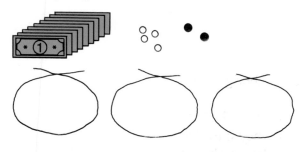

How many ones can be placed in each group?

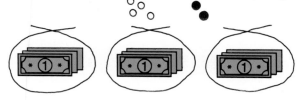

How many dimes can be placed in each group?

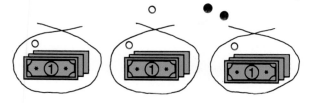

Regroup 1 dime as 10 pennies.
How many pennies can be placed in each group?

$$
\begin{array}{r}
3. \\
3\overline{)\$9.42} \\
9 \\
\hline
0
\end{array}
$$
← 3 ones in each group
← 9 ones shared in all

$$
\begin{array}{r}
3.1 \\
3\overline{)\$9.42} \\
9 \\
\hline
04 \\
3 \\
\hline
1
\end{array}
$$
← 1 dime in each group
← 3 dimes shared in all
← 1 dime left over

$$
\begin{array}{r}
\$3.14 \\
3\overline{)\$9.42} \\
9 \\
\hline
04 \\
3 \\
\hline
12 \\
12 \\
\hline
0
\end{array}
$$
← 4 pennies in each group
← 12 pennies shared in all
← 0 pennies left over

TRY IT OUT

Divide. Use play money.

1. $10.24 ÷ 4   **2.** $9.56 ÷ 2   **3.** $12.50 ÷ 5   **4.** $0.65 ÷ 5

Dividing Decimals

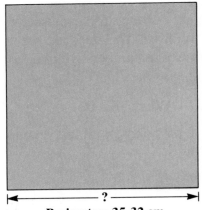

Perimeter: 35.32 cm

EXPLORE **Analyze the Process**

What is the length of each side of the square shown at the right?

Because each side of a square has the same length, we divide.

Divide the whole number part.	Place the decimal point. Divide the tenths.	Divide the hundredths.
$$\begin{array}{r} 8 \\ 4)\overline{3\ 5.3\ 2} \\ \underline{3\ 2} \\ 3 \end{array}$$	$$\begin{array}{r} 8.8 \\ 4)\overline{3\ 5.3\ 2} \\ \underline{3\ 2} \\ 3\ 3 \\ \underline{3\ 2} \\ 1 \end{array}$$	$$\begin{array}{r} 8.8\ 3 \\ 4)\overline{3\ 5.3\ 2} \\ \underline{3\ 2} \\ 3\ 3 \\ \underline{3\ 2} \\ 1\ 2 \\ \underline{1\ 2} \\ 0 \end{array}$$

TALK ABOUT IT

1. Where does the 3 below the 2 come from in the first step?
2. How does the position of the decimal point in the dividend compare to its position in the quotient?

Other Examples

A
$$\begin{array}{r} 2\ 6.5 \\ 7)\overline{1\ 8\ 5.5} \\ \underline{1\ 4} \\ 4\ 5 \\ \underline{4\ 2} \\ 3\ 5 \\ \underline{3\ 5} \\ 0 \end{array}$$

B
$$\begin{array}{r} 0.5\ 3\ 7 \\ 2)\overline{1.0\ 7\ 4} \\ \underline{1\ 0} \\ 0\ 7 \\ \underline{6} \\ 1\ 4 \\ \underline{1\ 4} \\ 0 \end{array}$$

C
$$\begin{array}{r} 0.1\ 6\ 4 \\ 6)\overline{0.9\ 8\ 4} \\ \underline{6} \\ 3\ 8 \\ \underline{3\ 6} \\ 2\ 4 \\ \underline{2\ 4} \\ 0 \end{array}$$

D
$$\begin{array}{r} 0.0\ 0\ 7 \\ 4)\overline{0.0\ 2\ 8} \\ \underline{2\ 8} \\ 0 \end{array}$$

Divide.

1. $3)\overline{8.52}$ 2. $5)\overline{0.875}$ 3. $2)\overline{1.672}$ 4. $5)\overline{3.205}$

Divide and check.

1. $2\overline{)3.16}$ **2.** $3\overline{)1.095}$ **3.** $4\overline{)18.48}$ **4.** $5\overline{)41.5}$ **5.** $6\overline{)14.94}$

6. $4\overline{)7.28}$ **7.** $3\overline{)73.08}$ **8.** $7\overline{)16.8}$ **9.** $5\overline{)23.25}$ **10.** $4\overline{)2.348}$

11. $8\overline{)0.984}$ **12.** $9\overline{)34.56}$ **13.** $7\overline{)3.822}$ **14.** $5\overline{)31.45}$ **15.** $4\overline{)0.852}$

16. Find 0.7654 divided by 2.   **17.** Find the quotient of 16.048 and 4.

Use **mental math** to find each quotient.

18. $32.08 \div 8$ **19.** $448 \div 4$ **20.** $9.54 \div 9$ **21.** $2.50 \div 5$

APPLY

MATH REASONING

22. Copy and complete the following statement.

To check a division problem, multiply the __?__ by the __?__ . Add the __?__ .

23. Why is the remainder in this problem not a whole number?

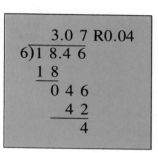

PROBLEM SOLVING

24. Tara put a wire fence around her square garden. When she finished, she had 8.5 m of wire fence left. She started with a total of 40.5 m of fence. How long was each side of the garden?

25. The perimeter of the square below is shown. What is the length of each side?

P: 5.44 cm

MIXED REVIEW

Use mental math and the distributive property to find the products.

26. 7×14 **27.** 3×45 **28.** 2×54 **29.** 6×24 **30.** 3×43

Give the missing measure for each rectangle.

31. length: 3.5 cm
width: 3 cm
area: ▥

32. length: 4 cm
width: ▥
area: 8 cm²

33. length: ▥
width: 8 m
area: 128 m²

More Practice, page 509, set A

Problem Solving
Determining Reasonable Answers

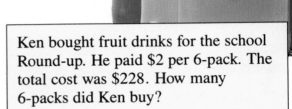

UNDERSTAND
ANALYZE DATA
PLAN
ESTIMATE
SOLVE
EXAMINE

LEARN ABOUT IT

A very important part of evaluating your thinking and your work when you solve problems is checking your work. The chart below shows some ways you can do this.

Check Your Work
■ Is the arithmetic correct?
■ Did you use strategies correctly?
■ Is your answer reasonable?

Ken bought fruit drinks for the school Round-up. He paid $2 per 6-pack. The total cost was $228. How many 6-packs did Ken buy?

Miriam used her calculator and got this answer:

$$38$$

Is the answer reasonable?

> I can use multiplication to check division. I can round to estimate the product.

> My check shows a total cost much less than the total given in the problem.

38 x 2 is about
40 x 2, or $80.

The answer is
not reasonable.

TRY IT OUT

Do not solve the problems. Decide whether the answer shown on the calculator is reasonable. If it is not reasonable, tell why not.

1. It takes 0.24 kilowatt hours (kwh) of energy to make a biodegradable milk carton. How much energy is needed to make 150 cartons?

   Tina's answer

2. The energy needed to make 6 aluminum cans is 7.68 kwh. How much energy is needed to make 1 can? Joel's answer

Solve. Use any problem solving strategy.

1. It takes 5.04 kwh to make 6 paper cups. How many kilowatt hours does it take to make 1 paper cup?

2. One kilowatt hour is equal to 860 food calories. How many food calories would it take to equal 2.5 kwh?

Use data from the table below for problems 3, 4, and 5.

Type of container	Energy needed to make container
milk carton	0.24 kwh
steel can	0.58 kwh
returnable glass bottle	1.42 kwh
nonreturnable glass bottle	0.85 kwh

3. What is the difference in the number of kilowatt hours it takes to make a returnable glass bottle and a nonreturnable glass bottle?

4. The tomato juice Melanie drinks for her lunch 3 times a week comes in a steel can. How many kilowatt hours does it take to make the cans in a 6-pack of tomato juice?

5. What is the total number of kilowatt hours needed to make 100 steel cans and 100 returnable glass bottles?

6. Jon bought a 6-pack of apple juice for $1.88. About how much did he pay for each can of juice?

7. Julio said, "If you divide the number of returnable glass bottles of juice I bought for the party by 3 and add 13 to the quotient, you get 25." How many bottles did Julio buy?

8. Janet paid $89.00 for 100 cartons of milk for the day camp. What was the cost per carton?

9. **Understanding the Operations** Name the operation you would use. Show with objects or drawings why that operation makes sense for the problem.

   Teresa had 39 recyclable paper cups to use at the party. That was 3 times the number of guests who were going to attend. How many guests were going to attend the party?

Applied Problem Solving
Group Decision Making

UNDERSTAND
ANALYZE DATA
PLAN
ESTIMATE
SOLVE
EXAMINE

Group Skill:
Disagree in an Agreeable Way

Your school is having a pancake breakfast to raise money for a field trip. You will be offering a short stack of 2 pancakes and a tall stack of 3 pancakes. How much will you charge for each?

Facts to Consider

- To the right are the prices of items you will need.

Item	Cost/Information
Pancake mix	$1.79
	8 cups of mix per box.
Milk	$0.42 per quart
Syrup	$2.89 per bottle
	1 bottle serves about 20 people.
Butter	$1.29 for 4 sticks
	1 stick contains 8 tablespoons.
Orange juice	$0.95 for 1 quart
	1 quart makes 8 servings.
Paper plates	$1.49 for 100
Plastic forks	$0.45 for 24 forks
Paper cups	$1.15 for 50 cups
Napkins	$0.92 for 100 napkins

204

- The recipe for pancakes calls for the following ingredients:

	Pancake mix	Milk
For 16 pancakes:	2 cups	2 cups

- Juice will be included with each pancake breakfast.
- You will give 1 tablespoon of butter per pancake.

1. How many pancakes can you make from a box of mix? What is the cost per pancake?
2. How much would the butter for a short stack cost?
3. When a customer orders a short stack, how much does it cost you altogether to serve it to him or her?
4. How much profit do you want to make on each breakfast you serve? Is your price reasonable?

What Is Your Decision?

Make a poster advertising the pancake breakfast. Include all prices. On a separate paper, show how you decided on your prices.

205

WRAP UP

Sharing Equally

Tell the place of the first digit in these quotients:
thousands, hundreds, tens, or **ones.**

1. $7\overline{)578}$ **2.** $6\overline{)49}$ **3.** $4\overline{)2,108}$ **4.** $8\overline{)9,305}$

Without dividing, tell whether the given quotient is
reasonable or **not reasonable.**

5. $9\overline{)365}$ 8 R4   **6.** $7\overline{)79}$ 10 R9   **7.** $5\overline{)467}$ 93 R2   **8.** $4\overline{)315}$ 177 R7

Sometimes, Always, Never

Complete each statement by writing **sometimes,
always,** or **never.** Explain your choices.

9. To find the average of six numbers you can __?__
find their sum and divide by 2.

10. Compatible numbers can __?__ be used to find an
exact quotient.

11. If $a - b = c$, then we can __?__ say that
$b + c = a$.

12. You __?__ can find a product mentally by
"breaking apart" the dividend.

13. The number of zeros in the dividend __?__ equals
the number of zeros in the quotient.

14. If the dividend has 3 digits and the divisor has 1
digit, the quotient will __?__ have 2 digits.

Project

Find four books of different sizes. Find the length of
each book. What is the average length of the group
of books? What would happen if one book were 6 in.
longer? What would happen if you added a fifth
book that was 5 inches shorter than the average?

Power Practice/Test

Part 1   Understanding

1. How would you use mental math to find 368 ÷ 4?

2. Which gives an estimate of 4,729 ÷ 7 by using compatible numbers?

   A. 4,600 ÷ 7   B. 4,700 ÷ 7

   C. 4,800 ÷ 7   D. 4,900 ÷ 7

Part 2   Skills

In which place do you start dividing? Write **hundreds** or **tens.**

3. 5)342   4. 8)165   5. 4)630   6. 7)921

Divide and check.

7. 6)705   8. 3)127   9. 4)883   10. 5)8,024

11. 7)2,156   12. 4)21.72   13. 6)0.450   14. 8)5.672

Give the average of each set of numbers.

15. 27, 31, 22, 28   16. 168, 142, 182   17. 14, 17, 25, 19, 30

Part 3   Applications

18. Elena went shopping. She spent half of her money on groceries. Then she spent $9.63 at the bakery. She had $3.21 left. How much did she start with?

19. When Carlos was 7, his mother was four times as old as he was. Carlos is now 16. Is it reasonable to think that his mother is now 64 years old?

20. Elliot has 200 photographs. The photo album he wants can hold 4 photos on each page. If each album has 12 pages, how many albums does Elliot need for all of his photographs?

21. **Challenge.** A company claims that the average annual salary of its employees is $50,000. There are 10 employees. 9 of them earn $20,000 a year each. What is the salary of the other employee?

ENRICHMENT
Short Division

Since he started his baseball card collection 6 years ago, Richard has collected 3,068 cards. His younger sister, Rita, is helping him put the cards in plastic sheets that have 8 pockets in each sheet. How many sheets will Richard need? He used **short division** to solve the problem.

A. $\overset{3}{8)\overline{3,068}}$ → B. $\overset{3}{8)\overline{3,0\,^{6}68}}$ → C. $\overset{3\ 8}{8)\overline{3,0\,^{6}6\,^{2}8}}$ → $\overset{3\ 8\ 3\ R4}{8)\overline{3,0\,^{6}6\,^{2}8}}$

Answer the questions about Richard's work.

1. What is the meaning of the small 6 between the 0 and the 6 in step A.

2. What is the meaning of the small 2 between the 6 and the 8 in step B?

3. What numbers did Richard divide in step C?

Use short division to divide.

4. $8)\overline{675}$ 5. $4)\overline{258}$ 6. $6)\overline{2,439}$ 7. $5)\overline{4,762}$

8. $9)\overline{2,881}$ 9. $7)\overline{5,235}$ 10. $3)\overline{1,962}$ 11. $4)\overline{3,473}$

12. $3)\overline{2,956}$ 13. $8)\overline{6,739}$ 14. $6)\overline{1,848}$ 15. $3)\overline{4,760}$

CUMULATIVE REVIEW

1. To estimate
   $41.3 + 39.21 + 40.15 + 41.47$
   using clustering,

   A. round to tenths, then add.

   B. add only the whole numbers.

   C. add whole numbers, round
   decimals.

   D. multiply 4×40.

2. Which expression is shown
   by the model?

   A. 0.7×0.1

   B. 0.4×0.8

   C. 0.7×0.4

   D. 0.6×0.3

   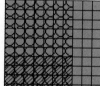

3. Find the area of a rectangular
   room 14.8 m by 12.6 m.

   A. 54.8 m^2

   B. 186.48 m^2

   C. 745.92 m^2

   D. 27.4 m^2

Multiply.

4. 8.6×0.12

   A. 0.258

   B. 2.472

   C. 1.022

   D. 1.032

5. 14.28×100

   A. 0.1428

   B. 1.428

   C. 142.8

   D. 1,428

6. A flower shop sells 4 different
   kinds of plants in 3 types of pots.
   How many different combinations
   are there?

   A. 7   B. 12   C. 4   D. 3

7. A double bar graph

   A. shows trends in data.

   B. is used to make predictions.

   C. compares two sets of data.

   D. uses pictures to show data.

8. Which interval would you use on
   the scale of a line graph to show
   the number of campers?

Year	Campers
1987	185
1988	193
1989	208
1990	214

   A. 5

   B. 50

   C. 100

   D. 1991

Choose the missing numbers.

9. 2,647 m = ▓ km

   A. 2.647 km

   B. 26.47 km

   C. 264.7 km

   D. 0.2647 km

10. 543 s = ▓ min ▓ s

    A. 22 min 15 s

    B. 12 min 3 s

    C. 9 min 3 s

    D. 90 min 3 s

11. 4 d 15 h = ▓ h

    A. 111   B. 255   C. 63   D. 100

12. To estimate the height of a door
    using the unitizing method,

    A. compare it to a known
    measurement.

    B. estimate larger parts.

    C. estimate smaller equal parts.

    D. mark off 100 cm, then
    estimate.

8

MORE DIVISION: WHOLE NUMBERS AND DECIMALS

THEME: THE HUMAN BODY

MATH AND SCIENCE

DATA BANK

Use the Science Data Bank on page 471 to answer the questions.

1 How many more red blood cells than white blood cells are in a drop of blood? How many more red blood cells than platelets are in a drop of blood?

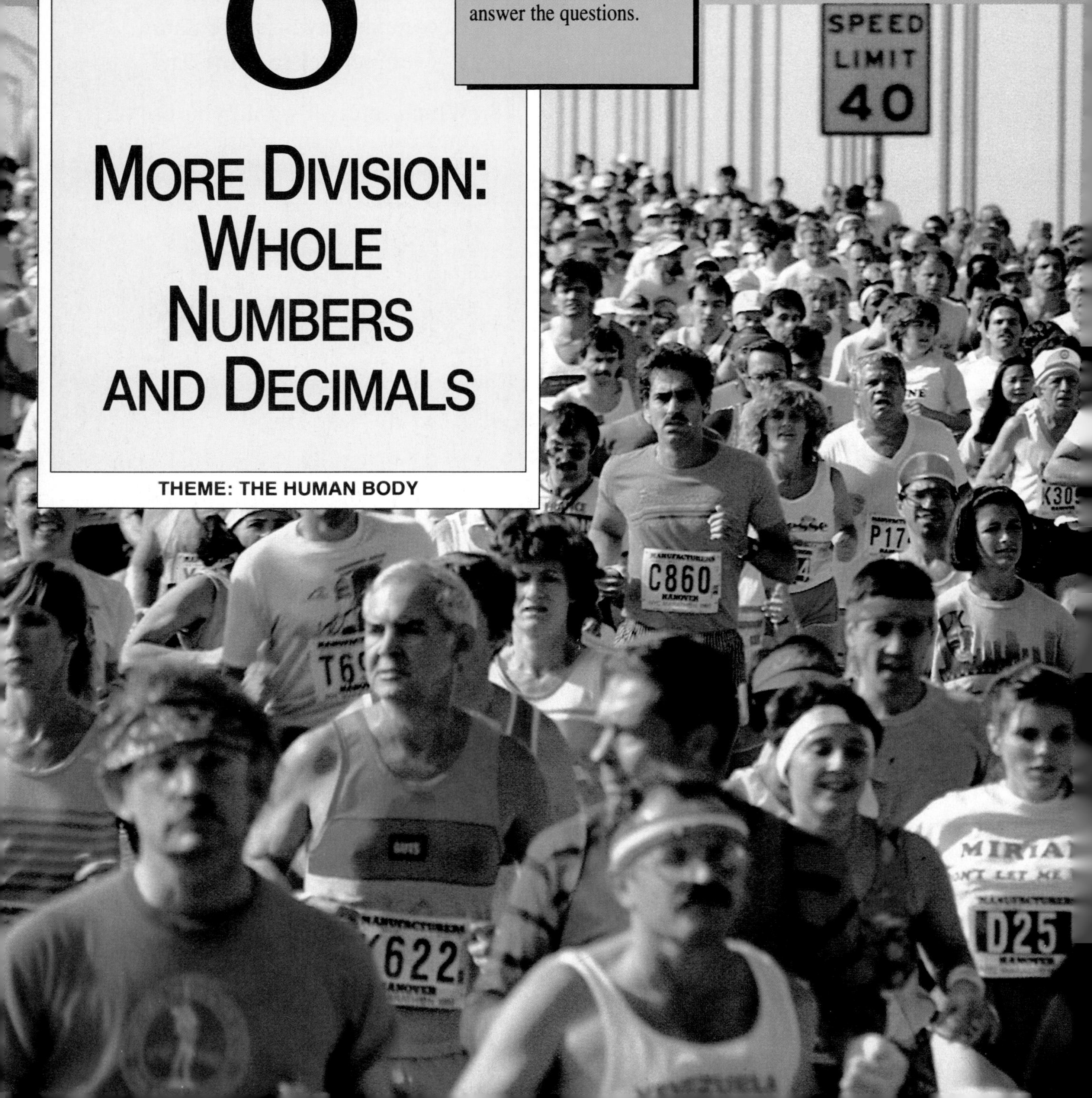
SPEED
LIMIT
40
C860
622
D25

2 About how many liters of blood does the heart of an average person pump per hour when the person is at rest?

3 About how many milliliters of air does the average person breathe in per minute? How many liters of air is this?

4 **Using Critical Thinking** Compare the amount of air a person at rest breathes in with the amount after hard exercise. What can you say about hard exercise and your body's need for oxygen?

Women and men of all ages turn out to share the pleasure of running in long-distance races.

Mental Math
Special Quotients

Bags of Trash Collected During Cleanup Week

Mon.

Tues.

Wed.

Thurs.

Fri.   ?

= 50 bags

You can use basic facts and properties to find quotients like $350 \div 50$.

EXPLORE Solve to Understand

Suppose you are making this pictograph to show the number of bags of trash your class collected. On Friday, your class collected 350 bags. How many bags should be shown on the graph for Friday?

TALK ABOUT IT

1. What data do you need to graph the number of bags for Friday?
2. How can you use guess and check to find a number you can multiply mentally by 50 to get 350?

When both the dividend and the divisor are divided by the same number, the resulting numbers will have the same quotient.

To find	$350 \div 50$
Think	$35 \div 5 = 7$
So	$350 \div 50 = 7$

Divide both the dividend and the divisor by 10.

Check: $7 \times 50 = 350$, so the quotient 7 is correct.

Other Examples

A $2,800 \div 40$.
$2,800 \div 40$
$2,800 \div 40 = 70$

Think about dividing each number by 10.

B $4,900 \div 70$.
$4,900 \div 70$
$4,900 \div 70 = 70$

Think about dividing each number by 10.

Use mental math to find each quotient. Check by multiplying.

1. $540 \div 60$ **2.** $2,000 \div 20$ **3.** $3,500 \div 70$ **4.** $6,300 \div 90$ **5.** $2,500 \div 50$

212

Divide and check.

1. $42 \div 6$
$420 \div 60$

2. $64 \div 8$
$640 \div 80$

3. $35 \div 7$
$350 \div 70$

4. $56 \div 8$
$560 \div 80$

5. $72 \div 9$
$720 \div 90$

6. $45 \div 5$
$450 \div 50$

7. $36 \div 4$
$360 \div 40$

8. $49 \div 7$
$490 \div 70$

9. $30 \div 6$
$300 \div 60$

10. $81 \div 9$
$810 \div 90$

Divide and check.

11. $80 \div 10$

12. $60 \div 30$

13. $40 \div 20$

14. $90 \div 10$

15. $100 \div 50$

16. $210 \div 70$

17. $160 \div 80$

18. $150 \div 30$

19. $180 \div 20$

20. $240 \div 40$

21. $30\overline{)1,200}$

22. $50\overline{)1,500}$

23. $60\overline{)2,400}$

24. $70\overline{)5,600}$

25. $80\overline{)400}$

26. $10\overline{)200}$

27. $90\overline{)2,700}$

28. $10\overline{)1,000}$

29. $70\overline{)6,300}$

30. $80\overline{)4,800}$

APPLY

MATH REASONING

Write two multiplication equations and two division equations for each family of numbers.

31. 40; 2,400; 60

32. 30; 2,100; 70

33. 70; 3,500; 50

34. 90; 4,500; 50

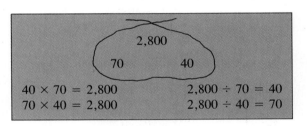

$40 \times 70 = 2,800$
$70 \times 40 = 2,800$

$2,800 \div 70 = 40$
$2,800 \div 40 = 70$

PROBLEM SOLVING

35. Recycling carts hold 240 aluminum cans. One carton holds 40 cans. How many cartons can be placed on a cart?

36. Use the pictograph on page 212. How many fewer cans were collected on Monday than on Tuesday?

▶ **USING CRITICAL THINKING   Give a Counterexample**

37. Bill noticed that the factors of 8 are 1, 2, 4, and 8 and the factors of 10 are 1, 2, 5, and 10. He concluded, "All numbers have an even number of factors." Can you find and give the factors of a number that would show that Bill's statement is not correct?

More Practice, page 509, set B

Estimating Quotient Digits

LEARN ABOUT IT

Front-end estimation and compatible number estimation can help you estimate quotient digits.

EXPLORE Study the Data

A clothing store manager has decided to spend $375 per week on television advertising. Here are the ad costs.

Time of Day	Cost of a 30-Second Television Ad
Morning	$ 40
Midday	$ 70
Late afternoon	$ 90
Evening news	$300
Evening	$200

TALK ABOUT IT

1. What operation can you use to find how many morning ads the store manager can buy for $375?

2. How can you use guess and check to estimate the number of midday ads the manager can buy for $375?

The example below shows one way to estimate the number of midday ads that could be bought for $375.

- **To estimate the quotient digit,** $70\overline{)375}^{\,?}$

  look at front-end digits and divide. $\underline{7}0\overline{)\underline{37}5}^{\,5}$

  > The compatible numbers 7 and 35 help you estimate the quotient.

- **Check the estimate by multiplying.** $5 \times 70 = 350$

You can buy about 5 midday ads for $375.

TRY IT OUT

Copy these exercises and underline the front-end digits you would use to estimate the quotient digit.

1. $40\overline{)258}$ 2. $60\overline{)438}$ 3. $80\overline{)743}$ 4. $50\overline{)421}$

5. Rewrite exercises 1−4 to show how you would substitute compatible numbers to find the estimated quotient digit.

Estimate the number of these ads you could buy with $375.

6. morning   7. late afternoon   8. evenings news   9. evening

214

Copy these exercises. Underline the front-end digits you
would use to estimate the quotient digit.

1. $50\overline{)328}$ 2. $30\overline{)249}$ 3. $60\overline{)308}$ 4. $40\overline{)252}$ 5. $70\overline{)363}$

6. $90\overline{)281}$ 7. $20\overline{)88}$ 8. $40\overline{)230}$ 9. $30\overline{)281}$ 10. $80\overline{)273}$

Estimate the quotient. Multiply to check.

11. $20\overline{)152}$ 12. $40\overline{)291}$ 13. $70\overline{)432}$ 14. $30\overline{)195}$ 15. $60\overline{)248}$

16. $80\overline{)340}$ 17. $50\overline{)464}$ 18. $90\overline{)385}$ 19. $40\overline{)218}$ 20. $70\overline{)578}$

21. $30\overline{)286}$ 22. $60\overline{)382}$ 23. $20\overline{)170}$ 24. $80\overline{)660}$ 25. $90\overline{)288}$

MATH REASONING

Tell which estimate is closest to the exact answer.

26. $40\overline{)2,783}$ 7, 70, or 700

27. $60\overline{)495}$ 8, 80, or 800

28. $30\overline{)9,105}$ 3, 30, or 300

29. $70\overline{)2,216}$ 3, 30, or 300

PROBLEM SOLVING

Use the data on page 214 as needed.

30. Suppose you have $1,250. About how
many 30-second ads can you buy
during the evening news?

31. Suppose you have $1,850. About how
many 30-second ads can you buy
during the evening?

▶ **ALGEBRA**

Choose the correct meaning (A or B) of each algebraic expression.

32. $X - 5$ **A.** 5 more than a number **B.** a number less 5

33. $H \div 4$ **A.** 4 divided by a number **B.** a number divided by 4

34. $12M$ **A.** 12 times a number **B.** 21 more than a number

35. $Y - 23$ **A.** 23 less than a number **B.** 23 take away a number

More Practice, page 509, set C

Dividing
1-Digit Quotients

EXPLORE **Analyze the Process**

Alcott Middle School has 238 students. How many homerooms are needed if no homeroom can have more than 28 students?

Since the maximum number of students for each room is the same, we divide.

To solve this problem, divide 238 by 28. Here is how to do it.

Decide where to start.	Estimate the first quotient digit.	Divide the ones.
28)238	28)238	$\begin{array}{r} 8\ \text{R}14 \\ 28\overline{)238} \\ 224 \\ \hline 14 \end{array}$ ■ Divide. ■ Multiply. ■ Subtract. ■ Compare.
$28 > 2$ $28 > 23$ $28 < 238$ Divide the ones.	Think 30)240	Check: $\begin{array}{r} 28 \\ \times\ 8 \\ \hline 224 \\ +\ 14 \\ \hline 238 \end{array}$

TALK ABOUT IT

1. Why is the first digit in the quotient in the ones place?
2. What two numbers are multiplied to give 224?
3. Why is $240 \div 30$ a better estimate of the first digit in the quotient than $210 \div 30$?

Other Examples

A (30) $\begin{array}{r} 6\ \text{R}9 \\ 31\overline{)195} \\ 186 \\ \hline 9 \end{array}$

B (80) $\begin{array}{r} 4\ \text{R}9 \\ 78\overline{)321} \\ 312 \\ \hline 9 \end{array}$

C (40) $\begin{array}{r} 8 \\ 44\overline{)352} \\ 352 \\ \hline 0 \end{array}$

Divide and check.

1. 41)85
2. 22)156
3. 57)191
4. 42)175
5. 63)189

Divide and check.

1. 37)89   **2.** 22)66   **3.** 43)90   **4.** 51)162   **5.** 32)160

6. 12)49   **7.** 26)78   **8.** 45)207   **9.** 63)174   **10.** 82)328

11. 57)248   **12.** 73)511   **13.** 88)225   **14.** 94)190   **15.** 31)254

16. $212 \div 41$ **17.** $354 \div 68$ **18.** $600 \div 74$ **19.** $382 \div 39$ **20.** $809 \div 81$

21. Find the quotient of 262 divided by 91.   **22.** 482 divided by 59 is what number?

APPLY

MATH REASONING

23. Jered solved $341 \div 42$ and checked his work. It checked. Did Jered solve the problem correctly? If not, what did he do wrong?

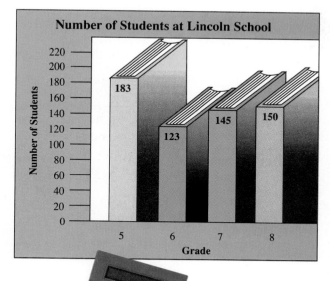

PROBLEM SOLVING

24. About how many students are in grades 5 through 8 at Lincoln School?

25. How many 5th grade homerooms are needed if each homeroom is to have no more than 24 students?

26. Data Hunt   How many students are in your grade at your school? How many homerooms are needed if each homeroom is to have no more than 23 students?

Number of Students at Lincoln School

▶ **CALCULATOR**

27. Solve the problem $192 \div 24$ on your calculator by using any number keys but only the $[-]$ operations key.

28. Solve the problem 5×28 on your calculator by using any number keys but only the $[+]$ operations key.

More Practice, page 509, Set D

Changing Estimates

LEARN ABOUT IT

EXPLORE Analyze the Process

At rest, an adult takes about 14 breaths per minute. If you take 28 breaths a minute while jogging slowly, how many minutes have you run by the time you have taken 168 breaths?

Decide where to start.	Estimate the first quotient digit.	Estimate again if necessary.
$28)\overline{168}$ Think $30)\overline{150}$	$\begin{array}{r} 5 \\ 28)\overline{168} \\ \underline{140} \\ 28 \end{array}$ 5 is not correct. This difference must be less than 28.	$\begin{array}{r} 6 \\ 28)\overline{168} \\ \underline{168} \end{array}$

TALK ABOUT IT

1. Why is the first quotient digit in the ones place?

2. How can you tell that the estimate of 5 is not correct?

3. Give an answer to the Explore problem in a complete sentence.

Other Examples

A
$$\begin{array}{r} 3 \\ 28)\overline{117} \\ \underline{84} \\ 33 \end{array} \rightarrow \begin{array}{r} 4 \\ 28)\overline{117} \\ \underline{112} \\ 5 \end{array}$$

Try $30)\overline{100}$.   3 is too low.

B
$$\begin{array}{r} 7 \\ 51)\overline{344} \\ \underline{357} \end{array} \rightarrow \begin{array}{r} 6 \\ 51)\overline{344} \\ \underline{306} \\ 38 \end{array}$$

Try $50)\overline{350}$.   7 is too high.

TRY IT OUT

Decide which estimates must be changed. Give the correct estimates for the ones that need to be changed.

$\begin{array}{r} 4 \\ 18)\overline{89} \end{array}$
    2. $\begin{array}{r} 6 \\ 83)\overline{490} \end{array}$
    3. $\begin{array}{r} 5 \\ 25)\overline{161} \end{array}$
    4. $\begin{array}{r} 2 \\ 94)\overline{201} \end{array}$
    5. $\begin{array}{r} 6 \\ 54)\overline{318} \end{array}$

Divide and check.

1. $31\overline{)96}$ **2.** $20\overline{)180}$ **3.** $18\overline{)161}$ **4.** $30\overline{)255}$ **5.** $14\overline{)104}$

6. $53\overline{)315}$ **7.** $60\overline{)500}$ **8.** $29\overline{)105}$ **9.** $32\overline{)275}$ **10.** $43\overline{)354}$

11. $22\overline{)156}$ **12.** $43\overline{)330}$ **13.** $70\overline{)452}$ **14.** $51\overline{)427}$ **15.** $25\overline{)169}$

16. $298 \div 75$ **17.** $628 \div 80$ **18.** $835 \div 91$ **19.** $529 \div 67$ **20.** $594 \div 82$

21. Find the quotient when 874 is divided by 38.

APPLY

MATH REASONING

Use **estimation** to decide whether the exact quotient is less than ($<$) or greater than ($>$) the given number.

22. $476 \div 66$ < 7 OR > 7?   **23.** $592 \div 71$ < 8 OR > 8?

24. $361 \div 81$ < 5 OR > 5?   **25.** $228 \div 39$ < 6 OR > 6?

PROBLEM SOLVING

26. Homeroom 7 collected money for a science field trip from a walkathon. They made the same amount the next week with a pledge run. After paying $25 for expenses, they had $225. How much did they make from the walkathon?

27. Homeroom 12 sold $425 worth of adult tickets and $183 worth of children's tickets for the science fair. Each of the 32 members sold tickets worth the same amount. What was the value of the tickets sold by each student?

28. **Science Data Bank** If you take 35 breaths a minute after hard exercise, about how much air would you be taking in with each breath? See page 471.

► CALCULATOR

Use a calculator to find the missing numbers.

29. $n \div 21 = 4$ R2   **30.** $n \div 40 = 6$ R22

31. $n \div 37 = 5$ R10   **32.** $358 \div n = 7$ R8

More Practice, page 510, set A

Finding Larger Quotients

Area 11,070 ft²	Area 11,316 ft²	Area 10,947 ft²
Lot 16	Lot 17	Lot 18
◄— 90 ft —►	◄— 92 ft —►	◄— 89 ft —►

EXPLORE   Analyze the Process

The lots on the north side of Elm Street are rectangular. Mr. and Mrs. Sanchez bought lot 17. How long is their lot?

To solve this problem, divide 11,316 by 92. Here is how to do it.

Decide where to start.	Divide the hundreds.	Divide the tens.	Divide the ones.
$92\overline{)11{,}316}$ 92 > 11 Not enough thousands. 92 < 113 Divide the hundreds.	⑨⓪ 1 $92\overline{)11{,}316}$ 92 21 ■ Divide. ■ Multiply. ■ Subtract. ■ Compare.	⑨⓪ 12 $92\overline{)11{,}316}$ 9 2↓ 211 184 27 ■ Bring down. ■ Divide. ■ Multiply. ■ Subtract. ■ Compare.	123 $92\overline{)11{,}316}$ 92 211 184↓ 276 276 0 ■ Bring down. ■ Divide. ■ Multiply. ■ Subtract. ■ Compare.

TALK ABOUT IT

1. What do the words "Not enough thousands" mean?
2. Give the answer to the Explore problem in a complete sentence.

Other Examples

A
```
      58 R3
41)2,381
   205
    331
    328
      3
```

B
```
       435 R10
53)23,065
   212
    186
    159
    275
    265
     10
```

Divide and check.

1. $31\overline{)458}$ 2. $52\overline{)3{,}796}$ 3. $23\overline{)14{,}763}$ 4. $62\overline{)1{,}954}$

220

Divide and check. Remember to estimate the quotient first.

1. $68\overline{)775}$ 2. $44\overline{)977}$ 3. $21\overline{)319}$ 4. $24\overline{)534}$

5. $45\overline{)560}$ 6. $36\overline{)1,476}$ 7. $50\overline{)2,872}$ 8. $18\overline{)1,574}$

9. $35\overline{)1,166}$ 10. $53\overline{)1,863}$ 11. $82\overline{)1,776}$ 12. $45\overline{)2,000}$

13. $3,422 \div 27$ 14. $5,891 \div 76$ 15. $2,335 \div 37$ 16. $8,626 \div 54$

17. $5,579 \div 54$ 18. $5,300 \div 63$ 19. $3,237 \div 67$ 20. $6,549 \div 85$

APPLY

MATH REASONING

Copy the problems and show what digit should be placed in each ▦ .

21.
```
              2 ▦
  ▦ ▦ ) 1 , 9 5 0
        ▦   ▦ ▦
        ─────────
          4 5 0
        ▦ ▦ ▦
        ─────────
              0
```

22.
```
            1 8 ▦  R ▦
  4 ▦ ) ▦ , 6 ▦ 3
        4 ▦
        ──────
        ▦ 4 ▦
        ▦ 3 6
        ──────
            ▦ 3
            8 4
            ────
              9
```

PROBLEM SOLVING

23. How many rectangles with sides that are a whole number of units in length have an area of 1,155 square units?

24. What is the width of a rectangle with an area equal to 7,260 in.² and a length of 165 in.?

MIXED REVIEW

Give the number of units for each ▦ .

25. $2,354 \text{ mL} = ▦ \text{ L}$ 26. $3.2\text{L} = ▦ \text{ mL}$ 27. $54\text{L} = ▦ \text{ mL}$ 28. $698 \text{ ml} = ▦ \text{ L}$

Find the quotient.

29. $975 \div 8$ 30. $592 \div 9$ 31. $321 \div 3$ 32. $719 \div 2$ 33. $227 \div 6$

Problem Solving
Choosing a Calculation Method

UNDERSTAND	
ANALYZE DATA	
PLAN	
ESTIMATE	
SOLVE	
EXAMINE	

LEARN ABOUT IT

Look carefully at the numbers in a problem. The size of the numbers and the kinds of numbers help you to choose a calculation method.

Calculation Methods

- Paper and Pencil
- Calculator
- Mental Math

Sharon scored 1,050 in 10 games. What was her average score?

Since the divisor is 10, I can use mental math to solve this.

TRY IT OUT

Choose an appropriate calculation method and tell why. Then solve.

1. $475 \div 25$
2. $235 \div 7$
3. $560 \div 7$
4. $1,137 \div 6$
5. $2,700 \div 90$
6. $128 \div 4$
7. $546 \div 9$
8. $1,720 \div 42$
9. $490 \div 70$
10. $1,248 \div 6$
11. $640 \div 8$
12. $436 \div 4$

13. Sharon and her dad are in a parent-child bowling league. Sharon scored 85, 117, and 104 in 3 games. What was her average score?

14. A night of bowling (5 games) costs $7.50 for Sharon's father and only $2.75 for Sharon. They usually spend another $5 on refreshments. What does it cost them for a night of bowling?

15. A regular game of bowling costs $1.75 at a certain bowling alley. About how many games could you bowl if you had $10?

16. Suppose you bowled 5 games that cost $2.15 per game. You rented shoes for $0.75. What did it cost you to bowl?

17. The manager told Sharon he used 5,100 bowling pins in 5 years. There are 15 lanes in this bowling alley. What was the average number of pins used per lane?

More Practice, page 510, set C

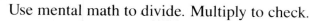

POWER PRACTICE/QUIZ

Use mental math to divide. Multiply to check.

1. 80 ÷ 40 **2.** 360 ÷ 60 **3.** 600 ÷ 20 **4.** 2,400 ÷ 30 **5.** 630 ÷ 70

6. 240 ÷ 60 **7.** 3,500 ÷ 70 **8.** 4,800 ÷ 60 **9.** 900 ÷ 30 **10.** 2,700 ÷ 90

11. $90\overline{)540}$ **12.** $60\overline{)4,200}$ **13.** $80\overline{)800}$ **14.** $90\overline{)3,600}$ **15.** $80\overline{)1,600}$

Estimate each quotient. Multiply to check whether the estimate is reasonable.

16. $30\overline{)256}$ **17.** $5\overline{)263}$ **18.** $80\overline{)177}$ **19.** $70\overline{)496}$ **20.** $9\overline{)463}$

21. $40\overline{)372}$ **22.** $7\overline{)445}$ **23.** $20\overline{)164}$ **24.** $50\overline{)264}$ **25.** $60\overline{)497}$

26. $40\overline{)290}$ **27.** $90\overline{)756}$ **28.** $60\overline{)561}$ **29.** $30\overline{)159}$ **30.** $70\overline{)588}$

Divide and check.

31. $54\overline{)267}$ **32.** $78\overline{)310}$ **33.** $44\overline{)386}$ **34.** $32\overline{)4,000}$ **35.** $80\overline{)700}$

36. $72\overline{)3,520}$ **37.** $26\overline{)9,224}$ **38.** $67\overline{)563}$ **39.** $15\overline{)8,935}$ **40.** $44\overline{)9,855}$

PROBLEM SOLVING

41. During a two-week vacation, Andrew's family drove a total of 2,700 km. About how many kilometers per day was that?

42. A hamster's heart beats about 450 times in 1 minute. About how many times is that per second?

43. Boston's average rainfall about 110 cm per year. About how many centimeters is that per month?

44. A queen termite can lay about 350 eggs in 1 hour. About how many eggs is that per minute?

45. Maya jogged 83 km in 9 days. Estimate the average number of kilometers she jogged each day.

Dividing
Special Cases

LEARN ABOUT IT

EXPLORE   Analyze the Process

The heart of an adult elephant may be as heavy as 15,912 g. This is about 52 times as heavy as the heart of a human. About how heavy is the heart of a human?

To solve the problem, we find 15,912 ÷ 52.

Decide where to start.	Divide the hundreds.	Divide the tens.	Divide the ones.
$52\overline{)15{,}912}$	$52\overline{)15{,}912}$ with quotient 3 15 6 3	$52\overline{)15{,}912}$ with quotient 30 15 6↓ 31 0 31	$52\overline{)15{,}912}$ with quotient 306 15 6 31 0↓ 312 312 0

Decide where to start:
$52\overline{)15{,}912}$
52 > 15 Not enough thousands.
52 < 159 Divide the hundreds.

Divide the hundreds:
$$\begin{array}{r} 3 \\ 52\overline{)15{,}912} \\ \underline{15\,6} \\ 3 \end{array}$$
■ Divide.
■ Multiply.
■ Subtract.
■ Compare.

Divide the tens:
$$\begin{array}{r} 30 \\ 52\overline{)15{,}912} \\ \underline{15\,6}\downarrow \\ 31 \\ \underline{0} \\ 31 \end{array}$$
Remember! Every time you bring down, you must divide.

Divide the ones:
$$\begin{array}{r} 306 \\ 52\overline{)15{,}912} \\ \underline{15\,6} \\ 31 \\ \underline{0}\downarrow \\ 312 \\ \underline{312} \\ 0 \end{array}$$

TALK ABOUT IT

1. Why is a 0 written below the 31 in the third step?
2. How could you estimate that the answer is about 300?

Other Examples

A
$$\begin{array}{r} 4\,0\,0\text{ R5} \\ 56\overline{)2\,2{,}4\,0\,5} \\ \underline{2\,2\,4} \\ 0\,0 \\ \underline{0} \\ 0\,5 \\ \underline{0} \\ 5 \end{array}$$

B
$$\begin{array}{r} \$2.4\,6 \\ 3\,2\overline{)\$7\,8.7\,2} \\ \underline{6\,4} \\ 1\,4\,7 \\ \underline{1\,2\,8} \\ 1\,9\,2 \\ \underline{1\,9\,2} \\ 0 \end{array}$$

Divide as with whole numbers. Show dollars and cents, so the answers make sense.

TRY IT OUT

Divide and check.

1. $42\overline{)8{,}736}$
2. $60\overline{)12{,}250}$
3. $78\overline{)47{,}270}$
4. $38\overline{)\$153.14}$

Divide and check.

1. $18\overline{)546}$ 2. $23\overline{)478}$ 3. $32\overline{)1,283}$ 4. $48\overline{)5,113}$

5. $52\overline{)6,780}$ 6. $60\overline{)\$125.40}$ 7. $22\overline{)13,308}$ 8. $56\overline{)16,820}$

9. $31\overline{)2,114}$ 10. $72\overline{)30,275}$ 11. $91\overline{)6,211}$ 12. $44\overline{)\$159.28}$

13. $47,651 \div 68$ 14. $33,708 \div 54$ 15. $65,271 \div 81$ 16. $\$592.90 \div 77$

Estimate each quotient.

17. $82\overline{)3,296}$ 18. $33\overline{)13,472}$ 19. $85\overline{)5,952}$ 20. $47\overline{)19,500}$ 21. $60\overline{)36,360}$

APPLY

MATH REASONING

22. Copy and complete the problem to give the quotient shown. Use each of the numbers in the box exactly one time.

$$\overset{7\ 0\ 5}{4\ \text{▓}\ \overline{)3\ \text{▓}\ ,\ \text{▓}\ \text{▓}\ \text{▓}}} \qquad \boxed{0\ 2\ 3\ 4\ 6}$$

PROBLEM SOLVING

23. During its lifetime a red blood cell makes 75,000 trips between lungs and body cells at a rate of 625 trips per day. How many days is the lifetime of a red blood cell?

24. **Science Data Bank** How many times more platelets than white blood cells are there in a drop of blood? See page 471.

▶ **MENTAL MATH**

Use one or more of the mental math techniques you have learned to complete the exercises below.

Mental Math Techniques
■ Counting On/Back
■ Breaking Apart Numbers
■ Choosing Compatible Numbers
■ Using Compensation

25. $198 + 327$ 26. $216 \div 4$ 27. $278 - 99$

28. $19 + 58 + 81$ 29. 23×5 30. $324 \div 3$

31. $541 - 302$ 32. 6×54 33. $4 \times 9 \times 25$

More Practice, page 510, set D

Problem Solving
Look for a Pattern

UNDERSTAND
ANALYZE DATA
PLAN
ESTIMATE
SOLVE
EXAMINE

LEARN ABOUT IT

You may find a pattern in the data to help you solve some problems. Making a table may help you discover the pattern. This problem-solving strategy is called **Look for a Pattern.**

> Tom's soccer coach believes drills are very important. She divided the players into groups of 7. Each player in the group has to do the dribbling drill with every other player in the group. How many drills does each group do in all?

> I'll start with a simpler problem.

1 —— 2   2 players → 1 drill.

3 players → 3 drills.

4 players → 6 drills.

Players	Drills
2	1
3	3
4	6

> I can continue a table and look for a pattern. I see! Each time the difference increases by 1.

Players	Drills
2	1
3	3
4	6
5	10
6	15
7	21

In Tom's group, they did 21 drills in all.

TRY IT OUT

When Hari and her father practice soccer, she wants to score 1 goal the first day, 3 goals the second day, 5 goals the third day, and so on. After the sixth day, how many goals would she have scored in all?

Day	Goals	Total Goals
1	1	1
2	3	4
3	5	9
4	7	—
5	—	—
6	—	—

- How many goals did Hari want to score the second day?

- What was the total number of goals Hari should have scored after 2 days?

- Copy the table. Look for patterns to complete the table and solve the problem.

226

Look for a pattern to help you solve each problem.

1. At the end-of-season soccer tournament, all teams play each other once. There are 8 teams. How many games are played in all?

2. At their soccer games, the Booters scored 2 goals their first game, 4 their second, and 6 their third. If they continue to score at this rate, how many goals will they have scored in all after 5 games?

MIXED PRACTICE

Choose a strategy from the strategies list or use other strategies you know to solve these problems.

3. Nina's mother is one of 49 soccer referees. There are 98 parents serving as coaches. There are 15 times as many players as coaches. How many players are there?

4. The banner for the Kicking Kings soccer team shows soccer balls in a pyramid shape. There is 1 ball in the top row, 2 in the second row, 4 in the third row, and 7 in the fourth row. There were 7 rows. How many balls does the banner show?

5. The banner for the Fleet Feet team cost $2.48 for edging and $11.98 for felt. The coach's gift cost $45.50. How much were all the expenses?

6. The printing shop had the following digits available for the Fleet Feet's jerseys: 1, 3, 5, and 7. How many different 2-digit numbers can Kimo choose from for his soccer jersey?

7. The Fleet Feet scored 103 points during the 1989 season. They scored 121 points during the 1990 season. How many more points did they score in 1990?

Some Strategies	
Act Out	Make a Table
Use Objects	Solve a Simpler Problem
Choose an Operation	Make an Organized List
Draw a Picture	Work Backward
Guess and Check	Look for a Pattern

8. Use the graph to find about how many players signed up for soccer in the 10 and 11 year old age groups altogether.

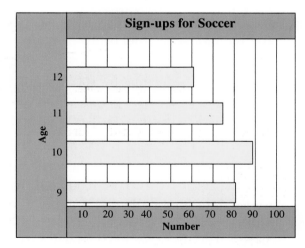

9. Last year 274 children signed up to play soccer. There had to be 15 players on each team. How many full teams could be formed?

10. The Tri-County League had 10 teams. There were 20 players on each team. How many players were there in the league?

More Practice, page 525, set A

227

Mental Math
Dividing Decimals by 10, 100, and 1,000

LEARN ABOUT IT

EXPLORE Discover a Pattern

Work in groups and use a calculator to try the following.

- Choose several decimals such as 534.6 and divide them first by 10, then by 100, and then by 1,000.

- Make a table and record the results. The table should show each decimal you choose and the quotients that result when the decimal is divided by 10, 100, and 1,000.

TALK ABOUT IT

Look for patterns in your table. How would you complete the following statements?

1. To divide a decimal by 10 mentally, "move" the decimal point __?__ places to the __?__ .

2. To divide a decimal by 100 mentally, "move" the decimal point __?__ places to the __?__ .

3. To divide a decimal by 1,000 mentally, "move" the decimal point __?__ places to the __?__ .

The pattern explored above shows that the number of zeros in a divisor of 10, 100, or 1,000 tells us how many places we need to "move" the decimal point in the dividend in order to show the correct quotient. For example, to solve $34.5 \div 100$ we move the decimal point two places to the left of where it is in 34.5. So, $34.5 \div 100 = 0.345$.

TRY IT OUT

Use mental math to find the missing number in each equation.

1. $34.69 \div 10 = n$ 2. $57.83 \div 100 = b$ 3. $687.2 \div 1,000 = y$ 4. $879 \div 100 = x$

5. $56.4 \div 100 = a$ 6. $298 \div 10 = c$ 7. $0.76 \div 10 = z$ 8. $436.6 \div 100 = w$

228

Use mental math to find the missing number in each equation.

1. $276.8 \div 10 = a$ **2.** $109.5 \div 100 = b$

3. $0.47 \div 10 = n$ **4.** $764.5 \div 1,000 = x$

5. $1,050 \div 100 = c$ **6.** $62.75 \div 1,000 = n$

7. $5.68 \div 10 = y$ **8.** $43.89 \div 100 = z$

9. $95.7 \div 10 = l$ **10.** $553.4 \div 1,000 = r$

11. $22.2 \div 100 = s$ **12.** $0.05 \div 10 = d$

13. $3,176 \div 1,000 = f$ **14.** $990.9 \div 100 = t$

15. $41.4 \div 10 = v$ **16.** $0.37 \div 100 = p$

APPLY

MATH REASONING

Tell whether the divisor in each is 10, 100, or 1,000.

17. $456.6 \div n = 45.66$ **18.** $1,234.2 \div n = 1.2342$ **19.** $24.5 \div n = 0.0245$

20. $265.6 \div n = 2.656$ **21.** $0.01 \div n = 0.0001$ **22.** $51.7 \div n = 0.0517$

PROBLEM SOLVING

23. How many dimes (10¢) could you get if you had 450 pennies?

24. How many dollar bills (100¢) could you get if you had 34,200 pennies?

25. A package of 10 computer disks cost $47.50. Each disk costs the same amount. What is the cost of each disk?

26. A census taker can put 100 names on a page. How many pages will be needed for 27,500 names?

MIXED REVIEW

Give the number for each ▓ .

27. $850 \text{ g} = $ ▓ $ \text{ kg}$ **28.** $3,240 \text{ g} = $ ▓ $ \text{ kg}$

29. $2.3 \text{ kg} = $ ▓ $ \text{ g}$ **30.** $0.5 \text{ kg} = $ ▓ $ \text{ g}$

Divide.

31. $24.9 \div 6$ **32.** $312.9 \div 3$ **33.** $50.44 \div 4$ **34.** $67.27 \div 7$ **35.** $329.4 \div 9$

More Practice, page 510, set E

Problem Solving
Estimating the Answer

| UNDERSTAND |
| ANALYZE DATA |
| PLAN |
| ESTIMATE |
| SOLVE |
| EXAMINE |

Before solving a problem, it is
important to decide what would be
a reasonable answer. You can do
this by estimating the answer.

> Stephie and her father took a bike trip
> from New York to Washington, D.C.
> They rode 32 miles (mi) each day.
> How many days did it take?

	Atlanta	Chicago	Dallas	Miami	New York	San Francisco	Washington
Atlanta	—	722	800	688	896	2,515	**672**
Chicago	722	—	933	1,410	831	2,205	753
Dallas	800	933	—	1,348	1,576	1,761	1,352
Miami	688	1,410	1,348	—	1,352	3,147	1,128
New York	896	831	1,576	1,352	—	2,996	**224**
San Fran.	2,515	2,205	1,761	3,147	2,996	—	2,922
Wash., D.C.	672	753	1,352	1,128	**224**	2,922	—

Before solving the problem, estimate the answer.

I'll start by rounding 32 miles.

$$32 \rightarrow 30$$

I'll substitute a compatible number for the
distance from New York to Washington, D.C.

$$224 \rightarrow 210$$

I'll use these numbers to estimate how
many days the trip took.

$$210 \div 30 = 7$$

Now I'll solve the problem.

$$224 \div 32 = 7$$

7 is a reasonable answer because it is the same as my estimate.

Before solving each problem, estimate the answer. Then solve
the problem and decide whether your answer is reasonable.

1. Jack's mother bicycled from Atlanta to
   Washington, D.C. Her average speed
   was 12 miles per hour (mph). How
   many hours did the trip take?

2. Maria's mother took 44.1 hours to
   drive from one city to another. Her
   average speed was 50 mph. What two
   cities did she travel between?

3. What is the distance from Miami to
   Dallas and back to Miami?

4. Jeannie wants to jog from Dallas to
   Atlanta to raise money for her favorite
   charity. She plans to jog about 21 mi
   each day. How many full days should
   she plan to be jogging?

Solve. Use any problem solving strategy.

1. How much farther is it from Dallas to New York than from Miami to New York?

2. Carlos took a trip in the family camper that was 654 miles farther than 3 times the distance from New York to Chicago. What two cities did they travel between?

3. Tony, who had a kidney transplant when he was very young, walked from Chicago to Washington, D.C., to raise money for kidney research. He walked at a speed of 3 mph. How many hours did it take him?

4. Julie's family took a trip from Dallas to Atlanta. The gasoline cost $0.92 per gallon. They drove 16 hours. On the average, how many miles did they travel per hour?

5. On a bike trip from Cincinnati to Cleveland, Yang rode at a speed of 10.5 mph. He rode for 24.5 hours. How far is it from Cincinnati to Cleveland?

6. Tom made a map showing the distances between 9 different cities. He connected every city to every other city. How many lines did he draw?

7. How far did Ms. Fraser travel when she drove from New York to Chicago to San Francisco to Dallas and back to New York?

8. Mr. Golden drove from San Francisco to Miami at an average speed just above 50 mph. About how many hours of driving time was that?

9. Five students had a bicycle race. Dan finished ahead of Carmen, but Carmen was not last. Betty finished far ahead of Carmen, and Ed finished just behind Betty. If Ralph finished last, who finished next to last?

10. **Understanding the Operations**
Tell what operation you would use. Explain why. Then solve the problem.

Jane traveled to 42 cities. This is 3 times the number of cities she had seen before the trip. How many cities had Jane seen before the trip?

Data Collection and Analysis
Group Decision Making

UNDERSTAND
ANALYZE DATA
PLAN
ESTIMATE
SOLVE
EXAMINE

Doing a Questionnaire
Group Skill:
Encourage and Respect Others

All of the members of your group are on a committee to choose older students to give help to others in an after-school program. Prepare a questionnaire for the older students to answer.

Collecting Data

1. Have a brainstorming discussion about the kind of person a good student helper should be. Make a list of at least ten qualities a good helper should have.
2. Use your list to make a questionnaire that asks students to rate their personal qualities. Some examples are given below.

Questionnaire

How would you rate yourself on the following personal qualities?

	very low	low	average	high	very high
1. Patience	1	2	3	4	5
2. Helpfulness	1	2	3	4	5
3. Self-confidence	1	2	3	4	5

3. Give your questionnaire to at least 3 or 4 students. Make changes if they find that it is unclear in any way.
4. Distribute the revised questionnaire to at least 10 students.

Organizing Data

5. One way your group can decide which students would make the best tutors is to find out who rated themselves highest on the questionnaire. You can do this by adding the ratings given by each student to get a total rating for each one. Make a list of the students in order from the one with the highest rating to the one with the lowest rating.

Presenting Your Analysis

6. Write a paragraph explaining why you think this is or is not a fair way to evaluate students for the job of helping others.

7. Be ready to tell what else your group could do to find out which students would be good student helpers.

233

WRAP UP

Division Time

1. Write these steps for dividing 8,976 by 5 in order.

   A. Bring down tens.

   B. Divide thousands, multiply, subtract, compare.

   C. Divide ones, multiply, subtract, compare.

   D. Write the remainder.

   E. Bring down hundreds.

   F. Divide tens, multiply, subtract, compare.

   G. Bring down ones.

   H. Divide hundreds, multiply, subtract, compare.

Sometimes, Always, Never

Complete each statement by writing **sometimes, always,** or **never.** Explain your choices.

2. The quotient is __?__ larger than the divisor.

3. When both the dividend and the divisor are divided by the same number, the quotient of the new numbers is __?__ the same as the quotient of the original numbers.

4. When dividing, you __?__ work from right to left.

5. The quotient is __?__ smaller than the dividend.

6. To divide a decimal by 100, you should __?__ move the decimal point two places to the left.

Project

Use the digits 1, 2, 4, 5, and 6 to make a 5-digit number. Divide it by 9 and record the remainder. Do this at least 5 times. What do you notice? Can you explain why it happens?

Try to find 5 other digits that give the same results.

POWER PRACTICE/TEST

Part 1   Understanding

What compatible numbers could you use to estimate each quotient?

1. $70\overline{)586}$ **2.** $47\overline{)246}$ **3.** $32\overline{)251}$

Which method would you choose: paper and pencil, calculator, or mental math? Explain.

4. $2,465 \div 57$ **5.** $1,632 \div 8$ **6.** $759 \div 8$

Part 2   Skills

Use mental math to find each quotient.

7. $4,200 \div 70$ **8.** $3,600 \div 40$ **9.** $527.04 \div 10$ **10.** $0.073 \div 10$

Is the first estimate correct? Give the correct estimate for exercises that need a second estimate.

11. $36\overline{)168}^{\,4}$ **12.** $89\overline{)530}^{\,6}$ **13.** $35\overline{)321}^{\,8}$

Divide.

14. $47\overline{)294}$ **15.** $62\overline{)506}$ **16.** $28\overline{)701}$

17. $71\overline{)15,416}$ **18.** $94\overline{)19,275}$ **19.** $39\overline{)\$327.60}$

Part 3   Applications

20. A mail carrier drove 4,820 km in 83 working days. Is it reasonable to estimate that the carrier drove 600 km per day? If not, find a reasonable estimate.

21. Challenge. This large triangle is made up of small triangles. How many small triangles are in the large triangle? How is the number of small triangles related to the number of rows?

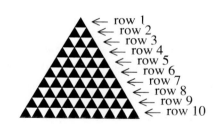

← row 1
← row 2
← row 3
← row 4
← row 5
← row 6
← row 7
← row 8
← row 9
← row 10

ENRICHMENT
Divisibility

We say 624 is **divisible** by 2 because the remainder is 0 when 624 is divided by 2. Look for patterns to discover some **divisibility tests.**

- *Divisibility test for 2.* Here are some numbers that are divisible by 2: 24; 316; 1,508; 570; and 92.

1. Find 5 other numbers that are divisible by 2.

2. Copy and complete the following:
   "A number is divisible by 2 if its last digit is ___?___."

- *Divisibility test for 5.* Here are some numbers that are divisible by 5: 30; 635; 75; 320; and 5,125.

3. Find 5 other numbers that are divisible by 5.

4. Copy and complete the following:
   "A number is divisible by 5 if its last digit is ___?___."

- *Divisibility test for 3.* Here are some numbers that are divisible by 3: 84; 72; 126; 513; 1,302; and 3,351.

5. Find 5 other numbers that are divisible by 3.

6. Copy and complete the following:
   "A number is divisible by 3 if the sum of its digits is ___?___."

Discover a Rule!

Find some examples to help you discover the number that should be written in place of the variable to make a divisibility rule.

7. A number is divisible by x if twice the tens digit plus its ones digit is divisible by x.

8. A number is divisible by y if it is divisible by 2 and 3.

CUMULATIVE REVIEW

Solve using mental math.

1. 400 × 80 × 20

   A. 32,000   B. 640,000

   C. 160,000   D. 1,280,000

2. 23 × 8

   A. 40   B. 180

   C. 160   D. 184

3. 5,400 ÷ 9

   A. 600   B. 60

   C. 6   D. 6,000

4. 8.46 × 100

   A. 846   B. 0.846

   C. 84.6   D. 8,460

Give the missing numbers.

5. 82.4 m = ▓ cm

   A. 8.24   B. 824

   C. 0.824   D. 8,240

6. 397 mm = ▓ cm

   A. 3.97   B. 397

   C. 39.7   D. 3,970

7. 4,521 mL = ▓ L

   A. 45.21   B. 452.1

   C. 4.521   D. 4,521

8. 0.47 kg = ▓ g

   A. 4.7   B. 470

   C. 47   D. 4,700

9. What would be the best choice for estimating the quotient of 2,286 ÷ 3?

   A. 2,000 ÷ 3   B. 1,800 ÷ 3

   C. 3,000 ÷ 3   D. 2,100 ÷ 3

10. In which place do you start dividing to find the quotient of 824.6 ÷ 7?

   A. hundreds   B. ones

   C. tens   D. tenths

Divide.

11. 4)2,129

   A. 53 R9   B. 53

   C. 532 R1   D. 532 R3

12. 8)3,685

   A. 46 R5   B. 410 R5

   C. 461   D. 460 R5

13. Jennifer scored 87, 82, 92, 84, and 90 on her last five math tests. What was her average score for these tests?

   A. 85   B. 87

   C. 86   D. 88

14. There are 464 campers staying at Camp Whynot this summer. There are 8 campers and 2 counselors in each cabin. How many cabins are occupied?

   A. 46   B. 57

   C. 50   D. 58

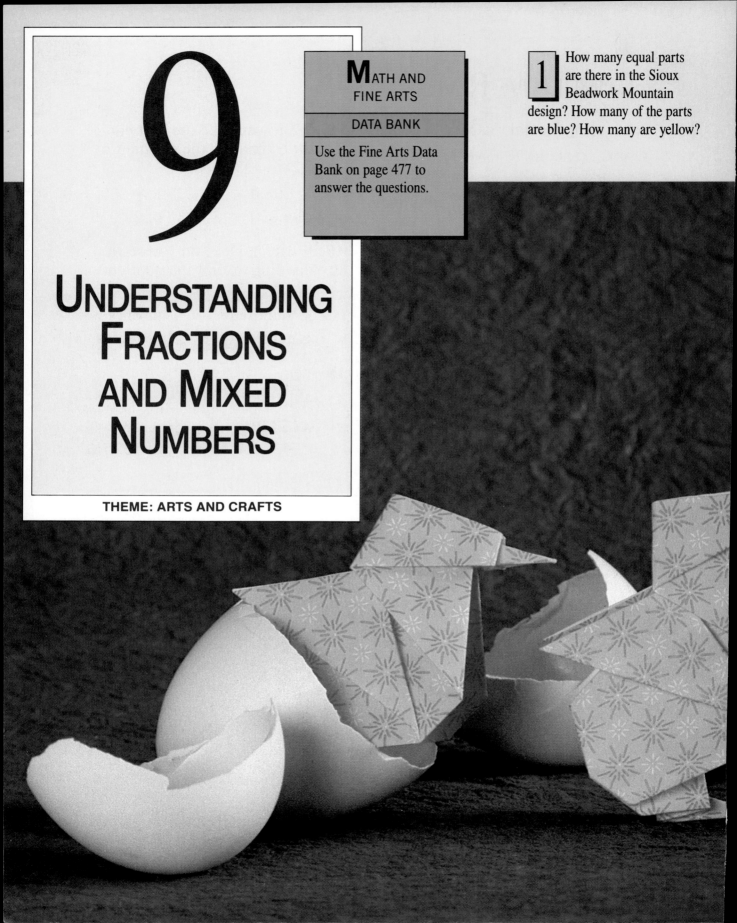

9

UNDERSTANDING FRACTIONS AND MIXED NUMBERS

THEME: ARTS AND CRAFTS

MATH AND FINE ARTS

DATA BANK

Use the Fine Arts Data Bank on page 477 to answer the questions.

1 How many equal parts are there in the Sioux Beadwork Mountain design? How many of the parts are blue? How many are yellow?

2 Which of the Origami Basic Forms show folds into equal parts? How many equal parts are there in Basic Form 4?

3 In the Sioux Beadwork Dragonfly design the number of yellow parts is how many times greater than the number of black parts?

4 **Using Critical Thinking** Suppose the color pattern in the Sioux Horse Track design is continued so that there are a total of 3 tracks. How many of all the equal parts will be blue? Explain.

These lively looking chicks are examples of the paper-folding art known as *origami*.

239

Reviewing the Meaning of Fractions

LEARN ABOUT IT

You can use fractions to tell about parts of a region or parts of a set.

Bright mosaics decorate the outer walls of Mexico's University Library, near Mexico City.

EXPLORE Consider the Examples

Mosaic is an art form that uses small pieces of colored stone, glass, or other material to make pictures. You can use fractions to describe the mosaic region and the sets of mosaic pieces shown at the right.

TALK ABOUT IT

1. In box A, is each part of the region the same size? How many parts are blue? red?
2. In box B, are the mosaic pieces all the same size? How many are green? How many are tan? How many are there in all?
3. How many sets are shown by the string and color?

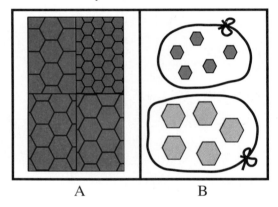

A   B

Remember how we read and write fractions. 3 of the 4 equal parts of the region are red.

We say: "three fourths"   We write: $\dfrac{3}{4}$ numerator
denominator

$\dfrac{3}{4}$ of the region is red. $\dfrac{1}{4}$ is blue.

TRY IT OUT

1. What fraction of all the pieces in box B above are green?

2. Write the fraction that is colored.

A.

B.

C.

D.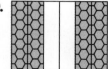

240

Give the fraction of the region that is colored.

1.  **2.** ⊗ **3.**  **4.**

Give the fraction of each set that is colored.

5. ●○● **6.** ▢▢▢▢▢ ▢▢▢▢▢ **7.** △▽▲▽ ▲ ▲ **8.** ◆◆◆◆ ◆◆◇◆

Write the fractions.

9. two thirds **10.** three fourths **11.** one half **12.** two fifths

Write the word name for each fraction.

13. $\frac{7}{10}$ **14.** $\frac{9}{12}$ **15.** $\frac{6}{8}$ **16.** $\frac{1}{6}$ **17.** $\frac{3}{7}$

MATH REASONING

Show each fraction as part of a region and as part of a set.

18. $\frac{3}{5}$ **19.** $\frac{2}{6}$ **20.** $\frac{3}{8}$ **21.** $\frac{7}{10}$ **22.** $\frac{5}{12}$

PROBLEM SOLVING

23. A bag of 250 mosaic pieces cost $2.25. There were 100 green pieces in the bag. What fraction of the pieces were green?

24. Elena spent $1\frac{1}{2}$ h putting 75 mosaic pieces in place. Then she spent 30 min drawing another design. What fraction of the total time did she spend drawing?

▶ **ESTIMATION**

Estimate the fraction of each figure that is shaded.

25.   **26.**   **27.** 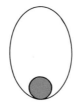 **28.**  **29.**

Equivalent Fractions

EXPLORE Use Fraction Pieces

- Work in groups. Use fraction pieces to find different ways to cover $\frac{1}{2}$ exactly.

- Use fraction pieces to find different ways to cover $\frac{3}{4}$ exactly.

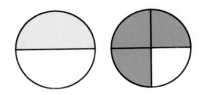

TALK ABOUT IT

1. What fractions did you find that show the same amount as $\frac{1}{2}$?

2. What fractions did you find that show the same amount as $\frac{3}{4}$?

Fractions that name the same amount of a region or set are called **equivalent fractions.**

We use an equal sign to show that two fractions are equivalent. The pictures below show that $\frac{2}{3} = \frac{6}{9}$.

     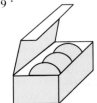 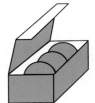 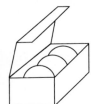

2 out of 3 boxes are colored.   **6 out of 9 bulbs are colored.**

Use fraction pieces to show each of the following.

1. $\frac{1}{4} = \frac{2}{8}$ **2.** $\frac{3}{5} = \frac{6}{10}$ **3.** $\frac{5}{6} = \frac{10}{12}$ **4.** $\frac{2}{4} = \frac{1}{2}$

Use fraction pieces to help you find the missing numerator or denominator.

5. $\frac{1}{2} = \frac{\text{\rule{0.5cm}{0.15mm}}}{6}$ **6.** $\frac{1}{2} = \frac{4}{\text{\rule{0.5cm}{0.15mm}}}$ **7.** $\frac{2}{3} = \frac{\text{\rule{0.5cm}{0.15mm}}}{6}$ **8.** $\frac{3}{4} = \frac{6}{\text{\rule{0.5cm}{0.15mm}}}$

Write two fractions that name the shaded part of each region or set.

1.

2.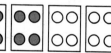

3.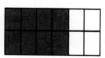

4.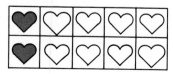

5.

6.

Use fraction pieces to show each of the following.

7. $\frac{1}{5} = \frac{2}{10}$ **8.** $\frac{1}{3} = \frac{2}{6}$ **9.** $\frac{3}{4} = \frac{6}{8}$ **10.** $\frac{5}{6} = \frac{10}{12}$

Use counters of two colors to show each of the following.

11. $\frac{1}{2} = \frac{3}{6}$ **12.** $\frac{3}{4} = \frac{6}{8}$ **13.** $\frac{2}{3} = \frac{4}{6}$ **14.** $\frac{2}{5} = \frac{4}{10}$

MATH REASONING

Use fraction pieces to find the missing number.

15. $\frac{2}{4} = \frac{4}{\text{||||}}$ **16.** $\frac{1}{\text{||||}} = \frac{2}{12}$ **17.** $\frac{1}{\text{||||}} = \frac{4}{12}$ **18.** $\frac{2}{5} = \frac{4}{\text{||||}}$

PROBLEM SOLVING

19. Out of 16 sections in a basketball arena, 4 sections are for reserved seats. Todd said $\frac{4}{16}$ of the seats are reserved. Gail said only $\frac{1}{4}$ are reserved. Who is correct?

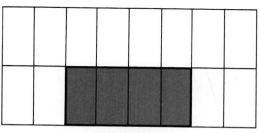

RESERVED

MIXED REVIEW

Divide. Check by using multiplication.

20. $1,864 \div 8$ **21.** $3,246 \div 6$ **22.** $2,395 \div 5$ **23.** $2,427 \div 3$

24. $1,624 \div 4$ **25.** $4,501 \div 7$ **26.** $7,515 \div 9$ **27.** $3,070 \div 5$

Finding Equivalent Fractions

LEARN ABOUT IT

EXPLORE Solve to Understand

Keith bought paper for making origami figures. He bought 2 packages of orange paper and 3 packages of yellow paper. What fraction of the papers were orange?

TALK ABOUT IT

1. How many packages of each color did Keith buy?

2. How many papers are in each package?

3. How many papers did Keith buy altogether?

orange 3 sheets	yellow 3 sheets
6 sheets in all	**9 sheets in all**

2 of the 5 packages were orange. $\frac{2}{5}$ of the packages were orange.

6 of the 15 papers were orange. $\frac{6}{15}$ of the papers were orange.

You can find a fraction that is equivalent to another fraction by multiplying or dividing the numerator and denominator by the same nonzero number.

$$\frac{2}{5} = \frac{6}{15}$$

Think: $\frac{2}{5} \overset{\times 3}{=} \frac{6}{15}$ (× 3)

$$\frac{9}{12} = \frac{3}{4}$$

Think: $\frac{9}{12} \overset{\div 3}{=} \frac{3}{4}$ (÷ 3)

TRY IT OUT

Find equivalent fractions by multiplying the numerator and denominator by 2.

1. $\frac{1}{2} = \frac{}{}$ 2. $\frac{1}{6} = \frac{}{}$ 3. $\frac{2}{3} = \frac{}{}$ 4. $\frac{1}{8} = \frac{}{}$ 5. $\frac{3}{5} = \frac{}{}$

Find the equivalent fractions by multiplying the numerator and denominator by 3.

6. $\frac{5}{8} = \frac{}{}$ 7. $\frac{1}{5} = \frac{}{}$ 8. $\frac{5}{6} = \frac{}{}$ 9. $\frac{3}{4} = \frac{}{}$ 10. $\frac{3}{8} = \frac{}{}$

244

Find equivalent fractions by multiplying the numerator and denominator by 4.

1. $\frac{1}{4} = \frac{|||||}{|||||}$ **2.** $\frac{3}{4} = \frac{|||||}{|||||}$ **3.** $\frac{2}{5} = \frac{|||||}{|||||}$ **4.** $\frac{1}{10} = \frac{|||||}{|||||}$ **5.** $\frac{5}{12} = \frac{|||||}{|||||}$

Tell what number the numerator and denominator were multiplied or divided by to get the equivalent fraction.

6. $\frac{5}{6} = \frac{15}{18}$ **7.** $\frac{3}{7} = \frac{9}{21}$ **8.** $\frac{12}{30} = \frac{2}{5}$ **9.** $\frac{4}{5} = \frac{12}{15}$ **10.** $\frac{16}{36} = \frac{4}{9}$

Give the next three equivalent fractions. What pattern did you use to find them?

11. $\frac{1}{2} = \frac{|||||}{|||||}, \frac{|||||}{|||||}, \frac{|||||}{|||||}$ **12.** $\frac{1}{3} = \frac{|||||}{|||||}, \frac{|||||}{|||||}, \frac{|||||}{|||||}$ **13.** $\frac{1}{6} = \frac{|||||}{|||||}, \frac{|||||}{|||||}, \frac{|||||}{|||||}$ **14.** $\frac{2}{3} = \frac{|||||}{|||||}, \frac{|||||}{|||||}, \frac{|||||}{|||||}$

MATH REASONING

Look for a pattern. Use a calculator to find the next three fractions.

15. $\frac{36}{97}, \frac{72}{194}, \frac{144}{388}, \frac{|||||}{|||||}, \frac{|||||}{|||||}, \frac{|||||}{|||||}$ **16.** $\frac{17}{23}, \frac{51}{69}, \frac{153}{207}, \frac{|||||}{|||||}, \frac{|||||}{|||||}, \frac{|||||}{|||||}$

PROBLEM SOLVING

17. Stan Wilson made 12 baskets out of 20 shots in last night's basketball game. What fraction of his shots did he make? Give two fractions equivalent to this, one of which has a denominator of 100.

18. Fine Arts Data Bank What fraction of the origami figures show a single fold into two halves? Give an equivalent fraction. See page 477.

▶ USING CRITICAL THINKING   Discover a Relationship

You can find the **cross products** by multiplying the red numbers and by multiplying the black numbers. Look for a relationship between the red numbers and the black numbers in the equivalent fractions. Complete the following sentence.

19. "If two fractions are equivalent, then the __?__ __?__ are __?__ ."

Equivalent fractions

$\frac{5}{8} = \frac{10}{16}$ $\frac{3}{4} = \frac{6}{8}$

Not equivalent fractions

$\frac{2}{3} \neq \frac{6}{8}$ $\frac{1}{6} \neq \frac{6}{32}$

Greatest Common Factor

EXPLORE **Analyze the Process**

There are 18 fifth graders and 24 sixth graders on the playground. The leader wants to divide the students from each grade into teams. She wants all the teams to be the same size and have as many players as possible. How can she do it?

TALK ABOUT IT

1. What are some sizes the teams might be? Explain.
2. Have you found the greatest possible number of players for each team? Try to prove it.

A number is a **factor** of another number if it divides into the number with remainder zero. In the problem above, the answer, 6, is the **greatest common factor (GCF)** of 18 and 24 because it is the largest number that is a factor of both numbers. Here is how to find the GCF of 24 and 36.

List the factors of each number.	List the common factors (the factors in both lists).	Find which common factor is the greatest.
24: 1, 2, 3, 4, 6, 8, 12, 24 36: 1, 2, 3, 4, 6, 9, 12, 18, 36	1, 2, 3, 4, 6, 12	12

You can also use a **Venn diagram** to think about the greatest common factor.

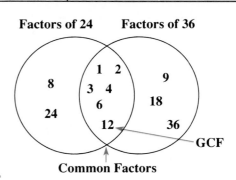

Factors of 24   Factors of 36

GCF

Common Factors

List the factors of each number. Then give the GCF.

1. $\frac{28}{42}$ 2. $\frac{18}{27}$ 3. $\frac{9}{12}$ 4. $\frac{14}{25}$

List the factors of each number. Then give the greatest common factor.

1. $\frac{9}{12}$ **2.** $\frac{8}{20}$ **3.** $\frac{9}{15}$ **4.** $\frac{7}{13}$ **5.** $\frac{10}{14}$ **6.** $\frac{9}{27}$

7. $\frac{40}{50}$ **8.** $\frac{20}{25}$ **9.** $\frac{16}{24}$ **10.** $\frac{15}{18}$ **11.** $\frac{15}{25}$ **12.** $\frac{8}{14}$

13. $\frac{18}{24}$ **14.** $\frac{9}{10}$ **15.** $\frac{18}{30}$ **16.** $\frac{10}{30}$ **17.** $\frac{3}{21}$ **18.** $\frac{15}{21}$

Try a Shortcut!
- List only the factors of the smaller number.
- Find the largest of these that is a factor of the other number.

19. $\frac{12}{15}$ **20.** $\frac{18}{45}$ **21.** $\frac{28}{16}$ **22.** $\frac{42}{18}$ **23.** $\frac{16}{36}$ **24.** $\frac{18}{32}$

MATH REASONING

25. Brian said, "If 6 is a factor of a number, then 2 and 3 are also factors of the number." Do you think Brian is right? Why or why not?

PROBLEM SOLVING

26. One hundred campers made a list of 145 camp songs they knew. They decided to sing each song once during the 12 days they would be at camp. How many did they need to sing each day if they sang about the same number each day?

▶ **ALGEBRA**

Algebraic expressions involving multiplication can be written in different ways. $5 \times n$, $5 \cdot n$, $5(n)$, and $5n$ all mean "five times a number."

> Remember, if an algebraic expression involves multiplication together with addition or subtraction, multiply first, then add or subtract.

Evaluate each expression.

27. $6m - 4$ when $m = 2$ **28.** $8 + 3g$ when $g = 4$ **29.** $12 - 5y$ when $y = 0$

30. $5 \times n$ when $n = 3$ **31.** $28 \div z$ when $z = 7$ **32.** $6w + 4$ when $w = 2$

Lowest-Terms Fractions

EXPLORE Solve to Understand

Mrs. DeGroat weaves rugs in her spare time. One rug she wove has 6 rows of squares with 4 squares in each row. It has 18 brown squares and 6 green squares. The brown squares and green squares are divided evenly among the rows. What fraction of the squares in each row are brown?

TALK ABOUT IT

1. What two operations could you use to find the total number of squares in the blanket? What is the total number?

2. What fraction of all the squares are brown?

3. What operation can you use to find how many squares in each row are brown? What fraction of all squares in the row is this?

A fraction is in **lowest terms** when the greatest common factor of the numerator and the denominator is 1. Here are two ways to find an equivalent fraction in lowest terms.

- Divide both terms by common factors until the greatest common factor is 1.

$$\frac{18 \div 2}{24 \div 2} = \frac{9}{12} = \frac{9 \div 3}{12 \div 3} = \frac{3}{4}$$ ← lowest-terms fraction

- Divide both terms by their greatest common factor.

$$\frac{18 \div 6}{24 \div 6} = \frac{3}{4}$$ 6 is the greatest common factor of 18 and 24.

Other Examples

A $\frac{2}{6} = \frac{1}{3}$ Think: $\frac{2}{6} \overset{\div 2}{\underset{\div 2}{=}} \frac{1}{3}$

B $\frac{70}{100} = \frac{7}{10}$

Reduce to lowest terms when not already in lowest terms.

1. $\frac{12}{30}$ 2. $\frac{4}{12}$ 3. $\frac{4}{15}$ 4. $\frac{9}{27}$ 5. $\frac{7}{24}$ 6. $\frac{12}{18}$

Tell whether the fraction is in lowest terms. Write **yes** or **no.**

1. $\frac{1}{5}$ 2. $\frac{2}{66}$ 3. $\frac{5}{10}$ 4. $\frac{3}{12}$ 5. $\frac{12}{18}$ 6. $\frac{4}{9}$

7. $\frac{3}{8}$ 8. $\frac{6}{8}$ 9. $\frac{9}{15}$ 10. $\frac{8}{20}$ 11. $\frac{6}{13}$ 12. $\frac{6}{18}$

Reduce to lowest terms when not already in lowest terms.

13. $\frac{6}{8}$ 14. $\frac{9}{12}$ 15. $\frac{18}{45}$ 16. $\frac{3}{15}$ 17. $\frac{7}{8}$ 18. $\frac{8}{20}$

19. $\frac{3}{24}$ 20. $\frac{12}{15}$ 21. $\frac{2}{18}$ 22. $\frac{2}{3}$ 23. $\frac{35}{42}$ 24. $\frac{8}{14}$

Use **mental math** to reduce each fraction to lowest terms.

25. $\frac{5}{10}$ 26. $\frac{6}{60}$ 27. $\frac{10}{35}$ 28. $\frac{8}{400}$ 29. $\frac{4}{100}$

APPLY

MATH REASONING

Write **true** or **false** for each of the following statements.

30. If the numerator of a fraction is 1, the fraction is in lowest terms.

31. If the numerator of a fraction is not 1, the fraction can always be reduced to lowest terms.

PROBLEM SOLVING

32. In the Explore problem on page 248, what fraction names the part of the total squares that are green? What is this fraction reduced to lowest terms?

33. Fine Arts Data Bank What fraction in lowest terms names the part of the total squares in the Sioux Horse Tracks design that is yellow? See page 477.

DATA BANK

▶ **ESTIMATION**

Replace the terms of the fractions with **compatible numbers** to give an estimate for each fraction.

Example: $\frac{11}{23}$ is about $\frac{12}{24}$ or $\frac{1}{2}$.

34. $\frac{15}{22}$ **35.** $\frac{4}{26}$ **36.** $\frac{7}{27}$ **37.** $\frac{12}{35}$

Exploring Algebra
More About Variables

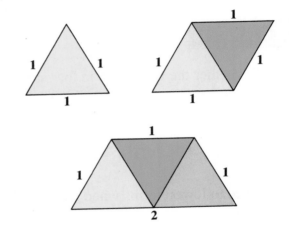

You have learned that a **variable** can stand for a single unknown number. A variable can also be used to stand for a **range of numbers.**

LEARN ABOUT IT

Work in groups.
Copy and complete the table at the right. Make or draw triangles if you find that helpful. Look for patterns.

Number of triangles	1	2	3	4	5	6	7	8	9	10
Perimeter	3	4	5							

TALK ABOUT IT

1. What is the perimeter when there are 6 triangles?

2. What is the perimeter when there are 10 triangles?

3. If you know the number of triangles, how can you find the perimeter?

In the table above, the number of triangles varies from 1 to 10. The perimeter varies from 3 to 12. Suppose N stands for the number of triangles and P stands for the perimeter. N and P are variables.

TRY IT OUT

Copy the tables. Look for patterns you can use to complete them. Describe the patterns you use.

1.

B	1	2	3	4	5	6
C	6	12	18			

2.

A	1	2	3	4	5	6
B	3	6	9			

3.

A	1	2	3	4	5	6
S	1	3	5			11

4.

W	10	20	30	40	50	60
B	21	41				121

250

Write two fractions to name the part that is colored. Write
two fractions to name the part that is not colored.

1.   2. 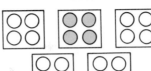   3.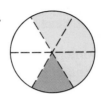

Decide whether the fractions are equivalent. Write **yes** or **no.**

4. $\frac{3}{8} \stackrel{?}{=} \frac{6}{16}$ 5. $\frac{1}{2} \stackrel{?}{=} \frac{5}{8}$ 6. $\frac{2}{3} \stackrel{?}{=} \frac{4}{9}$ 7. $\frac{4}{6} \stackrel{?}{=} \frac{6}{9}$

8. $\frac{4}{5} \stackrel{?}{=} \frac{6}{10}$ 9. $\frac{7}{8} \stackrel{?}{=} \frac{14}{16}$ 10. $\frac{1}{3} \stackrel{?}{=} \frac{4}{12}$ 11. $\frac{6}{9} \stackrel{?}{=} \frac{3}{4}$

List the factors of each number. Then give the greatest
common factor.

12. 6   13. 5   14. 12   15. 10   16. 18
    8   9   4   15   12

Is the fraction in lowest terms? Write **yes** or **no.**

17. $\frac{3}{10}$ 18. $\frac{5}{15}$ 19. $\frac{10}{12}$ 20. $\frac{2}{7}$ 21. $\frac{3}{24}$

Reduce each fraction to lowest terms.

22. $\frac{4}{6}$ 23. $\frac{5}{15}$ 24. $\frac{9}{24}$ 25. $\frac{2}{14}$ 26. $\frac{6}{9}$

PROBLEM SOLVING

27. "I am a fraction. My numerator is 6 less than my
denominator. In lowest terms, I reduce to $\frac{3}{5}$. What
fraction am I?"

28. Mario practiced piano 45 minutes. Brian practiced
trumpet 40 minutes. Write the lowest-term fractions
to show what part of an hour each boy practiced.

Problem Solving
Use Logical Reasoning

UNDERSTAND
ANALYZE DATA
PLAN
ESTIMATE
SOLVE
EXAMINE

LEARN ABOUT IT

To solve some problems, you may need to write what you know in a table. Then you can reason logically to complete the table. This problem solving strategy is **Use Logical Reasoning.**

> Abe, Ben, Carol, and Dino each wrote a report on a different kind of whale. The reports were about blue whales, fin whales, humpbacks, and bowheads. Carol and Dino did not write about humpbacks. Ben wrote about fin whales. Abe did not write about blue whales, and Dino did not write about bowheads. Who wrote about each type of whale?

First I'll make a table of what I know.

I can use what I know to find more information.

Hmmm...Now I know!

	Blue	Fin	Hump	Bow
Abe	no			
Ben		yes		
Carol			no	
Dino			no	no

	Blue	Fin	Hump	Bow
Abe	no	no	yes	no
Ben	no	yes	no	no
Carol		no	no	
Dino		no	no	no

	Blue	Fin	Hump	Bow
Abe	no	no	yes	no
Ben	no	yes	no	no
Carol	no	no	no	yes
Dino	yes	no	no	no

Abe: humpbacks; Ben: fins; Carol: bowheads; Dino: blue

TRY IT OUT

Ed and Nita each did two reports on animals. They did not write about any of the same animals. The animals were the elephant, bobcat, leopard, and gorilla. Ed did not write about the elephant. Nita did not write about the gorilla. The person who wrote about the gorilla did not write about the leopard. Which animal did each write about?

- Which animal did Ed not write about? Which did Nita not write about?

	Ed	Nita
Elephant	no	yes
Bobcat		
Leopard		
Gorilla	yes	no

- Copy and complete the table. Use logical reasoning to solve the problem.

Use logical reasoning to help you solve these problems.

1. At Renaldo's house each person is in charge of recycling something different. One person recycles cans, another recycles newspapers, another bottles, and another boxes. Renaldo recycles cans. Maria does not recycle newspapers. Juanita does recycle bottles. What does Tina recycle?

2. Lee and Ron found information about conservation of wildlife, trees, energy, and water. Each boy chose two topics different from the other boy's topics. Lee did not study energy. Ron did not study trees. The one who studied animals did not study energy. Which topics did each boy study?

MIXED PRACTICE

Choose a strategy from the strategies list or use other strategies you know to solve these problems.

Some Strategies	
Act Out	Make a Table
Use Objects	Solve a Simpler Problem
Choose an Operation	Make an Organized List
Draw a Picture	Work Backward
Guess and Check	Look for a Pattern
Use Logical Reasoning	

Garbage Content

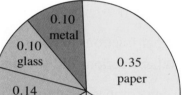

0.10 metal
0.10 glass
0.35 paper
0.14 other
0.15 food waste
0.16 yard waste

3. For every ton of paper recycled, 17 small trees are saved. Tim's school recycled 336 tons of paper last year. How many small trees did they save?

4. Karen recycled 47 cans in January and February. She recycled 7 more in January than in February. How many did she recycle in February?

5. There were about 225 thousand blue whales before man started hunting them. There are only about 15 thousand now. About how many fewer blue whales are there now?

6. Each person makes about 4.5 lb of garbage a day. How many pounds does each person make in a year?

7. Use the circle graph above. What decimal part of the garbage is paper, yard waste, and food waste combined?

8. It takes 182 gallons of water to wash 12 loads of laundry. How many gallons of water does it take to wash 1 load?

9. Gwen, Sarah, Bob, and Nelda were the heads of 4 committees for Conservation Day. One was in charge of food, another drinks, another booths, and another cleanup. Gwen and Sarah did not do drinks or food. Sarah did not do booths. Bob did not do food. What committee was each person in charge of?

Comparing and Ordering Fractions

EXPLORE Use Fraction Pieces
Work with a partner.

- Use your fraction pieces. Find at least three fractions you can use to complete the statement. Write each statement using the "is less than" (<) symbol.

- Use the number line. Find at least three fractions you can use to complete the statement. Write each statement using the "is greater than" (>) symbol.

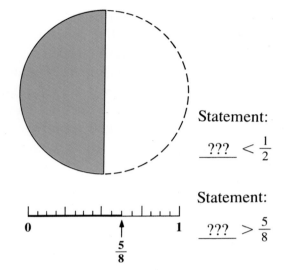

Statement:

$$\underline{???} < \frac{1}{2}$$

Statement:

$$\underline{???} > \frac{5}{8}$$

TALK ABOUT IT

1. What fractions did you find that are less than $\frac{1}{2}$?
2. What fractions did you find that are greater than $\frac{5}{8}$?

You can compare fractions using fraction pieces or the number line. You can also compare fractions by finding equivalent fractions with a common denominator. You can order fractions by comparing them two at a time.

Look at the denominators.	Write equivalent fractions with a common denominator.	Compare the numerators.	The fractions compare the same way the numerators compare.
$\frac{3}{8}$ Not the same $\frac{2}{3}$	$\frac{3}{8} = \frac{9}{24}$ The same $\frac{2}{3} = \frac{16}{24}$	$9 < 16$	$\frac{9}{24} < \frac{16}{24}$ so $\frac{3}{8} < \frac{2}{3}$

TRY IT OUT

Give the correct sign (<, >, or =) for each ▦ .

1. $\frac{1}{2}$ ▦ $\frac{3}{7}$ 2. $\frac{10}{12}$ ▦ $\frac{5}{6}$ 3. $\frac{4}{5}$ ▦ $\frac{3}{4}$ 4. $\frac{5}{8}$ ▦ $\frac{2}{3}$ 5. $\frac{3}{4}$ ▦ $\frac{7}{10}$

Give the correct sign ($<$, $>$, or $=$) for each 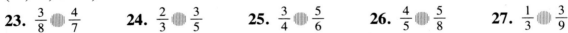 .

1. $\frac{1}{5}$ 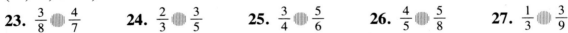 $\frac{1}{4}$ **2.** $\frac{3}{4}$ 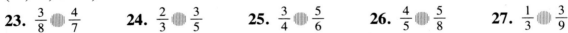 $\frac{5}{6}$ **3.** $\frac{1}{2}$ 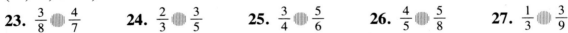 $\frac{2}{3}$ **4.** $\frac{4}{5}$ 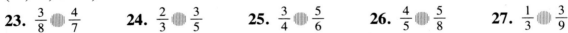 $\frac{5}{8}$ **5.** $\frac{7}{8}$ 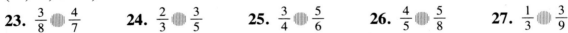 $\frac{7}{10}$

6. $\frac{3}{10}$ 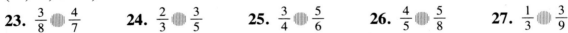 $\frac{9}{30}$ **7.** $\frac{1}{3}$ 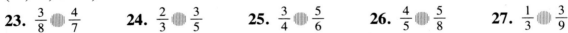 $\frac{1}{2}$ **8.** $\frac{5}{6}$ 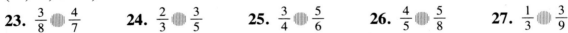 $\frac{7}{8}$ **9.** $\frac{7}{12}$ 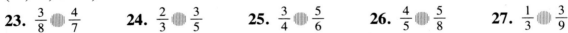 $\frac{2}{3}$ **10.** $\frac{7}{10}$ 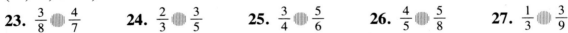 $\frac{3}{4}$

11. $\frac{1}{4}$ 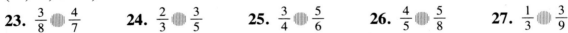 $\frac{1}{3}$ **12.** $\frac{3}{5}$ 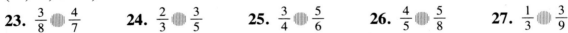 $\frac{2}{3}$ **13.** $\frac{1}{3}$ 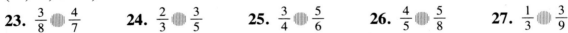 $\frac{3}{8}$ **14.** $\frac{1}{5}$ 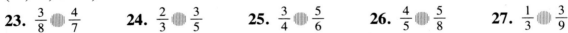 $\frac{20}{100}$ **15.** $\frac{8}{10}$ 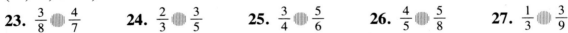 $\frac{79}{100}$

Compare the fractions two at a time. Then write them in order from least to greatest.

16. $\frac{1}{2}, \frac{3}{8}, \frac{2}{5}$ **17.** $\frac{5}{8}, \frac{3}{5}, \frac{2}{3}$ **18.** $\frac{3}{4}, \frac{2}{3}, \frac{7}{12}$ **19.** $\frac{2}{3}, \frac{3}{4}, \frac{2}{5}$

MATH REASONING

20. True or **False**? If the numerators of the fractions are the same, the fraction with the larger denominator is the smaller of the two.

PROBLEM SOLVING

21. In 1989, $\frac{5}{8}$ of the fifth grade students at Mott school said they plan to go to college. In 1987, $\frac{7}{12}$ of the students said they plan to go to college. In which year did the greater fraction of students say they plan to go to college?

22. The Wildcats won $\frac{3}{4}$ of their games. The Owls won $\frac{5}{6}$ of their games. The Dolphins won $\frac{7}{8}$ of their games. Which team won the greatest fraction of their games? the least?

▶ **CALCULATOR**

We can read a fraction like $\frac{3}{4}$ as "3 divided by 4." We can change a fraction to a decimal by dividing the numerator by the denominator. (On a calculator, $3 \div 4 = 0.75$.)

Use a calculator to compare these fractions. Change each fraction to a decimal, rounded to the nearest hundredth. Then compare the decimals. Give the correct sign ($<$, $>$, or $=$) for each 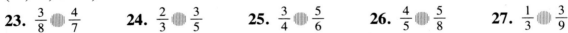 .

23. $\frac{3}{8}$ 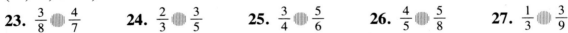 $\frac{4}{7}$ **24.** $\frac{2}{3}$ 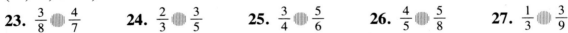 $\frac{3}{5}$ **25.** $\frac{3}{4}$ 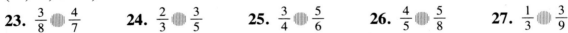 $\frac{5}{6}$ **26.** $\frac{4}{5}$ 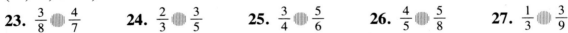 $\frac{5}{8}$ **27.** $\frac{1}{3}$ 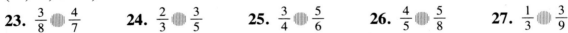 $\frac{3}{9}$

More Practice, page 512, set A

Improper Fractions and Mixed Numbers
Using Manipulatives

Fractions can be used for amounts greater than 1.

EXPLORE Use Fraction Pieces
Work in groups. Find fraction pieces to match the pictures.

Mr. Verga had 2 full wheels and $\frac{5}{8}$ of a wheel of Romano cheese in the display case. He cut the whole amount into eighths for packaging.

TALK ABOUT IT

1. How many pieces of cheese does Mr. Verga get from each full wheel?

2. How many pieces of cheese does Mr. Verga have after he cuts all the cheese into eighths?

Fractions with a numerator greater than or equal to the denominator are called **improper fractions.** Examples of improper fractions are $\frac{5}{3}$ and $\frac{5}{2}$. A whole number and a fraction make up a **mixed number.** Examples of mixed numbers are $1\frac{2}{3}$ and $2\frac{1}{2}$.

Mixed number: $2\frac{5}{8}$ (two and five eighths)

Improper fraction: $\frac{21}{8}$ (twenty-one eighths)

TRY IT OUT

Use fraction pieces or draw pictures to show each equation.

1. $1\frac{1}{5} = \frac{6}{5}$ 2. $\frac{11}{4} = 2\frac{3}{4}$ 3. $3 = \frac{9}{3}$ 4. $4\frac{1}{2} = \frac{9}{2}$

5. $\frac{11}{6} = 1\frac{5}{6}$ 6. $3\frac{1}{2} = \frac{7}{2}$ 7. $\frac{8}{4} = 2$ 8. $1\frac{1}{8} = \frac{9}{8}$

Write the improper fraction and mixed number for the colored part of each picture.

1.    **2.**    **3.**

4.   **5.**   **6.**

Write each as an improper fraction. Use objects or pictures if necessary.

7. $1\frac{1}{5}$ **8.** $3\frac{1}{2}$ **9.** $4\frac{1}{5}$ **10.** $2\frac{1}{4}$ **11.** $6\frac{2}{3}$ **12.** $4\frac{1}{3}$

Write each as a mixed number. Use objects or pictures if necessary.

13. $\frac{15}{6}$ **14.** $\frac{10}{3}$ **15.** $\frac{9}{2}$ **16.** $\frac{23}{6}$ **17.** $\frac{17}{5}$ **18.** $\frac{33}{8}$

APPLY

MATH REASONING

19. Draw a picture that shows the improper fraction for $2\frac{5}{6}$.

20. Draw a picture that shows the mixed number for $\frac{18}{5}$.

PROBLEM SOLVING

21. Ann, Don, Bo, and Gina each like one kind of cheese. One likes Brie, one likes Swiss, one likes Cheddar, and one likes Edam. Ann does not like Edam. Bo and Gina do not like Swiss. Don likes Brie. Gina dislikes Cheddar. Who likes which kind of cheese?

▶ **COMMUNICATION** **Writing to Learn**

22. Write a sentence that describes how to change a mixed number to an improper fraction.

23. Write a sentence that describes how to change an improper fraction to a mixed number.

More Practice, page 512, set B

More Improper Fractions and Mixed Numbers

EXPLORE Examine the Picture

The amount of grapefruit in the picture at the right can be named using an improper fraction or a mixed number.

TALK ABOUT IT

1. How many whole grapefruits are shown?
2. Each grapefruit is made up of how many "half" grapefruits?
3. What mixed number can be used to name the amount of grapefruit?
4. What improper fraction can be used to name the amount of grapefruit?

Here is how to change improper fractions to mixed numbers and mixed numbers to improper fractions.

To change an improper fraction to a mixed number:

Divide the numerator by the denominator.

$$\frac{9}{2} \rightarrow 2\overline{)9} \rightarrow 4\frac{1}{2}$$
$$\quad\quad \frac{8}{1}$$

To change a mixed number to an improper fraction:

Multiply the denominator by the whole number and add the numerator.

$$4\frac{1}{2} \rightarrow \begin{array}{c} 4 \text{ times } 2 \\ \text{plus } 1 \end{array} \rightarrow \frac{9}{2}$$

Other Examples

A $\frac{11}{4} = 2\frac{3}{4}$ **B** $\frac{12}{3} = 4$ **C** $1\frac{7}{10} = \frac{17}{10}$ **D** $15\frac{1}{2} = \frac{31}{2}$

Rename mixed numbers as improper fractions. Rename improper fractions as mixed numbers in lowest terms.

1. $\frac{10}{3}$ 2. $3\frac{1}{2}$ 3. $\frac{15}{4}$ 4. $7\frac{5}{6}$ 5. $\frac{17}{5}$ 6. $6\frac{3}{10}$

Copy and complete.

1. $2 = \frac{\text{▥}}{3}$ **2.** $4 = \frac{\text{▥}}{5}$ **3.** $3 = \frac{\text{▥}}{3}$ **4.** $5 = \frac{\text{▥}}{2}$ **5.** $1 = \frac{\text{▥}}{4}$

Rename each as a whole number or mixed number. Reduce to lowest terms.

6. $\frac{27}{3}$ **7.** $\frac{8}{2}$ **8.** $\frac{15}{4}$ **9.** $\frac{18}{3}$ **10.** $\frac{13}{10}$ **11.** $\frac{4}{3}$

12. $\frac{46}{10}$ **13.** $\frac{20}{4}$ **14.** $\frac{25}{8}$ **15.** $\frac{28}{6}$ **16.** $\frac{17}{3}$ **17.** $\frac{24}{5}$

Rename each mixed number as an improper fraction.

18. $8\frac{1}{10}$ **19.** $3\frac{1}{2}$ **20.** $4\frac{1}{5}$ **21.** $2\frac{1}{4}$ **22.** $6\frac{2}{3}$ **23.** $4\frac{1}{3}$

24. $9\frac{3}{8}$ **25.** $12\frac{2}{5}$ **26.** $8\frac{1}{5}$ **27.** $2\frac{3}{4}$ **28.** $7\frac{5}{6}$ **29.** $11\frac{1}{4}$

MATH REASONING

Give a mixed number and an improper fraction for the points.

30.

31.

PROBLEM SOLVING

32. A box of eggs contains 4 cartons. Each carton holds 1 dozen eggs. Rob has $3\frac{1}{2}$ boxes. How many cartons of 1 dozen does he have? How many eggs does he have?

MIXED REVIEW

Use mental math to find the quotients.

33. $720 \div 8$ **34.** $200 \div 40$ **35.** $2{,}100 \div 7$ **36.** $5{,}400 \div 6$

Find the quotients and remainders.

37. $42\overline{)2{,}852}$ **38.** $63\overline{)5{,}495}$ **39.** $57\overline{)3{,}876}$ **40.** $29\overline{)2{,}387}$

More Practice, page 512, set C

Problem Solving
Using Data from a Table

| UNDERSTAND |
| ANALYZE DATA |
| PLAN |
| ESTIMATE |
| SOLVE |
| EXAMINE |

LEARN ABOUT IT

To solve some problems you have to locate the data you need in a table.

How many times longer is Daniel's boot size than Joey's?

Jackson Family Rental of Skis, Boots, and Poles						
	Skis (cm)	Wt. (lb)	Age/Ht.	Boot Size (mm)	Pole Size (cm)	Binding Setting
Julia	140	98	41 yr 5 ft 2 in.	270	42	$3\frac{1}{2}$
Michele	130	82	11 yr 4 ft 6 in.	290	40	2
Tom	120	59	8 yr 4 ft 2 in.	260	36	2
Daniel	180	177	40 yr 6 ft 2 in.	330	50	$6\frac{1}{2}$
Joey	90	35	$3\frac{1}{2}$ yr 3 ft 8 in.	110	no	1

I'll find the data I need from the table.

Now I can solve the problem.

Daniel's boot size   330 mm

Joey's boot size   110 mm

$$110\overline{)330}$$
$$3$$
$$330$$
$$0$$

Daniel's boot size is 3 times longer than Joey's.

TRY IT OUT

Solve.

1. How much heavier is the person whose bindings are set at $6\frac{1}{2}$ than the person whose bindings are set at $3\frac{1}{2}$?

2. Daniel's brother Larry rented boots that are 1.2 times as long as Tom's. How long are Larry's boots?

260

Solve. Use any problem solving strategy.

1. The longest run at Birkwood Valley ski resort is 3.5 miles. The longest run at Snow Haven is 1.8 times as long. How many miles is the longest run at Snow Haven?

2. How much would the Jacksons pay for ski-lift tickets for a half day?

	Lift Tickets	
	Full Day	Half Day
Adult	$24	$16
Child (under 12)	$12	$ 8

3. Julia, Michele, Tom, and Daniel each like different ski resorts. One likes White Cliffs, one likes Snow Haven, one likes Birkwood, and one likes Mountain Land. Daniel does not like Birkwood. Tom and Michele do not like Snow Haven. Julia likes White Cliffs. Tom does not like Birkwood. Who likes each resort?

Use the table below for problems 4-6.

Snow Haven Chair Lifts		
Chair Lift	Minutes	Rise (ft)
West Bowl	9	1,836
Champion	4	375
Powder Run	6	1,132
Boulder	10	1,498

4. Jeff got in line for the West Bowl chair at 3:25 p.m. He waited in line for 43 minutes before getting onto the lift. When did he get to the top of the chair lift?

5. How much higher does the West Bowl chair lift go than the Champion chair lift?

6. Suzu starts skiing down Powder Run at 1:45 p.m. She takes 9 minutes. Then she waits in line at Boulder chair for 24 minutes. When does she get to the top of Boulder chair?

7. The Jacksons rented skis, boots, and poles for 3 days. Each adult's set of equipment cost $18 per day. Each child's set of equipment cost $12 per day. Instead of renting by the day, they got a group rate that cost them $86 in all. How much did they save by getting the group rate?

8. **Suppose** Tell which of the following facts would change the solution to problem 7.

   A. The prices will be going up next year.

   B. Joey has a $\frac{1}{2}$-off coupon.

   C. The Jacksons paid with a credit card.

   D. They decided to rent the equipment for 1 day.

More Practice, page 525, set D

Applied Problem Solving
Group Decision Making

UNDERSTAND
ANALYZE DATA
PLAN
ESTIMATE
SOLVE
EXAMINE

Group Skill:
Listen to Others

The world you are growing up in today is much different from the world of 50, 20, or even just 10 years ago. Many of the big differences have been brought about by advances in technology. As shown in the graph below, there is a growing demand for workers who have been trained to use computers and other technical equipment.

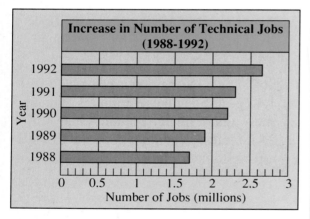

Increase in Number of Technical Jobs (1988-1992)

Do you know people whose jobs involve working with computers or other complex equipment such as copiers or recorders? Do you think you might like to work at a technical job after you finish school?

Facts to Consider

To help her decide whether it would be a good idea to plan for a career in technology after finishing high school, Jay's older sister, Miriam, made a list of what she thought were the main advantages and disadvantages of a technology career. She gave a point rating of 5, 4, 3, 2, or 1 to each advantage or disadvantage she listed. A rating of 5 meant "very important" and a rating of 1 meant "not important at all."

Advantages	Rating
Good salary and benefits	4
College degree not required	3
Many jobs available, usually	4
Suits my abilities	5
No hard physical labor	2
Disadvantages	
Some special training needed	2
Usually work alone	1
Sometimes sudden layoffs	3
Limited chances for management jobs	4
Little chance for creativity	2

1. How many rating points did Miriam give to advantages of a technology career? to disadvantages?

2. If you were trying to make a decision about a job, what point rating would you give to each of the items in the list Miriam made?

3. Can you name some other things you think would be important in trying to make a career decision?

Using your own point ratings for the advantages and disadvantages in Miriam's list, do you think a career in technology would be a good idea for you? Explain your decision.

WRAP UP

What Is It?

Find the correct match for each term.

1. fraction
2. lowest terms fraction
3. improper fraction
4. terms of a fraction
5. equivalent fractions
6. greatest common factor

A. fractions that name the same amount

B. a fraction in which the greatest common factor of the numerator and denominator is 1

C. the numerator and the denominator of a fraction

D. a number that names a part compared to a whole unit

E. the largest number that is a factor of both the numerator and denominator

F. a fraction in which the numerator is equal to or greater than the denominator

Sometimes, Always, Never

Complete each statement by writing **sometimes, always,** or **never.** Explain your choices.

7. The numerator of a fraction is __?__ smaller than the denominator.

8. If two fractions have the same nonzero numerator, the fraction with the smaller denominator is __?__ the larger fraction.

9. You can __?__ use cross products to find whether or not two fractions are equivalent.

Project

Give the lowest-terms fraction for the part of all the whole numbers from 1 to 50 that are:

10. even numbers
11. odd numbers
12. factors of 18
13. multiples of 4
14. multiples of 5

POWER PRACTICE/TEST

Part 1   Understanding

Draw pictures to show the fractions in items 1–5.

1. $\frac{2}{3}$ of a set

2. $\frac{1}{8}$ of a region

3. $\frac{3}{5} = \frac{9}{15}$

4. $3\frac{2}{3} = \frac{11}{3}$

5. $\frac{19}{4} = 4\frac{3}{4}$

6. Complete the table. Describe the pattern.

Give the number for each variable.

7. $\frac{5}{12} = \frac{n}{36}$

8. $\frac{3}{4} = \frac{a}{20}$

x	4	5	6	7	8	9
y	16	20	24			

Part 2   Skills

Give the greatest common factor.

9. $\frac{15}{25}$

10. $\frac{18}{36}$

Reduce to lowest terms.

11. $\frac{8}{12}$

12. $\frac{15}{21}$

Write as a mixed number.

13. $\frac{11}{4}$

14. $\frac{23}{8}$

Write as an improper fraction.

15. $4\frac{2}{3}$

16. $8\frac{4}{5}$

17. Order $\frac{2}{3}$, $\frac{5}{8}$, and $\frac{3}{4}$ from greatest to least.

Part 3   Applications

18. Dennis, Rachel, Mia, and Craig each wrote down one of these numbers: 394; 9,892; 56,146; 2,473. Use the clues to find the number each person wrote.

- Dennis's number does not have 4 digits.

- Rachel's number has more even digits than odd digits.

- If you multiply Mia's number by 4, you get Craig's number.

19. Which person has about twice as many goldfish as George?

Person	Number of Goldfish
Suzanne	29
George	15
Eve	7
Stan	10

20. Challenge. Draw 24 small squares. Color $\frac{1}{8}$ of the squares red, $\frac{1}{3}$ blue, and $\frac{1}{2}$ yellow. How many squares are not colored?

ENRICHMENT
Finding Prime Factors

Problem: How many ways can you find to express 60 as a product of two or more factors?

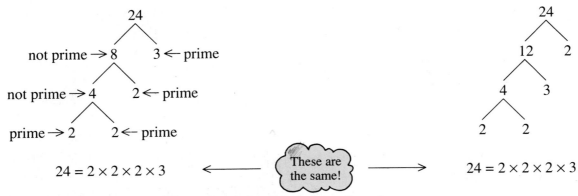

Hey Khala! I found two ways to use multiplication to get a product of 60!... 3×20 and 4×3×5.

There are more ways than that!

Some Facts
- A **prime number** is a whole number that has exactly two factors.
- The 2 factors of a prime number are the number itself and 1.
  Examples: 7 is a prime number. Its two factors are 7 and 1.
  6 is not a prime number. Its factors are 1, 2, 3, and 6.
- A number greater than 1 that is not prime is a **composite number.**
- A composite number can be expressed as a product of only one set of prime numbers. This expression is the **prime factorization** of the number.

You can use a **factor tree** to find the prime factorization of a number. Here are two factor trees for 24.

not prime → 8   3 ← prime

not prime → 4   2 ← prime

prime → 2   2 ← prime

$$24 = 2 \times 2 \times 2 \times 3$$

These are the same!

$$24 = 2 \times 2 \times 2 \times 3$$

Make a factor tree to find the prime factors of each number. If the number given is prime, write **prime.**

1. 20   **2.** 30   **3.** 45   **4.** 23   **5.** 60   **6.** 1,000

CUMULATIVE REVIEW

1. Find the area of a rectangle that is 23.4 cm long and 12.2 cm wide.
   - A. 71.2 cm^2
   - B. 285.48 cm^2
   - C. 35.6 cm^2
   - D. 142.74 cm^2

2. Which estimate must be changed?
   - A. $34\overline{)177}$ with 6
   - B. $61\overline{)446}$ with 7
   - C. $75\overline{)659}$ with 8
   - D. $93\overline{)375}$ with 4

Give the missing numbers.

3. 12.74 m = ▦ m ▦ cm
   - A. 127 m 4 cm
   - B. 1 m 274 cm
   - C. 1,274 m 0 cm
   - D. 12 m 74 cm

4. 4,627 mL = ▦ L
   - A. 4.627
   - B. 46.27
   - C. 462.7
   - D. 0.4627

5. The picture shows the result after dividing. Choose the original division problem.

    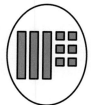 

   - A. 36 ÷ 3
   - B. 72 ÷ 3
   - C. 96 ÷ 3
   - D. 108 ÷ 3

Divide.

6. $6\overline{)44.4}$
   - A. 74
   - B. 0.74
   - C. 7.4
   - D. 0.074

Divide.

7. 7,200 ÷ 80
   - A. 9
   - B. 90
   - C. 900
   - D. 9,000

8. 527.6 ÷ 100
   - A. 52.76
   - B. 5.276
   - C. 0.5276
   - D. 5,276

9. $37\overline{)227}$
   - A. 6 R5
   - B. 5 R42
   - C. 5 R5
   - D. 6 R4

10. $86\overline{)42,507}$
    - A. 424 R43
    - B. 49 R4
    - C. 424 R23
    - D. 494 R23

11. When Maria's dog had a litter of puppies, Maria sold half the litter to the pet store. Then she gave half of the rest to her uncle and half of what was left to Sue. She had one puppy left for herself. How many puppies were in the original litter?
    - A. 16
    - B. 4
    - C. 8
    - D. 12

12. Suppose you tear a piece of paper in half and give half to another person. Then each person with paper tears it in half and passes half on to another person. How many people would have a piece of paper after 10 rounds of tearing and passing?
    - A. 320
    - B. 256
    - C. 512
    - D. 1,024

10

ADDITION AND SUBTRACTION: FRACTIONS AND MIXED NUMBERS

THEME: PROSE AND POETRY

MATH AND LANGUAGE ARTS

DATA BANK

Use the Language Arts Data Bank on page 469 to answer the questions.

1 Is the fractional part of the content of Reading Series A that is poetry greater than or less than the part that is poetry in Reading Series B?

2 List the poems on Side 2 of the *Treasury of Great Poems* that you can listen to in $1\frac{1}{2}$ minutes or less.

3 Order the fractions for the types of writing in Reading Series A from least to greatest. Order those in Reading Series B from greatest to least.

4 **Using Critical Thinking** Pat said, "It's easy to estimate that the total playing time for Side 1 of the record is longer than the time for Side 2." Do you agree with that conclusion? Explain.

Students sharpen communication skills as they record readings from a book of poems by Nikki Giovanni.

Adding and Subtracting Fractions
Like Denominators

EXPLORE Analyze The Process

The contents of the reading book used by Mr. Emerson's class are $\frac{3}{5}$ prose fiction and $\frac{1}{5}$ poetry. How much greater is the part that is fiction than the part that is poetry?

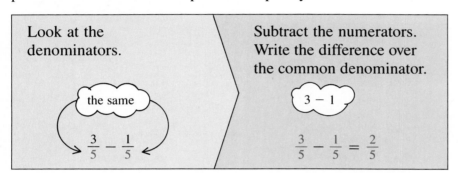

Look at the denominators.

the same

$$\frac{3}{5} - \frac{1}{5}$$

Subtract the numerators. Write the difference over the common denominator.

$3 - 1$

$$\frac{3}{5} - \frac{1}{5} = \frac{2}{5}$$

TALK ABOUT IT

1. What do you do to the numerators when subtracting fractions with like denominators?
2. What do you do to the denominators?
3. Write the answer to the Explore problem in a complete statement.

Other Examples

A $1 + 3$

$$\frac{1}{6} + \frac{3}{6} = \frac{4}{6} = \frac{2}{3}$$

B

$$\frac{7}{8} - \frac{3}{8} = \frac{4}{8} = \frac{1}{2}$$

C

$$\frac{3}{4} + \frac{2}{4} = \frac{5}{4} = 1\frac{1}{4}$$

Add or subtract. Reduce to lowest terms.

1. $\frac{5}{6} - \frac{1}{6}$ 2. $\frac{7}{8} + \frac{3}{8}$ 3. $\frac{12}{8} - \frac{10}{8}$ 4. $\frac{4}{12} + \frac{6}{12}$ 5. $\frac{7}{10} - \frac{3}{10}$

Add. Reduce sums to lowest terms.

1. $\frac{1}{5} + \frac{2}{5}$

2. $\frac{1}{3} + \frac{1}{3}$

3. $\frac{1}{10} + \frac{7}{10}$

4. $\frac{3}{8} + \frac{3}{8}$

5. $\begin{array}{r} \frac{1}{8} \\ + \frac{3}{8} \\ \hline \end{array}$

6. $\begin{array}{r} \frac{5}{10} \\ + \frac{3}{10} \\ \hline \end{array}$

7. $\begin{array}{r} \frac{2}{4} \\ + \frac{1}{4} \\ \hline \end{array}$

8. $\begin{array}{r} \frac{5}{12} \\ + \frac{1}{12} \\ \hline \end{array}$

9. $\begin{array}{r} \frac{2}{6} \\ + \frac{2}{6} \\ \hline \end{array}$

Subtract. Reduce differences to lowest terms.

10. $\frac{2}{3} - \frac{1}{3}$

11. $\frac{5}{12} - \frac{1}{12}$

12. $\frac{4}{5} - \frac{2}{5}$

13. $\frac{9}{10} - \frac{3}{10}$

14. $\begin{array}{r} \frac{3}{8} \\ - \frac{2}{8} \\ \hline \end{array}$

15. $\begin{array}{r} \frac{13}{15} \\ - \frac{4}{15} \\ \hline \end{array}$

16. $\begin{array}{r} \frac{7}{8} \\ - \frac{5}{8} \\ \hline \end{array}$

17. $\begin{array}{r} \frac{11}{12} \\ - \frac{4}{12} \\ \hline \end{array}$

18. $\begin{array}{r} \frac{15}{16} \\ - \frac{9}{16} \\ \hline \end{array}$

19. Find the sum of $\frac{4}{10}$ and $\frac{6}{10}$.

20. Subtract $\frac{1}{6}$ from $\frac{5}{6}$.

MATH REASONING

Evaluate each expression when the variable has the given value.

21. $x + \frac{3}{5}$ when $x = \frac{4}{5}$

22. $m - \frac{1}{4}$ when $m = \frac{5}{4}$

23. $h + \frac{3}{10}$ when $h = \frac{5}{10}$

PROBLEM SOLVING

24. Ogden Nash's poem, "The Octopus," took up $\frac{1}{4}$ of the page in a reading book. A picture took up $\frac{3}{4}$ of the page. How much greater was the fraction of the page taken up by the picture?

25. Language Arts Data Bank How much greater is the fraction of the contents that are stories in Reading Series B than the fraction that are stories in Reading Series A? See page 469.

DATA BANK

▶ ALGEBRA

Write the algebraic expression. Use the letter n for the unknown number.

26. a number increased by $\frac{1}{2}$

27. $\frac{3}{5}$ less than a number

28. 5 times a number

29. the sum of a number and $\frac{4}{5}$

More Practice, page 512, set D

Least Common Multiple

LEARN ABOUT IT

EXPLORE Solve to Understand

Kara collects payments from her morning newspaper customers every 6 days. She collects from her afternoon customers every 8 days. Today she collected payments from all of her customers. How many days will it be before she again collects from her morning and afternoon customers on the same day?

TALK ABOUT IT

1. On what days will she collect from her morning customers?
2. On what days will she collect from her afternoon customers?
3. When is the first day she will collect from morning and afternoon customers on the same day?

The numerical part of the answer to the problem above is the **least common multiple (LCM)** of 6 and 8. Here is how to find the least common multiple of 4 and 6.

List some multiples of each number. (Do not list 0.)	List the common multiples (the numbers in both lists).	Choose the smallest of these common multiples.
4: 4, 8, 12, 16, 20, 24 **6:** 6, 12, 18, 24, 30, 36	→ **12, 24**	**12**

The least common multiple of 4 and 6 is 12.
For the fractions $\frac{1}{4}$ and $\frac{1}{6}$, the **least common denominator** is 12.

Other Examples

multiples of 4: 4, 8, 12
multiples of 8: 8, 16, 24   LCM is 8.

multiples of 5: 5, 10, 15, 20
multiples of 3: 3, 6, 12, 15, 18   LCM is 15.

TRY IT OUT

Find the least common multiple for each pair of numbers.

1. 3 and 4   **2.** 3 and 5   **3.** 4 and 12   **4.** 8 and 10   **5.** 6 and 10

Find the least common multiple (LCM) for each pair of numbers.

1. 8 and 12   **2.** 4 and 5   **3.** 2 and 3   **4.** 6 and 8   **5.** 3 and 8

6. 6 and 9   **7.** 5 and 6   **8.** 4 and 6   **9.** 8 and 10   **10.** 9 and 12

Find the least common denominator (LCD) for each pair of fractions.

11. $\frac{1}{2}, \frac{2}{3}$ **12.** $\frac{2}{5}, \frac{5}{10}$ **13.** $\frac{1}{4}, \frac{1}{2}$ **14.** $\frac{2}{3}, \frac{5}{6}$ **15.** $\frac{5}{8}, \frac{7}{16}$

APPLY

MATH REASONING

- Try a shortcut! Start a list of multiples of the larger number of a pair whose LCM you want to find. Check each number to see if it is also a multiple of the smaller number. The smallest multiple of each is the LCM.

Use the shortcut to find the LCD for these fractions.

16. $\frac{1}{8}, \frac{5}{6}$ **17.** $\frac{2}{3}, \frac{3}{4}$ **18.** $\frac{3}{5}, \frac{1}{6}$ **19.** $\frac{1}{4}, \frac{5}{12}$ **20.** $\frac{5}{6}, \frac{49}{100}$

PROBLEM SOLVING

21. Myra collects from her morning newspaper customers every 5 days. She collects from her afternoon customers every 8 days. Today is February 1, and she collected from both customers today. Is there another day in February when she will again collect from both customers on the same day?

CALCULATOR

You can use the counting constant on a calculator to find the LCM of two numbers. For example: Find the LCM of 24 and 18.

Find 5 or 6 multiples of the larger number:
[ON/AC] [+] 24 [=] [=], and so on.
Find multiples of 18: [ON/AC] [+] 18 [=] [=], and so on.
The first multiple on the display that is also a multiple of 24 is the LCM of 18 and 24.

Find the LCM of these numbers.

22. 24 and 26   **23.** 48 and 64   **24.** 18 and 48   **25.** 36 and 20

Adding and Subtracting Fractions
Making the Connection

EXPLORE Use Fraction Pieces

Work with a partner.

- Pick a pair of fractions from those in the box.
- One partner shows each fraction using fraction pieces.
- The other partner puts together the two groups.
- Trade fraction pieces for equivalent pieces. Write the fraction that names the total.
- Write a number sentence that shows what you did.
- Repeat this several times changing roles and using different pairs of fractions.

$\frac{1}{6}$ and $\frac{1}{3}$	$\frac{1}{2}$ and $\frac{1}{4}$
$\frac{3}{5}$ and $\frac{1}{10}$	$\frac{1}{3}$ and $\frac{5}{12}$
$\frac{1}{2}$ and $\frac{3}{8}$	$\frac{1}{6}$ and $\frac{7}{12}$
$\frac{1}{4}$ and $\frac{3}{8}$	$\frac{5}{12}$ and $\frac{1}{2}$

TALK ABOUT IT

1. Use one of the pairs of fractions above. Tell what trade had to be made to write the total.

2. Why do you have to rename one of the fractions for each of the pairs above?

3. Use fraction pieces to find the total for $\frac{1}{2}$ and $\frac{1}{3}$. Explain any trades that had to be made.

You have put fraction pieces together, traded, and found the fraction that names the total. Now you will see a way to record what you have done. We can use fraction pieces to show $\frac{1}{4} + \frac{5}{8}$.

What You Do

Show each fraction.

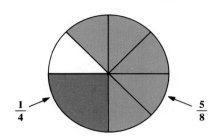

$\frac{1}{4}$ $\frac{5}{8}$

What You Record

$$\frac{1}{4}$$
$$+\frac{5}{8}$$

Can you change the fractions so they have the same denominator?

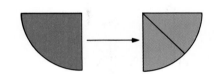

Change $\frac{1}{4}$ to an equivalent fraction.

$$\frac{1}{4} = \frac{2}{8}$$
$$+\frac{5}{8} = \frac{5}{8}$$

How many eighths are there altogether?

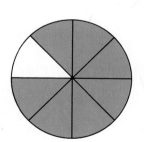

Add the numerators. Write the sum over the common denominator.

$$\frac{2}{8}$$
$$+\frac{5}{8} \quad 2+5=7$$
$$\frac{7}{8}$$

TRY IT OUT

Use fraction pieces to find each sum or difference. Rename one fraction so they both have the same denominator. Record what you did.

1. $\frac{1}{2} - \frac{1}{4}$ **2.** $\frac{2}{5} + \frac{3}{10}$ **3.** $\frac{2}{3} - \frac{1}{6}$ **4.** $\frac{2}{6} + \frac{3}{12}$ **5.** $\frac{1}{4} + \frac{3}{8}$

6. $\frac{1}{4} - \frac{1}{8}$ **7.** $\frac{1}{2} + \frac{1}{4}$ **8.** $\frac{5}{6} - \frac{2}{3}$ **9.** $\frac{4}{5} + \frac{1}{10}$ **10.** $\frac{3}{4} - \frac{1}{8}$

Adding and Subtracting Fractions
Unlike Denominators

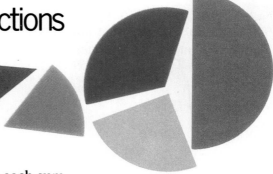

EXPLORE **Estimate Using Objects**

Work in groups. Use fraction pieces to estimate each sum.

■ $\frac{1}{2}$ and $\frac{1}{3}$ is about ___?___ .   ■ $\frac{3}{5}$ and $\frac{1}{2}$ is about ___?___ .   ■ $\frac{3}{4}$ and $\frac{5}{8}$ is about ___?___ .

Here is how to add fractions with unlike denominators.

Look at the denominators.	Find the least common denominator.	Write equivalent fractions with this denominator.	Add the fractions.
$\frac{1}{4}$ ← Not the same $+\frac{3}{8}$ ←	Multiples of 4: 4, 8 Multiples of 8: 8	$\frac{1}{4} = \frac{2}{8}$ $+\frac{3}{8} = \frac{3}{8}$	$\frac{2}{8}$ $+\frac{3}{8}$ $\frac{5}{8}$

TALK ABOUT IT

1. Will the LCD always be one of the denominators in the given fraction?
2. How could you estimate that the sum will be less than 1?

Other Examples

A $\frac{2}{3} = \frac{8}{12}$
$+\frac{3}{4} = \frac{9}{12}$
Rename → $\frac{17}{12} = 1\frac{5}{12}$

B $\frac{5}{6} = \frac{20}{24}$
$-\frac{3}{8} = \frac{9}{24}$
$\frac{11}{24}$

C $\frac{3}{5} = \frac{12}{20}$
$-\frac{1}{4} = \frac{5}{20}$
$\frac{7}{20}$

Add or subtract.

1. $\frac{1}{8}$
    $+\frac{3}{4}$

2. $\frac{1}{3}$
    $+\frac{2}{5}$

3. $\frac{2}{3}$
    $-\frac{1}{4}$

4. $\frac{7}{8}$
    $-\frac{5}{10}$

5. $\frac{2}{3}$
    $+\frac{3}{5}$

276

Add or subtract. Reduce answers to lowest terms.

1. $\frac{2}{5}$
$+\frac{3}{10}$

2. $\frac{4}{5}$
$-\frac{1}{2}$

3. $\frac{1}{6}$
$+\frac{1}{3}$

4. $\frac{3}{4}$
$+\frac{1}{2}$

5. $\frac{5}{6}$
$-\frac{2}{3}$

6. $\frac{1}{4}$
$+\frac{3}{8}$

7. $\frac{2}{3}$
$-\frac{1}{12}$

8. $\frac{7}{8}$
$-\frac{3}{4}$

9. $\frac{1}{5}$
$+\frac{1}{2}$

10. $\frac{1}{3}$
$+\frac{3}{4}$

11. $\frac{9}{10} + \frac{3}{100}$

12. $\frac{3}{4} - \frac{2}{3}$

13. $\frac{3}{10} + \frac{9}{20}$

14. $\frac{1}{6} - \frac{1}{8}$

15. $\frac{3}{10} + \frac{49}{100}$

16. $\frac{4}{5} - \frac{3}{10}$

17. $\frac{9}{100} + \frac{9}{10}$

18. $\frac{83}{100} + \frac{7}{10}$

19. What is the sum of $\frac{5}{6}$ and $\frac{5}{8}$?

20. What is $\frac{4}{5}$ less than $\frac{7}{8}$?

MATH REASONING

Evaluate each expression for the values given.

21. $m + \frac{2}{3}$ for $m = \frac{3}{5}$ and for $m = \frac{1}{8}$

22. $n - \frac{1}{4}$ for $n = \frac{4}{5}$ and for $n = \frac{3}{10}$

PROBLEM SOLVING

23. Plant C grew $\frac{2}{3}$ in. more than Plant D in a science experiment. Plant D grew $\frac{7}{8}$ in. How much did Plant C grow?

24. Plant B grew $\frac{1}{2}$ in. more than Plant A. Plant C grew $\frac{2}{3}$ in. less than Plant B. Plant D grew $\frac{1}{2}$ in. more than Plant C. Plant D grew $\frac{9}{10}$ in. How much did each plant grow?

Divide.

25. $72 \div 23$ **26.** $587 \div 68$ **27.** $629 \div 74$ **28.** $388 \div 54$ **29.** $471 \div 49$

Give the next three equivalent fractions.

30. $\frac{1}{3}$ **31.** $\frac{3}{5}$ **32.** $\frac{1}{10}$ **33.** $\frac{2}{7}$

More Practice, page 513, set A

Problem Solving
Problems Without Solutions

UNDERSTAND
ANALYZE DATA
PLAN
ESTIMATE
SOLVE
EXAMINE

LEARN ABOUT IT

All the problems you have seen so far have had solutions. Some problems do not have solutions.

> Danielle's father bought her 5 coins for her collection of American coins. None of the coins was a half dollar. Could the total face value of the coins be $1.00?

> I can make an organized list to help me find the possibilities. I'll use Q for quarter, D for dime, and N for nickel.

Q	D	N	Face Value
5	0	0	$1.25
4	1	0	$1.10
4	0	1	$1.05
3	1	1	$ .90
2	3	0	$ .80

None of the possibilities adds up to $100.

This problem has no solution.

You cannot get exactly $1.00 with 5 coins if one is not a half dollar.

TRY IT OUT

If the problem has a solution, find it. If it has no solution, explain why not.

1. Ray has a collection of old U.S. coins. He bought 4 more old coins. Their face value is 75¢. None is a quarter. What coins did he buy?

2. Rosa was looking at two facing pages in a book about old Spanish "pieces of eight." Just for fun, she quickly added the numbers of the pages and got 24. Did she add correctly?

3. At the coin show, Jeff's father set up a rectangular table to sell coins. The perimeter of the table was 210 in. One side was 52 in. What was the length of the other side?

4. Tommy just bought 5 coins for his collection. They were all pennies, nickels, or quarters. When he added their face values, he got 55¢ as the total. Did he add correctly?

MIXED PRACTICE

Solve. Choose a strategy from the list or use other strategies that you know.

Some Strategies

Act Out	Make a Table
Use Objects	Solve a Simpler Problem
Choose an Operation	Make an Organized List
Draw a Picture	Work Backward
Guess and Check	Look for a Pattern
Use Logical Reasoning	

1. Denise has $\frac{1}{2}$ page of Lincoln pennies and $\frac{2}{3}$ page of buffalo nickels. How many pages does she have altogether?

2. Divers who discovered a Spanish ship that was wrecked in 1622 found two chests. One weighed 137 pounds and contained 2,516 coins. Another weighed 124 pounds and contained 7,139 coins. How many coins did the divers find?

3. Jim bought 10 Greek coins for $27.50. Each coin cost the same amount. How much did each coin cost?

4. How much do you save by buying the off-center coins together instead of one at a time?

Off-center Lincoln penny	$ 0.99
Off-center Jefferson nickel	$ 3.95
Off-center Roosevelt dime	$ 3.95
Off-center Washington quarter	$ 9.95
A complete set of 4 (one of each)	$16.95

5. Elsa keeps her coin collection in a special case. The area of the case's cover is 17 in.^{2}. The width and the length are both a whole number of inches. What are the length and the width of the case?

6. Martin gave $\frac{1}{5}$ of his collection of old coins to his brother. He gave $\frac{3}{4}$ to his friend Sam. What part of his collection did he give away altogether?

7. Elena could get 3 half-dimes for $13. How much would 15 half-dimes cost her?

8. Ms. Braun has a large collection of coins. She has 48 coins in one book, 54 in another book, 45 in a third book, and 57 in a fourth book. About how many coins does Ms. Braun have altogether in the four books?

9. **Talk About Your Solution** Jennifer spent $\frac{1}{2}$ of her money on Washington quarters. Then she spent $3 on coin books. She had $2.12 left. How much did she have to start with? Explain your solution to a classmate. Compare your solutions.

Estimating Fraction Sums and Differences

LEARN ABOUT IT

EXPLORE **Examine the Map**
Roberto made a map to show
some distances between several
cities in the United States and
Mexico. He wrote his measurements on the map.

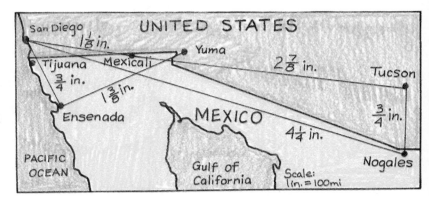

TALK ABOUT IT

1. What whole number of inches on the map is closest to
   the distance between Tucson and Mexicali?

2. How would you estimate the distance in miles between
   Tucson and Mexicali? between Nogales and San Diego?

   Estimate the sum: $\frac{3}{4} + 4\frac{5}{8} + 1\frac{3}{8} + 2\frac{7}{8}$

- **Using rounding**
  Round to whole numbers. $1 + 5 + 1 + 3 = 10$

  Round **down** if the fraction part is
  less than $\frac{1}{2}$. Round **up** if the fraction
  part is greater than or equal to $\frac{1}{2}$.

- **Using compatible numbers**
  Substitute whole numbers or $\frac{1}{2}$. $1 + 4\frac{1}{2} + 1\frac{1}{2} + 3 = 10$

TRY IT OUT

Use the estimation method of your choice.

1. $6\frac{1}{4} - 2\frac{5}{6}$ 2. $12\frac{1}{8} - 4\frac{3}{4}$ 3. $2\frac{3}{5} + 1\frac{1}{2} + 5\frac{3}{8}$

4. $1\frac{7}{8} + \frac{9}{16} + 3\frac{4}{9}$ 5. $7\frac{5}{6} - 2\frac{2}{3}$ 6. $3\frac{1}{8} + \frac{3}{4} + 4\frac{1}{6}$

7. Estimate the distance in miles between Ensenada
   and Yuma.

8. Estimate the distance in miles if you travel from Tucson
   to Ensenada through Mexicali and San Diego.

POWER PRACTICE/QUIZ

Find the least common multiple (LCM) for each pair of numbers.

1. 2, 3   **2.** 8, 4   **3.** 18, 6   **4.** 9, 5   **5.** 10, 4   **6.** 3, 7

Suppose you showed these four problems using fraction pieces.

7. For which problems can you rename the fractions using sixths to find the answer?

A. $\frac{2}{3} + \frac{5}{6}$ **B.** $\frac{1}{2} + \frac{1}{3}$

C. $\frac{7}{8} - \frac{1}{8}$ **D.** $\frac{5}{9} - \frac{1}{6}$

8. For which problems can the final answer be reduced?

Add or subtract. Reduce answers to lowest terms.

9. $\frac{3}{5} + \frac{1}{5}$ **10.** $\frac{5}{12} + \frac{5}{12}$ **11.** $\frac{1}{6} + \frac{1}{4}$ **12.** $\frac{2}{3} + \frac{1}{6}$

13. $\frac{3}{8} + \frac{5}{8}$ **14.** $\frac{5}{6} - \frac{1}{6}$ **15.** $\frac{7}{9} - \frac{5}{18}$ **16.** $\frac{9}{10} - \frac{3}{8}$

17. $\frac{9}{10}$ $- \frac{3}{10}$ **18.** $\frac{3}{4}$ $- \frac{1}{4}$ **19.** $\frac{3}{5}$ $- \frac{1}{3}$ **20.** $\frac{5}{6}$ $+ \frac{4}{15}$ **21.** $\frac{7}{12}$ $- \frac{5}{12}$

22. $\frac{3}{4}$ $+ \frac{1}{2}$ **23.** $\frac{2}{3}$ $+ \frac{3}{4}$ **24.** $\frac{5}{7}$ $+ \frac{1}{7}$ **25.** $\frac{7}{8}$ $- \frac{5}{6}$ **26.** $\frac{11}{12}$ $- \frac{1}{4}$

PROBLEM SOLVING

Solve the fraction riddles. If there is no solution, tell how you know.

27. "My numerator is 3 less than my denominator. When you add me to $\frac{3}{4}$, my sum is 1."

28. "My denominator is 6 more than my numerator. When you subtract me from $\frac{7}{12}$, the difference is $\frac{1}{4}$."

29. "I am equivalent to $\frac{3}{8}$. When you double my numerator you get my denominator."

30. "I am in lowest terms. When you double my numerator and my denominator the result is $\frac{10}{15}$."

Adding and Subtracting Mixed Numbers
Making the Connection

EXPLORE Use Fraction Pieces

Work with a partner.

- Pick a pair of mixed numbers from those at the right.
- One partner shows each mixed number using fraction pieces.
- The other partner puts together the two groups to find the total.
- Pick another pair of mixed numbers.
- One partner shows only the larger of the two numbers using fraction pieces.
- The other partner takes away an amount represented by the smaller mixed number.

$$1\frac{1}{4} \qquad 2\frac{1}{4} \qquad 3\frac{1}{4}$$

$$2\frac{1}{2} \qquad 1\frac{1}{2} \qquad 2\frac{3}{4}$$

$$3\frac{3}{4} \qquad 3\frac{1}{2} \qquad 1\frac{3}{4}$$

TALK ABOUT IT

1. Use one pair of mixed numbers. What trades had to be made when the two groups were put together?
2. Use one pair of mixed numbers. What trades had to be made when taking the smaller amount away from the larger amount?
3. Explain how 1 whole unit can be traded for fraction pieces.

You have put together and taken away fraction pieces to find sums and differences. Now you will see a way to record what you have done. We can use fraction pieces to show $3\frac{1}{4} - 1\frac{3}{4}$.

What You Do

Show the greater mixed number.

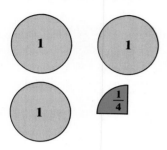

What You Record

$$3\frac{1}{4}$$
$$-1\frac{3}{4}$$

Can you take away $\frac{3}{4}$? If not, trade.

Trade

$$3\frac{1}{4} = 2\frac{5}{4}$$
$$-1\frac{3}{4} = 1\frac{3}{4}$$

Take away the fraction part. Take away the whole number part.

$$2\frac{5}{4}$$ Subtract the fractions.
$$-1\frac{3}{4}$$ Subtract the whole numbers.
$$1\frac{2}{4} = 1\frac{1}{2}$$

TRY IT OUT

Use fraction pieces to find each sum or difference. Record what you do.

1. $3\frac{2}{3} - 1\frac{1}{3}$ **2.** $1\frac{1}{5} + 1\frac{3}{5}$ **3.** $3\frac{1}{6} - 1\frac{5}{6}$ **4.** $1\frac{4}{5} + 1\frac{3}{5}$

5. $2\frac{1}{2} + 2\frac{1}{4}$ **6.** $1\frac{5}{8} + 1\frac{3}{4}$ **7.** $4\frac{2}{3} - 1\frac{1}{6}$ **8.** $3\frac{1}{5} - 1\frac{7}{10}$

283

Adding Mixed Numbers

LEARN ABOUT IT

EXPLORE Analyze the Process

Jan and Dean spent $1\frac{3}{4}$ h decorating a valentines box. They spent $2\frac{1}{2}$ h making valentines. Altogether, how much time did they spend on these jobs?

Here is how to find the answer.

Look at the denominators.	Find equivalent fractions with like denominators.	Add the fractions.	Add the whole numbers.
$1\frac{3}{4}$ *Not the same* $+\,2\frac{1}{2}$	$1\frac{3}{4} = 1\frac{3}{4}$ $+\,2\frac{1}{2} = 2\frac{2}{4}$	$1\frac{3}{4}$ $+\,2\frac{2}{4}$ $\dfrac{5}{4}$	$1\frac{3}{4}$ $+\,2\frac{2}{4}$ $3\frac{5}{4} = 4\frac{1}{4}$ *Rename*

TALK ABOUT IT

1. How do you know that the LCD was 4?
2. Why are the fractions added first?

Other Examples

$$\text{A} \qquad \begin{aligned} 12\tfrac{1}{5} &= 12\tfrac{3}{15} \\ +\,17\tfrac{2}{3} &= 17\tfrac{10}{15} \\ \hline &\ \ \ 29\tfrac{13}{15} \end{aligned}$$

$$\text{B} \qquad \begin{aligned} 7\tfrac{1}{2} &= 7\tfrac{10}{20} \\ 5\tfrac{4}{5} &= 5\tfrac{16}{20} \\ +\,2\tfrac{3}{4} &= 2\tfrac{15}{20} \\ \hline &\ 14\tfrac{41}{20} = 16\tfrac{1}{20} \end{aligned}$$

TRY IT OUT

Add. Reduce sums to lowest terms.

1. $\begin{aligned} 4\tfrac{4}{5} \\ +\,2\tfrac{3}{5} \end{aligned}$

2. $\begin{aligned} 5\tfrac{5}{6} \\ +\,8\tfrac{1}{3} \end{aligned}$

3. $\begin{aligned} 9\tfrac{3}{4} \\ +\,14\tfrac{5}{6} \end{aligned}$

4. $\begin{aligned} 34\tfrac{5}{6} \\ +\,25\tfrac{4}{5} \end{aligned}$

5. $\begin{aligned} 8\tfrac{3}{4} \\ +\,5\tfrac{1}{3} \\ +\,6\tfrac{1}{6} \end{aligned}$

284

Add. Reduce sums to lowest terms.

1. $3\frac{2}{3}$
   $+6\frac{2}{3}$

2. $8\frac{5}{6}$
   $+2\frac{4}{6}$

3. $11\frac{5}{7}$
   $+7\frac{6}{7}$

4. $4\frac{7}{12}$
   $+8\frac{5}{6}$

5. $19\frac{1}{2}$
   $+2\frac{3}{4}$

6. $92\frac{3}{5}$
   $88\frac{3}{5}$
   $+9\frac{3}{5}$

7. $27\frac{1}{4}$
   $46\frac{3}{4}$
   $+50\frac{1}{2}$

8. $27\frac{1}{2}$
   $18\frac{5}{8}$
   $+12\frac{1}{4}$

9. $48\frac{1}{10}$
   $65\frac{3}{5}$
   $+74\frac{1}{2}$

10. $40\frac{4}{5}$
    $23\frac{5}{6}$
    $+8\frac{10}{15}$

Estimate each sum.

11. $5\frac{4}{5} + 12\frac{1}{8}$

12. $9\frac{4}{5} + 8\frac{3}{10}$

13. $4\frac{3}{10} + 7\frac{7}{8}$

14. $8\frac{2}{3} + 7\frac{1}{8}$

MATH REASONING

15. Give the number for each ▦ . $▦\frac{3}{5} + 8\frac{5}{▦} = 14\frac{13}{▦}$

PROBLEM SOLVING

16. Jan and Dean used $3\frac{1}{4}$ yd of red ribbon and $3\frac{5}{8}$ yd of white ribbon for their valentine box. How many yards of ribbon did they use altogether?

17. Three boxes full of valentines were weighed. Their weights were $1\frac{1}{2}$ lb, $2\frac{1}{8}$ lb, and $1\frac{3}{4}$ lb. What was the total weight of these boxes?

▶ **MENTAL MATH**

You can use **compatible numbers** to add mixed numbers.
For example:

$4\frac{4}{5} + 2\frac{1}{2} + 3\frac{1}{5}$ $\qquad 4\frac{4}{5} + 3\frac{1}{5}$ are easy to add mentally:

$$4 + 3 + 1 = 8; \quad 8 + 2\frac{1}{2} = 10\frac{1}{2}$$

Decide which you can solve using mental math. Find those sums only.

18. $8\frac{1}{4} + 4\frac{1}{2} + 1\frac{3}{4}$

19. $1\frac{7}{8} + 2\frac{3}{4} + 4\frac{1}{2}$

20. $6\frac{5}{6} + 7\frac{3}{4} + 3\frac{1}{6}$

More Practice, page 513, set B

Subtracting Mixed Numbers

EXPLORE Analyze the Process

Mortimer Mouse won the high jump with a jump of $9\frac{1}{4}$ in. Miranda Mouse jumped $7\frac{1}{2}$ in. How much higher was Mortimer's jump?

Here is how to find the answer.

Look at the denominators.	Find equivalent fractions with like denominators.	Rename if necessary. Subtract the fractions.	Subtract the whole numbers.
$9\frac{1}{4}$ ← Not the same $-7\frac{1}{2}$	$9\frac{1}{4} = 9\frac{1}{4}$ $-7\frac{1}{2} = 7\frac{2}{4}$	$9\frac{1}{4} = 8\frac{5}{4}$ $-7\frac{2}{4} = 7\frac{2}{4}$ $\frac{3}{4}$	$8\frac{5}{4}$ $-7\frac{2}{4}$ $1\frac{3}{4}$

TALK ABOUT IT

1. Why was $9\frac{1}{4}$ renamed?
2. How could you have estimated the difference?
3. Give the answer to the Explore problem in a complete sentence.

Other Examples

A $\begin{aligned} 14 &= 13\frac{3}{3} \\ -12\frac{2}{3} &= 12\frac{2}{3} \\ \hline & 1\frac{1}{3} \end{aligned}$

B $\begin{aligned} 12\frac{1}{3} &= 12\frac{2}{6} = 11\frac{8}{6} \\ -9\frac{5}{6} &= 9\frac{5}{6} = 9\frac{5}{6} \\ \hline &\phantom{=9\frac{5}{6} =} 2\frac{3}{6} = 2\frac{1}{2} \end{aligned}$

Subtract.

1. $6\frac{1}{3}$ $-3\frac{2}{3}$

2. 11 $-6\frac{3}{5}$

3. $7\frac{2}{5}$ $-3\frac{7}{10}$

4. $9\frac{2}{3}$ $-6\frac{5}{6}$

5. $11\frac{3}{4}$ $-5\frac{3}{8}$

286

Subtract. Reduce answers to lowest terms.

1. $6\frac{1}{5}$ 2. $8\frac{1}{4}$ 3. $10\frac{1}{3}$ 4. 22 5. $32\frac{1}{6}$
$-3\frac{5}{10}$ $-3\frac{3}{4}$ $-4\frac{2}{3}$ $-9\frac{5}{8}$ $-10\frac{5}{12}$

6. $47\frac{5}{8}$ 7. $41\frac{1}{2}$ 8. $86\frac{1}{3}$ 9. $60\frac{1}{6}$ 10. $52\frac{3}{8}$
$-11\frac{3}{4}$ $-7\frac{1}{10}$ $-38\frac{3}{4}$ $-7\frac{4}{5}$ $-27\frac{4}{5}$

Estimate each difference.

11. $67\frac{3}{5} - 48\frac{1}{3}$ 12. $60\frac{3}{4} - 26$ 13. $87\frac{1}{5} - 16\frac{9}{10}$ 14. $43\frac{1}{4} - 29\frac{5}{8}$

MATH REASONING

Use **mental math** to write the number for each ▒.

15. $5\frac{3}{8} + 7\frac{1}{6} = 12\frac{13}{24} \rightarrow 5\frac{3}{8} + 5\frac{1}{6} = $ ▒

16. $8\frac{4}{5} - 3\frac{1}{2} = 5\frac{3}{10} \rightarrow 10\frac{4}{5} - 3\frac{1}{2} = $ ▒

PROBLEM SOLVING

17. Mortimer Mouse set a new pole vault record of 15 in. The old record was only $8\frac{1}{4}$ in. By how much did he break the record?

18. Miranda Mouse broke the old record for the long jump event by a length of $3\frac{3}{4}$ in. The old record was $18\frac{5}{8}$ in. How far did Miranda jump?

Give the correct sign ($>$, $<$, or $=$) for each ▒.

19. $\frac{2}{4}$ ▒ $\frac{2}{4}$ 20. $\frac{3}{4}$ ▒ $\frac{2}{5}$ 21. $\frac{7}{8}$ ▒ $\frac{14}{16}$ 22. $\frac{4}{16}$ ▒ $\frac{2}{4}$

Divide and check.

23. $24,805 \div 41$ 24. $22,790 \div 53$ 25. $12,749 \div 61$ 26. $\$329.67 \div 37$

More Practice, page 513, set C

More Adding and Subtracting
Whole Numbers, Fractions, and Mixed Numbers

EXPLORE Analyze the Process

On a recording of readings of popular poems, "Gunga Din" lasts $4\frac{1}{2}$ min, "The Owl and the Pussycat" lasts $1\frac{3}{4}$ min, and "The Highwayman" lasts 7 min. What is the total time needed for listening to these three poems?

To solve the problem, add 7, $1\frac{3}{4}$, and $4\frac{1}{2}$. Here is how.

Look at the denominators.	Find equivalent fractions with like denominators.	Add or subtract the fractions.	Add or subtract the whole numbers.
$4\frac{1}{2}$ $\underset{\text{Not the same}}{\Longleftarrow}$ $1\frac{3}{4}$ $+7$	$4\frac{1}{2} = 4\frac{2}{4}$ $1\frac{3}{4} = 1\frac{3}{4}$ $+7 = 7$	$4\frac{2}{4}$ $1\frac{3}{4}$ $+7$ $\frac{5}{4}$	$4\frac{2}{4}$ $1\frac{3}{4}$ $+7$ $12\frac{5}{4} = 13\frac{1}{4}$

TALK ABOUT IT

1. What is the least common denominator for the fractions?
2. Give the answer to the Explore problem in a complete sentence.

Other Examples

A
$$\frac{5}{6} = \frac{25}{30}$$
$$+3\frac{1}{5} = 3\frac{6}{30}$$
$$3\frac{31}{30} = 4\frac{1}{30}$$

B
$$8 = 7\frac{3}{3}$$
$$-4\frac{2}{3} = 4\frac{2}{3}$$
$$3\frac{1}{3}$$

C
$$16 = 15\frac{5}{5}$$
$$-\frac{4}{5} = \frac{4}{5}$$
$$15\frac{1}{5}$$

Add or subtract. Reduce answers to lowest terms.

1.
$$\frac{3}{4}$$
$$+6\frac{5}{8}$$

2.
$$23$$
$$-4\frac{7}{10}$$

3.
$$30\frac{4}{5}$$
$$-12\frac{5}{6}$$

4.
$$9\frac{3}{5}$$
$$+\frac{9}{10}$$

5.
$$12\frac{1}{2}$$
$$+\frac{7}{8}$$

Add or subtract. Reduce answers to lowest terms.

1. $9\frac{1}{3}$
$+ 4\frac{1}{6}$

2. $6\frac{7}{8}$
$- \frac{2}{4}$

3. 12
$- 7\frac{1}{5}$

4. $14\frac{2}{5}$
$+ 8$

5. $26\frac{5}{6}$
$+ 14\frac{1}{6}$

6. $32\frac{1}{3}$
$- 16\frac{5}{15}$

7. 62
$+ 34\frac{4}{12}$

8. $\frac{9}{12}$
$+ \frac{3}{8}$

9. 48
$- 31\frac{7}{10}$

10. 28
$- 2\frac{5}{8}$

11. $37\frac{2}{3}$
$+ 68\frac{3}{5}$

12. $\frac{21}{4}$
$+ \frac{55}{8}$

13. $\frac{13}{8} - \frac{2}{3}$

14. $26\frac{4}{8} + 4 + \frac{3}{5}$

15. $73 - 6\frac{3}{8}$

16. $13\frac{4}{5} + 20\frac{2}{3} + 10$

Estimate each sum or difference.

17. $49\frac{7}{8} + 24\frac{6}{12}$

18. $38\frac{2}{3} - 27\frac{5}{6}$

19. $14\frac{1}{8} + 11\frac{9}{10}$

20. $28\frac{1}{4} - 5\frac{5}{6}$

MATH REASONING

Write a mixed number that will give a sum or difference in the given range.

21. $5\frac{5}{8} + x\frac{y}{z}$ is between 9 and 10.

22. $12\frac{1}{3} - x\frac{y}{z}$ is between 6 and 7.

PROBLEM SOLVING

23. A public reading of two poems at the library took 15 min. When Luis read the same two poems silently it took him only $8\frac{1}{4}$ min. How much less was the silent reading time?

24. Language Arts Data Bank On the recording *A Treasury of Great Poems,* how much less time does the poem by Lear take than the poem by Poe? How much less time than the poem by Hay? See page 469.

▶ **USING CRITICAL THINKING   Discover a Pattern**

Give the missing numbers.

25. $4\frac{1}{2}$, 6, $7\frac{1}{2}$, ▓▓▓, ▓▓▓

26. $3\frac{1}{3}$, 5, $6\frac{2}{3}$, ▓▓▓, ▓▓▓

27. ▓▓▓, ▓▓▓, $32\frac{1}{2}$, 25, $17\frac{1}{2}$

28. $\frac{1}{8}$, $\frac{1}{4}$, $\frac{3}{8}$, ▓▓▓, ▓▓▓

29. $1\frac{1}{4}$, $2\frac{1}{2}$, $3\frac{3}{4}$, ▓▓▓, ▓▓▓

30. 6, $4\frac{7}{8}$, $3\frac{3}{4}$, ▓▓▓, ▓▓▓

Problem Solving
Choosing a Calculation Method

UNDERSTAND
ANALYZE DATA
PLAN
ESTIMATE
SOLVE
EXAMINE

LEARN ABOUT IT

Before using paper and pencil to add or subtract fractions, look carefully at the fractions. Some fractions can be added or subtracted easily using mental math.

> Three soil samples were collected for a science experiment. The weights of the samples were $12\frac{1}{4}$ oz, $7\frac{1}{2}$ oz, and $10\frac{3}{4}$ oz. What was the total weight of the soil samples?

I need an exact answer. Here's what I need to find.

$12\frac{1}{4} + 7\frac{1}{2} + 10\frac{3}{4}$

$\frac{1}{4}$ and $\frac{3}{4}$ are compatible fractions. I can use mental math.

Think: $12\frac{1}{4} + 10\frac{3}{4}$
is $12 + 10 + 1$, or 23.
23 and $7\frac{1}{2}$ is $30\frac{1}{2}$.

The total weight of the soil samples was $30\frac{1}{2}$ oz.

TRY IT OUT

Solve. Explain your choice of calculation method.

1. Tamara started an experiment with 12 oz. of water. At the end she had $2\frac{1}{2}$ oz. How much water did she use for her experiment?

2. The rectangular lid of a soil sample box is $3\frac{1}{4}$ in. long and $2\frac{1}{2}$ in. wide. What is its perimeter?

3. A half an orange weighs $7\frac{1}{4}$ oz. When it has been dried out completely, it weighs $2\frac{2}{5}$ oz. How heavy was the water in the orange slice?

4. The total weight of two soil samples is $10\frac{3}{4}$ oz. One sample weighs $7\frac{1}{4}$ oz. What is the weight of the other sample?

Solve. Use any problem solving strategies to solve the problems. Use data from the table as needed.

Sizes of Mice		
	Length in Inches	
Mouse	Head and Body	Tail
White-footed	$3\frac{3}{4}$	$3\frac{1}{5}$
Grasshopper	$2\frac{1}{2}$	$1\frac{7}{10}$
Meadow	$6\frac{7}{8}$	$3\frac{1}{4}$

1. How much longer is the head and body of the white-footed mouse than the head and body of the grasshopper mouse?

2. Hamsters take 75 breaths per minute. A hamster's heart beats 260 to 600 times per minute. How many breaths do hamsters take in an hour?

3. Terry, Roger, and Amy Bolt bought the supplies for their guinea pig. They each paid the same amount. How much was that?
$3.99 water bottle $2.19 vegetables
$2.99 dish $1.78 pellet food

4. A guinea pig's normal temperature is 99.5°F. A human's temperature is 98.6°F. How many degrees less is a human's normal temperature?

5. About how much shorter is the head and body of the white-footed mouse than the head and body of the meadow mouse?

6. Alice, Bunky, Marv, and Rick have rodents for pets. One has a mouse, one a hamster, one a rat, and one a guinea pig. Bunky does not have a mouse. Rick has a rat. The name of the kind of pet Marv has does not start with the letter **g**. Alice would not like to own a hamster or a mouse. What pet does each person have?

7. What is the total length of the grasshopper mouse from head to tail?

8. Anita's golden hamster eats 16 oz of dry food in a month. Anita has 68 oz of that food at home. How many full months of food is this?

9. Finishing the Solution Linda's white-footed mouse's total length was 4 in. when she bought it. It grew $\frac{1}{2}$ in. the first month she had it and $\frac{1}{8}$ in. less than that during the second, third, and fourth months. What was its total length at the end of the fourth month? Copy and complete the table.

	Start	1st Month	2nd Month	3rd Month	4th Month
Length at beginning of month	4 in.	4 in.	$4\frac{1}{2}$ in.		
Growth during month	0	$\frac{1}{2}$ in.	$\frac{3}{8}$ in.		
Length at end of month	4 in.	$4\frac{1}{2}$ in.			

More Practice, page 514, set B; page 526, set A

Data Collection and Analysis
Group Decision Making

UNDERSTAND
ANALYZE DATA
PLAN
ESTIMATE
SOLVE
EXAMINE

Doing a Survey
Group Skill:
Check for Understanding

In your school, who would like to have a dog as a pet, more girls or more boys? Who thinks dogs are hard to take care of, girls or boys? Make some predictions and then conduct a survey to find out.

Collecting Data

1. Work with your group to think of two questions to ask in a survey about dogs as pets. Write the questions so that the answer is a rating from 1 to 10.

   Sample Question:
   On a scale from 1 to 10, how much do you like playing with a dog? (1 means **not at all** and 10 means **very much**.)

2. You will need at least 15 girls and 15 boys so that you can compare these groups. Talk about how to make sure that your sample fairly represents the students in your school.

3. Conduct your survey. Make a table to record your results, as in the sample shown.

Survey Results	
Question 1	Boys' Ratings: 2, 9, 9, 5, 6, 10, 7, 5, 5, 3, 9, 10, 8, 6, 8 Girls' Ratings: 4, 6, 10, 4, 8, 1, 7, 6, 7, 3, 9, 2, 3, 6, 5, 4
Question 2	Boys' Ratings: Girls' Ratings:

4. Find the sums of the boys' ratings for each question and the sums of the girls' ratings for each question. Make a double bar graph to show the sums.

Question 1   Sum of the boys' ratings: 102
Sum of the girls' ratings: 85

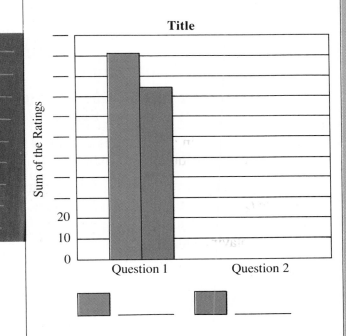

Title

Sum of the Ratings

20

10

0

Question 1   Question 2

Presenting Your Analysis

5. Write a summary to tell about your survey. Be sure to include the questions you asked, how you selected your sample, and what you found.

6. Give two or three reasons that you think led to the results that you found.

293

WRAP UP

Come to Terms with Fractions

Choose the term that correctly completes each sentence.

1. To add or subtract fractions with like denominators, add or subtract the numerators and write the answer over the __?__.

2. To find the least common denominator for two fractions, find the __?__ of the denominators.

3. To add or subtract fractions with unlike denominators, first rename the fractions as __?__ with common denominators.

4. When adding mixed numbers, if the sum of the fractional parts is greater than 1 you should __?__.

A. rename

B. least common multiple

C. common denominator

D. equivalent fractions

Sometimes, Always, Never

Complete each statement by writing **sometimes**, **always**, or **never**. Explain your choices.

5. A problem __?__ has a solution.

6. If two fractions have the same denominator, their sum is __?__ the sum of the numerators over the sum of the denominators.

7. The least common denominator (LCD) of two fractions is __?__ the same as the least common multiple (LCM) of the two denominators.

8. You __?__ need to rename a mixed number before subtracting.

Project

Find these sums. What pattern do you notice? What are the next three sums?

A. $\frac{1}{2} + \frac{1}{4}$

B. $\frac{1}{2} + \frac{1}{4} + \frac{1}{8}$

C. $\frac{1}{2} + \frac{1}{4} + \frac{1}{8} + \frac{1}{16}$

D. $\frac{1}{2} + \frac{1}{4} + \frac{1}{8} + \frac{1}{16} + \frac{1}{32}$

E. $\frac{1}{2} + \frac{1}{4} + \frac{1}{8} + \frac{1}{16} + \frac{1}{32} + \frac{1}{64}$

POWER PRACTICE/TEST

Part 1   Understanding

1. Show how to estimate $3\frac{1}{8} + 4\frac{11}{12} + 2\frac{3}{5}$ using compatible numbers. Substitute whole numbers or $\frac{1}{2}$.

2. Show how to estimate $8\frac{7}{8} - 3\frac{1}{4}$ using rounding.

Use fraction pieces to find each sum or difference. Record what you did. Reduce answers to lowest terms.

3. $\frac{7}{12} - \frac{2}{6}$

4. $3\frac{1}{2} + 4\frac{5}{6}$

5. $8\frac{1}{2} - 5\frac{3}{8}$

Part 2   Skills

Find the least common multiple for each set of numbers.

6. 3 and 7

7. 5 and 8

8. 2 and 15

Add or subtract. Reduce answers to lowest terms.

9. $\frac{5}{4} + \frac{1}{2}$

10. $\frac{5}{12} - \frac{1}{12}$

11. $\frac{3}{8} + \frac{3}{6}$

12. $\frac{7}{10} - \frac{1}{6}$

13. $\begin{array}{r} 15\frac{1}{3} \\ + 23\frac{1}{2} \\ \hline \end{array}$

14. $\begin{array}{r} 8 \\ + 4\frac{2}{3} \\ \hline \end{array}$

15. $\begin{array}{r} 50\frac{7}{8} \\ - 41\frac{2}{3} \\ \hline \end{array}$

16. $\begin{array}{r} 7 \\ - 2\frac{1}{9} \\ \hline \end{array}$

Part 3   Applications

17. Marsha's dog weighed $67\frac{1}{4}$ lb. It now weighs $72\frac{5}{6}$ lb. How much weight did it gain?

18. Byron needs $4\frac{3}{8}$ ft of blue ribbon and $2\frac{1}{2}$ ft of white ribbon. How much ribbon does he need in all?

19. If the problem has a solution, give it. If it has no solution, explain why not.
Eva spent exactly $4.35 on stamps. She bought only $0.25 stamps. How many stamps did she buy?

20. **Challenge.** A unit fraction is a fraction with a numerator of 1. $\frac{1}{6}$ and $\frac{1}{2}$ are unit fractions. All fractions can be written as the sum of unit fractions. Find two unit fractions that have a sum of $\frac{7}{12}$. Try some others on your own.

ENRICHMENT
Fractions Between Fractions

You can make rulers to find numbers between numbers. To find a number halfway between 3 and 8, label a paper ruler as shown and fold it so the 8 falls on the 3.

Where is the fold?

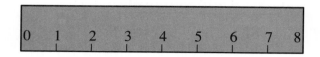

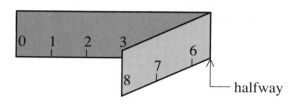

Think: $3 + 2\frac{1}{2} = 5\frac{1}{2}$

$8 - 2\frac{1}{2} = 5\frac{1}{2}$

$5\frac{1}{2}$ is halfway between 3 and 8, so the fold is at about $5\frac{1}{2}$.

There is always another fraction between any two fractions. You can make fraction rulers to find fractions halfway between fractions. To find a number halfway between $\frac{1}{4}$ and $\frac{2}{3}$, label a paper ruler as shown and fold it so $\frac{2}{3}$ falls on $\frac{1}{4}$. Where is the fold?

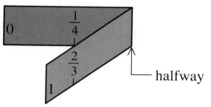

To find the name of the fraction halfway between $\frac{1}{4}$ and $\frac{2}{3}$:

Step 1
Write equivalent fractions using the least common denominator, 12.

$\frac{1}{4} = \frac{3}{12}$ Can you tell what is

$\frac{2}{3} = \frac{8}{12}$ halfway between? No.

Step 2
Try another pair of equivalent fractions. Multiply both fractions by $\frac{2}{2}$.

$\frac{3}{12} \times \frac{2}{2} = \frac{6}{24}$ $6 + 5 = 11$

$\frac{8}{12} \times \frac{2}{2} = \frac{16}{24}$ $16 - 5 = 11$

$\frac{11}{24}$ is halfway between $\frac{1}{4}$ and $\frac{2}{3}$.

Find a fraction halfway between each pair of fractions.

1. $\frac{5}{9}$ and $\frac{6}{9}$

2. $\frac{6}{15}$ and $\frac{7}{15}$

3. $\frac{1}{9}$ and $\frac{2}{3}$

4. $\frac{2}{3}$ and $\frac{4}{5}$

5. $\frac{3}{4}$ and $\frac{4}{5}$

6. $\frac{1}{2}$ and $\frac{1}{3}$

296

CUMULATIVE REVIEW

1. Which fraction is equivalent to $\frac{9}{12}$?

   A. $\frac{6}{9}$ **B.** $\frac{2}{3}$ **C.** $\frac{10}{13}$ **D.** $\frac{6}{8}$

2. Rename $4\frac{5}{9}$ as an improper fraction.

   A. $\frac{36}{9}$ **B.** $\frac{41}{9}$ **C.** $\frac{36}{5}$ **D.** $\frac{41}{5}$

3. What pattern can you use to complete this table?

B	5	10	15	20	25	30
W	17	32	47	62		

   A. $W = B - 12$

   B. $W = (3 \times B) + 2$

   C. $W = B + 22$

   D. $W = (2 \times B) + 7$

Divide.

4. $4,800 \div 80$

   A. 6   **B.** 60   **C.** 600   **D.** 6,000

5. $37\overline{)1,999}$

   A. 54 R1   **B.** 540 R1

   C. 49 R5   **D.** 495 R1

6. Choose the greatest common factor of 32 and 24.

   A. 12   **B.** 6   **C.** 4   **D.** 8

7. What improper fraction names the shaded part?

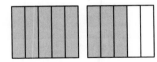

   A. $\frac{8}{5}$ **B.** $\frac{10}{8}$ **C.** $\frac{8}{2}$ **D.** $\frac{8}{10}$

8. Reduce $\frac{32}{72}$ to lowest terms.

   A. $\frac{16}{36}$ **B.** $\frac{8}{18}$

   C. $\frac{4}{9}$ **D.** $\frac{5}{6}$

9. Find the average of this set of data:
4,252; 5,016; 358; 7,914.

   A. 7,556   **B.** 2,305

   C. 17,540   **D.** 4,385

10. What compatible numbers would you use to divide 5,745 by 8?

   A. $5,700 \div 8$ **B.** $5,600 \div 8$

   C. $6,400 \div 10$ **D.** $4,800 \div 8$

11. Which answer is reasonable? A truck delivered 625 watermelons to the supermarket. If the average weight of each melon is 20 lb, about how many pounds of melons were delivered?

   A. 120   **B.** 1,200

   C. 12,000   **D.** 120,000

12. Eileen, Joyce, Ray, and Dawn are two sets of twins. One is a veterinarian, one a computer operator, one a musician, and one a truck driver. The musician is not female. Eileen and Joyce have lunch every week with the computer operator. Joyce's sister is her cat's veterinarian. Who is the truck driver?

   A. Eileen   **B.** Joyce

   C. Ray   **D.** Dawn

11

CUSTOMARY MEASUREMENT

THEME: SEA CREATURES

MATH AND SCIENCE

DATA BANK

Use the Science Data Bank on page 472 to answer the questions.

1 Look at the graph showing the sizes of full-grown whales. Which would be the better estimate of the length of a full-grown right whale, 60 feet or 80 feet?

Conservation efforts of recent decades have led to population increases for some endangered species of whales.

2 What kind of full-grown whale is 12 times the length of a young dolphin that is only 5 feet long?

3 On an average day about how many waves per hour strike the beach described in the article on the movement of beach sands?

4 **Using Critical Thinking** Julio said, "I can see that 2 grown fin whales would have a total weight greater than that of 1 grown blue whale." Do you believe Julio is correct? Explain your answer.

Customary Units of Length

LEARN ABOUT IT

EXPLORE Make a Measurement
Work in groups. Measure each of your heights to the nearest inch. What different units can you use to record your height—inches, feet, yards?

1 foot (ft) = 12 inches (in.)
1 yard (yd) = 3 ft = 36 in.

TALK ABOUT IT

1. How many inches tall are you?
2. Give your height in feet and inches.
3. Is your height closest to 4 ft, 5 ft, or 2 yd? Explain your answer.

Sometimes we use two units instead of one to give a measure. It is usually easier to think about a person's height as 5 ft 2 in. rather than 62 in. Here is how to change units like these.

To change smaller units to larger units, divide.

Example: Change 59 in. to feet and inches.

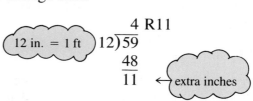

12 in. = 1 ft

$$\begin{array}{r} 4\ \text{R}11 \\ 12\overline{)59} \\ 48 \\ \hline 11 \end{array}$$ ← extra inches

So 59 in. = 4 ft 11 in.

To change larger units to smaller units, multiply.

Example: Change 6 ft 5 in. to inches.

$$\begin{array}{r} 12 \\ \times\ 6 \\ \hline 72 \end{array}$$ ← 12 in. = 1 ft

$$\begin{array}{r} 72 \\ +\ 5 \\ \hline 77 \end{array}$$ ← extra inches

So 6 ft 5 in. = 77 in.

TRY IT OUT

Change the units in each measurement.

1. 97 in. = ▦ ft ▦ in.

2. 114 in. = ▦ ft ▦ in.

3. 50 in. = ▦ ft ▦ in.

4. 7 ft 4 in. = ▦ in.

5. 3 ft 5 in. = ▦ in.

6. 4 ft 7 in. = ▦ in.

300

Change each measure to inches.

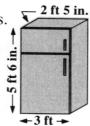

1. refrigerator height
2. refrigerator width
3. refrigerator depth

4. dresser width
5. dresser depth
6. dresser height

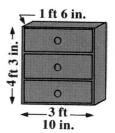

Change each measure to feet and inches.

7. TV width
8. TV height
9. TV depth

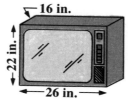

10. van width
11. van length
12. van height

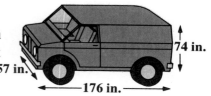

APPLY

MATH REASONING

Does this make sense? Write **yes** or **no**. Tell why or why not.

13. A basketball player 7 ft 4 in. tall has a bed 78 in. long.

14. A curtain 54 in. wide covers a window 4 ft 3 in. wide.

15. An extension cord 3 yd long is used to reach a distance of 8 ft 6 in.

PROBLEM SOLVING

16. Mary needed 100 in. of ribbon. She bought a roll with 9 ft of ribbon. Was there enough ribbon? If so, how much will she have left over?

17. **Suppose** Tell which of the following items of information would change the solution to problem 16.
   A. Mary needed 75 in. of ribbon.
   B. The package had 10 ft of ribbon.
   C. The ribbon was 1 inch wide.

► **MENTAL MATH**

You can often use mental math to add measurements given in feet and inches. First think how many feet and how many inches. Then change units if necessary.

Try this method to add these measurements.

3 ft 5 in. + 4 ft 9 in. = 7 ft 14 in.
(7 ft) *(14 in.)* *(14 in. = 1 ft 2 in.)*
or 8 ft 2 in.

18. 4 ft 8 in. + 2 ft 8 in.
20. 7 ft 2 in. + 2 ft 10 in.

19. 1 ft 10 in. + 3 ft 6 in.
21. 6 ft 3 in. + 7 ft 8 in.

Length
Parts of an Inch

EXPLORE Examine the Data

Paul recorded the length of the horseshoe crab, with and without its tail, in 4 different ways.

	Whole crab (with tail)	Crab's body
Nearest inch	4 in.	2 in.
Nearest $\frac{1}{2}$ inch	$3\frac{1}{2}$ in.	$2\frac{1}{2}$ in.
Nearest $\frac{1}{4}$ inch	$3\frac{1}{2}$ in.	$2\frac{1}{2}$ in.
Nearest $\frac{1}{8}$ inch	$3\frac{5}{8}$ in.	$2\frac{3}{8}$ in.

TALK ABOUT IT

1. Why can different measurements be given for the length of the whole crab?
2. Why are some of the measurements for the body length the same?
3. For each length, which measurement is the most accurate?

The smaller the part of a unit in a measurement, the more precise the measurement. In the data above, $3\frac{5}{8}$ in. is a more precise measurement than $3\frac{1}{2}$ in.

TRY IT OUT

Measure your math book cover to the nearest inch or the given part of an inch.

Width

1. nearest inch
2. nearest $\frac{1}{2}$ inch
3. nearest $\frac{1}{4}$ inch
4. nearest $\frac{1}{8}$ inch

Length (height)

5. nearest inch
6. nearest $\frac{1}{2}$ inch
7. nearest $\frac{1}{4}$ inch
8. nearest $\frac{1}{8}$ inch

Which of the objects shown at the right measure

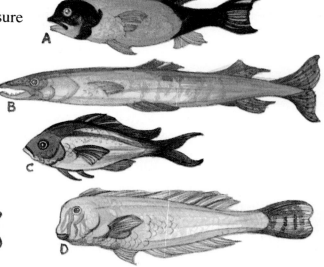

1. between 2 in. and 3 in. long?

2. 2 in. long to the nearest inch?

3. $2\frac{1}{2}$ in. long to the nearest $\frac{1}{2}$ inch?

4. 3 in. long to the nearest $\frac{1}{2}$ inch?

5. $2\frac{3}{4}$ in. long to the nearest $\frac{1}{4}$ inch?

6. $3\frac{3}{8}$ in. long to the nearest $\frac{1}{8}$ inch?

APPLY

MATH REASONING

Which is the more precise measurement for each length?
Explain why.

7.

   A. $1\frac{7}{8}$ in.   **B.** 2 in.

8.

   A. $2\frac{5}{8}$ in.   **B.** $2\frac{3}{4}$ in.

DATA BANK

PROBLEM SOLVING

9. Paul is building a frame for a model of a tidepool. He cut a board $34\frac{1}{2}$ in. long from a board 4 ft long. How long was the piece that was left over?

10. **Science Data Bank**   Do you think that lengths listed for the whales on this graph are measurements to the nearest one foot, five feet, or ten feet? See page 472.

▶ **ALGEBRA**

Remember, the formula for finding the area of a rectangle is
$A = l \times w$.

11. Find the length of a rectangle if $A = 240$ in.^{2} and $w = 12$ in.

12. Find the width of a rectangle if $A = 144$ in.^{2} and $l = 14.4$ in.

13. Find the area of a rectangle if $l = 20$ in. and $w = 16$ in.

More Practice, page 514, set D

Length
Feet, Yards, and Miles

LEARN ABOUT IT

You have worked with the foot as a unit of measurement.
Here you will work with larger units.

EXPLORE Make Some Estimates

A 1-inch segment is shown at the right.
Use this to help you make the following
estimates.

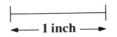
← 1 inch →

- My math book is about ▒ inches long.
- A baseball bat is about ▒ inches long.
- A baseball bat is about ▒ math books long.

TALK ABOUT IT

1. Explain how you made your decisions for each situation.
2. Which of your estimates do you think is closest to the
   actual length? Explain why you think so.
3. Which estimate was most difficult to make? Why?

The **yard (yd)** is a customary unit of
length.

A baseball bat is about a yard long.
1 yd = 3 ft = 36 in.

The **mile (mi)** is a customary unit of
length used for measuring long distances.

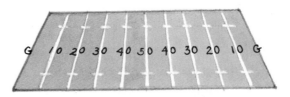
G 10 20 30 40 50 40 30 20 10 G

15 football fields laid end to end would be
about 1 mile long.
1 mi = 1,760 yd = 5,280 ft

TRY IT OUT

Which unit would you use? Write in., ft, yd, or mi.

1. An airplane might fly 6 __?__ high.
2. An automobile is about 14 __?__ long.
3. A long step might be about 1 __?__ long.

Write the unit (in., ft, yd, mi) you would use to measure the following.

1. the length of your classroom
2. the length of a train track
3. the length of a city block
4. the distance of an hour's bike ride
5. the height of a flagpole
6. the distance across a river
7. the height of a skyscraper
8. the perimeter of your school building
9. the distance you walk each week
10. the distance between two cities

APPLY

MATH REASONING

Use mental math to give the number for each ▦ .

11. 6 yd = ▦ ft
12. 2 yd = ▦ in.
13. 10 mi = ▦ ft

14. 24 ft = ▦ yd
15. 100 yd = ▦ ft
16. 10 yd = ▦ in.

PROBLEM SOLVING

Tell whether the distance described in problems 17 and 18 is **more than, less than,** or **about** 1 mile.

17. distance around your school playground

18. distance around a large city park

19. **Data Hunt** About how many fifth grade students standing fingertip to fingertip with arms stretched out would it take to make 1 mi?

MIXED REVIEW

Rename each mixed number as an improper fraction.

20. $4\frac{2}{3}$
21. $3\frac{3}{8}$
22. $7\frac{4}{5}$
23. $3\frac{1}{3}$
24. $2\frac{5}{6}$
25. $3\frac{3}{10}$

Subtract. Reduce to lowest terms.

26. $\frac{5}{6}$ $-\frac{1}{6}$
27. $\frac{7}{10}$ $-\frac{4}{10}$
28. $\frac{7}{12}$ $-\frac{5}{12}$
29. $\frac{5}{6}$ $-\frac{2}{6}$
30. $\frac{4}{5}$ $-\frac{3}{5}$
31. $\frac{5}{8}$ $-\frac{3}{8}$

More Practice, page 515, set A

Problem Solving
Problems with More Than One Answer

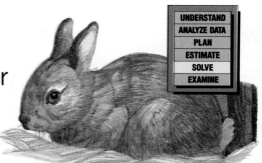

UNDERSTAND
ANALYZE DATA
PLAN
ESTIMATE
SOLVE
EXAMINE

LEARN ABOUT IT

Some problems have more than one answer. After you find one answer to a problem, ask yourself if other answers are possible.

> I could use guess and check to find an answer.

> I should check for other answers. I can organize my work in a table.

The floor of the rabbit hutch Rick is building is 48 ft². Each side is a whole number of feet. What is the perimeter of the floor?

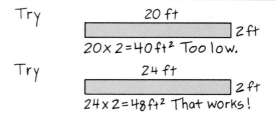

Try   20 ft   2 ft
20 x 2 = 40 ft² Too low.

Try   24 ft   2 ft
24 x 2 = 48 ft² That works!

length	width	area	perimeter
1	48	48	98
2	24	48	52
3	16	48	38
4	12	48	32
5	(will not work)		
6	8	48	28
7	(will not work)		
8	6 (same as 6 and 8)		

There are 5 possible answers for the perimeter of the floor.
The perimeter could be 98 ft, 52 ft, 38 ft, 32 ft, or 28 ft.

TRY IT OUT

Solve. Find as many answers as possible.

1. To make a coaster car, Gretchen used a piece of plywood with an area of 24 ft². The length of each side of the plywood is a whole number of feet. What is the perimeter of the piece?

2. The workbench Adam and Marti made had a perimeter of 20 ft. Each side was a whole number of feet. How wide and how long was the workbench?

3. Rico entered a coaster car in a race. There were 3-wheeled cars and 4-wheeled cars. He counted 26 wheels in all. How many 3-wheeled and 4-wheeled cars did he see?

4. The raft Harry built is 35 ft². The length of each side is a whole number of feet. What is the perimeter?

MIXED PRACTICE

Solve. Choose any of the listed strategies or use any other strategy you know.

1. The following people got on the raft Harry built:

Name	Weight	Age
Mingel	102 lb	10 years old
Ben	127 lb	11 years old
Tommy Lee	132 lb	9 years old
Ben's father	212 lb	41 years old
Margy	113 lb	10 years old

What was the average weight of the children on the raft?

2. What is the total height of one of the stilts that Rudy built?

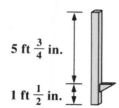

5 ft $\frac{3}{4}$ in.

1 ft $\frac{1}{2}$ in.

3. Gail spent a total of $35 for lumber to build a workbench and a raft. She spent $9 more on the lumber for the raft. How much did she pay for the lumber for the workbench?

4. Joe had a piece of lumber 3 ft 5 in. long. He sawed off a piece 9 in. long to make a sign. How long was the piece of lumber that was left?

Some Strategies	
Act Out	Make a Table
Use Objects	Solve a Simpler Problem
Choose an Operation	Make an Organized List
Draw a Picture	Work Backward
Guess and Check	Look for a Pattern
Use Logical Reasoning	

5. Peter made a set of blocks for his little brother Mo. He sawed a piece of wood 8 in. long into pieces of a whole number of inches of the same length. How many pieces did he saw the wood into?

6. Peter built Mo some steps with blocks. It took 1 block to make 1 step, 3 blocks to make 2 steps, and so on. How many steps did he make with 36 blocks?

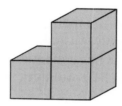

7. Chris needed a piece of wood $5\frac{3}{4}$ ft long for his puppet theater. About how much wood will he have left from a piece of lumber that is $8\frac{1}{12}$ long?

8. **Developing a Plan**   Tell what steps you could follow to solve this problem. Find all of the correct choices. Sandra bought 12 pieces of lumber at $2.99 each. Sandra and 3 of her friends split the cost equally. How much did each pay?
   A. Divide $2.99 by 4. Multiply by 12.
   B. Multiply 12 times $2.99. Divide by 4.
   C. Divide $2.99 by 12. Multiply by 4.

Temperature
Degrees Fahrenheit

LEARN ABOUT IT

EXPLORE Study the Situation

When Joni didn't feel well on Sunday night, her father took her body temperature. The thermometer her father used shows a mark for every 0.2 degrees.

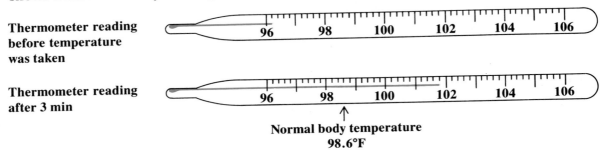

Thermometer reading before temperature was taken

Thermometer reading after 3 min

↑
**Normal body temperature
98.6°F**

TALK ABOUT IT

1. What did the thermometer read before Joni's temperature was taken?
2. What was her temperature at the end of 3 min?
3. How much above normal is Joni's temperature?

TRY IT OUT

Joni's temperature readings for two days are shown below. Give each temperature to the nearest tenth of one degree.

	Monday	Tuesday
8:00 a.m.	1.	2.
1:00 p.m.	3.	4.
7:00 p.m.	5.	6.

7. Give the day and the time that Joni's temperature was the highest.

More Practice, page 515, set B

POWER PRACTICE/QUIZ

Change each measure to feet and inches.

1. 72 in.   **2.** 40 in.   **3.** 27 in.   **4.** 50 in.

5. Which of the measures in exercises 1−4 are longer than a yard?

Measure each side of the triangle.

6. What is the measure of side A to the nearest inch?

7. What is the measure of side B to the nearest half inch?

8. What is the measure of side C to the nearest quarter inch?

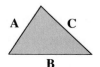

Decide which unit—in., ft, yd, or mi—would be most reasonable to use to measure the following lengths or distances.

9. from your desk to the door

10. your walking step

11. a 1-hour bike ride

12. length of your foot

13. from your home to school

14. from Florida to Iowa

15. length of a football field

16. width of your notebook

PROBLEM SOLVING

Solve. Find as many solutions as you can.

17. Stuart measured a board and found that its surface area was 48 in². The board's length and width were both a whole number of inches. What are the possible measures of the length and the width?

18. Connie owed her sister 75¢. She repaid her with 5 coins. What coins might Connie have given to her sister?

19. The top of a bookcase that Ms. Kelley built has a perimeter of 16 ft. The top is a whole number of feet in length and width. What might its area be in square feet?

Customary Units of Capacity

You often need to use multiplication or division to help you change customary units of capacity.

EXPLORE Solve to Understand

Arlene needs to put 6 gal (gallons) of water in her fish tank. She is using a quart jar to put the water into the tank. How many times will she need to fill the jar to get enough water?

TALK ABOUT IT

Units of Capacity
2 tablespoons (tbsp) = 1 fluid ounce (fl oz)
8 fl oz = 1 cup (c)
2 c = 1 pint (pt)
2 pt = 1 quart (qt)
2 qt = $\frac{1}{2}$ gallon (gal)
4 qt = 1 gal

1. How many quarts are in one gallon?

2. What operation did you use to find how many times Arlene needed to fill the quart jar?

3. If Arlene told you she had put 16 qt into the tank, how could you find how many gallons that was?

To change smaller units to larger units, you can divide.

Example: Change 8 pt to gallons.

8 pt = 4 qt

First change to quarts. 8 ÷ 2 = 4

4 qt = 1 gal

So 8 pt = 1 gal

To change larger units to smaller units, you can multiply.

Example: Change 3 gal to cups.

3 gal = 12 qt

First change to quarts. 3 × 4 = 12

12 qt = 24 pt

Next change to pints. 2 × 12 = 24

24 pt = 48 c

Next change to cups. 2 × 24 = 48

So 3 gal = 48 c

Give the number for each ▦ .

1. $\frac{1}{2}$ gal = ▦ c

2. 3 qt = ▦ c

3. 16 fl oz = ▦ pt

4. 32 c = ▦ qt

5. $\frac{1}{2}$ pt = ▦ fl oz

6. 1 c = ▦ tbsp

Give the number for each ▦ .

Juice
1 qt 14 oz

Milk
1 gal

Vanilla extract
14 fl oz

Bottled water
1 gal

1. ▦ tablespoons of vanilla extract

2. ▦ cups of bottled water

3. ▦ fluid ounces of juice

4. ▦ pints of milk

Do the pictures show the correct amount for items 5–8?
Explain why or why not.

5. 1 pt sour cream

6. 1 gal milk

7. 1 pt salad dressing

8. 3 c vinegar

vinegar
1 pt

sour cream
16 fl oz

salad dressing
8 fl oz

milk
1 qt

milk
1 qt

milk
1 qt

APPLY

MATH REASONING

Do the statements below make sense? Tell why or why not.

9. A quart jar holds $\frac{1}{2}$ gallon of milk.

10. A gallon jug holds 7 pints of lemonade.

PROBLEM SOLVING

11. Millie and Jose have put 6 qt of water into their fish tank. It holds 4 gal. How many more quarts of water do they need to put into the tank?

12. **Science Data Bank** Ben wants to buy these tropical fish: 1 velvet swordtail, 2 neon tetras, and 2 angelfish. How many gallons of water will he need in a tank for these fish? See page 472.

▶ CALCULATOR

13. Imagine that you have a leaky faucet that drips 2 fl oz of water each hour. About how many gallons of water would you lose from the faucet in 1 week? in 1 month? in 1 year?

More Practice, page 515, set C

311

Customary Units of Weight

The **ounce** (oz), **pound** (lb), and **ton** (T) are frequently used customary units of weight.

about 1 oz

about 1 lb
16 oz = 1 lb

about 1 T
2,000 lb = 1 T

EXPLORE Make Some Estimates

Work in groups. Find some objects that you estimate weigh about 1 oz, about 1 lb, or about 5 lb. Then weigh the objects.

TALK ABOUT IT

1. Were your estimates too high, too low, or about right?
2. Describe your method for estimating weights.

Sometimes we use two units instead of one to give a measure. For instance, we would usually state a baby's weight as 10 lb 3 oz rather than 163 oz.

To change a smaller unit to a larger unit, you can divide.
Example: Change 36 oz to pounds and ounces.

$$16 \text{ oz} = 1 \text{ lb} \quad 16\overline{)36} \quad \begin{array}{r} 2 \text{ R4} \\ \hline \end{array}$$
$$\frac{32}{4} \leftarrow \text{remaining oz}$$

So 36 oz = 2 lb 4 oz

To change a larger unit to a smaller unit, you can multiply.
Example: Change 8 lb 11 oz to ounces.

$$16 \leftarrow 16 \text{ oz} = 1 \text{ lb} \qquad 128$$
$$\times \ \ 8 \qquad\qquad\qquad + \ \ 11 \leftarrow \text{extra oz}$$
$$\overline{128} \qquad\qquad\qquad \overline{139}$$

So 8 lb 11 oz = 139 oz

TRY IT OUT

Give the number for each ▥ .

1. 35 oz = ▥ lb ▥ oz

2. 50 oz = ▥ lb ▥ oz

3. 3 lb 4 oz = ▥ oz

4. 2 lb 8 oz = ▥ oz

5. 3 T = ▥ lb

6. 2,500 lb = ▥ T ▥ lb

Give the number for each ▦ .

1. pancake mix: ▦ lb ▦ oz
2. baked beans: ▦ lb ▦ oz
3. relish: ▦ lb ▦ oz
4. bread: ▦ lb ▦ oz
5. peanut butter: ▦ oz
6. rice: ▦ oz
7. applesauce: ▦ oz
8. cereal: ▦ oz

APPLY

MATH REASONING

Do you have enough? Tell why or why not.

9. You need 1 lb of grapes.
   You have 26 oz.

10. You need 1 T of cement.
    You have four 200-lb bags.

PROBLEM SOLVING

11. How much less does the small bunch of grapes weigh than the large bunch of grapes?

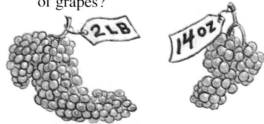

12. **Missing Data** Make up the missing data, then solve. Four students in Mrs. Sutton's class divided a bag of clay equally among them. How much clay did each student get? Give your answer in pounds and ounces.

MIXED REVIEW

Rename each improper fraction as a whole number or as a mixed number in lowest terms.

13. $\frac{16}{4}$
14. $\frac{7}{3}$
15. $\frac{12}{3}$
16. $\frac{10}{4}$
17. $\frac{7}{2}$
18. $\frac{32}{10}$

Add. Reduce to lowest terms.

19. $\frac{2}{3}$
    $+\frac{2}{3}$

20. $\frac{1}{4}$
    $+\frac{3}{4}$

21. $\frac{2}{9}$
    $+\frac{4}{9}$

22. $\frac{5}{8}$
    $+\frac{1}{8}$

23. $\frac{5}{6}$
    $+\frac{5}{6}$

24. $\frac{7}{12}$
    $+\frac{1}{12}$

More Practice, page 515, set D

Problem Solving
Deciding When to Estimate

UNDERSTAND
ANALYZE DATA
PLAN
ESTIMATE
SOLVE
EXAMINE

LEARN ABOUT IT

Chad's class did a social studies project on "Human Rights Leaders." As they worked on the project, they needed to find some lengths and areas. The purpose of the measurement helped them decide whether to estimate or make an actual measurement.

Portrait stamps honor the leadership of Abraham Lincoln, Susan B. Anthony, Mahatma Gandhi, and Martin Luther King, Jr.

Problem 1 Chad needs to get enough paper to cover the bulletin boards that will display data about the leaders. Should he estimate or measure the bulletin board area?

Chad needs to know whether 1 roll of paper will be enough. An estimate is ok.

Problem 2 To buy frames for pictures of the leaders, should Jean estimate or measure the pictures' dimensions?

Since Jean needs to get frames that fit the pictures, she needs to measure.

TRY IT OUT

Explain whether you would estimate or measure.

1. Carl is using a map of India to find how far Gandhi traveled on one of his trips. Should he measure or estimate?

2. Lita is cutting some rolls of crepe paper to make borders for the bulletin boards. Should she measure or estimate the length of paper needed?

3. Mindy is making a scale model of the Lincoln Memorial in Washington, D.C. Should she estimate or measure to mark the dimensions of her model?

4. Should Joel estimate or measure to find how many miles of highway are named for Martin Luther King, Jr. in his state?

314

Solve. Use any problem solving strategy.

1. The project bulletin board display showed this information on some of the leaders. How many years did each live?

> Abraham Lincoln (1809–1865)
> Susan B. Anthony (1820–1906)
> Mahatma Gandhi (1869–1948)
> Martin Luther King (1929–1968)

2. Gandhi once fasted for 21 days to help bring freedom to India. For how many hours did his fast last?

3. In 1868 Susan B. Anthony issued a publication that demanded voting rights for women. The 19th Amendment, which guaranteed women's right to vote, became law 52 years later. In what year did the amendment become law?

4. Martin Luther King once spent 5 days in a Birmingham jail because he led a nonviolent demonstration supporting racial justice. How many hours did he spend in jail?

5. Kerry had 175 copies of a sheet with data about the leaders made at the copy shop. The cost for copying was $0.07 per sheet. What was the total cost?

6. Leilani wrote 3 paragraphs of her project report on Monday, 5 on Tuesday, 7 on Wednesday, and so on. At this rate, how many paragraphs in all will she have written by the end of Saturday?

7. On Friday, 47 people attended the open house and came to see the project display. Geraldo told his friend that 6 more than twice that number came to see the project on Saturday. How many people visited the project during those two days?

8. **Developing a Plan** Class committees worked on the project for 43 h in all. The displays committee worked 3 times as long as the publicity committee. The reports committee worked 3 h more than the other two committees combined. How many hours did each committee work?
   A. List two or more strategies you think might help you solve this problem.

   B. Solve the problem.
   C. Look back at your solution. What strategies did you use?

More Practice, page 526, set C

Applied Problem Solving
Group Decision Making

UNDERSTAND
ANALYZE DATA
PLAN
ESTIMATE
SOLVE
EXAMINE

Group Skill:
Check for Understanding

Your class is going to build a puppet theater for the children's wing of the hospital near your school. One of your classmates brought in the plans for the theater. Your group is to look over the plans and decide what lumber to buy.

Facts to Consider

■ This diagram shows the different parts of the theater.

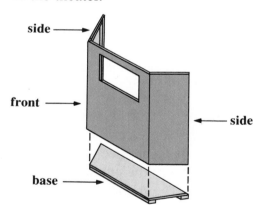

■ The diagrams below show the measurements of the large pieces of wood and of the narrow framing pieces needed to make the theater.

View from the front

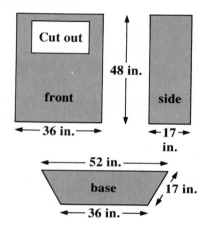

View from the back showing narrow framing pieces

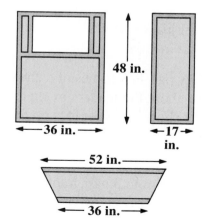

- The front and sides of the theater will be made from hardwood. Hardwood comes in sheets that are 4 ft wide and 8 ft long.
- The base will be made from plywood. Plywood comes in sheets that are 4 ft wide and 8 ft long.
- The framing pieces are used to reinforce the hardwood and the plywood. They are narrow strips of wood 1 in. high, 2 in. wide, and 8 ft long.

1. Will one piece of hardwood be enough to build the front and sides of the theater?

2. How many 4 foot long framing pieces will you need? How much lumber will you buy to cut these pieces from?

3. How could drawing a picture or a diagram help you figure out the total number of 8 foot long framing pieces you will need?

What Is Your Decision?

Make a list of the kinds and sizes of lumber you will need to buy.

317

WRAP UP

Unit/Number Match

Match the words and numbers.

1. inches in a foot
2. quarts in a gallon
3. inches in a yard
4. yards in a mile
5. cups in a pint
6. pounds in a ton
7. ounces in a pound
8. fluid ounces in a cup
9. feet in a mile
10. feet in a yard

A. 3   B. 2,000   C. 36   D. 2   E. 1,760   F. 8   G. 4   H. 16   I. 12   J. 5,280

Sometimes, Always, Never

Complete each statement by writing **sometimes**, **always**, or **never**. Explain your choices.

11. When you change from a smaller customary unit to a larger one, the number __?__ gets larger.

12. 6 pints of sour cream will __?__ fit in a quart container.

13. To change from smaller units to larger units, you can __?__ multiply by a whole number.

Project

Choose a model that you think has a volume of about 1 in.³ Use it to try to find larger objects, such as boxes, that are about 12 times the length, width, and height of the cubic inch. What would be the approximate volume of the larger objects?

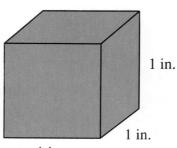

1 in.
1 in.
1 in.

Now try to find some objects that are about 3 times as long, wide, and high as the boxes. What would be the approximate volume of these objects? List as many objects as you can find in school or in your neighborhood that you estimate to have this volume. How can you check your estimates?

POWER PRACTICE/TEST

Part 1 Understanding

Give the most appropriate customary unit of measure for each.

1. Heat of boiling water

2. Weight of a white mouse

3. Distance from Chicago to Houston

4. Length of a football field

5. Amount of flour in a loaf of bread

6. Amount of water in a bathtub

Part 2 Skills

Give the missing numbers.

7. 15 ft 6 in. = ▓▓ in.

8. 150 in. = ▓▓ ft ▓▓ in

9. 2 c = ▓▓ tbsp

10. 3 gal = ▓▓ qt

11. 40 fl oz = ▓▓ qt ▓▓ fl oz

12. 4 T = ▓▓ lb

Measure the line segment.

13. to the nearest $\frac{1}{4}$ inch

14. to the nearest $\frac{1}{8}$ inch

Give each temperature to the nearest tenth of one degree.

15.

16.

Part 3 Applications

17. Duane built a rectangular deck with an area of 48 yd^2. The length of each side is a whole number. What could the perimeter of the deck be?

18. Challenge. In liquid measures, 1 gal contains 231 in.^{3} How many cubic inches are in a quart?

319

ENRICHMENT
Estimating Length

Pia is estimating the length of her arm from her shoulder to her fingertips.

Hand, about 5 inches
Wrist to elbow, about 7 inches
Elbow to shoulder, about 9 inches

1. Use Pia's estimates. What is the length of her arm?

2. Describe the method Pia used to estimate her arm length.

3. This method of estimating lengths, heights, and distances is called **chunking**. Why do you think it was given such a name?

Use the chunking method to make each estimate.

4. height in feet of your classroom wall

5. height in inches of your chair

6. height in inches of a door

7. length in feet of your classroom

8. length in feet of the chalkboard

9. length of your leg from your heel to your hipbone

10. length in inches of your teacher's desk

11. height in inches of a window

12. length of the hall outside your classroom

CUMULATIVE REVIEW

1. What fraction of the region is shaded?

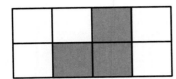

   A. $\frac{3}{8}$ B. $\frac{5}{3}$ C. $\frac{5}{8}$ D. $\frac{3}{5}$

2. Rename $\frac{15}{4}$.

   A. 4 B. $3\frac{3}{4}$ C. $3\frac{1}{2}$ D. $4\frac{1}{4}$

3. By what was $\frac{5}{12}$ multiplied to get $\frac{20}{48}$?

   A. $\frac{5}{4}$ B. $\frac{3}{4}$ C. $\frac{4}{6}$ D. $\frac{4}{4}$

Divide.

4. $68\overline{)435}$

   A. 60 R27 B. 6 R27
   C. 5 R12 D. 51 R27

5. $74\overline{)\$446.22}$

   A. \$603.00 B. \$60.30
   C. \$0.603 D. \$6.03

6. $381.62 \div 100$

   A. 38.162 B. 3,816.2
   C. 3.8162 D. 0.38162

7. Mai is reading two facing pages in her English book. The product of the page numbers is 42. What are the numbers of the pages she is reading?

   A. 6 and 8 B. 7 and 8
   C. 8 and 9 D. 6 and 7

Add or subtract. Reduce answers to lowest terms.

8. $14 - 6\frac{1}{3}$

   A. $7\frac{2}{3}$ B. $8\frac{2}{3}$ C. $7\frac{1}{3}$ D. $8\frac{1}{3}$

9. $26\frac{3}{4} + 35\frac{1}{12}$

   A. $61\frac{1}{3}$ B. $61\frac{10}{12}$ C. $61\frac{5}{6}$ D. 62

10. $6\frac{2}{3} + 2\frac{2}{5}$

   A. $9\frac{1}{15}$ B. $8\frac{11}{15}$ C. $8\frac{1}{15}$ D. $9\frac{4}{15}$

11. $41\frac{1}{8} - 27\frac{5}{6}$

   A. $13\frac{7}{24}$ B. $14\frac{17}{24}$ C. $13\frac{1}{6}$ D. $14\frac{7}{24}$

12. How many more points did Andrea score than Rae? Use the table.

Player	Andrea	Mia	Rae
Points	62	59	48

   A. 3 B. 11 C. 14 D. 110

13. Gail drank $8\frac{1}{4}$ oz of water in the morning, $7\frac{5}{8}$ oz in the afternoon, and $12\frac{3}{4}$ oz in the evening. What method would you use to find out how much water Gail drank?

   A. estimation
   B. calculator
   C. mental math
   D. paper and pencil

12

MULTIPLICATION AND DIVISION OF FRACTIONS

THEME: MUSIC

MATH AND FINE ARTS

DATA BANK

Use the Fine Arts Data Bank on page 478 to answer the questions.

1 What fraction of all the musical instruments shown in the diagram of an orchestra are brass instruments? What fraction are woodwinds?

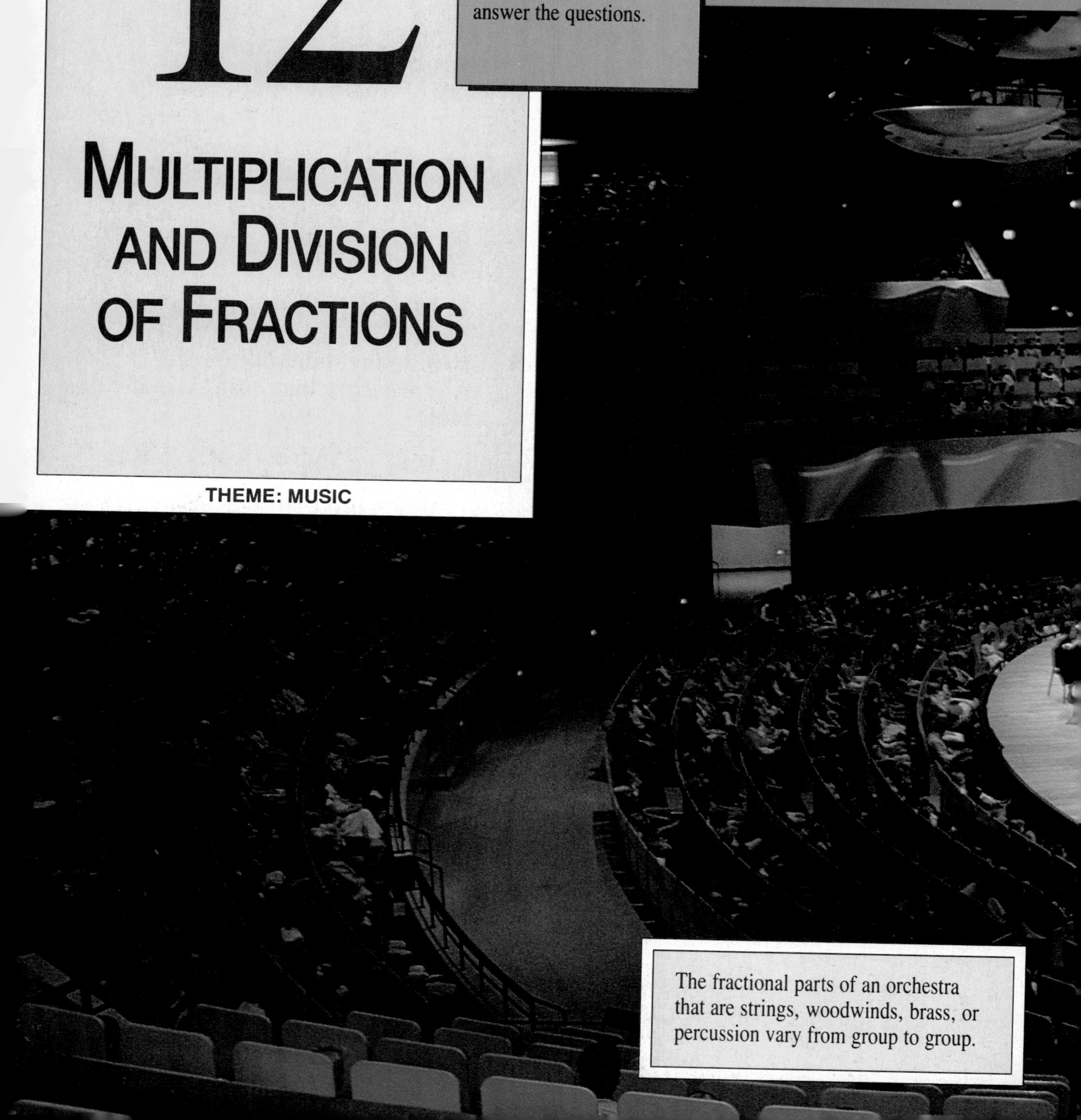

The fractional parts of an orchestra that are strings, woodwinds, brass, or percussion vary from group to group.

2 Violins are what fraction of all the string instruments in the orchestra?

3 What fraction of all the violins in the orchestra are first violins? Give the fraction in lowest terms.

4 **Using Critical Thinking** Do you think it would be easier to find a job as a violin player or as a tuba player in a large orchestra? Explain your thinking.

Multiplying a Fraction and a Whole Number

You can use what you know about division of whole numbers to help you think about finding a fraction of a whole number.

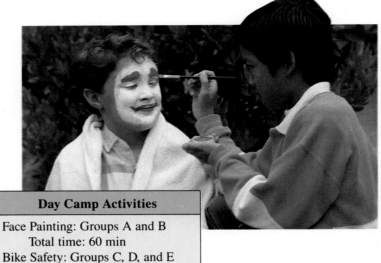

EXPLORE Make a Decision

Work in groups. Your group is in charge of planning activities at a day camp for young children. Use the data to decide how many minutes each group will spend on each activity if the time is shared equally.

Day Camp Activities

Face Painting: Groups A and B
    Total time: 60 min
Bike Safety: Groups C, D, and E
    Total time: 60 min
Nature Study: Groups F, G, H, and I
    Total time: 60 min

TALK ABOUT IT

The situation above shows one way to think about finding a fraction of a number. The pictures below also show how to think about finding a fraction of a whole number.

$\frac{1}{3}$ of 18

**1 out of 3
equal groups**

$\frac{2}{3}$ of 18

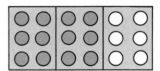

**2 out of 3
equal groups**

$\frac{1}{3} \times 18 = 6$ Divide 18 by 3.

$\frac{2}{3} \times 18 = 12$ Divide 18 by 3.
Multiply by 2.

Other Examples   **A** $\frac{1}{2} \times 20 = 10$ **B** $\frac{2}{5} \times 30 = 12$ **C** $\frac{5}{8} \times 16 = 10$

Multiply.

1. $\frac{1}{2} \times 18$ **2.** $\frac{3}{4} \times 12$ **3.** $\frac{1}{5} \times 40$ **4.** $\frac{2}{3} \times 24$

Multiply.

1. $\frac{1}{2} \times 8$ 2. $\frac{1}{3} \times 15$ 3. $\frac{2}{3} \times 12$ 4. $\frac{1}{4} \times 16$ 5. $\frac{2}{5} \times 10$

6. $\frac{3}{4} \times 20$ 7. $\frac{1}{8} \times 32$ 8. $\frac{3}{5} \times 30$ 9. $\frac{1}{6} \times 42$ 10. $\frac{2}{3} \times 21$

11. $\frac{1}{10} \times 50$ 12. $\frac{5}{6} \times 18$ 13. $\frac{3}{8} \times 40$ 14. $\frac{4}{5} \times 35$ 15. $\frac{3}{7} \times 14$

16. Find three fifths of twenty-five.   17. Find nine tenths of one hundred.

MATH REASONING

Tell the value for the variable that will make the equation true.

18. $\frac{1}{x} \times 20 = 10$ 19. $\frac{1}{n} \times 16 = 2$ 20. $\frac{2}{m} \times 12 = 8$

PROBLEM SOLVING

21. Last month 60 students came to day camp. $\frac{2}{3}$ of the students signed up for art. How many of the students signed up for art?

22. This year 40 students signed up for swimming. Only 15 of these had lessons last year. $\frac{1}{5}$ of those who did not have lessons last year said they were not afraid of the water. How many are not afraid of the water?

▶ **USING CRITICAL THINKING**   Discover a Relationship

$3 \times 4 = 4 + 4 + 4$

Use this way to think about multiplication to find each of the following.

23. $5 \times \frac{2}{15}$ 24. $6 \times \frac{1}{12}$ 25. $8 \times \frac{3}{4}$ 26. $4 \times \frac{9}{10}$

More Practice, page 515, set E

Estimating a Fraction of a Number

Instruments in the Junior Symphony

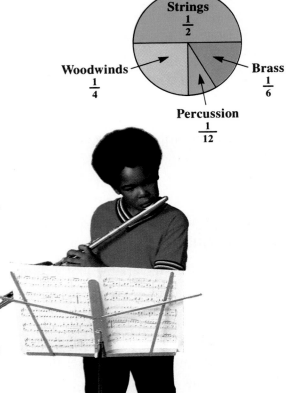

EXPLORE Study a Graph

Melissa's class did some research on the instruments in the Junior Symphony. They made a circle graph to show the results.

TALK ABOUT IT

1. Suppose the Junior Symphony has 50 members. How many of the instruments are played by the members of the strings section?

2. Suppose the Junior Symphony has 60 members. How many of the instruments would be played by members of the brass section?

3. Suppose the Junior Symphony has 40 members. What number close to 40 is divisible by 6? Can you use this fact to estimate the number of instruments in the brass section?

You can estimate a fraction of a whole number by substituting compatible numbers. For example, estimate $\frac{1}{6} \times 52$.

Betsy's estimate:

$\frac{1}{6}$ of 54 is 9, so $\frac{1}{6}$ of 52 is about 9.

Todd's estimate:

$\frac{1}{5}$ of 50 is 10, so $\frac{1}{6}$ of 52 is about 10.

Both are reasonable ways to estimate the product.

TRY IT OUT

Substitute compatible numbers to estimate each.

1. $\frac{1}{3} \times 23$
2. $\frac{1}{5} \times 33$
3. $\frac{1}{4} \times 30$
4. $\frac{1}{8} \times 43$

5. $\frac{1}{12} \times 86$
6. $\frac{1}{6} \times 50$
7. $\frac{2}{3} \times 19$
8. $\frac{3}{4} \times 34$

Substitute compatible numbers to estimate each.

1. $\frac{1}{5} \times 38$ **2.** $\frac{1}{2} \times 17$ **3.** $\frac{1}{3} \times 236$ **4.** $\frac{2}{3} \times 118$

5. $\frac{2}{3} \times 29$ **6.** $\frac{1}{4} \times 41$ **7.** $\frac{3}{4} \times 35$ **8.** $\frac{1}{2} \times 27$

9. $\frac{2}{3} \times 53$ **10.** $\frac{1}{10} \times 57$ **11.** $\frac{5}{6} \times 19$ **12.** $\frac{3}{4} \times 57$

Estimate each. Write **+** if the exact answer is greater than your estimate.

13. $\frac{2}{5} \times 53$ **14.** $\frac{1}{2} \times 67$ **15.** $\frac{1}{4} \times 43$ **16.** $\frac{3}{10} \times 73$

17. $\frac{1}{3} \times \$61.89$ **18.** $\frac{4}{5} \times \$27.95$ **19.** $\frac{3}{4} \times \$53.21$ **20.** $\frac{1}{2} \times \$32.75$

APPLY

MATH REASONING

Write a fraction or whole number that could replace the variable.

21. x of 27 is about 4. **22.** y of 67 is about 11. **23.** z of 143 is about 14.

24. m of 27 is about 21. **25.** $\frac{3}{5}$ of a is about 36. **26.** $\frac{3}{4}$ of b is about 21.

PROBLEM SOLVING

27. One year the Junior Symphony had 56 members. About how many of the members played brass instruments that year? See the graph on page 326.

28. Fine Arts Data Bank What fraction of all the instruments in a typical symphony orchestra are the violins? See page 478.

DATA BANK

▶ **CALCULATOR**

You can find a fraction of a whole number using a calculator. Example:

Find $\frac{3}{4} \times 120$. Key code: [ON/AC] 3 [×] 120 [÷] 4 [=] ⬚ 90

Use a calculator to find each.

29. $\frac{5}{6} \times 78$ **30.** $\frac{1}{2} \times 62$ **31.** $\frac{1}{3} \times 42$ **32.** $\frac{2}{3} \times 72$

Multiplying Fractions
Making the Connection

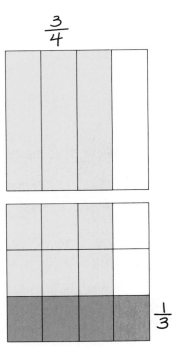

$\frac{3}{4}$

$\frac{1}{3}$

EXPLORE **Draw to Understand**
   Work with a partner.

■ One partner divides a square into any
   number of equal vertical sections like
   the one at the right, then shades and
   names the fraction.

■ The other partner divides the same
   square into any number of equal
   horizontal sections, then shades and
   names the fraction.

■ Together, the partners decide how
   many small rectangles are in the
   original square and name the fraction
   of the square that is shaded twice.

TALK ABOUT IT

1. Is the fraction represented by the region shaded twice
   greater than or less than each of the original fractions?

2. How can you find the total number of rectangles the
   square will be divided into by thinking about the
   denominators of the original fractions?

3. How can you find the number of squares shaded twice
   by looking at the numerators of the original fractions?

You have drawn pictures to find a fraction of a fraction. Here you will see how to record what you have done. Here is how to find $\frac{2}{3} \times \frac{6}{8}$.

What You Do	**What You Record**

Show $\frac{6}{8}$.

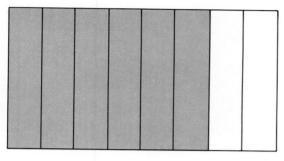

$$\frac{2}{3} \times \frac{6}{8}$$

Can you divide $\frac{6}{8}$ into thirds?

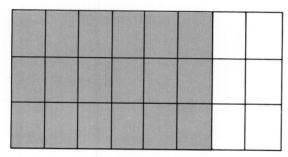

$$\frac{2}{3} \times \frac{6}{8}$$

How much is $\frac{2}{3}$ of $\frac{6}{8}$?

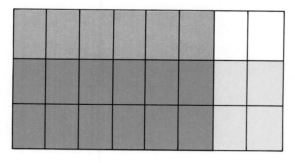

$$\frac{2}{3} \times \frac{6}{8} = \frac{12}{24}$$

TRY IT OUT

Draw pictures to show each product.

1. $\frac{1}{2} \times \frac{4}{8}$ 2. $\frac{1}{3} \times \frac{3}{5}$ 3. $\frac{1}{2} \times \frac{5}{8}$ 4. $\frac{3}{4} \times \frac{1}{6}$

Multiplying Fractions

LEARN ABOUT IT

In the previous lesson, you drew pictures to multiply fractions. Here you will learn how to do this using only symbols.

EXPLORE Analyze the Process
Suppose you have to spray the grass in the Huff's yard with a weed killer. Their yard is $\frac{2}{3}$ grass. What part of an acre do you need to spray?

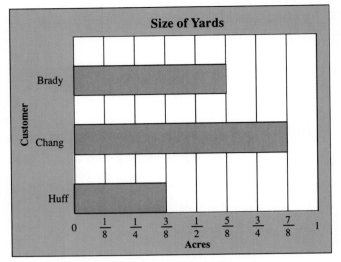

Size of Yards

Tell why multiplication is the operation needed to solve this problem. Here is how to find the answer.

Multiply the numerators.	Multiply the denominators.	Reduce if possible.
$\frac{2}{3} \times \frac{3}{8} = \frac{6}{\_}$	$\frac{2}{3} \times \frac{3}{8} = \frac{6}{24}$	$\frac{2}{3} \times \frac{3}{8} = \frac{6}{24} = \frac{1}{4}$

TALK ABOUT IT

1. Could you multiply denominators before the numerators?
2. Do you need to have like denominators to multiply two fractions?
3. Give the answer to the Explore problem in a complete sentence.

Other Examples

A $\frac{1}{2} \times \frac{3}{4} = \frac{3}{8}$ **B** $\frac{3}{4} \times \frac{5}{2} = \frac{15}{8} = 1\frac{7}{8}$ **C** $\frac{2}{3} \times 5 = \frac{2}{3} \times \frac{5}{1} = \frac{10}{3} = 3\frac{1}{3}$

TRY IT OUT

Multiply.

1. $\frac{3}{5} \times \frac{2}{3}$ **2.** $8 \times \frac{1}{3}$ **3.** $\frac{3}{10} \times \frac{7}{10}$ **4.** $\frac{4}{9} \times 9$

330

Multiply. Reduce to lowest terms.

1. $\frac{1}{4} \times \frac{2}{5}$ **2.** $\frac{6}{1} \times \frac{3}{4}$ **3.** $\frac{3}{2} \times \frac{1}{4}$ **4.** $\frac{1}{3} \times \frac{5}{8}$

5. $\frac{5}{6} \times \frac{1}{2}$ **6.** $9 \times \frac{2}{3}$ **7.** $\frac{2}{3} \times \frac{3}{8}$ **8.** $\frac{1}{5} \times \frac{3}{10}$

9. $16 \times \frac{5}{8}$ **10.** $\frac{3}{4} \times \frac{4}{3}$ **11.** $\frac{2}{5} \times 12$ **12.** $8 \times \frac{9}{10}$

APPLY

MATH REASONING

Using each number only once, write 1, 2, 3, or 4 for each ▦ to make:

13. the largest product possible.
14. the smallest product possible.
15. a product close to 1.

$$\frac{\text{▦}}{\text{▦}} \times \frac{\text{▦}}{\text{▦}} = ?$$

Write $+$, $-$, or $\times$ for each ▦.

16. $\frac{1}{2}$ ▦ $\frac{1}{2} = 0$ **17.** $\frac{1}{2}$ ▦ $\frac{1}{2} = \frac{1}{4}$ **18.** $\frac{1}{2}$ ▦ $\frac{1}{2} = 1$ **19.** $\frac{3}{4}$ ▦ $\frac{2}{3} = 1\frac{5}{12}$

PROBLEM SOLVING

20. How many acres of yard do the Bradys and Changs have together? Use the graph on page 330.

21. The Smiths have a 1-acre yard. How much larger is this than the Bradys' yard?

22. The Changs live next to the Huffs. Together their yards are $\frac{3}{4}$ grass. How many acres of grass is this?

23. Unfinished Problem   Write and answer a question about this data. The Jones family have $\frac{1}{8}$ acre more yard than the Huff family. The yard is $\frac{7}{8}$ grass.

MIXED REVIEW

24. $\frac{3}{4}$ $+ \frac{1}{8}$ **25.** $\frac{2}{3}$ $+ \frac{1}{2}$ **26.** $\frac{5}{6}$ $+ \frac{1}{3}$ **27.** $\frac{3}{8}$ $+ \frac{5}{12}$ **28.** $\frac{7}{10}$ $+ \frac{3}{5}$

More Practice, page 516, set B

331

Exploring Algebra
Informal Algebra in Problem Solving

LEARN ABOUT IT

You can guess and check, draw pictures,
or use objects to help you solve many
problems.

Solve.

One more than twice Sal's age is 25.
How old is Sal?

$$\boxed{?} + \boxed{?} + 1 \rightarrow 25$$

Try 8: 8+8+1=17   Too low!
Try 12: 12+12+1=25 Correct!

TALK ABOUT IT

1. What do the question marks represent? Why are there
   two of them?

2. Give a guess that Sal might have made that is too high.

3. Give the answer to the problem above in a complete sentence.

TRY IT OUT

Draw pictures, use objects, or guess and check to help you
solve each.

1. Bob's parrot is 6 years older than Bob.
   The parrot is 21 years old. How old is
   Bob?

2. If you add Donna's and Wanda's ages
   you get 21. If you multiply their ages
   you get 110. What age is each girl?

3. In 7 more years, Marie will be 21.
   How old is Marie now?

4. 2 less than 3 times Turk's weight is 178
   pounds. How much does Turk weigh?

5. Tom's weight is 2 times his brother's
   weight. Tom weighs 54 pounds. How
   much does his brother weigh?

6. If you add Yolanda's age and Teresa's
   age you get 54. If you subtract their
   ages you get 14. What age is each?

7. Terri is half as old as her sister. Terri is
   13. How old is her sister?

8. 5 more than half Paul's age is 13. How
   old is Paul?

POWER PRACTICE/QUIZ

Multiply.

1. $\frac{1}{9} \times 45$ **2.** $\frac{3}{8} \times 24$ **3.** $\frac{4}{5} \times 20$ **4.** $\frac{2}{7} \times 42$

5. $\frac{1}{3} \times 18$ **6.** $\frac{3}{4} \times 12$ **7.** $\frac{2}{5} \times 10$ **8.** $\frac{1}{6} \times 30$

Substitute compatible numbers to estimate each. Write +
after an estimate if the exact answer is greater than your
estimate.

9. $\frac{2}{3} \times 17$ **10.** $\frac{1}{5} \times 46$ **11.** $\frac{1}{8} \times 50$ **12.** $\frac{3}{4} \times 29$

13. $\frac{1}{4} \times 11$ **14.** $\frac{2}{3} \times 25$ **15.** $\frac{1}{6} \times 35$ **16.** $\frac{3}{8} \times 15$

Multiply. Write each product in lowest terms.

17. $\frac{1}{2} \times \frac{2}{3}$ **18.** $\frac{2}{3} \times \frac{3}{5}$ **19.** $\frac{3}{4} \times \frac{4}{9}$ **20.** $\frac{1}{3} \times \frac{6}{8}$

21. $\frac{1}{6} \times \frac{8}{9}$ **22.** $\frac{2}{3} \times \frac{2}{3}$ **23.** $\frac{7}{10} \times 15$ **24.** $\frac{2}{5} \times \frac{3}{8}$

25. $\frac{3}{5} \times \frac{1}{4}$ **26.** $\frac{2}{3} \times \frac{3}{4}$ **27.** $\frac{5}{6} \times \frac{3}{5}$ **28.** $\frac{3}{8} \times \frac{2}{3}$

PROBLEM SOLVING

29. A recipe calls for $\frac{3}{4}$ lb of butter. How many ounces of
butter are needed? (1 lb = 16 oz)

30. Gayle walked $\frac{1}{3}$ mi and then jogged 9 times that
distance. What is the distance she jogged?

31. Gretchen ran $\frac{1}{3}$ the distance Gayle jogged. What is the
distance Gretchen ran?

32. Grace rides her bike between home and school 8 times
a week. The distance is $\frac{3}{4}$ mi. How many miles does
she ride in a week?

Problem Solving
Multiple-Step Problems

UNDERSTAND
ANALYZE DATA
PLAN
ESTIMATE
SOLVE
EXAMINE

LEARN ABOUT IT

Some problems can be solved using two or more operations (addition, subtraction, multiplication, and division). These problems are called **multiple-step** problems.

The student council decided to sell school T-shirts and sweatshirts. $\frac{2}{5}$ of the fifth graders and $\frac{1}{6}$ of the sixth graders bought shirts the first week. What was the total number of fifth and sixth graders who bought T-shirts the first week?

Fifth grade: 65 students enrolled
Sixth grade: 72 students enrolled

First I'll find out how many fifth graders bought T-shirts.

$$\frac{2}{5} \times 65 = 26$$

Next I'll find out how many sixth graders bought T-shirts.

$$\frac{1}{6} \times 72 = 12$$

Then I'll add them together.

$$26 + 12 = 38$$

38 fifth and sixth graders bought T-shirts the first week.

TRY IT OUT

Solve. Use the T-shirt cost data table as needed.

1. Jack ordered 80 T-shirts for the school store the first month. The second month he ordered only $\frac{1}{4}$ that number. What was the cost of the shirts he ordered the second month?

2. How much would the student council save by buying one batch of 100 T-shirts instead of buying 2 different batches of 50 T-shirts each?

Cost for One T-Shirt or Sweatshirt					
Number of shirts	1−24	25−60	61−96	97−144	145−200
T-shirts	$6.90	$6.45	$6.05	$5.65	$5.25
Sweatshirts	$7.70	$7.20	$6.75	$6.35	$5.85

Use any strategy to solve the problems.

1. The students at Penrose Elementary voted on what symbol to use on their school T-shirts. $\frac{1}{2}$ of the students who wanted the bulldog also wanted a black T-shirt. What part of the students who voted wanted a bulldog on a black shirt?

Symbol Survey
Fifth and Sixth Grade Voting Results

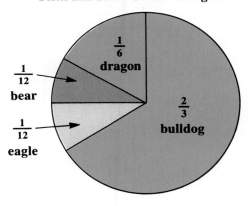

2. There are 96 fifth and sixth graders at Penrose. How many voted for the bulldog and the dragon altogether?

3. Ari works at the school store. He sold $\frac{1}{2}$ of the T-shirts at the store in the first month. He sold 27 more the second month. At that point he had 12 shirts left. How many T-shirts did he start out with?

4. What part of the students voted for the bear and the eagle altogether?

5. Marta collected $27.75 when she sold 3 sweatshirts. How much would she collect if she sold 4 sweatshirts at the same price per shirt?

6. Tops T-Shirt Store has been open for 3 days. $\frac{2}{3}$ of the T-shirts they ordered have arrived. $\frac{1}{3}$ of those shirts have been priced and put on the shelves. What part of the T-shirts that have been ordered are priced and on the shelves?

7. How much would 21 T-shirts cost on sale?

The Tops Sale
3 for $11

8. **Finding Another Way** The following digits could be used for the backs of the Bear Cubs' baseball shirts: 2, 4, 7, 9. Each player will have a 2-digit number. How many different numbers can be put on the shirts? Corita solved this problem by drawing a picture. Find, and show another way to solve the problem.

Multiplying Mixed Numbers

You can use what you know about multiplying fractions to help you multiply mixed numbers.

EXPLORE Analyze the Process

A city architect is planning a new housing and parklands project. It will cover a rectangular section of land $2\frac{1}{3}$ mi long and $1\frac{1}{4}$ mi wide. What is its area?

Why is multiplication the operation needed to solve this problem?

Here is how to find the exact answer.

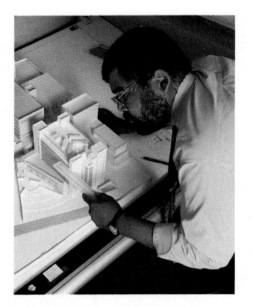

Write the mixed numbers as improper fractions.	Multiply the fractions. Reduce to lowest terms.
$2\frac{1}{3} \times 1\frac{1}{4} = \frac{7}{3} \times \frac{5}{4}$	$\frac{7}{3} \times \frac{5}{4} = \frac{35}{12} = 2\frac{11}{12}$

TALK ABOUT IT

1. What steps did you follow to multiply the fractions?
2. What might you have estimated the product to be?
3. Give a reasonable answer to the Explore problem in a complete sentence.

Other Examples

A $3\frac{1}{3} \times 1\frac{3}{4} = \frac{10}{3} \times \frac{7}{4} = \frac{70}{12} = 5\frac{5}{6}$ **B** $\frac{1}{3} \times 3\frac{2}{5} = \frac{1}{3} \times \frac{17}{5} = \frac{17}{15} = 1\frac{2}{15}$

C $2\frac{1}{4} \times 5 = \frac{9}{4} \times \frac{5}{1} = \frac{45}{4} = 11\frac{1}{4}$ **D** $5 \times 4\frac{3}{8} = \frac{5}{1} \times \frac{35}{8} = \frac{175}{8} = 21\frac{7}{8}$

Multiply.

1. $3\frac{2}{3} \times 1\frac{2}{5}$ 2. $1\frac{3}{8} \times 6$ 3. $1\frac{5}{6} \times 3\frac{7}{8}$ 4. $8 \times 2\frac{1}{4}$

Multiply. Reduce to lowest terms.

1. $1\frac{1}{3} \times 2\frac{1}{2}$ **2.** $2\frac{1}{3} \times 1\frac{1}{4}$ **3.** $\frac{3}{4} \times 1\frac{1}{2}$ **4.** $5 \times 1\frac{2}{5}$

5. $2\frac{1}{5} \times 1\frac{1}{4}$ **6.** $10 \times 2\frac{1}{2}$ **7.** $1\frac{1}{3} \times \frac{2}{3}$ **8.** $2\frac{1}{8} \times \frac{1}{4}$

9. $1\frac{3}{4} \times 1\frac{2}{3}$ **10.** $8\frac{1}{2} \times 4$ **11.** $1\frac{2}{3} \times 12$ **12.** $2\frac{1}{2} \times 1\frac{3}{4}$

APPLY

MATH REASONING

13. Use the digits 1, 2, 3, 4, 5, or 6 in place of each ▓ to make a problem with a product close to 8.

PROBLEM SOLVING

14. A new park band shell has a stage that is 60 ft long and $40\frac{1}{2}$ ft wide. What is the area of the stage?

15. The symphony gave 6 free concerts in the park. The concerts lasted an average of $2\frac{3}{4}$ h each. What was the total number of hours of free concerts?

16. Fine Arts Data Bank Suppose half of the second violin players in a typical orchestra are women. How many women would that be? See page 478.

▶ ### ESTIMATION

Use one or more of the techniques you have learned to estimate these products.

17. $4\frac{1}{3} \times 5\frac{5}{8}$ **18.** $12\frac{1}{5} \times 7\frac{1}{8}$

19. $\frac{2}{3} \times 3\frac{1}{2}$ **20.** $4\frac{1}{5} \times 2\frac{2}{3}$

Estimation Techniques
■ Front-end
■ Rounding
■ Compatible numbers
■ Clustering

Problem Solving
Using a Calculator

UNDERSTAND
ANALYZE DATA
PLAN
ESTIMATE
SOLVE
EXAMINE

LEARN ABOUT IT

Toni's mother has taught her how to make many traditional American Indian dishes. Toni also likes to try out traditional recipes of other cultures.

> Toni uses $2\frac{1}{2}$ c of flour to make bread for 4 people. How many cups would she use to make bread for 14 people?

She can use a calculator that does fraction computations to solve the problem.

> Since I know $2\frac{1}{2}$ c are enough for 4 people, I'll divide $2\frac{1}{2}$ by 4 to find how much I need for 1 person.

[ON/AC] 2 [Unit] 1/2 [÷] 4 [=] 5/8

> Now I can multiply $\frac{5}{8}$ c by 14 to find how much I need to use to make enough for 14 people.

[×] 14 [=] 70/8

[Ab/c] 8 u 6/8 [Simp] [=] 8 u 3/4

Toni would use $8\frac{3}{4}$ c of flour.

TRY IT OUT

Solve. Use a fraction calculator.

1. Paul brought some Cajun food to a picnic. His chicken recipe called for using $2\frac{1}{4}$ lb of chicken for 8 people. How many pounds would he need for 6 people?

2. Yee's recipe for Chinese almond cookies calls for $2\frac{1}{4}$ c of flour. He needs to use only $\frac{2}{3}$ of that amount. How many cups of flour does he need?

3. Audra is using an African recipe for Injera bread that calls for 5 c of flour. The recipe makes enough bread to serve 8 people. How much flour should Audra use to make enough for 12 people?

4. Simca made a Malaysian dessert that has $\frac{3}{4}$ lb of grated coconut. If coconut costs $5.96 per pound, what would be the cost of $\frac{3}{4}$ lb?

Solve. Use the data in the recipe and any
of the strategies.

AFRICAN YAM FRITTERS

Ingredients

$1\frac{1}{2}$ lb yams, boiled and mashed

1 egg, beaten

$\frac{1}{2}$ tsp salt

$\frac{1}{4}$ tsp black pepper

$\frac{1}{4}$ tsp thyme

pinch of cayenne pepper

$\frac{1}{2}$ green chili, seeded and minced

1 medium onion, chopped fine

1 medium tomato, chopped fine

$\frac{1}{2}$ c bread crumbs

peanut oil for frying

*Makes 4 servings.

Some Strategies

Act Out	Make a Table
Use Objects	Solve a Simpler Problem
Choose an Operation	Make an Organized List
Draw a Picture	Work Backward
Guess and Check	Look for a Pattern
	Use Logical Reasoning

1. Carla wants to make 12 servings of
   fritters. How many pounds of yams
   should she use? How many green
   chilis should she use?

2. What is the total amount of salt,
   thyme, and black pepper Terri needs
   to use to make 8 servings of fritters?

3. Yams cost $0.68 per pound at the
   market where Aaron shops. What will
   the yams cost if Aaron buys enough to
   make 10 servings of fritters?

4. Leona bought 3 whole green chilis.
   She used enough of the chilis to make
   8 servings of fritters. How many chilis
   does she have left?

5. Harriet has 72 recipe cards in a box.
   Each is for a dessert or a main dish.
   She has twice as many dessert recipes
   as main dish recipes. How many of
   each type does she have?

6. Tom used half as many eggs in one
   recipe as he used in another recipe.
   He dropped 3 eggs and could not use
   them. There are 3 eggs left in the
   carton. If the carton had 2 dozen eggs
   to begin with, how many eggs did he
   use in each recipe?

7. **Data Hunt** Find a recipe that has
   been a favorite of your family or
   relatives. How much of each item
   would you use to make $2\frac{1}{2}$ times the
   amount called for in the recipe?

More Practice, page 526, set D

Dividing Fractions
Using Objects and Pictures

You can think about what it means to divide whole numbers to help you divide fractions. For example, $15 \div 3$ can mean, "How many threes are in 15?" $2 \div \frac{1}{2}$ can mean, "How many halves are in 2?"

EXPLORE **Solve to Understand**

Work in groups.

- The pictures below show how to use fraction pieces to find how many halves are in 2, or $2 \div \frac{1}{2}$.

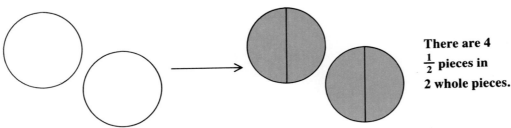

There are 4 $\frac{1}{2}$ pieces in 2 whole pieces.

- Draw a picture to show how many eighths are in $\frac{3}{4}$, that is, $\frac{3}{4} \div \frac{1}{8}$.

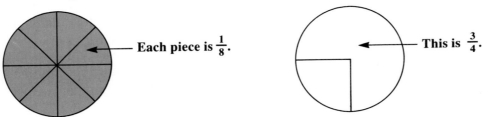

Each piece is $\frac{1}{8}$.

This is $\frac{3}{4}$.

TALK ABOUT IT

1. How many $\frac{1}{2}$ pieces are in 2? What is $2 \div \frac{1}{2}$?
2. How many $\frac{1}{8}$ pieces are in $\frac{3}{4}$? What is $\frac{3}{4} \div \frac{1}{8}$?

Use fraction pieces or draw pictures to find each.

1. How many thirds in 2? $2 \div \frac{1}{3} = $ ▒

2. How many thirds in $\frac{2}{3}$? $\frac{2}{3} \div \frac{1}{3} = $ ▒

340

Find the quotients. Check by multiplying.

1. How many fourths are in 2?

$$2 \div \frac{1}{4} = n$$

2. How many sixths are in $\frac{2}{3}$?

$$\frac{2}{3} \div \frac{1}{6} = n$$

Use fraction pieces or draw pictures to find each quotient.
Check by multiplying.

3. How many halves are in 2?

$$2 \div \frac{1}{2} = n$$

4. How many fourths are in 3?

$$3 \div \frac{1}{4} = n$$

5. How many eighths are in $\frac{1}{2}$?

$$\frac{1}{2} \div \frac{1}{8} = n$$

6. How many eighths are in $\frac{1}{4}$?

$$\frac{1}{4} \div \frac{1}{8} = n$$

7. How many thirds are in 3?

$$3 \div \frac{1}{3} = n$$

8. How many fourths are in $\frac{1}{2}$?

$$\frac{1}{2} \div \frac{1}{4} = n$$

MATH REASONING

Look for a **pattern** in the pairs of problems. Copy and
complete the next two pairs of problems.

9. $\frac{1}{2} \div \frac{1}{8} = 4$ $\frac{1}{2} \times \frac{8}{1} = 4$

$\frac{5}{6} \div \frac{2}{3} = 1\frac{1}{4}$ $\frac{5}{6} \times \frac{3}{2} = 1\frac{1}{4}$

$\frac{1}{2} \div \frac{3}{8} = 1\frac{1}{3}$ $\frac{1}{2} \times \text{▥} = \text{▥}$

10. $\frac{3}{4} \div \frac{1}{4} = 3$ $\frac{3}{4} \times \frac{4}{1} = 3$

$\frac{3}{4} \div \frac{3}{8} = 2$ $\frac{3}{4} \times \frac{8}{3} = 2$

$\frac{1}{6} \div \frac{1}{3} = \frac{1}{2}$ $\frac{1}{6} \times \text{▥} = \text{▥}$

PROBLEM SOLVING

11. Write Your Own Problem   Write a division question
using this data. Jan was making a snack for her friends.
She cut 4 oranges into sixths.

► **ALGEBRA**

You can write algebraic expressions involving division. The
expression for "a number divided by 5" is $n \div 5$ or $\frac{n}{5}$.◄ — The "bar" means
divided by.

Write an algebraic expression for each.

12. six and one half plus a number

13. twelve divided by a number

14. three fourths of a number

15. a number divided by 5

Data Collection and Analysis
Group Decision Making

UNDERSTAND
ANALYZE DATA
PLAN
ESTIMATE
SOLVE
EXAMINE

Making a Questionnaire
Group Skill:
Encourage and Respect Others

Are there household jobs that you now do or could do? Helping with chores around the house gives you the satisfaction of knowing you are doing your part as a member of your family. It also helps to prepare you for many responsibilities you will have later in your life. Do most of the students in your school do things to help out around the house? Make a questionnaire to find out.

Collecting Data

1. Work with your group to make a list of at least ten things you now do or could do to help out at home.

2. Use the items in your list to prepare a questionnaire that will help you find out what kinds of chores students do and how often they do them.

Questionnaire

How often do you help out at home by doing any of the listed items? Check the box that best applies.

	Daily	Sometimes	Never
1. Help in kitchen	☐	☐	☐
2. Care for pets	☐	☐	☐
3. Make bed	☐	☐	☐
4. Take out garbage	☐	☐	☐
5. Help with cleaning	☐	☐	☐
6. Run errands	☐	☐	☐
7. Care for younger children	☐	☐	
Others (List below.)			
_____	☐	☐	☐
_____	☐	☐	☐

3. Check your questionnaire by having two or three people fill it out. Make sure each person who answers your questionnaire will understand how to complete it properly. Revise your questionnaire if necessary.

4. Make copies of the questionnaire for each person in your group. Find at least 25 students in your school who will be willing to provide responses.

Organizing Data

5. Sort the completed questionnaires into groups according to responses:
   1) students who do some of the listed activities daily
   2) students who never do any of the activities daily but sometimes do some of the activities
   3) students who never do any of the activities

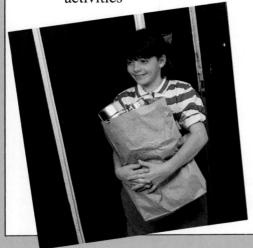

6. Count the number of students in each of the three groups. Make a pictograph that shows how many students are in each group. Design your own symbol to use on the graph.

Presenting Your Analysis

7. Write a short paragraph describing how you decided which students to ask to complete the questionnaire. Was your sample selected randomly?

8. Tell how you decided on the design for the symbol to use in your graph.

9. Prepare a short summary of your results to share with the class.

WRAP UP

Fraction Fill-In

Choose the word from the box that completes each sentence. Some words will not be used.

less	greater	divide
sixths	compatible	five
multiply	thirds	four

1. You can estimate a fraction of a whole number by substituting __?__ numbers.

2. To find $\frac{3}{5}$ of 40, __?__ 40 by 5, then __?__ by 3.

3. Two thirds of one half is two __?__.

4. Five eighths of 32 is __?__ than two sixths of 54.

Sometimes, Always, Never

Complete each statement by writing **sometimes**, **always**, or **never**. Explain your choices.

5. When you multiply two fractions between 0 and 1, the product is __?__ smaller than either fraction.

6. When you divide one fraction by another, the quotient is __?__ a fraction.

7. To multiply two mixed numbers, you should __?__ multiply the whole numbers, multiply the fractions, then add the two products.

Project

Use the digits 1 through 8 as often as you like to write two fractions with the given product and sum. Make up four others to exchange with a partner.

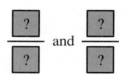

8. Product: $\frac{1}{5}$
Sum: $\frac{9}{10}$

9. Product: $\frac{1}{10}$
Sum: $\frac{13}{20}$

10. Product: $\frac{1}{9}$
Sum: $\frac{5}{6}$

11. Product: $\frac{5}{8}$
Sum: $1\frac{7}{12}$

POWER PRACTICE/TEST

Part 1 Understanding

Use the digits 4, 5, 6, and 7 only once in each ▨ to make: $\frac{▨}{▨} \times \frac{▨}{▨}$

   1. the largest possible product   **2.** the smallest possible product

Draw a picture for each. Give the answer.

   3. $\frac{1}{2} \times \frac{3}{5}$ **4.** The number of eighths in $\frac{3}{4}$

                                                         $\frac{3}{4} \div \frac{1}{8}$

Part 2 Skills

Multiply.

   5. $\frac{3}{4} \times 16$ **6.** $\frac{2}{3} \times 27$ **7.** $\frac{1}{4} \times 36$

   8. $\frac{6}{7} \times \frac{5}{12}$ **9.** $\frac{5}{8} \times \frac{3}{10}$ **10.** $\frac{7}{8} \times \frac{4}{5}$

  11. $2\frac{5}{6} \times 1\frac{7}{8}$ **12.** $8\frac{1}{2} \times 4\frac{2}{3}$ **13.** $2\frac{1}{3} \times 3\frac{3}{7}$

Estimate each.

  14. $\frac{1}{2} \times 19$ **15.** $\frac{2}{3} \times 25$ **16.** $\frac{4}{5} \times 48$

  17. $\frac{1}{5} \times 24$ **18.** $\frac{3}{4} \times 29$ **19.** $\frac{3}{8} \times 15$

Find the quotients. Check by multiplying.

  20. How many thirds are in 1?   **21.** How many fifths are in 2?

      $1 \div \frac{1}{3} = n$ $2 \div \frac{1}{5} = n$

Part 3 Applications

  22. If you add Jim's and Kara's ages, you get 26. If you multiply their ages, you get 168. What are their ages?

  23. Kee had 56 books. He donated $\frac{3}{8}$ of them to the hospital library and $\frac{1}{4}$ of them to the school library. How many books did he keep for himself?

  24. Challenge A $1 bill is $2\frac{5}{8}$ in. wide and about $6\frac{1}{8}$ in. long. How many stacks of $1 bills will fit into a briefcase that is 14 in. wide and 22 in. long?

345

ENRICHMENT
Following Flow Chart Directions

Find the missing numbers.

1.

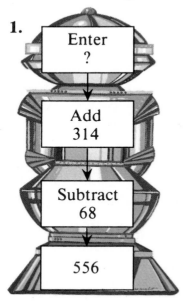

Enter
?

Add
314

Subtract
68

556

2.

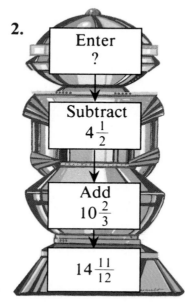

Enter
?

Subtract
$4\frac{1}{2}$

Add
$10\frac{2}{3}$

$14\frac{11}{12}$

3.

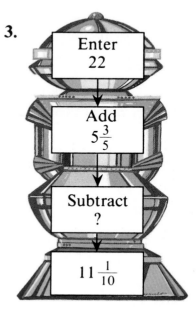

Enter
22

Add
$5\frac{3}{5}$

Subtract
?

$11\frac{1}{10}$

4.

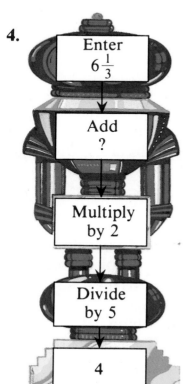

Enter
$6\frac{1}{3}$

Add
?

Multiply
by 2

Divide
by 5

4

5.

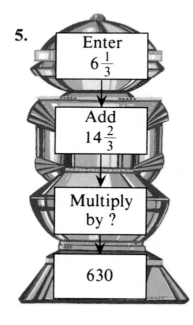

Enter
$6\frac{1}{3}$

Add
$14\frac{2}{3}$

Multiply
by ?

630

6.

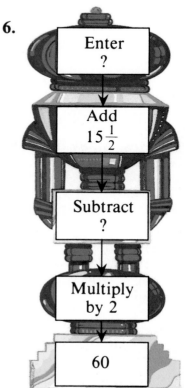

Enter
?

Add
$15\frac{1}{2}$

Subtract
?

Multiply
by 2

60

CUMULATIVE REVIEW

1. What fraction of the set is shaded?

- A. $\frac{7}{12}$
- B. $\frac{5}{7}$
- C. $\frac{5}{12}$
- D. $\frac{7}{5}$

2. Which unit would you use to measure the length of your backyard?

- A. inch
- B. pound
- C. yard
- D. mile

Add or subtract. Reduce answers to lowest terms.

3. $\frac{11}{12} - \frac{5}{12}$

- A. $\frac{1}{2}$
- B. $\frac{16}{12}$
- C. $1\frac{1}{3}$
- D. $\frac{7}{12}$

4. $\frac{2}{5} + \frac{3}{4}$

- A. $1\frac{3}{20}$
- B. $\frac{9}{20}$
- C. $\frac{7}{20}$
- D. $\frac{5}{9}$

5. $86\frac{1}{5} - 27\frac{1}{3}$

- A. $58\frac{8}{15}$
- B. $58\frac{13}{15}$
- C. $62\frac{8}{15}$
- D. $62\frac{13}{15}$

6. Which answer is *not* a possible answer for this problem?

Angela counted 44 wheels. Some belonged to bicycles and some to tricycles. How many bicycles and tricycles did she see?

- A. 4 and 12
- B. 11 and 7
- C. 10 and 8
- D. 16 and 4

7. Which line measures $1\frac{3}{4}$ in. to the nearest $\frac{1}{4}$ inch?

- A. _____
- B. _____
- C. _____
- D. _____

8. Which fraction is equivalent to $\frac{5}{6}$?

- A. $\frac{15}{12}$
- B. $\frac{10}{18}$
- C. $\frac{15}{36}$
- D. $\frac{20}{24}$

9. Which fraction is less than $\frac{2}{3}$?

- A. $\frac{4}{5}$
- B. $\frac{8}{9}$
- C. $\frac{9}{12}$
- D. $\frac{5}{8}$

Give the missing numbers.

10. 85 in. = ▦ ft ▦ in.

- A. 6 ft 13 in.
- B. 7 ft 5 in.
- C. 8 ft 5 in.
- D. 7 ft 1 in.

11. 1 gal = ▦ c

- A. 16
- B. 8
- C. 4
- D. 2

12. 5 lb 12 oz = ▦ oz

- A. 80
- B. 92
- C. 86
- D. 98

13. Which would you be most likely to estimate?

- A. the length of drapes for a window
- B. the length of rope for a clothesline
- C. the length of a picture frame for a special picture
- D. the length of your foot when buying shoes

13

GEOMETRY

MATH AND
HEALTH AND FITNESS

DATA BANK

Use the Health and
Fitness Data Bank on
page 476 to answer
the questions.

1 Which of the sports playing areas has sides that
are all the same length?
Which area is only half as wide
as it is long?

THEME: PLAYING FIELDS

2 Most sports are played on fields that have rectangular shapes. Which sport uses playing fields that are not rectangular?

3 Is the diamond on a baseball field the same shape as a boxing ring? Is a boxing ring the same shape as a karate area?

4 **Using Critical Thinking** Use the clues to solve the riddle. "It is more than 3 yards long. It is less than 40 feet wide. It is not a square. Which sports playing area is it?"

Football is an action-packed sport whose beginnings can be traced back to games played in ancient Egypt.

349

Analyzing Solid Figures

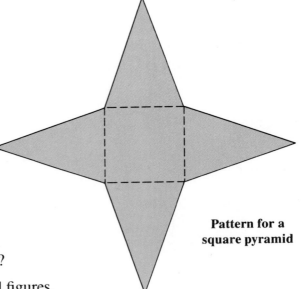

LEARN ABOUT IT

Geometric solid figures are used to make many useful objects.

EXPLORE Make a Model
Trace this figure on your paper. Then cut it out, fold on dashed lines, and tape the edges together to make a solid figure.

Pattern for a square pyramid

TALK ABOUT IT

1. A straight edge of a solid is a **line segment.** How many line segments can you find on your solid?

2. The flat surfaces of your model are its **faces.** Each of its faces is a **polygon.** What kinds of polygons are the faces of your model?

3. A corner of a solid is a **point,** or **vertex.** How many vertices does your solid have?

Here are some of the different types of solid figures.

   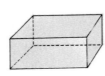 

| cylinder | sphere | rectangular prism | triangular prism | cone | rectangular pyramid |

TRY IT OUT

1. Name a solid figure above that has the figure named below as one or more of its flat surfaces.

   A. square   **B.** triangle   **C.** rectangle

2. A **cube** is a rectangular prism with square faces. How many faces, edges, and vertices does a cube have?

Name a real object that is shaped like each solid figure below.

1.
2.
3.
4.

Name a solid figure that has these flat surfaces.

5. 2 circles

6. 2 squares, 4 rectangles

7. 4 triangles

8. no flat surfaces

9. 2 triangles, 3 rectangles

10. 1 circle

11. Copy and complete this chart for faces, edges, and vertices of solid figures.

Solid Figure	Faces	Edges	Vertices
Rectangular Prism			
Triangular Pyramid			
Triangular Prism			

APPLY

MATH REASONING

12. Do you see a pattern in the table above? (Hint: Add the number of faces to the number of vertices.) How many edges would there be on a solid that has 7 faces and 10 vertices?

PROBLEM SOLVING

13. The cup shaped like a cylinder holds 3 times as much as the cup shaped like a cone. If the cone-shaped cup holds 198 mL, how much does the other cup hold?

14. A tent floor is 4 yd long and 3 yd wide. If twice the area of the floor is needed to set up the tent, how many square yards of ground are needed?

▶ USING CRITICAL THINKING   Analyze the Situation

15. What figure do you predict will appear on the screen? What if the cylinder is replaced with the sphere? the cone?

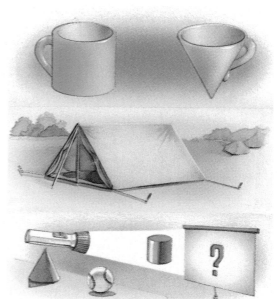

Exploring Triangles

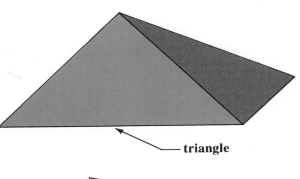

triangle

You have seen that the face of a pyramid is a triangle. In this lesson you will explore the properties of triangles.

EXPLORE **Construct Models**

Work in groups. Fold a sheet of paper. Make a triangle by cutting twice on the folded side. Can you cut a triangle that has

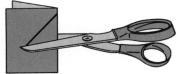

A. exactly 2 sides the same length?
C. a square corner?

B. all 3 sides the same length?
D. a triangle with no sides the same length?

TALK ABOUT IT

1. Which of the triangles above cannot be cut from folded paper? Why?

2. How many angles does a triangle have?

3. Use this picture and your cutout triangles to show a **line of symmetry** of each of the triangles. Can you cut a triangle from folded paper so that the triangle has no line of symmetry?

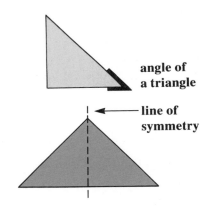

angle of a triangle

line of symmetry

Three types of triangles are shown below.

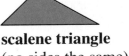

scalene triangle
(no sides the same)

isosceles triangle
(at least two sides the same)

equilateral triangle
(three sides the same)

TRY IT OUT

1. Draw a picture to show the lines of symmetry for each triangle above.

2. Can every triangle be divided by a line into 2 "square corner" triangles? Draw a picture of each type of triangle to explain.

Is the triangle **equilateral, isosceles,** or **scalene?**

1. 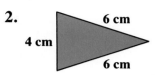 6 cm   3 cm
8 cm

2. 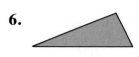 6 cm
4 cm
6 cm

3.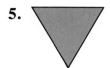

4.

5.

6.

MATH REASONING

Complete the following with **equilateral, scalene,** or **isosceles.**

7. Every __?__ triangle is also an isosceles triangle.
8. No __?__ triangle is also an isosceles triangle.
9. Some __?__ triangles are also equilateral triangles.

PROBLEM SOLVING

10. Draw an isosceles triangle and show a line of symmetry.

11. Use this figure to trace an equilateral, a scalene, and an isosceles triangle. Tell which type each triangle is.

12. How many triangles can you find in this figure? There are more than 6.

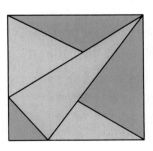

▶ **USING CRITICAL THINKING   Evaluate the Assumptions**

Jim said, "You can draw straight lines and divide any figure into triangles." "I'm not so sure," said Jeryl. "It depends on what you mean by *figures.*"

13. What might Jim have assumed about "figures"? What other assumptions might be made?

14. Is Jim's statement true for all polygons? Draw some pictures to support your conclusion.

More Practice, page 517, set C

Measuring Angles

The size or amount of opening of an angle is measured using a unit called a **degree.** Each of the red angles has a **measure** of 90°.

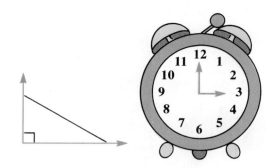

EXPLORE Analyze a Diagram

∠XYZ is an **acute** angle. Acute angles have measures less than 90°.

∠PQR is an **obtuse** angle. Obtuse angles have measures greater than 90°.

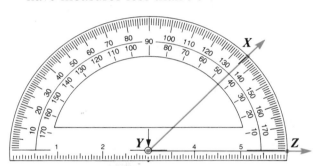

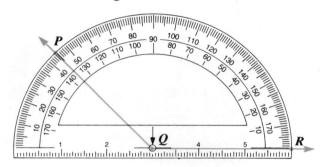

TALK ABOUT IT

1. An angle with a measure of 90° is called a **right** angle. Where would X be in ∠XYZ if ∠XYZ were a right angle?
2. What is the measure of ∠XYZ? How did you decide?
3. What is the measure of ∠PQR? How did you decide?

We use a **protractor** to measure angles. Steps 1, 2, and 3 tell how to use a protractor.

③ **Read the measure of the angle.**

The measure of ∠ABC is 47°

② **Place the zero edge of the protractor along one side of the angle.**

① **Place the arrow on the vertex of the angle.**

TRY IT OUT

Draw 4 angles, 2 acute and 2 obtuse. First estimate, then measure each angle. Record your results in a table.

Estimate	Measure	Difference

354

First **estimate** the measure of each angle. Then use a protractor to check your estimate. Trace the angle and draw longer sides if necessary.

1.
2.
3.
4.

MATH REASONING

Tell if the angle is **right, acute,** or **obtuse.** Choose the best estimate for its measure. Then measure with a protractor. Was your estimate reasonable?

5.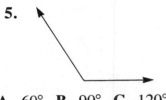

A. 60° **B.** 90° **C.** 120°

6.

A. 15° **B.** 45° **C.** 90°

7.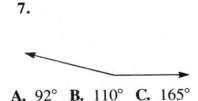

A. 92° **B.** 110° **C.** 165°

PROBLEM SOLVING

8. Explain why the hands of a clock do *not* form a right angle at 12:15 p.m.

9. Give two times when the hands of a clock *do* form a right angle.

▶ ESTIMATION

Estimate whether each angle is closest to 15°, 30°, 45°, 60°, or 90°. Use a protractor to check your estimates.

10.

11.

12.

13.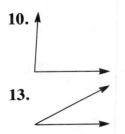

14.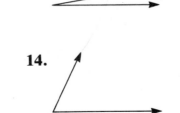

15.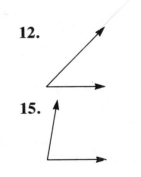

Quadrilaterals

EXPLORE **Make a Figure**

Trace and cut out 4 copies of this right triangle. How many 4-sided figures of different shapes can you make by putting two triangles together? four triangles together? Draw pictures to show your figures.

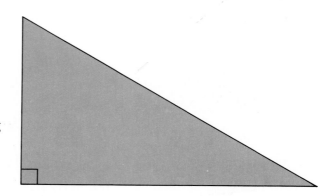

TALK ABOUT IT

1. Can you name your figures? Do some figures have more than one name?
2. Do you think you have made all the possible 4-sided figures? Explain.
3. Can all 4-sided figures be divided into two triangles? Draw pictures to justify your answer.

Four-sided polygons are called **quadrilaterals.**
Here are some different types of quadrilaterals.

Square

Rhombus

Rectangle

All sides the same length
All angles right angles

All sides the same length

Two pairs of sides the same length
All angles right angles

Parallelogram

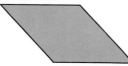

Trapezoid

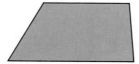

Kite

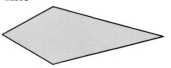

Two pairs of sides the same length
Two pairs of parallel sides

Exactly one pair of parallel sides

Two pairs of touching sides the same length

Copy and complete each statement.

1. A square is also a __?__ .

2. A rhombus is also a __?__ .

Write the name that best describes each figure: **square, rectangle, parallelogram, rhombus, trapezoid,** or **kite.**

1.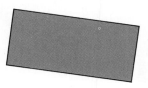

2.

3.

4.

5.

6.

MATH REASONING

Which quadrilateral has

7. all sides the same length and four right angles?

8. only one pair of parallel sides?

9. no right angles, but two pairs of parallel sides?

PROBLEM SOLVING

10. How many *different* rectangles can be found on a 5 by 5 geoboard? Here are some rules and hints.

- Sides do not have to be parallel to the sides of the geoboard.

- The same rectangle in a different position does not count as different.

- There are more than 10 but less than 20.

- Squares are a type of rectangle.

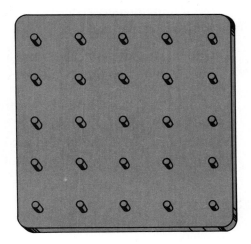

▶ **USING CRITICAL THINKING** Test a Conjecture

11. Myron said, "Every rectangle is a square." Barry said, "No, you're wrong. Every square is a rectangle." Write a paragraph supporting the statement you think is correct.

More About Quadrilaterals

Jai alai is a popular sport in Mexico and Florida. Players can hurl the ball, called a *pelota*, at speeds up to 150 mph.

LEARN ABOUT IT

A jai alai court is a quadrilateral. It is also a rectangle. In this lesson you will learn more about other quadrilaterals.

EXPLORE Try Some Paper-Folding

Work in groups. Fold a sheet of paper and cut out a piece like this. What kind of a figure will it be when you unfold it? Try to cut out pieces that unfold to make

A. a square.

B. a rectangle.

C. a rhombus.

D. a trapezoid.

E. a kite.

F. a parallelogram that is not a square, a rectangle, or a rhombus.

TALK ABOUT IT

1. Which quadrilaterals did you find cannot be cut from a folded piece of paper?

2. Can all of the quadrilaterals that you were able to cut out be folded so that two halves match exactly? Explain.

A quadrilateral has a **line of symmetry** if it can be folded so that the two halves match exactly. Some quadrilaterals have no lines of symmetry. Others have more than one line of symmetry.

TRY IT OUT

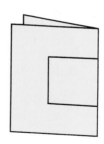

1. Tell what this figure will be when cut out and unfolded.

2. Give the total number of lines of symmetry for the unfolded figure.

Give the number of lines of symmetry for each geometric
shape. Trace and fold the shape if necessary.

1. 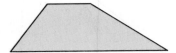   **2.**   **3.**

4.   **5.**    **6.**

APPLY

MATH REASONING

Draw what you would cut from the folded paper in order to
get a figure that when unfolded would be

7. a long thin rectangle **8.** a square folded on the diagonal

9. a thin rhombus **10.** a trapezoid with one very short side

PROBLEM SOLVING

11. Here is a horizontally symmetric
word and a vertically symmetric
word. Give another example of each.

12. Health and Fitness Data Bank How many lines
of symmetry are drawn on a basketball court? Find
another line of symmetry on the court. See page 476.

MIXED REVIEW

Multiply. Reduce answers to lowest terms.

13. $\frac{2}{3} \times \frac{1}{5}$ **14.** $\frac{3}{8} \times \frac{2}{4}$ **15.** $\frac{5}{7} \times \frac{3}{5}$ **16.** $\frac{2}{7} \times \frac{3}{4}$

17. $\frac{5}{6} \times \frac{1}{2}$ **18.** $\frac{3}{4} \times \frac{1}{8}$ **19.** $\frac{1}{2} \times \frac{2}{3}$ **20.** $\frac{3}{5} \times \frac{3}{4}$

21. $\frac{2}{3} \times 1\frac{1}{4}$ **22.** $1\frac{1}{2} \times 3\frac{1}{3}$ **23.** $\frac{3}{4} \times 2\frac{1}{5}$ **24.** $2\frac{1}{4} \times 1\frac{1}{3}$

Using Critical Thinking

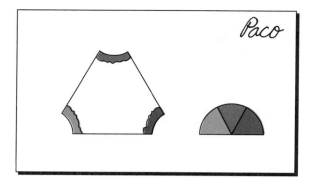

Paco

Paco made a poster to show something he discovered about the angles of a triangle. "I cut off the corners of an equilateral triangle," he explained. "Since the three angles fill half a circle and it can be folded to form two right angles, I've proved that the sum of the angles of a triangle is 180°. The angles fit into a **straight angle!**"

"But look at the triangles on my poster," said Sally. "You used an equilateral triangle. My triangles aren't equilateral, so I'm not sure you've proved what you say you did."

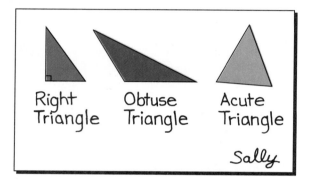

Right Triangle   Obtuse Triangle   Acute Triangle

Sally

TALK ABOUT IT

1. Do you think Sally has a good point? Explain.

2. How could you help support the conclusion that the sum of the measures of the angles of any triangle is 180°?

TRY IT OUT

Try an experiment that helps support Paco's conclusion. Measure the angles and find the sum of the angle measures of each triangle. Do the results agree with your earlier conclusion?

1.

2.

3.

4. A triangle has a 47° angle and a 26° angle. What is the measure of the other angle?

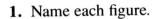

POWER PRACTICE/QUIZ

1. Name each figure.

2. What shapes are the faces in in figure **A**?

3. How many faces, edges, and vertices are in figure **B**?

A   B   C   D

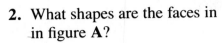

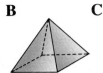

Which of the triangles below are

4. scalene?

5. equilateral?

6. isosceles?

A.   B.   C.   D.

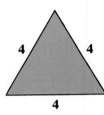
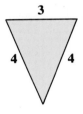
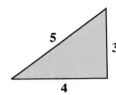

Which of the triangles above have

7. a right angle?

8. an acute angle?

9. an obtuse angle?

Estimate the angle measure each angle is closest to: 15°, 30°, 45°, 60°, or 90°. Then use a protractor to check.

10.

11.

12.
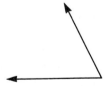

PROBLEM SOLVING

13. A triangle has a right angle. What is the sum of the measures of its other angles?

14. A triangle has an obtuse angle and two sides that are the same length. Are the two sides that are the same length longer than or shorter than the third side?

15. A certain prism is 3 inches tall. The bottom face is in the shape of this hexagon. What is the shape of the top?

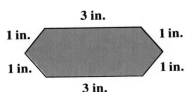

361

Congruent Figures and Motions

Two figures are **congruent** to each other if they have the same size and shape. In sports, rules require that certain playing fields be congruent. For example, every football field is congruent to other football fields and every professional soccer field is congruent to other professional soccer fields.

EXPLORE Make a Figure

Draw a scalene triangle on the left half of a sheet of paper.

TALK ABOUT IT

How can you use tracing paper to help you draw a figure on the right half that is

1. congruent to the top figure, but **turned** in a different direction?
2. congruent to the top figure, but **flipped** over?
3. a figure that has been neither turned nor flipped?

Two figures are **congruent** if you can slide, flip, or turn (rotate) one to make it fit exactly on the other.

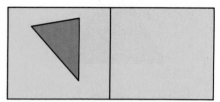
figure   turned

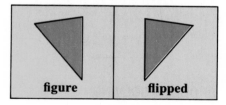
figure   flipped

TRY IT OUT

Use your tracing paper to decide whether figure A must be **slid, slid and turned,** or **slid and flipped** to fit on figure B.

1. A → B

2. A → B

3. A → B

4. A → B

Is figure A congruent to figure B? Use tracing paper to test.
Then tell which you had to do: **slide, slide and turn,** or
slide and flip.

1.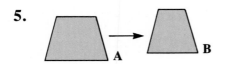

2.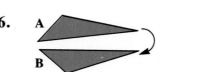

3.

4.

5.

6.

APPLY

MATH REASONING

7. Copy this figure on graph paper. Draw
the reflection image of the triangle by
flipping it across line *a*. Draw the
reflection image of the new triangle by
flipping it across line *b*. What single
motion would move the original triangle
onto the final triangle?

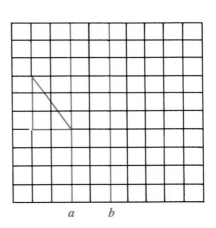

a   *b*

PROBLEM SOLVING

8. **Health and Fitness Data Bank**   In professional
baseball, what part of the field is congruent to the same
part of other fields? Can you find two stadiums that
seem to have congruent outfields? See page 476.

▶ **USING CRITICAL THINKING   Give a Counterexample**

Do you agree with the statement?
If not, give an example that shows that it is not true.

9. Dorcas said "All right angles are congruent."

10. Martin said "All right triangles are congruent."

Problem Solving
Using Data from a Picture

UNDERSTAND
ANALYZE DATA
PLAN
ESTIMATE
SOLVE
EXAMINE

LEARN ABOUT IT

To solve some problems, you must find the data you need in a picture.

The Sea Rovers are going on a sailing trip on an old ship named the *C. A. Thayer*. Dawn is making a model of the ship. She needs to know the measure of ∠C of the mizzensail.

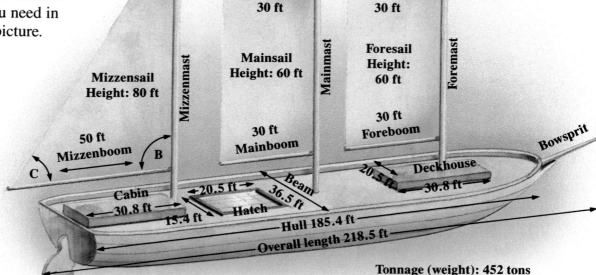

Tonnage (weight): 452 tons
Total area of canvas (sails): 7,292 ft

I'll find the data I need in the picture.

Now I can use the fact that the sum of the angles of a triangle is 180°.

I can add the angles I know. Then I can subtract from 180°.

Angle A is 30°.
Angle B is a right angle. It is 90°.

$$30° + 90° = 120°$$
$$180° - 120 = 60°$$

The measure of ∠C is 60°.

TRY IT OUT

1. How much greater is the overall length of the ship than the length of the hull?

2. What is the area of the top of the rectangular deckhouse?

364

Solve. Use any of the strategies. You may need data from page 364.

Some Strategies	
Act Out	Make a Table
Use Objects	Solve a Simpler Problem
Choose an Operation	Make an Organized List
Draw a Picture	Work Backward
Guess and Check	Look for a Pattern
Use Logical Reasoning	

1. The *C. A. Thayer* has 6 sails. The total area of the sails is about 7,292 ft². Another ship, the *Bowdoin,* has 4 sails with 2,566 ft² of sail area. About how much greater is the area of the sails on the *C. A. Thayer*?

2. What is the area of the rectangular mainsail on the *C. A. Thayer*?

3. Suppose the *Thayer's* mizzensail had been cut in one piece from a rectangular piece of canvas. What would the area of that piece of canvas have been?

4. What is the area of the *Thayer's* mizzensail? (You can use your answer to problem 3 to help you.)

5. The *Balclutha* weighs about 3.7 times as much as the *C. A. Thayer.* How much does the *Balclutha* weigh?

6. What is the perimeter of the deckhouse on the *C. A. Thayer*?

7. For the trip on the *C. A. Thayer,* the 65 Rovers are divided into crews. There are 13 in each crew. How many crews are there?

8. Roddy practiced knot tying for 5 minutes the first day, 10 minutes the second day, 15 minutes the third day, and so on. How many minutes would he have practiced in all at the end of the fifth day?

9. Janice needs to decide which one of the following crews she wants to be on: galley, linehandler, deckhand, fishing, rigger. She also needs to decide if she wants to be a sailor or an officer on her crew. How many different choices does she have?

10. On Eric's model of a ship, the hull is 10 in. long. The hull of the actual ship is 240 times as long. How many feet long is the hull of the actual ship?

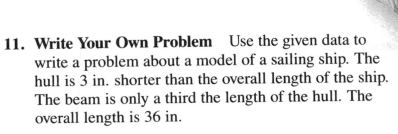

11. **Write Your Own Problem** Use the given data to write a problem about a model of a sailing ship. The hull is 3 in. shorter than the overall length of the ship. The beam is only a third the length of the hull. The overall length is 36 in.

Other Polygons
Tessellations

EXPLORE **Examine a Pattern**

Cathy's neighbor liked to make quilts.
Here are two of her patterns.

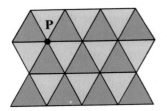

Pattern A

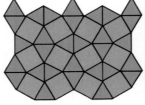

Pattern B

TALK ABOUT IT

1. What type of polygon was used to make pattern A? How
   many of these fit around point P?
2. Describe the types of polygons and their arrangements in
   pattern B.
3. How are patterns A and B alike? How are they different?

In geometry, quilt patterns of polygons like those above are
called **tessellations.** Some **regular polygons** (polygons
with all sides congruent and all angles congruent) can be
used to make tessellations. Equilateral triangles, squares,
hexagons, and octagons (with another polygon) can be used,
but pentagons cannot.

**pentagon
(5 sides)**

**hexagon
(6 sides)**

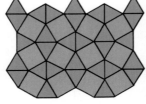

**octagon
(8 sides)**

TRY IT OUT

1. Look for examples of tessellations in your school and
   other places. Describe the kinds of polygons used.
2. Trace copies of the hexagon to make a tessellation that
   covers a square at least 3 in. on a side.

366

A

B

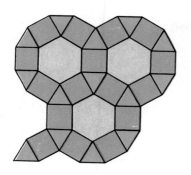

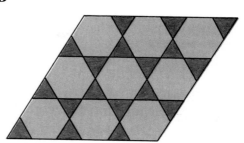

1. Name the polygons used to make tessellation A.
2. Name the polygons used to make tessellation B.
3. What polygon is on each side of every hexagon in A?
4. What polygon is on each side of every hexagon in B?

APPLY

MATH REASONING

5. Here is another tessellation. How is it like tessellations A and B? How is it different from tessellations A and B?

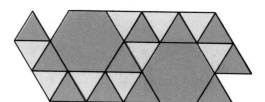

PROBLEM SOLVING

6. Lyle made a floor design using a square and an octagon. The design was a tessellation. Use tracing paper and draw a tessellation that covers a square 4 in. on a side.

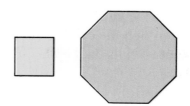

MIXED REVIEW

Give the number for each ▦.

7. $\frac{1}{2}$ gal = ▦ qt

8. 3 qt = ▦ pt

9. 32 fl oz = ▦ c

Multiply. Reduce to lowest terms.

10. $3\frac{1}{4} \times 2\frac{1}{3}$

11. $2\frac{1}{2} \times 3\frac{1}{3}$

12. $1\frac{1}{8} \times 2\frac{3}{4}$

13. $3\frac{1}{2} \times \frac{2}{3}$

14. $\frac{3}{8} \times 4$

More Practice, page 518, Set D

Circles

We see circles every day. Circles are useful in making a great many things, from tractor tires to colorful decorative designs.

EXPLORE Make Circular Designs

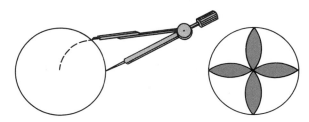

- Can you use a compass to make this design?

- Make a circular design of your own and color it.

TALK ABOUT IT

1. When you draw a circle with a compass, the compass tip is at the **center** of the circle. How are the points on the circle related to the center of the circle?

2. Draw a line segment with endpoints on the circle and which passes through the center. How does the length of the total segment compare to the length from the center to one of the endpoints? Do you think this is always true?

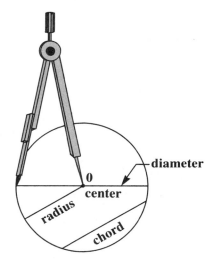

The distance the compass is open when you use it to draw a circle is the **radius** of the circle. The distance across the circle through the center is the **diameter.** A **chord** is a line segment with its endpoints on the circle.

TRY IT OUT

1. Draw several circles, each with a different radius. Measure with a centimeter ruler to complete a table like this.

Circle	radius (cm)	diameter (cm)
1	?	?
2	?	?

Look for a pattern to help you complete these statements.

2. The length of the diameter of a circle is __?__ the length of the radius.

3. The length of the radius of a circle is __?__ the length of the diameter.

Measure the diameter or radius shown in red to the nearest centimeter. Use this measure to find the other.

1.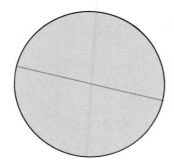

2.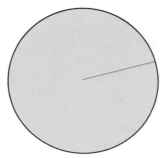

3.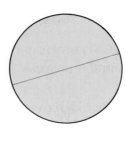

Use a compass and a centimeter ruler to draw a circle with

4. radius 5 cm.   **5.** diameter 6 cm.   **6.** diameter 4 cm.   **7.** radius 3 cm.

APPLY

MATH REASONING

8. Draw a circle in which the diameter is equal to the radius multiplied by itself.

PROBLEM SOLVING

9. How many circles can you make with a radius of 1 unit on the dot paper at the right? A unit is the vertical or horizontal distance between 2 dots. Copy the dot paper and show your circle.

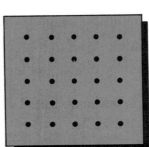

▶ **ESTIMATION**

10. A circular pool has a diameter of 6 m. About what distance would you go if you walked all the way around it?

Choose the best estimate.

A. 6 m   **B.** 12 m

C. 18 m   **D.** 24 m

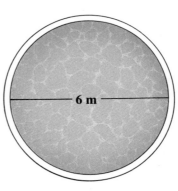

More Practice, page 518, set E

Circumference

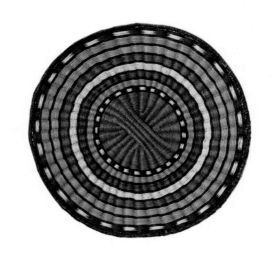

The **circumference** of a circle is the distance around the circle.

EXPLORE **Discover a Relationship**
Work in groups.

- Use a string and a ruler to find the circumference (C) and the diameter (d) of a can to the nearest millimeter. Record your measurements in a table like the one at the right.

- Divide the circumference by the diameter. Use a calculator to find the quotient to the nearest tenth. Record the quotient in the table.

- Repeat this activity with at least four other objects.

Object	C	d	$\frac{C}{d}$

TALK ABOUT IT

1. Is there a number around which your quotients appear to cluster?

2. Do you think this ratio $\left(\frac{C}{d}\right)$ will be the same regardless of the circular object you measure?

The ratio $\frac{C}{d}$ is the same for all circles. We call this ratio *pi* (symbol π). We know:

$$\pi = \frac{C}{d} = 3.1415926 \text{ (to seven decimal places)}$$

We can also write $C = \pi \times d$ (or $C = \pi d$). Since the diameter is twice the radius ($d = 2r$), we can also write $C = 2\pi r$. As approximations for π, we often use 3.14 or $3\frac{1}{7} = \frac{22}{7}$.

TRY IT OUT

Find the circumference. Use 3.14 for π.

1. $d = 12$ cm   2. $r = 8$ mm   3. $r = 8.5$ cm   4. $d = 12.1$ m

Find the circumference.

1.

Marker: $d = 1.8$ cm

2.

Quarter: $r = 12$ mm

3.

Glass: $d = 6.5$ cm

Estimate the circumference of each.

4.

Dime: $d = 17$ mm

5.

Cup: $r = 7.2$ cm

6.

Saucer: $d = 3.9$ cm

APPLY

MATH REASONING

Use a calculator to find the missing measurement to the nearest tenth.

7. $C = 85$ cm, $d = $ ▥   **8.** $C = 63$ cm, $r = $ ▥   **9.** $C = 6.28$ cm, $d = $ ▥

PROBLEM SOLVING

10. A playing field has the shape shown at the right. The ends of the field are half circles. Find the perimeter of the entire playing field.

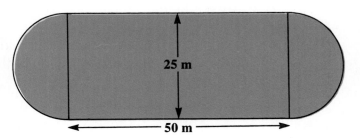

25 m

50 m

▶ **USING CRITICAL THINKING   Make a Conjecture**

11. Suppose the diameter of a circular memorial garden is doubled. Make a conjecture (general statement) about how this would change the circumference of the garden. Make up several examples to test your conjecture.

12. Suppose the radius of a circular garden is doubled. How would this change the circumference of the garden? Make a conjecture and test it.

Coordinate Geometry

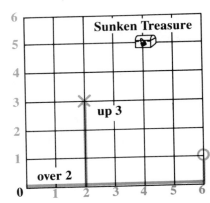

To find where to mark the point, start at 0 and go **over** 2 and **up** 3.

A mathematician named Descartes (1596−1650) invented a way to use pairs of numbers to show points on a grid. This idea has been used in mathematics and science ever since.

EXPLORE   Learn from a Game

- Try a game with a partner.

  Make a copy of the Sunken Treasure grid. Roll number cubes and use the pair of numbers to mark a point on the grid as shown with an **X.** Then your partner rolls the number cubes and marks the point with an **O.**

- The first person to land on the sunken treasure wins the game. Repeat the game several times.

Your Roll

Your Partner's Roll

TALK ABOUT IT

1. Does the number pair (3, 5) have the same location on the grid as (5, 3)? Explain.

2. What if you found a location for a number pair by going up first and then over? Would the location of the pair (2, 3) change? Explain.

Pairs of numbers like (3, 5) are called **coordinates** or **ordered pairs.** When you mark a point for the coordinates, you are **graphing the point.**

TRY IT OUT

1. Mark 4 points on a grid that form a trapezoid when the points are connected. Give the coordinates of the points.

2. Give a partner the coordinates for 3 points that form an isosceles triangle and ask him or her to graph the points and connect them.

Start with point *A* and give the coordinates of the vertices of each polygon in order. Name each polygon.

1.
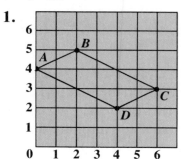

2.
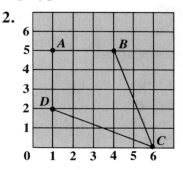

3.
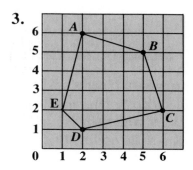

MATH REASONING

Graph these points. Connect them in order and name the polygon.

4. (1, 3), (3, 8), (5, 2), (1, 3)

5. (1, 6), (5, 10), (9, 6), (7, 1), (3, 1), (1, 6)

6. (3, 4), (3, 7), (6, 9), (9, 7), (9, 4), (6, 2), (3, 4)

7. (3, 9), (6, 9), (8, 7), (8, 4), (6, 2), (3, 2), (1, 4), (1, 7), (3, 9)

Graph these sets of points. Connect the points and show the lines of symmetry on the figures.

8. (7, 5), (5, 9), (1, 7), (3, 3), (7, 5)

9. (1, 1), (1, 3), (6, 3), (6, 1), (1, 1)

PROBLEM SOLVING

10. How many different squares can you find on a 5-by-5 geoboard? You may count congruent squares as different if their positions on the board are different.

▶ **ALGEBRA**

11. Use numbers less than 10 and show 5 more cards this machine would produce. Graph the coordinates on each card. What do you discover?

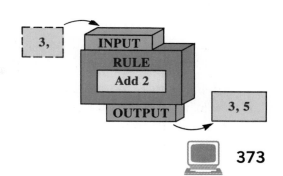

Applied Problem Solving
Group Decision Making

UNDERSTAND
ANALYZE DATA
PLAN
ESTIMATE
SOLVE
EXAMINE

Group Skill:
Disagree in an Agreeable Way

You have bought a new chair and have decided to rearrange your living room. Work with your group to copy on graph paper the outline of the room and each piece of furniture. Cut out the pieces of furniture.

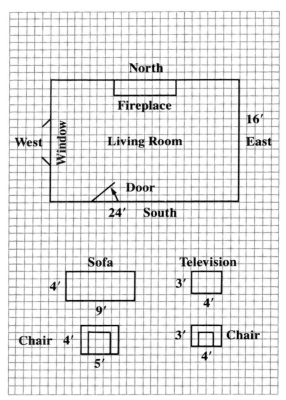

Facts to Consider

- You want to arrange the furniture so that someone sitting on the sofa or a chair can see the television set.
- You do not want any furniture directly in front of the fireplace.
- As you try different arrangements, you may want to record them so that you can remember which ones you have tried.
- There is a window in the west wall that you like to gaze through as you are sitting on the sofa or chair.

374

1. Is there enough room on the west wall to put the two chairs and the television?

2. Will the sofa fit against the south wall without getting hit by the opening door?

3. Can the television and the sofa be on the same side of the room?

4. How many different arrangements can you make?

Use graph paper to make a drawing of the arrangement that your group decided to use. Tell why you chose that arrangement.

WRAP UP

Word Scavenger Hunt

Each word described below can be found in this chapter. Give the word.

1. A 13-letter word that means four sided.

2. 10 letters that name an instrument used to measure angles.

3. A 9-letter word that describes a triangle with at least two equal sides.

Sometimes, Always, Never

Complete each statement by writing **sometimes**, **always**, or **never**. Explain your choices.

4. Solid figures  have straight edges.

5. A rectangle __?__ is a special parallelogram.

6. An isosceles triangle __?__ has three acute angles.

Project

Benny sometimes sees models of geometric ideas that remind him of situations he observes in everyday life. For example, a circle has points that continue in a repeating sequence again and again. The circle reminds him of the phases of the moon—new moon, quarter moon, half moon, three quarters moon, full moon—that occur regularly month after month. What other examples from everyday life can you think of that occur regularly over a period of time?

Parallel lines remind Amelia of events that happen at the same time but that are not really related. For example, she remembers an article she read about county fairs that were being held in Texas and Oklahoma during the same two weeks in August. What examples from your own experience suggest the idea of events that take place at the same time but are not related in other ways?

POWER PRACTICE/TEST

Part 1 Understanding

Name a solid figure that has exactly these flat surfaces.

1. 2 triangular surfaces

2. 1 circular surface

3. 2 circular surfaces

Draw an example of each quadrilateral.

4. parallelogram

5. trapezoid

6. rhombus

7. A triangle has angles that measure 45° and 37°. What is the measure of the third angle?

8. Draw a triangle. Use slide and flip to produce a congruent triangle.

9. Name the polygons used to make this tessellation.

10. Draw and label a scalene, an isosceles, and an equilateral triangle.

11. Mark 5 points on a grid that form a pentagon. Give the coordinates of the points.

Part 2 Skills

12. Draw a square. Then draw all of its lines of symmetry.

13. Use a compass and ruler to draw a circle with a diameter of 16 cm.

14. Find the circumference of a circle with radius 6.3 cm. Use 3.14 for π.

15. What is the measure of angle A?

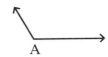

A

Part 3 Applications

16. Mrs. Herrera wants to fence in her garden. How much fencing does she need in addition to a 4-ft gate?

17. **Challenge** Which requires more fencing to go around it, a square garden plot with a side of 4 units or a circular garden plot with a radius of 2 units?

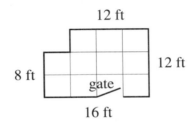

12 ft

8 ft

12 ft

gate

16 ft

ENRICHMENT
Top, Bottom, Front, and Side Views

Most space figures look different when viewed from different places.

Make a model of a triangular prism. Draw pictures to show what it would look like if you looked at it from the top, from the bottom, and from the front.

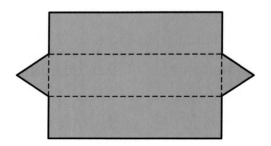

Make or use models of the following shapes. For each shape, draw the top view, bottom view, front view, and side view.

1. triangular pyramid

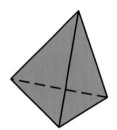

2. cube

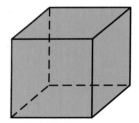

3. hexagonal prism

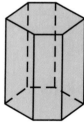

4. cylinder

5. rectangular prism

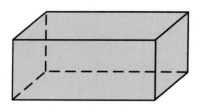

6. square pyramid

7. Which figure has four and only four identical views?

8. How are the top view of the triangular pyramid and the top view of the square pyramid alike?

CUMULATIVE REVIEW

Multiply.

1. $\frac{2}{3} \times 30$

    A. 20   B. 2   C. 15   D. 4

2. $\frac{5}{8} \times \frac{1}{4}$

    A. $\frac{1}{12}$ B. $\frac{3}{4}$ C. $\frac{5}{32}$ D. $\frac{2}{5}$

3. $15 \times \frac{3}{4}$

    A. $4\frac{1}{2}$ B. $11\frac{1}{4}$ C. $7\frac{1}{2}$ D. 20

4. $2\frac{3}{4} \times 1\frac{2}{3}$

    A. $4\frac{7}{12}$ B. $2\frac{2}{7}$ C. $3\frac{1}{2}$ D. 2

5. There are 40 people on the editorial staff of a local newspaper. $\frac{5}{8}$ are reporters and $\frac{1}{5}$ are photographers. How many people are *neither* reporters *nor* photographers?

    A. 33   B. 25   C. 8   D. 7

6. Which would you use to estimate this sum?

$$8\frac{1}{4} + 4\frac{7}{15} + 7\frac{9}{10}$$

    A. $9 + 4\frac{1}{2} + 8$ B. $9 + 5 + 8$

    C. $8 + 4\frac{1}{2} + 8$ D. $8 + 4 + 7$

Choose the missing numbers.

7. 65 oz = ▓ lb ▓ oz

    A. 4, 1 B. 5, 5 C. 8, 1 D. 16, 1

8. 8 ft 5 in. = ▓ in.

    A. 29   B. 293   C. 101   D. 74

9. 4 gal = ▓ c

    A. 32   B. 16   C. 48   D. 64

10. Which is the least common multiple of 3 and 7?

    A. 7   B. 21   C. 14   D. 28

11. To estimate $\frac{3}{8} \times 58$ using compatible numbers, find

    A. $\frac{1}{10}$ of 60, then multiply by 3

    B. $\frac{1}{7}$ of 56, then multiply by 3

    C. $\frac{1}{8}$ of 48, then multiply by 3

    D. $\frac{1}{8}$ of 56, then multiply by 3

12. What common denominator would you use to find the difference between $3\frac{1}{3}$ and $1\frac{3}{4}$?

    A. sixths   B. twelfths

    C. eighths   D. tenths

13. Rafe is 5 more than 3 times Wesley's age. If Rafe is 17, how old is Wesley?

    A. 4   B. 2

    C. 32   D. 7

14

RATIO AND PERCENT

THEME: WEATHER

MATH AND
SCIENCE

DATA BANK

Use the Science Data
Bank on page 473 to
answer the questions.

1 What was the average
number of degrees
Fahrenheit that the
temperature fell each hour
between noon and midnight
in Fairfield, Montana, on
December 24, 1924?

2 How many degrees did the temperature rise in Spearfish, South Dakota, between 7:30 am and 7:32 am? About how many degrees per minute was this?

3 At an altitude of 15,000 feet above sea level, about how many degrees colder would the air be than the air at sea level?

4 Using Critical Thinking
Study the graph of temperatures on the day of a storm. At what time do you think the storm began? About how long do you think the storm lasted?

Weather forecasters base predictions on data from land-based stations, ships at sea, and weather satellites.

381

Ratio

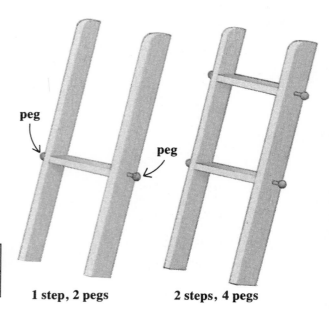

EXPLORE **Look for a Pattern**

Work in groups. Use dot paper to draw
ladders with different numbers of steps and
2 pegs for each step. Copy and complete the
table. Then graph the ordered pairs (steps,
pegs) on a coordinate grid.

Steps	1	2	3	4	5	6	7	8
Pegs	2	4						

1 step, 2 pegs   2 steps, 4 pegs

TALK ABOUT IT

1. What patterns do you see in the table?
2. If you connect the points for the ordered pairs, what
   would the new graph look like?
3. If there were 50 steps, how many pegs would there be?
   How do you know?

Two numbers can be compared by a **ratio.** A ratio can be
written in three ways. The ratio of the number of steps to
the number of pegs can be written:

In words	Colon notation	Fraction notation
1 to 2	1:2	$\frac{1}{2}$

Use the double ladder at the right to find
each ratio. Write each ratio in three ways.

1. number of steps to the number of
   pegs

2. number of steps to the number of
   bars

3. number of bars to the number of
   pegs

4. number of pegs to the number of bars

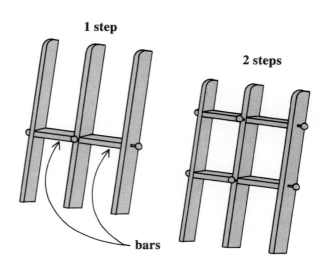

1 step

2 steps

bars

Write the ratio suggested by each picture in three ways.

1.

packs to cans

2.

tires to bicycles

3.

balls to cans

4.

oranges to glasses

5. Bananas: 89 cents for 3 pounds.

cents to pounds

6. 3 apples for 60 cents

cents to apples

APPLY

MATH REASONING

Write three different ratios for each picture or set of data.

7.

8.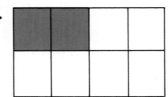

9.

Smith	10 pts
Denman	12 pts
Clark	6 pts
Ball	8 pt
Total	36 pts

PROBLEM SOLVING

10. Out of 29 students 11 listed soccer as their favorite sport. What ratio will compare the number of students who did not pick soccer to the total number of students?

11. How many different ratios can be formed using the numbers 8, 9, and 10? Each ratio must use 2 different numbers. Write the ratios.

▶ **ESTIMATION**

12. What ratio could be used to compare the size of rectangle A to rectangle B?

Ratio Tables

The same ratio may be shown
by different fractions.

EXPLORE **Study the Situation**

An LP record makes
5 complete turns every
9 seconds.

TALK ABOUT IT

1. What ratio compares the number of turns to the number
   of seconds?
2. How long would it take to make 10 complete turns?
   What is this ratio of turns to seconds?
3. Give one other ratio that compares turns to seconds for
   LP records.

Since 5 turns take 9 seconds, 10 turns would take 18
seconds, 15 turns would take 27 seconds, and so on. A
ratio table can be used to record the ratios. Here is an
example using the data about LP records.

	5×1	5×2	5×3	5×4	5×5	5×6
Number of turns	5	10	15	20	25	30
Number of seconds	9	18	27	36	45	54
	9×1	9×2	9×3	9×4	9×5	9×6

The ratios $\frac{5}{9}$, $\frac{10}{18}$, $\frac{15}{27}$, $\frac{20}{36}$, $\frac{25}{45}$, and $\frac{30}{54}$ are **equal ratios.**
They are named by equivalent fractions.

TRY IT OUT

Copy and complete the ratio table to solve this problem.

A record makes 3 turns every 4
seconds. How many seconds will it
take to make 15 turns?

	3×1	3×2	3×3	3×4	3×5
Turns	3	6	9	12	15
Seconds	4				
	4×1	4×2	4×3	4×4	4×5

384

Copy and complete each ratio table.

1.

1	2	3	4	5	6
8	16				

2.

2	4	6	8	10	12
7	14				

3.

8	16	24	32	40	48
3	6				

4.

1	2	3	4	5	6
25					

Write = or ≠ (not equal) for each pair of ratios. Use a ratio table if necessary.

5. $\frac{2}{3}$  $\frac{6}{10}$

6. $\frac{4}{12}$ $\frac{1}{4}$

7. $\frac{2}{5}$ $\frac{14}{35}$

8. $\frac{1}{10}$ $\frac{10}{100}$

9. $\frac{5}{6}$ $\frac{25}{36}$

10. $\frac{3}{10}$ $\frac{2}{5}$

11. $\frac{7}{8}$ $\frac{24}{32}$

12. $\frac{400}{800}$ $\frac{1}{2}$

APPLY

MATH REASONING

13. Make a ratio table with the data given in the bar graph. What two items are being compared?

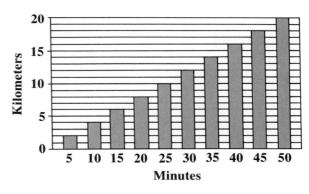

PROBLEM SOLVING

14. A cup of milk provides 2 mg (milligrams) of vitamin C. Make a ratio table that shows the vitamin C in 1, 2, 3, 4, and 5 cups of milk.

15. Samantha earned $19 by working 3 hours. About how many hours must she work to earn $100?

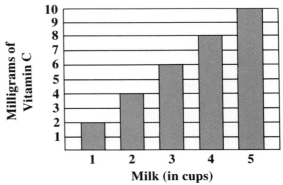

▶ **ALGEBRA**

16. Which expression can be used to find equal ratios when any nonzero number replaces the number n?

A. $\frac{2 + n}{3 + n}$ **B.** $\frac{2 \times n}{3 \times n}$

Proportions

EXPLORE Study the Information

A thunderstorm was raging near Gary's house. Gary's sister told him that for every 1 mile between him and the lightning, there would be a 5-s gap between lightning and thunder. Gary counted 20 s between the time he saw lightning and the time he heard thunder.

TALK ABOUT IT

1. What ratio compares the distance from the lightning strike to the seconds counted?
2. How many seconds did Gary count?

If you know the ratio of distance in miles to seconds passed, you can find how far away lightning is. You can use a ratio table, or you can write and solve a proportion. An equation showing that two ratios are equal is called a **proportion.** Here is how to solve a proportion.

Let n equal the miles between Gary and the thunder. Write an equation of equal ratios.

$$\frac{1}{5} = \frac{n}{20}$$

Since $5 \times 4 = 20$,
$1 \times 4 = n$.
So, $n = 4$.
The lightning is
4 mi away.

Other Examples

A $\frac{3}{5} = \frac{n}{40}$

$5 \times 8 = 40$
$3 \times 8 = 24$
$n = 24$

B $\frac{4}{9} = \frac{n}{45}$

$9 \times 5 = 45$
$4 \times 5 = 20$
$n = 20$

Solve.

1. $\frac{5}{6} = \frac{n}{24}$

2. $\frac{1}{4} = \frac{n}{20}$

3. $\frac{9}{10} = \frac{n}{50}$

4. $\frac{2}{3} = \frac{n}{18}$

5. $\frac{4}{3} = \frac{n}{9}$

6. $\frac{3}{4} = \frac{n}{20}$

7. $\frac{4}{7} = \frac{n}{28}$

8. $\frac{3}{8} = \frac{n}{48}$

Solve.

1. $\frac{9}{10} = \frac{n}{50}$ 2. $\frac{5}{2} = \frac{n}{10}$ 3. $\frac{1}{4} = \frac{n}{28}$ 4. $\frac{4}{5} = \frac{n}{25}$ 5. $\frac{7}{3} = \frac{n}{18}$

6. $\frac{7}{9} = \frac{n}{72}$ 7. $\frac{1}{2} = \frac{n}{60}$ 8. $\frac{2}{5} = \frac{n}{30}$ 9. $\frac{5}{12} = \frac{n}{48}$ 10. $\frac{3}{2} = \frac{n}{100}$

11. $\frac{6}{9} = \frac{n}{45}$ 12. $\frac{7}{6} = \frac{n}{42}$ 13. $\frac{1}{3} = \frac{n}{45}$ 14. $\frac{10}{9} = \frac{n}{27}$ 15. $\frac{9}{10} = \frac{n}{1000}$

APPLY

MATH REASONING

16. To find the ratio of the number of hits to the total times at bat, Kelly solved $\frac{1}{3} + \frac{2}{3}$. Did Kelly find the correct ratio? Explain. Draw pictures if you wish.

Kelly's Batting Record		
	Game 1	Game 2
hits	1	2
times at bat	3	3

PROBLEM SOLVING

17. In Becky's town, it rains 3 out of every 10 days during the spring. About how many rainy days should Becky expect out of 60 spring days?

18. Stormydale has thunderstorms 22 out of every 30 days. About how many days with thunderstorms could Stormydale expect to have out of 90 summer days?

19. **Science Data Bank**   What city has rain or snow about 1 out of every 10 days of the year? See page 473.

▶ **USING CRITICAL THINKING   Make a Generalization**

20. Find the products for the red numbers and the black numbers in each proportion. These products are called the **cross products.** Complete the statement below.

$\frac{2}{3} = \frac{6}{9}$ $\frac{4}{5} = \frac{12}{15}$ $\frac{15}{24} = \frac{5}{8}$ $\frac{3}{10} = \frac{30}{100}$

"When two ratios are equal, their cross products are __?__ ."

Problem Solving
Using Data from a Scale Drawing

UNDERSTAND
ANALYZE DATA
PLAN
ESTIMATE
SOLVE
EXAMINE

LEARN ABOUT IT

Maps, blueprints, and floor plans are examples of scale drawings. In this map, 1 cm on the map represents an actual distance of 10 km.

Jeremiah and his family went to Yellowstone National Park. They drove from Mammoth Hot Springs to Norris. How far did they drive?

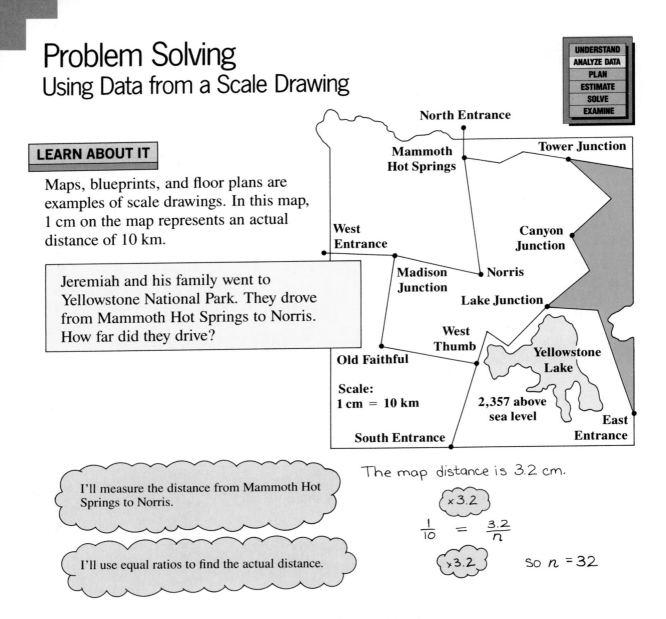

North Entrance

Tower Junction

Mammoth Hot Springs

West Entrance

Canyon Junction

Madison Junction

Norris

Lake Junction

West Thumb

Old Faithful

Yellowstone Lake

Scale:
1 cm = 10 km

2,357 above sea level

East Entrance

South Entrance

I'll measure the distance from Mammoth Hot Springs to Norris.

I'll use equal ratios to find the actual distance.

The map distance is 3.2 cm.

×3.2

$$\frac{1}{10} = \frac{3.2}{n}$$

×3.2

so $n = 32$

The actual distance from Mammoth Hot Springs to Norris is 32 km.

TRY IT OUT

1. Bart's family drove from the West Entrance to Madison Junction. How many kilometers did they drive?

2. Roman hiked along the road from Norris to Old Faithful Geyser. How long was the hike?

3. It is 20 km from Canyon Junction to Norris. How many centimeters would this road be on the map?

4. Nelly biked from Lake Junction to Tower Junction. How far did she bike?

Solve. Use any of the strategies.

1. How far would you drive if you made a trip from Old Faithful to West Thumb and back?

2. It took Marge $5\frac{1}{2}$ h to walk from Canyon Junction to Lake Junction. It took Grecia $4\frac{3}{4}$ h to walk the same distance. How much longer did Marge take?

3. Abe, Babs, Carol, and Don each like a different national park. One likes Rocky Mountain, another Yellowstone, another Acadia, and another Grand Canyon. Abe's favorite is not Yellowstone or Rocky Mountain. Babs likes Acadia. Don's favorite does not start with the letter Y. Which national park does each like best?

4. How much farther is it from Lake Junction to West Thumb than from Lake Junction to Canyon Junction?

5. Julie biked from Mammoth Hot Springs to Tower Junction. How far did she bike?

6. From Madison Junction to Canyon Junction is about 40 km. How many centimeters should this be on the map?

7. Yellowstone National Park, the oldest national park, became a park in 1872. How old was the park in 1990?

8. When Ted came in the North Entrance and Tom came in the East Entrance, they were 138 km apart. They are both traveling toward Canyon Junction. Ted has gone 34.2 km and Tom has gone 27.9 km. How far apart are they now?

9. Jake's family drove from West Thumb to the East Entrance. Their average speed was 58 kilometers per hour. How far did they drive?

10. To reach the park, Julio drove 8 times as far as the distance between the West Entrance and Madison Junction. How far did Julio drive?

11. **Write Your Own Problem** Write a problem that can be solved using equal ratios. Use data from the map on page 388.

389

Understanding Percent

EXPLORE **Make a Model**

EXPLORE **Make a Model**

Use your finger to trace a path through the maze from "Start" to "End." Is there more than one path?

Design a maze of your own. Shade squares on a 10 by 10 grid of paper to form a path from "Start" to "End." Trade mazes with classmates for some "a-maze-ment."

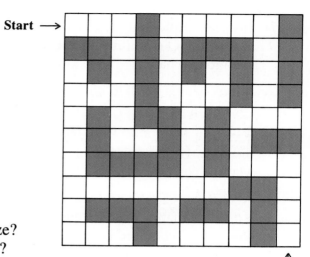

Start →

↑ End

TALK ABOUT IT

1. How many total squares are in your maze?
2. How many of the squares did you shade?
3. What ratio compares the shaded squares to all squares?
4. What ratio compares the unshaded squares to all squares?

To make the maze shown above, 41 out of 100 squares in the grid were shaded.

A ratio that compares a number to 100 can be expressed as a **percent.**
41 percent means 41 out of 100.
The word "percent" means "per hundred."

The symbol % is used with numbers as a symbol for percent. $41\% = \frac{41}{100}$

Other Examples

A 20% means 20 out of 100. $20\% = \frac{20}{100}$ **B** 1% means 1 out of 100. $1\% = \frac{1}{100}$

TRY IT OUT

Write as percents.

1. 3 out of 100   2. $\frac{19}{100}$ 3. 66 to 100   4. $\frac{100}{100}$

Write each percent as a ratio in fraction form.

5. 9%   6. 33%   7. 75%   8. 43%

Write a ratio as a fraction and a percent for the part of the region that is shaded.

1. 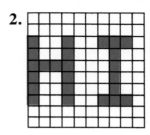 2. 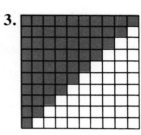 3. 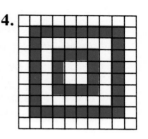 4.

Write each ratio as a percent. Write each percent as a fraction.

5. 3 to 100 **6.** $\frac{58}{100}$ **7.** 79 to 100 **8.** $\frac{85}{100}$ **9.** 1 to 100

10. 16% **11.** 29% **12.** 48% **13.** 20% **14.** 15.2%

APPLY

MATH REASONING

Estimate the percent for each point labeled on the number line.

15. 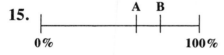 **16.**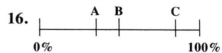

PROBLEM SOLVING

17. If you have 35 cents in change, what percent of a dollar do you have in change? What additional percent would you need in order to have a dollar?

18. Jenny had \$1. She spent 79¢. What percent of the dollar did she spend? What percent of a dollar does she have left?

MIXED REVIEW

Tell whether +, −, or × should be written in the ◯.

19. $\frac{3}{4} \bigcirc \frac{3}{4} = 1\frac{1}{2}$ **20.** $\frac{5}{6} \bigcirc \frac{2}{3} = \frac{1}{6}$ **21.** $\frac{2}{5} \bigcirc \frac{1}{2} = \frac{2}{10}$ **22.** $\frac{6}{8} \bigcirc 3\frac{2}{4} = 4\frac{1}{4}$

Write the number of sides for each polygon.

23. quadrilateral **24.** octagon **25.** triangle **26.** pentagon

More Practice, page 520, set A

Percents as Decimals or Fractions

LEARN ABOUT IT

When computing with percents, a fraction or a decimal is used for the percent.

EXPLORE Examine a Picture

Have you ever tried to solve a cross-number puzzle? Examine this example.

TALK ABOUT IT

1. How many squares are in the grid? What part of the total grid is shaded?

2. What decimal names the part of the grid that is shaded?

3. What percent of the grid is shaded?

In the picture above, 22 out of 100 squares are shaded. We can write a percent as a fraction and as a decimal.

$$22\% = \frac{22}{100} = 0.22$$

1	5	7	2			6	3	8	4
6	3		5	8	4	7		9	2
2	9	6	4		9	5	6	1	7
3		9	7		3	2	9		3
	7	8	9	5	6		8	5	
	1	3		4	2	9	3	7	
7		5	8	2		7	1		4
3	5	7	6	9		2	4	7	8
9	8		1	7	3	6		6	3
5	2	7	4			8	1	3	6

Other Examples

A $38\% = \frac{38}{100} = 0.38$ **B** $100\% = \frac{100}{100} = 1.00$ **C** $47\% = \frac{47}{100} = 0.47$

TRY IT OUT

Write a fraction and decimal for each percent.

1. 25%   **2.** 60%   **3.** 10%   **4.** 75%   **5.** 50%

Write as a percent.

6. 0.15   **7.** $\frac{33}{100}$ **8.** 0.07   **9.** $\frac{83}{100}$ **10.** 0.57

11. $\frac{105}{100}$ **12.** $\frac{35}{100}$ **13.** 0.19   **14.** $\frac{28}{100}$ **15.** 0.99

Write a fraction, a decimal, and a percent that tells what part of each 10 by 10 grid is shaded.

1. 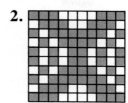   **2.** 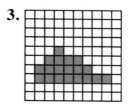   **3.** 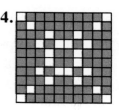   **4.**

Write each ratio as a percent and as a decimal.

5. 3 to 100   **6.** 23 to 100   **7.** 79 to 100   **8.** 94 to 100

9. $\frac{37}{100}$ **10.** $\frac{58}{100}$ **11.** $\frac{17}{100}$ **12.** $\frac{85}{100}$

Write each percent as a fraction and as a decimal.

13. 2%   **14.** 49%   **15.** 95%   **16.** 9%   **17.** 30%

Write a percent for each decimal.

18. 0.45   **19.** 0.07   **20.** 0.61   **21.** 0.01   **22.** 0.5

MATH REASONING

23. Which is greater, 0.08 or 80%?

24. Which number is the same as 100%?
A. 0.01 **B.** 100 **C.** 1.0 **D.** 0.100

PROBLEM SOLVING

25. Jill's batting average was 0.320. What percent of her times at bat did Jill get a hit?

26. In his last 75 times at bat, Garo has 20 hits. He expects to be at bat 25 more times this season. How many more hits does he need to have hits 30% of his times at bat?

▶ **MENTAL MATH**

What percent of 1 dollar is each of these U.S. coins?

27. penny   **28.** nickel

29. dime   **30.** quarter

More Practice, page 520, set B

Percents and Lowest-terms Fractions

EXPLORE **Examine a Graph**

Mrs. Alba's class made a circle graph to show how many days last year Austin had some rain or snow and how many days it had none.

TALK ABOUT IT

1. What fraction of the circle represents days with rain or snow?

2. What fraction of the circle represents days without rain or snow?

3. What percent of days do not have rain or snow?

Rainy or Snowy Days in Austin

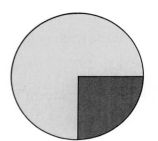

■ Days with rain or snow

□ Days without rain or snow

To write a fraction as a percent, find an equivalent fraction with a denominator of 100.

$\frac{3}{10} = \frac{30}{100}$ and $\frac{30}{100} = 30\%$ ($\times 10$)

$\frac{4}{5} = \frac{80}{100}$ and $\frac{80}{100} = 80\%$ ($\times 20$)

Percents can also be expressed as lowest-terms fractions.

$40\% = \frac{40}{100} = \frac{2}{5}$ ($\div 20$) $25\% = \frac{25}{100} = \frac{1}{4}$ $50\% = \frac{50}{100} = \frac{1}{2}$

TRY IT OUT

Give the percent for each fraction.

1. $\frac{1}{10}$ 2. $\frac{3}{5}$ 3. $\frac{7}{10}$ 4. $\frac{11}{25}$ 5. $\frac{19}{20}$

Give the lowest-terms fraction for each percent.

6. 60%   7. 12%   8. 2%   9. 45%   10. 64%

394

POWER PRACTICE/QUIZ

Gracie's math class has 6 boys for every 5 girls.
Copy and complete the ratio table.

Boys	6	12			
Girls	5	10			

1. Write the ratio of boys to girls in three ways.

2. If there are 12 boys, how many students are in the class?

Are these ratios equal? **3.** $\frac{6}{5}, \frac{15}{18}$

4. $\frac{30}{25}, \frac{24}{15}$

5. $\frac{10}{12}, \frac{30}{36}$

Solve for *n.*   **6.** $\frac{2}{3} = \frac{n}{9}$

7. $\frac{7}{4} = \frac{n}{28}$

8. $\frac{8}{9} = \frac{n}{900}$

9. What fraction of the square is shaded?

10. What percent of the square is shaded?

11. Write a fraction and a decimal for the part that is not shaded.

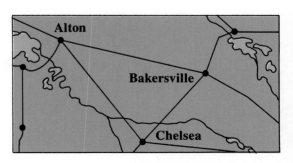

Write a percent for each.

12. $\frac{15}{100}$ **13.** 0.03   **14.** $\frac{80}{100}$ **15.** 0.20

16. 0.05   **17.** $\frac{1}{2}$ **18.** $\frac{4}{5}$ **19.** $\frac{2}{50}$

Write a lowest-terms fraction for each.

20. 25%   **21.** 64%   **22.** 90%   **23.** 6%

PROBLEM SOLVING

One centimeter on this map represents an actual distance of 20 km.

24. Find the map distance and the actual distance between:
    A. Alton and Bakersville
    B. Bakersville and Chelsea

25. Julio can ride his bike 16 km in 1 h. At that rate, how long will it take him to bike from Alton to Bakersville and back?

kilometers	16	32	
hours	1	2	

Mental Math and Estimation with Percents

EXPLORE **Draw a Picture**

You can use mental math to find some percents of numbers by substituting fractions for the percents before computing. Copy the dot pictures below. Draw a ring around dots to show the answers.

Percents		Fractions
$10\% = \frac{1}{10}$		$20\% = \frac{1}{5}$
$25\% = \frac{1}{4}$		$33\frac{1}{3}\% = \frac{1}{3}$
$50\% = \frac{1}{2}$		$75\% = \frac{3}{4}$

Find 50% of 30.

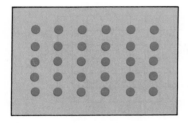

Find 10% of 60.

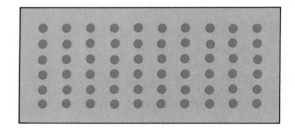

TALK ABOUT IT

1. How did you find 50% of 30? 10% of 60?

2. How does thinking about 50% as $\frac{1}{2}$ help you find 50% of 30 mentally?

You can estimate a percent of a number by substituting one of the percents given in the chart at the top of the page. You can also substitute compatible numbers.

Estimate: 27% of 48 is about 25% of 48, or $\frac{1}{4}$ of 48.
27% of 48 is about 12.

21% of 19 is about 20% of 20, or $\frac{1}{5}$ of 20.
21% of 19 is about 4.

TRY IT OUT

Solve. Use mental math, and estimation when appropriate.

1. 19% of 25
2. 50% of 18
3. 27% of 80
4. $33\frac{1}{3}\%$ of 15

Solve. Use mental math.

1. 10% of 30   **2.** 20% of 45   **3.** 25% of 8   **4.** 50% of 400

5. 25% of 40   **6.** $33\frac{1}{3}$% of 24   **7.** 75% of 20   **8.** 10% of 1,000

Estimate.

9. 24% of 32   **10.** 50% of 61   **11.** 32% of 21   **12.** 11% of 50

13. 9% of 80   **14.** 26% of 44   **15.** 10% of 199   **16.** $33\frac{1}{3}$% of 31

APPLY

MATH REASONING

Give 2 numbers that could replace each variable.

17. 23% of x is about 20.   **18.** 73% of y is between 40 and 50.

PROBLEM SOLVING

19. In Los Angeles, 10% of the days in a year have some rain. Is this number of days more than or less than the number of days in a 30-day month?

20. Science Data Bank What fraction of the days in a year have rain or snow in Juneau, Alaska? About what percent is this? See page 473.

DATA BANK

MIXED REVIEW

Write **oz, lb,** or **T** for the unit you would use to weigh each item.

21. a feather   **22.** a large ship   **23.** a truck   **24.** a jar of cinnamon

25. a sack of potatoes   **26.** yourself   **27.** a TV set   **28.** a tulip

Complete each sentence.

29. The distance across a circle is the ___?___ .

30. The distance around a circle is the ___?___ .

31. The distance from the center of a circle to a point on the circle is the ___?___ .

32. The symbol π represents the ratio of the ___?___ to the diameter of a circle.

Finding a Percent of a Number

EXPLORE Analyze a Situation

The members of the Sky Searchers Club want to buy a small telescope. They decided to buy the telescope shown in this advertisement in a local newspaper.

TALK ABOUT IT

1. What is the regular price of the telescope in the advertisement?

2. What is the meaning of the term "20% off"?

3. How can you use mental math to find 20% of $400?

Bring the heavens 200 times closer!

Regularly $395.00

Quality TELESCOPE NOW

20% OFF

You can multiply to find a percent of a number. Write percents as fractions or as decimals to multiply. Here is how to find 20% of $395.

20% of $395 is the same as 0.20 × $395.

$$\begin{array}{r} \$395 \\ \times\ 0.20 \\ \hline \$79.00 \end{array}$$

You can use the percent key on a calculator.
20 [%] [×] 395 [=]

Other Examples

A 25% of $128
$\frac{1}{4} \times 128 = 32$
25% of $128 is $32.

B 30% of $60
$0.30 \times 60 = 18.00$
30% of $60 is $18.

C 85% of $120
$0.85 \times 120 = 102.00$
85% of $120 is $102.

Find the percent of each number or amount.

1. 16% of 800
2. 80% of $64.95
3. 23% of 2,000
4. 75% of 400

5. 15% of 200
6. 60% of 150
7. 45% of 160
8. 30% of 600

Find the percent of each amount. Round answers to the nearest cent if necessary.

1. 15% of $90.00 **2.** 25% of $400.00 **3.** 75% of $160.00 **4.** 8% of $2,300

5. 3% of $72.00 **6.** 19% of $85.00 **7.** 11% of $72.85 **8.** 66% of $66.66

Find the amount saved.

9.

$210—30% off

10.

$49.95—40% off

11.

$75.00—33% off

12.

$9.95—5% off

13.

$72.00—18% off

14.

$28.00—15% off

APPLY

MATH REASONING

15. A video camera that usually costs $800 is on sale for 20% off. What is the sale price of the camera? (Hint: The new price will be what percent of the original price?)

PROBLEM SOLVING

16. A high-power flashlight regularly costs $29.95. It is on sale for 30% off. Is the sale price more or less than $25?

17. Jean correctly answered 85% of the 60 questions on a science test. On the same test Teresa correctly answered 95% of the items. How many fewer questions did Jean answer correctly?

▶ **USING CRITICAL THINKING   Support Your Conclusion**

18. The regular price of a junior telescope was $120.00. At a sale it was marked 25% off. When the telescope was not sold, it was marked, "Take 10% off the reduced price." Is this the same as taking 35% off the original price of $120.00? Explain.

More Practice, page 520, set E

Problem Solving
Finding Related Problems

UNDERSTAND
ANALYZE DATA
PLAN
ESTIMATE
SOLVE
EXAMINE

When you are solving a problem, sometimes it helps to think about a related problem.

Here are two related problems. They can both be solved using the same strategy.

> At Bud's Safety Gear Shop, hockey helmets come in 4 colors: white, black, blue, and yellow. They come in 3 brands: Racer, Brock, and Safe-T. How many different helmets can Ralph choose from?

white-Racer	black-Racer	blue-Racer	yellow-Racer
white-Brock	black-Brock	blue-Brock	yellow-Brock
white-Safe-T	black-Safe-T	blue-Safe-T	yellow-Safe-T

Ralph can choose from 12 different helmets.

> The players on Jan's team have 2-digit numbers on their jerseys. They used the digits 3, 4, and 5. How many different numbers could they make?

33 34 35   43 44 45   53 54 55

They could make 9 different 2-digit numbers.

TRY IT OUT

Solve. Tell which two problems are related.

1. Ms. Wong bought two hockey helmets—one for Sam and one for John. She paid $63 in all. Sam's helmet cost $11 more than John's. How much did John's cost?

2. Elvira spent 50% of her money for a bike helmet. Then she spent $2.19 on a water bottle. She had $3.55 left. How much money did she have before she bought those items?

3. On Monday 69 students rode bikes to school. 5 more of them wore helmets than rode without helmets. How many wore helmets?

Choose a strategy from the strategies list or use other strategies to solve these problems.

Use the circle graph to solve problems 1 and 2.

Some Strategies	
Act Out	Make a Table
Use Objects	Solve a Simpler Problem
Choose an Operation	Make an Organized List
Draw a Picture	Work Backward
Guess and Check	Look for a Pattern
Use Logical Reasoning	

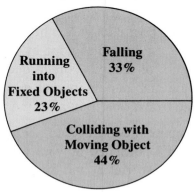

**Causes of Bicycle Injuries
(200 Injuries)**

Running into Fixed Objects 23%

Falling 33%

Colliding with Moving Object 44%

1. How many of the 200 injuries in the circle graph were from falls?

2. How many of the injuries were from running into a fixed object?

3. Jan bought her helmet at school. How much did she pay for it?

$32.95 regular price
20% off if you buy it at your school this week

4. Gina spent 25% of the $16 she had saved in order to buy a bicycle light. How much did the light cost?

5. Almost 9 out of 10 adults who do serious bicycle racing wear helmets. Out of 90 serious adult bikers, how many would probably wear helmets?

6. In which two age groups do about 56% of the bike injuries occur?

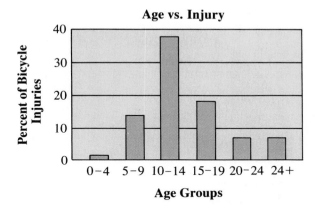

Age vs. Injury

Percent of Bicycle Injuries

Age Groups: 0–4 5–9 10–14 15–19 20–24 24+

7. 126 students from all the elementary schools met to discuss bicycle safety. They split into committees of 14 students. How many committees were there?

8. On Friday 75 students rode their bikes to school. 40% wore helmets. Only 14 bikes had current licenses. How many students wore helmets?

More Practice, page 527, set B

Data Collection and Analysis
Group Decision Making

UNDERSTAND
ANALYZE DATA
PLAN
ESTIMATE
SOLVE
EXAMINE

Doing an Investigation
Group Skill:
Explain and Summarize

A minute can seem like a very short time when you are playing a video game, or it can seem like a long time if you are waiting for a bus. Do you think you can estimate a minute? Conduct an investigation to see how well you can estimate a minute to find out whether you can improve your estimation skills with practice.

Collecting Data

1. Each person in your group will take turns estimating a minute. You will need a watch which gives time in seconds and a person to watch the time. Your group's timer says when to start, and the estimator says when he or she thinks a minute has gone by. The actual number of seconds is recorded in a table. Each person in your group gets three trials, one right after the other.

2. Compute the average number of seconds estimated by your group for trial 1, for trial 2, and for trial 3. Round each average to the nearest whole second.

Name	Number of seconds estimated		
	Trial 1	Trial 2	Trial 3
Len	34	45	. . . . .
Margie	. . . . .	. . . . .	. . . . .
Karin	. . . . .	. . . . .	. . . . .
Tommy	. . . . .	. . . . .	. . . . .

Organizing Data

3. Make a bar graph to show the average number of seconds estimated by the members of your group for each trial.

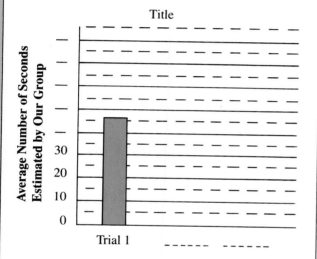

Title

Average Number of Seconds Estimated by Our Group

30
20
10
0

Trial 1

Presenting Your Analysis

4. Write a paragraph about your results. Did your group's average improve with practice?

5. Tell why you think your results turned out as they did. If you did the investigation again, what would you do differently?

WRAP UP

How Do You Do?

In your own words, tell how you do each of the following.

1. Find the missing number in $\frac{5}{6} = \frac{n}{30}$.

2. Write 60% as a fraction in lowest terms.

3. Use mental math to find 75% of 40.

4. Make a ratio table for the ratio 4:7.

5. Estimate 28% of 300.

6. Write $\frac{4}{5}$ as a percent.

Sometimes, Always, Never

Complete each statement by writing **sometimes**, **always**, or **never**. Explain your choices.

7. Percent is a special ratio that __?__ compares a number to a cent.

8. To change a fraction to a percent, you can __?__ divide the numerator by the denominator, then write the % sign.

9. The first number in a ratio is __?__ smaller than the second.

10. A ratio can __?__ be written as a percent.

Project

Draw the letters of the alphabet from A to Z in block letters on graph paper. Compare the areas of at least 5 different pairs of letters and express the ratios as fractions. Some pairs you can compare are:

E to F O to P S to T

POWER PRACTICE/TEST

Part 1   Understanding

1. Write the ratio that compares the number of triangles to the number of squares in three ways.

2. Write the ratio 9 out of 100 as a percent.

Write each as a percent.

3. 0.5   4. 0.41   5. $\frac{2}{5}$ 6. $\frac{3}{10}$

Write a lowest-terms fraction for each.

7. 12%   8. 4%   9. 80%   10. 75%

What strategy would you use to solve? Write a related problem.

11. Pablo walked south 6 blocks, east 4 blocks, and north 3 blocks. How far north and west does he have to walk to get back where he started?

Part 2   Skills

Solve.

12. $\frac{5}{6} = \frac{n}{30}$ 13. $\frac{3}{4} = \frac{n}{36}$ 14. 22% of 450

15. 35% of $65.40   16. $33\frac{1}{3}$% of 96   17. 75% of 80

Part 3   Applications

18. On the floor plan for Bart's room, 2 cm represents 1 m. How wide is the room if the floor plan width is 14 cm?

19. A recipe for 6 bran muffins calls for 2 teaspoons baking powder. Make a ratio table that shows teaspoons of baking powder needed for 12, 18, 24, and 36 muffins.

20. **Challenge** When a piece of clothing arrives at Rainy Day Discounts, the date and full price are marked on it. After 1 week, the price goes down 25%. After 2 weeks, another $33\frac{1}{3}$% is taken off the last price. After 3 weeks, 50% is taken off the last price. Give examples to show that the final price is $\frac{1}{4}$ of the original price.

ENRICHMENT
Percent Patterns Using Mental Math

If you know 10% of a number, you can find or estimate other percents of the number. Ms. Evans wanted to find 15% of $24, so she thought

> 10% is $2.40.
> 5% is $1.20.
> 15% is $3.60.

Study each of the problems below. Do you see a pattern?

$$\begin{array}{r} 60 \\ \times\, 0.10 \\ \hline 6 \end{array} \qquad \begin{array}{r} 240 \\ \times\, 0.10 \\ \hline 24 \end{array} \qquad \begin{array}{r} 160 \\ \times\, 0.10 \\ \hline 16 \end{array} \qquad \begin{array}{r} 3{,}400 \\ \times\, 0.10 \\ \hline 340 \end{array}$$

Use the products above to find each of these percents of a number.

1. 5% of 60

2. 5% of 240

3. 5% of 160

4. 5% of 3,400

5. 1% of 60

6. 1% of 240

7. 1% of 160

8. 1% of 3,400

Use reasoning and your answers above to find these.

9. 15% of 60

10. 11% of 60

11. 15% of 240

12. 11% of 240

13. 15% of 160

14. 11% of 160

15. 15% of 3,400

16. 11% of 3,400

Use 10%, 5%, and 1% to find the percent of each number.

17. 15% of 80

18. 15% of 800

19. 15% of 200

20. 6% of 200

21. 25% of 60

22. 30% of 70

23. 70% of 20

24. 15% of 360

CUMULATIVE REVIEW

1. Which line segment measures $2\frac{1}{4}$ inches to the nearest $\frac{1}{4}$ inch?

A. _____

B. _____

C. _____

D. _____

2. What does this picture show?

A. $\frac{1}{4} \times \frac{5}{6} = \frac{5}{24}$

B. $\frac{3}{4} \times \frac{5}{6} = \frac{5}{8}$

C. $\frac{1}{4} \times \frac{5}{24} = \frac{5}{96}$

D. $\frac{5}{24} \times \frac{5}{6} = \frac{25}{144}$

3. The diameter of a circle is

A. 3 times the radius

B. $\frac{1}{2}$ the radius

C. 3.14 times the radius

D. 2 times the radius

4. Which solid figure has two faces that are circles?

A. sphere B. cone

C. cylinder D. triangular pyramid

5. Find the number of twelfths in 2.

A. 24 B. 6 C. 36 D. 8

6. A triangle has a 52° angle and a right angle. What is the measure of the third angle?

A. 90° B. 142° C. 180° D. 38°

7. Which is the most likely temperature of a hot drink?

A. 32°F B. 70°F

C. 105°F D. 306°F

8. Which describes an isosceles triangle?

A. All three sides are equal.

B. No two sides are equal.

C. Two sides have equal length.

D. One angle measures 90°.

9. What is the first step in measuring an angle with a protractor?

A. Read the measure of the angle.

B. Place the point of the arrow on the vertex of the angle.

C. Place the zero edge along one side of the angle.

D. Follow one ray to the protractor.

10. Multiply $\frac{3}{4} \times 24$.

A. 72 B. 6 C. 18 D. 32

11. How much larger is the area of the barn than the area of the coop?

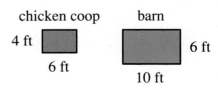

A. 24 ft^2 B. 60 ft^2

C. 20 ft^2 D. 36 ft^2

407

15

PROBABILITY

THEME: AMERICAN INDIAN GAMES

MATH AND
SOCIAL STUDIES

DATA BANK

Use the Social Studies
Data Bank on page 483 to
answer the questions.

1 Len and Barry are playing
Stick Game 1. There
are 51 sticks in the pile.
Len takes out 23 sticks. Barry
gets the rest. Who has more
sticks? Who wins the game?

The sport of blanket tossing began
as a hunting skill developed by
Native Alaskans.

2 Naomi is playing the Hidden Bean Game. How many ways can she make a wrong guess about where the bean is hidden? How many ways can she make a right guess?

3 Maria scored a total of 9 points in 3 turns while she was playing Stick Game 2. How could she have scored that total for 3 turns?

4 **Using Critical Thinking** Think carefully about the rules for Stick Game 1. Why do you think the players always began with an odd number of sticks in the pile?

Fair and Unfair Games

EXPLORE Learn from a Game

Play the game Odd-Even Products with a partner. You will need two number cubes with faces numbered 1 through 6. Follow these rules:

- One player is Odd and the other is Even.
- Each player takes a turn tossing the cubes and finding the product of the two numbers tossed.
- If the product is odd, the Odd player scores 1 point. If it is even, the Even player scores 1 point.
- The first player to get 10 points wins the game.
- Play the game at least 3 times.

TALK ABOUT IT

1. Who won more games, Odd or Even? Were the scores close?
2. Is the game of Odd-Even Products a fair or unfair game? Explain.
3. Make up a table of the possible products for this game. Explain how it can be used to decide whether this is a fair game.

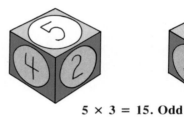

$5 \times 3 = 15$. Odd

$4 \times 2 = 8$. Even

A game in which each of two players has the same chance of winning is a **fair game.** Otherwise it is an **unfair game.** The Odd-Even Products game is not a fair game. The person choosing the even numbers has a better chance of winning.

TRY IT OUT

Change the rules of the game so that the **sum** instead of the product of the two numbers is used for Odd and Even. Play the game several times. Does this seem like a fair game?

Play each game with a classmate. Use a spinner divided into red and blue sections as shown. Decide whether each game is fair or unfair.

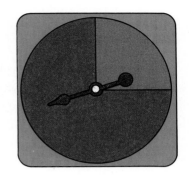

1. **Two-color Spinner Game**   *Rules:* One team is Red, the other Blue. Spin the spinner. The Red team scores 3 points if the pointer stops on red. The Blue team scores 1 point if it stops on blue. 24 points wins!

2. **Five-to-One Game**   *Rules:* The rules are the same as for the two-color spinner game except that the Red team gets 5 points when the spinner stops on red. The Blue team still gets 1 point when the spinner stops on blue.

APPLY

MATH REASONING

3. Make up point values for the sections in the spinner shown above so that the Spinner Game is fair. Make up other values so that it is unfair. How did you decide?

PROBLEM SOLVING

4. **Play a Strategy Game**   Place 15 dots in a straight line. Player 1 draws an X through any dot. Player 2 then circles any other dot on the line. The first player to mark a dot so that there are three consecutive marked dots is the winner. Try to find a winning strategy.

▶ **USING CRITICAL THINKING**   Analyzing a Game

5. **2-Chip Match Game**
   Materials: 2 chips. One chip is labeled "heads" on both sides. The other chip is labeled "heads" on one side and "tails" on the other.

   Rules: One team is the Match team. The other is the No-Match team. Toss both chips at once. If both chips come up heads, then the Match team scores one point. Otherwise, the No-Match team scores a point. 10 points wins!

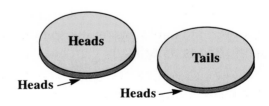

A. Which team would you want to be on, Match or No-Match? Why?

B. Tell why the game is fair or unfair.

Equally Likely Outcomes

American Indians played many tossing games with 2-sided sticks, shells, and bone pieces. When they tossed one of these, it landed on a decorated side or a plain side, so there were 2 possible equally likely results. When you toss a coin you have the same number of results, or **outcomes.**

EXPLORE **Try an Experiment**

Work in groups. Toss a coin 20 times. Keep a record of the outcomes.

Heads	
Tails	

TALK ABOUT IT

1. Did you get about the same number of heads as tails in the 20 tosses? Do you think that heads and tails have the same chance of coming up?
2. Predict how many times you would get heads in 50 tosses of a coin. Try tossing a coin 50 times. How close was your prediction?
3. Suppose you have tossed a fair coin 3 times and it came up tails each time. Do you think it is more likely to come up heads on the next toss than tails?

A head is just as likely to come up as a tail when a fair coin is tossed. The two outcomes are said to be **equally likely.** However, the outcomes on the spinner are not equally likely. Red is more likely than blue or yellow.

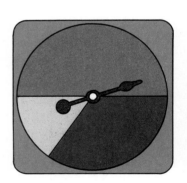

TRY IT OUT

Give all the outcomes for each experiment. Tell if they are equally likely or not.

1. Toss a number cube.

2. Spin the spinner.

3. Spin the spinner.

412

Try each activity. Decide if the outcomes are equally likely.

1. Toss a number cube 50 times. Keep a record of the number of times each outcome occurs.

2. Toss a paper cup 50 times. Keep a record of the way it lands.

Up   Down   Side

3. Toss 2 number cubes 50 times. An outcome is the sum of the 2 numbers tossed. Keep a record of the number of times each sum occurs.

4. Spin a spinner like this 50 times. Keep a record of the outcomes.

MATH REASONING

5. Make up a game using three numbers cubes where each outcome is equally likely.

DATA BANK

PROBLEM SOLVING

6. Local telephone numbers have seven digits, for example, 555-6842. What is the greatest sum possible for the last 4 digits? the smallest sum? Are all sums in between possible?

7. **Social Studies Data Bank** Give the name of a game played by American Indians that has the same number of outcomes as tossing a coin. See page 483.

▶ **ALGEBRA**

8. Toss a thumb tack many times (at least 25).
   Let **U** = number of times it lands with point **up.**
   Let **D** = number of times it lands point **down.**
   Let **T** = the number of **tosses.**

   Write the ratios $\frac{U}{T}$ and $\frac{D}{T}$.

   Which ratio is greater? Do you think the two outcomes are equally likely?

Up   Down

Probability of Outcomes

EXPLORE **Analyze a Situation**

The spinner is divided into four parts of equal size. The four outcomes, 1, 2, 3, and 4, are equally likely to happen. Suppose you spin the spinner 100 times.

TALK ABOUT IT

1. Which describes your chances of spinning a 3?
   A. 1 chance in 100
   B. 1 chance in 10
   C. 1 chance in 4
   D. 1 chance in 2

2. What are your chances of spinning the number 5?

3. What are your chances of spinning a number less than 5?

There is **1 chance in 4** of spinning the number 3 on the spinner. The **probability** of spinning a 3 is $\frac{1}{4}$.

We write: $P(3) = \frac{1}{4}$.

We say: The probability of 3 is $\frac{1}{4}$.

There are **3 chances in 4** of **not** spinning a 2.
$P(\text{not } 2) = \frac{3}{4}$.

There are **0 chances in 4** of spinning a 5.
$P(5) = \frac{0}{4} = 0$

There are **4 chances in 4** of spinning a number greater than 0.
$P(\text{number} > 0) = \frac{4}{4} = 1$.

The probability of any outcome is always a number from 0 through 1.

TRY IT OUT

Give the probability of each outcome.

1. Toss a coin.
   $P(\text{heads}) = $ ▨
   $P(\text{tails}) = $ ▨

2. Toss a number cube (1−6).
   $P(1) = $ ▨ $P(4) = $ ▨
   $P(2) = $ ▨ $P(5) = $ ▨
   $P(3) = $ ▨ $P(6) = $ ▨

Give the probability of the outcome.

1. Spin the spinner.

$P(4) = $ ▦

2. Toss a coin.

$P(\text{Tails}) = $ ▦

3. Toss a number cube.

$P(3) = $ ▦

4. Spin the spinner.

$P(C) = $ ▦

5. Toss a number cube.

$P(9) = $ ▦

6. Spin the spinner.

$P(\text{even number}) = $ ▦

MATH REASONING

Use the spinner at the right to complete Exercises 7–10.

7. $P(5) = $ ▦   **8.** $P(2) = $ ▦

9. $P(\text{odd number}) = $ ▦   **10.** $P(\text{even number}) = $ ▦

PROBLEM SOLVING

11. Laurie bought 5 tickets for a door prize. A total of 175 tickets were sold. What is the probability that Laurie will win the door prize?

12. You can win a large teddy bear if on one toss of a fair number cube, you get a 1 or a 6. What is the probability of **not** winning the bear?

Change the measures to pounds and ounces.

13. 54 oz   **14.** 49 oz   **15.** 29 oz   **16.** 24 oz   **17.** 63 oz

Solve each proportion.

18. $\frac{2}{3} = \frac{x}{9}$ **19.** $\frac{4}{10} = \frac{x}{30}$ **20.** $\frac{3}{6} = \frac{x}{42}$ **21.** $\frac{3}{12} = \frac{x}{48}$

More Practice, page 521, set A

Experimental and Mathematical Probabilities

When American Indians played games of chance such as tossing 2-sided sticks or other objects, they often tossed more than one at a time. If you toss more than one coin at a time, you can do coin-tossing experiments faster.

EXPLORE Try an Experiment
Work in groups. If you toss a penny 100 times, how many heads and how many tails do you think you will get? Try it.

TALK ABOUT IT

1. How many heads did your group get in 100 tosses?

2. Write the ratio: **number of heads to number of tosses.**
   Is this ratio close to $\frac{1}{2}$? Should it be close to $\frac{1}{2}$?

3. Combine your results with those of other groups and find the ratio of heads to tosses. Is this ratio closer to $\frac{1}{2}$?

We can compare the **experimental probability** for the penny tossing with the **mathematical probability.**

Mathematical Probability

$$P(\text{heads}) = \frac{50}{100} \quad \begin{array}{l} \leftarrow \text{ expected number} \\ \leftarrow \text{ of heads} \\ \leftarrow \text{ total tosses} \end{array}$$
$$= \frac{1}{2}$$

Experimental Probability

$$P(\text{heads}) = \frac{47}{100} \quad \begin{array}{l} \leftarrow \text{ actual number} \\ \leftarrow \text{ of heads} \\ \leftarrow \text{ total tosses} \end{array}$$

The experimental probability is close to the mathematical probability, because $\frac{47}{100}$ is close to $\frac{1}{2}$.

TRY IT OUT

1. Find the experimental and mathematical probabilities of tossing an even number with one number cube. Use at least 40 tosses.

2. Find the experimental and mathematical probabilities of getting a match of numbers when you toss two cubes numbered 1-6. Use at least 25 tosses.

Complete each probability activity. Give the experimental and the mathematical probabilities.

1. Spin the spinner 60 times.

$P(\text{number} < 4)$

2. Toss a number cube 60 times.

$P(6)$

3. Spin the spinner 100 times.

$P(\text{even number})$

APPLY

MATH REASONING

4. Estimate how many times you might have to roll a number cube before all 6 numbers have come up at least once each. Try the experiment several times. What is the least number of rolls you took?

5. Estimate how many times you might have to toss a coin before you get 3 heads in a row or 3 tails in a row. Then try the experiment and compare the actual number with your estimate.

PROBLEM SOLVING

6. Social Studies Data Bank How many outcomes are possible in the American Indians' Stick Game 2? Do you think each of the outcomes is equally likely? See page 483.

► **CALCULATOR**

7. Jeff and Jenny used a computer program to simulate tossing a coin 15,000 times. Then they used their calculators to find whose result was closer to the mathematical probability. Jeff's simulation gave heads 7,119 times. Jenny's gave heads 7,804 times. Whose simulation gave a result closer to the mathematical probability?

Using Critical Thinking

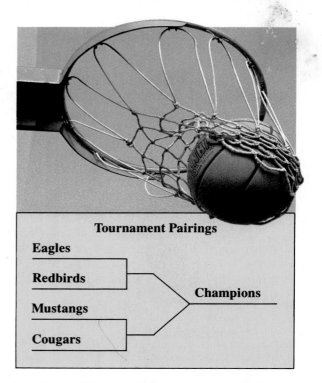

"Well," said the Redbirds' coach, "It looks like a tough tournament." "It really does," agreed the assistant coach. "Do you think we can beat the Eagles in the first round? If we do, what team do you predict we will play for the championship?"

The coach looked at the tournament pairings and the information sheet shown below. Then he whispered his prediction to the assistant coach.

Tournament Pairings

Eagles

Redbirds

Mustangs

Cougars

Champions

Scores for Season Games				Tournament Data
Redbirds	68	Cougars	67	The tournament is being played on the Redbirds' home court.
Eagles	75	Mustangs	58	
Redbirds	94	Mustangs	61	Freddie Flash, the Cougars' best player, will not be able to play. The Eagles are a young team, with no tournament experience.
Cougars	59	Eagles	57	
Eagles	74	Redbirds	73	
Cougars	68	Mustangs	60	

TALK ABOUT IT

1. How can the scores help the coach make his prediction?

2. How can the Tournament Data help the coach to make his prediction?

3. Is the probability of winning the tournament $\frac{1}{4}$ for each team? Why or why not?

4. Which team do you predict will win the tournament? Explain.

Choose a sports league you are interested in. Predict which team will win or have the best record. Give reasons for your predictions.

418

POWER PRACTICE/QUIZ

Use pictures A, B, and C for review items 1–4.

A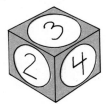

B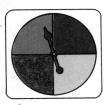

C

1. List the possible outcomes for each toss of the number cube or spin of a spinner. Tell whether the outcomes are equally likely.

2. Find these probabilities for the toss of the number cube.

   A. $P(3)$ **B.** $P(\text{odd number})$ **C.** $P(\text{number} < 7)$ **D.** $P(7)$

3. For spinners B and C, which outcomes have a probability of $\frac{1}{4}$?

4. After 1,000 spins of spinner C, would you expect
   A. more 10s or more 20s?   **B.** more 20s or more 30s?

This spinner was spun 100 times and produced the outcomes shown.

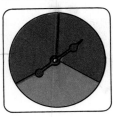

> **r** means the spinner pointed in the red area and **b** means it pointed in the blue.
>
> b b r r b b b r b b b b b b r r b r b b
> b b r b b r b r b b b r r b b r b r r b
> b b r r b b b r b b b r b b r b b b r b
> r b b b r b b r r b r b b b b b r b r b
> b b b r b r r b b b b r b b r b r r b b

5. What is the mathematical probability of $P(\text{red})$? of $P(\text{blue})$?

6. What was the experimental probability of each outcome?

PROBLEM SOLVING

Suppose you play games in which you and another player take turns spinning the red and blue spinner and score points only when you spin your chosen color. Blue begins. Decide which seem to be fair games.

7. Game 1: Blue scores 1 for each **b**; Red scores 2 for each **r**.

8. Game 2: Blue scores 1 for each **b**; Red scores 1 for each **r** and spins again.

Problem Solving
Using Data from an Order Form

UNDERSTAND
ANALYZE DATA
PLAN
ESTIMATE
SOLVE
EXAMINE

LEARN ABOUT IT

Joan and her family went on a tour of some historic sites. Afterward, they had pictures developed of themselves visiting places of special interest. How much did the 11 × 14 photos cost (without tax)?

Historic Sites Photographs					
Date	**Site**	**Frame #**	**Size (in.)**	**Quantity**	**Amount**
5/21/90	San Jacinto	27	8 × 10	2	$28.00
5/21/90	The Alamo	32	**11 × 14**	**3**	?
5/21/90	Mesa Verde	42	16 × 20	1	?

Prices

8 × 10	$14.00 each	Subtotal	?
11 × 14	**$19.50 each**		
16 × 20	$39.50 each	Tax (6%)	?
20 × 24	$59.50 each		
proofsheet	$12.00 each	Total Cost	?

> I'll find the data I need on the order form.

> Now I'll multiply to find the answer.

The cost of the 11 × 14 photos was $58.50.

11 x 14 photos cost $19.50 each. They bought 3 photos this size.

$19.50
  3
―――――
$58.50

TRY IT OUT

1. How much will the photos cost altogether before tax is added on?

2. How much tax must Joan and her friends pay in all? What is the total cost of the order?

Solve. Use a strategy from the strategies list or other strategies you know to solve these problems.

1. Barbara decided to buy one tour picture for $39.50. Is the area of her photo more or less than the area of two dozen 3 × 5 photos? How much more or less? Use the data on page 420.

Some Strategies	
Act Out	Make a Table
Use Objects	Solve a Simpler Problem
Choose an Operation	Make an Organized List
Draw a Picture	Work Backward
Guess and Check	Look for a Pattern
Use Logical Reasoning	

2. Bonita had two $50 bills. How much tax would she pay on an order of tour photos whose total cost is $95?

3. Joan's mother had twenty 8 × 10 photos of the tour lined up side-by-side in a row. What was the perimeter of the photo display?

4. Jon wanted a photo whose width was $\frac{4}{5}$ its length. Which sizes might he have bought?

5. Bob arranged some photos in squares of increasing size. How many photos did he need to make the fifth square?

6. How much would a dozen 11 × 14 photos cost before tax? Use the data on page 420.

7. Is the area of these two photos a little more or a little less than 55 in²?

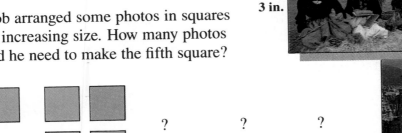

first   second   third   fourth   fifth

5 in.

3 in.

7 in.

5 in.

8. Developing a Plan A photo was enlarged so that each side of the new photo was double the length of the original. How many times larger was the area of the new photo than the original?

  A. List 2 or more strategies you think might help you solve this problem.

  B. Solve the problem.

  C. Look back at your solution. What strategies did you use?

More Practice, page 527, set C

Making Estimates by Sampling

EXPLORE **Analyze the Situation**

Suppose the drawing represents a photograph of a cluster of stars. What is your estimate of the total number of stars in the drawing?

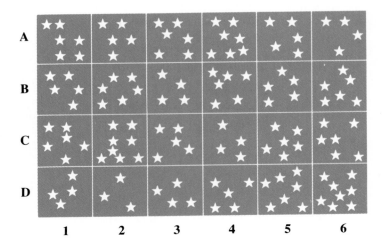

TALK ABOUT IT

1. How did you make your estimate?

2. How can the squares help you make your estimate?

3. Section **D1** contains 4 stars. If all sections contained 4 stars, how many stars would be in the photograph?

4. Section **D1** is a **sample** of the stars in the photograph. If you were asked to choose one section as a sample, which section would you choose? Why?

To make estimates of a large number of objects that are not easily counted, we can take **random samples.** For example, to choose one of the squares in the grid as a random sample, we could use a spinner with parts A, B, C, and D and toss a number cube with numbers 1 through 6.

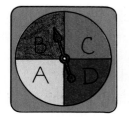

Outcome: B5

The spinner and number cube show an outcome of B5. Section B5 contains 5 stars. There are 24 sections.
Estimate: $5 \times 24 = 120$

TRY IT OUT

Estimate the number of stars using these sections.

1. C4   2. D1   3. A3   4. B6   5. D2

Use a spinner and a number cube like the ones shown on page 422 to choose 5 random samples of stars from the picture. Record the section and number of stars in a table.

1. What is the mean (or average) number of stars in your sample?

2. Estimate the total number of stars using the mean from your samples.

3. Count the number of stars in the picture. How close was your estimate?

	Section	Number of stars
Sample 1		
Sample 2		

Remember: The **mean** of a list of numbers is the total divided by the number in the list.

APPLY

MATH REASONING

4. Estimate what fraction of the pages in this book have a photograph. Then randomly select 20 pages and find the fraction of those that have photographs. How does this compare to your estimate? Randomly select 40 pages and find the fraction. Which number of pages is likely to give an estimate closer to the actual fraction for the entire book? Explain.

PROBLEM SOLVING

5. An overhead photograph of 1 mi² of forest is divided into 20 equal sections. You count the number of trees in 5 randomly chosen sections. You get these results: 53, 57, 60, 51, 59. What would be your estimate of the total number of trees in the square mile?

▶ COMMUNICATION   Writing to Learn

6. Find some ways to estimate the number of people in the photograph. Write a description of your method and why you think your estimate is a good one.

423

Simulations

Carlos had a 10-item true-false quiz in his French class. He wondered what he might score if he just guessed at all of the items (even though he would not really do it!). What would you predict?

EXPLORE **Try a Simulation**

Toss a coin 10 times, once for each test item. Let heads = true, tails = false. Check your outcomes against the answers shown in the box at the right. How many answers did you get correct?

True-False Quiz Answers				
1. T	**2.** T	**3.** F	**4.** T	**5.** F
6. F	**7.** F	**8.** F	**9.** F	**10.** F

TALK ABOUT IT

1. Do you think you would get at least half of the items correct by guessing? Why?

2. How likely are you to get all 10 correct just by guessing?

3. How many might you expect to get correct if there were 20 items rather than 10?

To decide the possible result in certain situations, you can make a model or **simulation** of the situation. The coin-tossing activity above was a simulation of guessing the answer to each item.

TRY IT OUT

1. Try the simulation described above 3 more times. Record the number of correct answers for each. Compare your results with those of your classmates. What is the greatest number of correct answers anyone found? What is the least number of correct answers anyone found?

2. Combine your number of correct answers with other students' results. Find the average number of correct answers for all the students in your class.

Guess   Answer

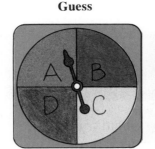
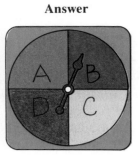

1. Work with a partner and try this simulation. Use a "Guess" spinner and an "Answer" spinner like the ones shown. One partner spins the "Guess" spinner 12 times and the other spins the "Answer" spinner 12 times. Keep a record of the outcomes. Then find out how many times the Guess outcome matches the Answer outcome. How many matches did you get out of 12 tries?

APPLY

MATH REASONING

2. A multiple-choice quiz has 12 questions. There are four choices of answers: A, B, C, and D. Suppose you just guessed at the answer to all 12 items. Estimate how many answers you would get correct. Use your results from exercise 1 to help you decide.

PROBLEM SOLVING

3. Combine the results of your simulation in Practice, Exercise 1, with the results obtained by 5 of your classmates. Find the average number of correct answers.

MIXED REVIEW

Write each ratio as a percent.

4. 4 to 100   **5.** 36 to 100   **6.** 44 to 100   **7.** 12 to 100

8. $\frac{85}{100}$ **9.** $\frac{61}{100}$ **10.** $\frac{10}{100}$ **11.** $\frac{73}{100}$

Write each percent as a lowest-terms fraction.

12. 45%   **13.** 60%   **14.** 30%

15. 75%   **16.** 15%   **17.** 25%

425

Applied Problem Solving
Group Decision Making

UNDERSTAND
ANALYZE DATA
PLAN
ESTIMATE
SOLVE
EXAMINE

Group Skill:
Check for Understanding

Your class is planning a field trip to the Museum of Natural History. Your group must make a schedule for the day that lists the starting and ending time for each of the day's activities.

Facts to Consider

- Your class cannot leave school before 8:30 a.m. and must be back by 3:30 p.m.
- The bus trip from your school to the museum takes 30 minutes.
- You must allow time in the schedule for lunch.
- You must allow time for afternoon or morning refreshments, washing up, and getting from one section of the museum to another.
- You and your classmates have already decided that you want to visit these sections of the museum:
  Hall of the Ancient Egyptians
  Hall of Chinese Jades
  Hall of Equatorial Africa
  Hall of American Indians
- You do not need to spend equal time in each hall, so you may want to do a brief survey to find out which exhibits are most interesting to your classmates.

Some Questions to Answer

1. About how much time is needed to go to and from the museum? (Be sure to allow time for getting on and off the bus and getting into and out of the museum.)

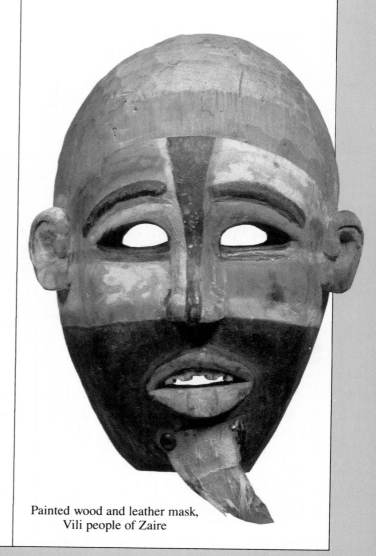

Painted wood and leather mask,
Vili people of Zaire

426

2. How much time should you allow for lunch? Do you want to allow time for a morning or afternoon refreshment break?

3. About how much extra time, if any, should you allow for unexpected delays?

4. How much time will be left for you to visit the exhibits? How will you divide this time among the four halls?

What Is Your Decision?

Use your decisions about times to make a possible schedule for the day. Get reactions from your classmates, and revise the schedule if necessary.

Wood mask,
Luba people of Zaire

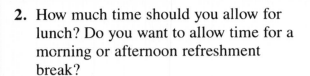

Coming-of-age mask,
Biombo people of Zaire

WRAP UP

Word Choice

Complete each sentence with the correct word or words from the box. Not all words will be used.

| mathematical |
| unfair |
| one |
| fair |
| zero |
| simulation |

1. A game in which all players have the same chance of winning is called __?__.

2. The probability of picking 1 blue marble from a bag of 6 red marbles is __?__.

3. The probability of picking 1 blue marble from a bag of 6 blue marbles is __?__.

4. A model of a situation is called a __?__.

Sometimes, Always, Never

Complete each statement by writing **sometimes**, **always**, or **never**. Explain your choices.

5. If an outcome is impossible, the probability is __?__ 1.

6. If an outcome is certain, the probability is __?__ 1.

7. If there are only two possible outcomes and both are equally likely, the probability of one of them occurring is __?__ $\frac{1}{2}$.

Project

Suppose you have 1 red cube, 1 blue cube, and 1 white cube. Predict how many different ways you can arrange them in a row. Try it! Use colored cubes or cut-out squares. Compare your prediction with your trial using models.

Try the same activity with 2 red cubes and 1 blue cube. First predict, then use models. What was your prediction? What was the result of your trial with models?

Make up your own predict-and-try problem. Give it to a classmate to do.

POWER PRACTICE/TEST

Part 1   Understanding

Explain why each game is fair or unfair.

1. **Vowel-Consonant** A bag contains 6 cards. Each card has one of these letters on it: A, E, I, B, O, U. A player chooses a card without looking. If it is a vowel, that player gets 1 point. If it is a consonant, the other player gets 1.

2. **Odd-Even** One player is *Odd* and the other is *Even*. Toss two number cubes that both have 1, 2, 2, 3, 3, and 4 on them. If the sum of the numbers is even, *Even* gets 1 point. If the sum is odd, *Odd* gets 1 point.

Part 2   Skills

Use the activities above. Find the probability of each.

Vowel-Consonant: 3. $P(A)$

4. $P(consonant)$ 5. $P(z)$

Odd-Even: 6. $P(5)$

7. $P(4)$ 8. $P(2)$

9. Would you be more likely to roll a 4 or a 7 in an **Odd-Even** game?

10. Find the experimental and mathematical probability of tossing a 7 in the **Odd-Even** game. Use 60 tosses.

Part 3   Applications

11. Estimate the number of dots using B4.

12. An order form states that Style 203 notebooks cost $1.50 each. There is a handling charge of $2.50 for each order. What payment must Myrna make for 6 notebooks?

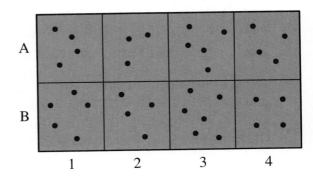

13. **Challenge** Suppose you took a multiple-choice test with 100 questions. There are 5 choices for each question. You decide to guess at every answer. How could you simulate this situation to estimate how many answers you would get correct?

ENRICHMENT
Combinations

Mindy, Charles, Leah, Sean, and Penny are all running for president of the student council. The person with the most votes will be president. The person with the second most votes will be vice president.

One way to find and show the different possible election results is by drawing a tree diagram. Here is the tree diagram if Mindy were elected president.

President	*Vice President*	*Combination*
	Charles	Mindy—Charles
	Leah	Mindy—Leah
Mindy	Sean	Mindy—Sean
	Penny	Mindy—Penny

1. Make similar tree diagrams in which Charles, Leah, Sean, and Penny are each elected president.

2. How many combinations are possible with Mindy as president? with Charles as president? with Leah? Sean? Penny? How many combinations are there in all? Can you see a pattern? Explain.

CUMULATIVE REVIEW

1. What compatible numbers would you use to estimate $\frac{1}{4} \times 39$?

   A. $\frac{3}{4} \times 36$
   B. $\frac{1}{4} \times 36$
   C. $\frac{3}{4} \times 40$
   D. $\frac{1}{4} \times 40$

2. Multiply $2\frac{2}{3} \times 3\frac{1}{4}$. Reduce to lowest terms.

   A. $6\frac{1}{6}$
   B. $8\frac{2}{3}$
   C. 8
   D. $6\frac{2}{3}$

3. Which is *not* a correct way to write a ratio?

   A. 4 to 7
   B. $\frac{4}{7}$
   C. $\frac{4}{7}\%$
   D. 4:7

4. Write 36% as a lowest-terms fraction.

   A. $\frac{36}{100}$
   B. $\frac{9}{25}$
   C. $\frac{1}{4}$
   D. $\frac{18}{50}$

5. Write 16:100 as a percent.

   A. 100%
   B. $\frac{16}{100}\%$
   C. 16%
   D. 25%

6. Which of the following is *not* a quadrilateral?

   A. rhombus
   B. parallelogram
   C. trapezoid
   D. octagon

7. Murray got 9 out of every 10 math problems correct. The test had a total of 40 problems. How many problems did Murray answer correctly?

   A. 9
   B. 18
   C. 27
   D. 36

8. Find the circumference of a circle with a diameter of 6.8 cm. Use 3.14 for π.

   A. 42.704 cm
   B. 21.352 cm
   C. 10.676 cm
   D. 64.056 cm

9. Solve $\frac{2}{3} = \frac{n}{24}$ for n.

   A. 16
   B. 14
   C. 12
   D. 18

10. Which regular polygon *cannot* be used in a tessellation?

    A. pentagon
    B. triangle
    C. hexagon
    D. octagon

11. Write 27% as a decimal.

    A. 2.70
    B. 27.00
    C. 0.27
    D. 0.027

12. Which number pair completes the ratio table?

3	6	9	12	15	
8	16	24	32	40	

    A. 18, 48
    B. 18, 44
    C. 17, 44
    D. 17, 48

13. Wanda is one third as old as her brother. Wanda is 6. How old is her brother?

    A. 2
    B. 3
    C. 12
    D. 18

14. Ian sliced 3 whole pizzas into equal sixths. How many sixths did he get altogether?

    A. 6
    B. 18
    C. 3
    D. 12

16

MATH AND
FINE ARTS

DATA BANK

Use the Fine Arts Data
Bank on page 479 to
answer the questions.

1 What is the length of the
base of the Parthenon to
the nearest meter? What
is the width of the base to the
nearest meter?

PERIMETER, AREA, AND VOLUME

THEME: FAMOUS STRUCTURES

2 Suppose you took a walk all the way around the base of the Parthenon. About how many meters would you have walked? About how many meters less than a kilometer is that?

3 Would a walk around the base of the Great Pyramid be longer or shorter than the walk around the Parthenon? About how many meters longer or shorter would it be?

4 **Using Critical Thinking** Leslie studied the Parthenon facts and said, "I can add the number of columns on each side to find how many outside columns there are in all." Do you agree?

The symmetry and proportions of ancient Greek buildings are admired and copied by architects today.

Perimeter

Many buildings and other structures have rectangular bases. You can use what you know about parallel sides of rectangles to help you find the perimeter of a rectangle.

EXPLORE **Find How Many Ways**

Work in groups. How many different rectangles with a perimeter of 24 units can you draw on graph paper? Each side should be a whole number of units.

TALK ABOUT IT

1. How could you find the perimeter of a rectangle without adding all four sides?
2. Are any of the rectangles you made squares? How can you find the perimeter of a square without adding?
3. If each side of a rectangle is a whole number, can the perimeter be an odd number?

One way to find the perimeter of a rectangle is to use a formula.

Perimeter $= (2 \times$ **length**$) + (2 \times$ **width**$)$
$$P = 2l + 2w$$

The formula for the perimeter of a square is $P = 4l$.

Example: Find the perimeter of a rectangle 14 cm long and 4 cm wide.
$$P = (2 \times 14) + (2 \times 4)$$
$$= 28 + 8 = 36$$
$$P = 36 \text{ cm}$$

TRY IT OUT

Find the perimeter of each figure. Write **yes** if you can use a formula.

1.
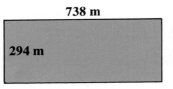
738 m
294 m

2.
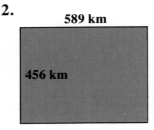
589 km
456 km

3.
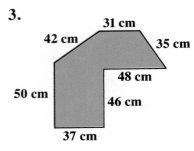
31 cm
42 cm
35 cm
48 cm
50 cm
46 cm
37 cm

434

PRACTICE

Find the perimeter of each figure. Write **yes** if you can use a formula.

1. basketball court

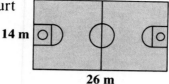

14 m

26 m

2. soccer field

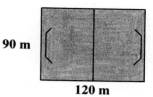

90 m

120 m

3. table tennis

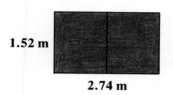

1.52 m

2.74 m

4. baseball field

5. baseball diamond

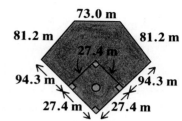

73.0 m

81.2 m   81.2 m

27.4 m

94.3 m   94.3 m

27.4 m   27.4 m

APPLY

MATH REASONING

Estimate the width of these rectangular figures.

6. $P = 260$ cm
$l = 82$ cm

7. $P = 90$ m
$l = 24$ m

8. $P = 20$ m
$l = 6.8$ m

PROBLEM SOLVING

9. The North Stone Pyramid of Egypt has a height of 99 m. The perimeter of its square base is 880 m. What is the length of each side of the base?

10. The Pentagon Building in Washington, D.C., has 5 equal sides. The distance from one corner to the next is 281 m. What is the perimeter of the building?

11. Fine Arts Data Bank   What is the perimeter of the Lincoln Memorial in Washington, D.C.? See page 479.

DATA BANK

MIXED REVIEW

Write a percent for each decimal.

12. 0.91   **13.** 0.45   **14.** 0.89   **15.** 0.63   **16.** 0.07   **17.** 0.39

Give the lowest-terms fraction for each percent.

18. 75%   **19.** 80%   **20.** 35%   **21.** 22%   **22.** 40%   **23.** 65%

More Practice, page 521, set B

435

Problem Solving
Estimating the Answer

UNDERSTAND
ANALYZE DATA
PLAN
ESTIMATE
SOLVE
EXAMINE

LEARN ABOUT IT

Before solving a problem, you often can estimate to decide what would be a reasonable answer.

The action and comedy movies at Midcity Video are next to each other on the wall. The wall space they cover is 6.35 m long and 1.8 m high. What is the area of the wall space they cover?

I'll begin by rounding both dimensions.

$$6.35 \longrightarrow 6$$
$$1.8 \longrightarrow 2$$

Then I'll use the numbers to estimate the area of the wall space.

$$6 \times 2 \longrightarrow 12$$

Now I'll solve the problem.

$$6.35 \times 1.8 \longrightarrow 11.43$$

The answer 11.43 m² is reasonable because it is close to 12.

TRY IT OUT

First estimate the answer. Then solve the problem and decide whether your answer is reasonable.

1. The narrow side of each videotape is 3.2 cm wide. Jan can fit exactly 39 tapes on a shelf. How long is each shelf?

2. The perimeter of the poster for foreign tapes is 298 cm. The length is 98 cm. What is the width?

3. Bing took some of his friends to a movie to celebrate his birthday. He paid $20.79 for 11 large lemonades. How much did each lemonade cost?

436

Solve. Choose a strategy from the list or use other strategies that you know.

1. The floor plan of Midcity Video is shown below. What is the area of the store?

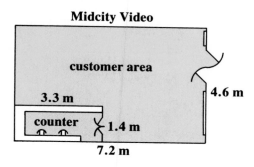

Midcity Video

customer area

3.3 m

4.6 m

counter

1.4 m

7.2 m

2. The owner of Midcity Video is going to enlarge his store by making it 3.2 m longer. What will its perimeter be then?

3. About how many movies are there in all at Midcity Video?

Midcity Video Movies	
Type	**Number**
Comedy	182
Children's	192
Drama	321
Horror	125
Science Fiction	81
Foreign	192
Action	183

4. While looking over the foreign movies, Julie, Serena, and Ivan realized that they each can speak a different foreign language—Italian, Spanish, and Japanese. None of them speaks a language that starts with the first letter of his or her first name. Serena does not speak Japanese. Which language does each person speak?

Some Strategies	
Act Out	Make a Table
Use Objects	Solve a Simpler Problem
Choose an Operation	Make an Organized List
Draw a Picture	Work Backward
Guess and Check	Look for a Pattern
Use Logical Reasoning	

5. It costs $29.50 to become a member at Midcity Video. When you pay for membership, you get a packet of tickets that allows you to rent 9 movies free. Videotape rentals normally cost $2.50 each. If you subtract the amount you save on rental costs, what does it cost to become a member?

6. The floor of a movie theater is a square. Its area is 16 m² and its perimeter is 16 m. How long is each side of the floor?

7. For the opening of the new theater, the manager put a giant balloon on each lamp post on the perimeter of the parking lot. The lamp posts are 22 m apart and the parking lot is 132 m on each side. How many balloons did she need?

8. The popcorn container shaped like a cylinder holds about 3 times as much popcorn as the container shaped like a cone. The cone-shaped holder holds 32.5 g of popcorn. About how much does the container shaped like a cylinder hold?

 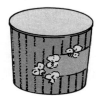

More Practice, page 527, set D

Area of Figures with Irregular Shapes

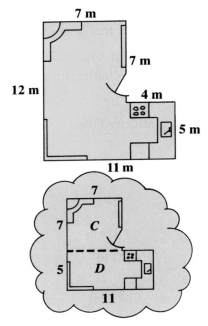

7 m

7 m

12 m

4 m

5 m

11 m

EXPLORE **Analyze a Plan**

When Carrie and David each found the area of the floor shown in the plan, they thought about it in different ways.

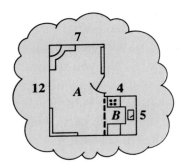

Carrie mentally divided the room into these 2 rectangles and found their areas.

David mentally divided the room into these 2 rectangles and found their areas.

TALK ABOUT IT

1. How can Carrie and David find the total area for the room? Is the area the same or different for the two methods?
2. How could the floor plan for the room be divided into 3 rectangles? Will you get the same total area?

This is one way to find the area of an irregular shape.

■ Break the shape into rectangular parts.
■ Find the area of each rectangle and add these areas to find the total area.

Calculator Key Code

To find the area of an irregular shape divided into two rectangles:

[ON/AC] length a [×] width a [=] [M+] length b [×] width b [=] [M+] [MR]

Trace this figure twice. Show two different ways to break the figure into 2 smaller rectangles. Find the total area for the figure.

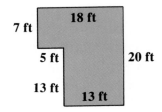

7 ft

18 ft

5 ft

20 ft

13 ft

13 ft

The students in room 5B want to paint only the walls of their classroom. Find the area of each wall to be painted.

1. North wall

2. East wall

3. South wall

4. West wall

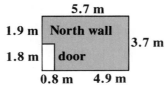

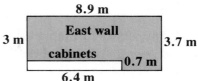

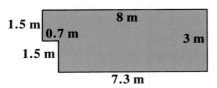

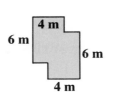

MATH REASONING

Estimate whether the area of each figure is a little more than or a little less than 24 m².

5.

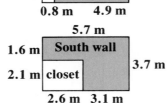

6.

7.

PROBLEM SOLVING

8. Carrie wants to buy carpet that costs $19.95 per square meter for this room. What is the area of the floor without the fireplace?

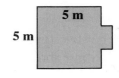

9. Data Hunt What is the area of your desk top or table top? Use a unit of measure of your choice.

▶ **CALCULATOR**

10. Use the **memory minus** [M−] key to find the area of the blue portion of this figure.

You can use this key code:

[ON/AC] length *a* [×] width *a* [=] [M+] length *b* [×] width *b* [=] [M−] [MR]

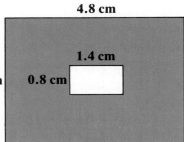

More Practice, page 521, set C

Using Critical Thinking

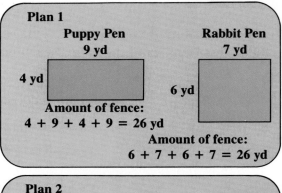

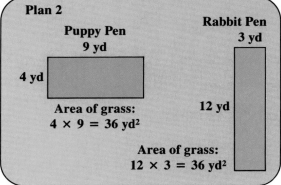

Mrs. Manypets used Plan 1 to make two pens. "I've used the same length of fence for each pen," she told her two children. "You will each have the same amount of pen area to care for."

As time passed, one of the children complained that the jobs were not equal. "It will be easy to fix this," said Mrs. Manypets, "I can just rearrange the fence according to Plan 2 and the areas of the pens will then be exactly the same."

TALK ABOUT IT

1. What two types of measures of figures are involved in deciding about the pens?

2. Do you agree with the conclusion Mrs. Manypets reached about Plan 1? Explain. Do you agree with the conclusion she reached about Plan 2? Explain.

3. What have you learned about perimeter and area of a rectangle from this story?

TRY IT OUT

1. Draw and label two rectangles, both with a perimeter of 24 ft, but with different areas.

2. Draw and label two rectangles, both with an area of 24 ft^2, but with different perimeters.

3. A rectangle has sides that are all whole numbers of units. Its area is 18 square units and its perimeter is 18 units. What are its length and width?

440

POWER PRACTICE/QUIZ

Find the perimeter and then find the area of each figure.

1.
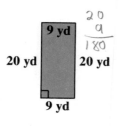

20
9
180

9 yd
20 yd   20 yd
9 yd

perimeter = ▦
area = ▦

2.
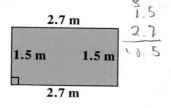

2.7 m
1.5 m   1.5 m
2.7 m

3.5
1.5
2.7
0.5

perimeter = ▦
area = ▦

3.
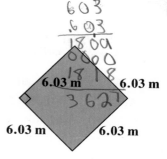

603
.603
1800
0000
18 8
3627

6.03 m   6.03 m
6.03 m   6.03 m

perimeter = ▦
area = ▦

4.
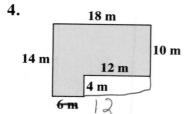

18 m
14 m
12 m
10 m
4 m
6 m 12

perimeter = ▦
area = ▦

5.
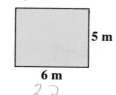

1.4 m
2.4 m 2.4 m
2.4 m 2.4 m
1.4 m   1.4 m
2.4 m 2.4 m
2.4 m 2.4 m
1.4 m

14
14
14
14
56

24
24
24
24
24
24
24

perimeter = ▦
area = ▦

6.

70 cm
20 cm
50 cm
30
10 cm   10 cm

perimeter = ▦
area = ▦

PROBLEM SOLVING

Gordon, Caryl, and Ann each planted rectangular gardens.

Gordon's Garden
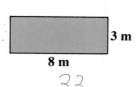
3 m
8 m
22

Caryl's Garden
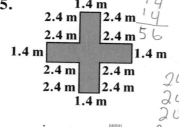
5 m
6 m
23

Ann's Garden
6 m
4 m

7. Which garden needs the least amount of fencing?

8. Which garden covers the greatest area?

9. Andy has 50 m of fencing for a garden. What is the greatest area he can fence in if his garden is rectangular and is a whole number of meters on each side?

10. Dawn used 36 m of fencing around her garden. Tim's garden covers an area of 56 m². Could both gardens be rectangular and have the same dimensions? Explain.

441

Area of Right Triangles

LEARN ABOUT IT

EXPLORE Make a Model

Work in groups. When you cut a rectangle along the diagonal, do the two right triangles you make always have the same area as each other? Try rectangles of different sizes to find out.

TALK ABOUT IT

1. What fractional part of the rectangle does each right triangle represent?
2. Is the area of each triangle the same as half the area of the rectangle? Explain.

You can find the area of a right triangle by first finding the area of a rectangle with the same base and height and then dividing by 2.

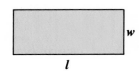

Area of a right triangle $= \frac{1}{2} \times$ base $\times$ height

$$A = \frac{1}{2} \times b \times h$$

Example: $A = \frac{1}{2} \times 8 \times 4$

$A = \frac{1}{2} \times 32 = 16$

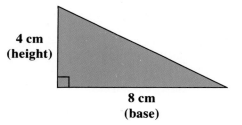

The area of the right triangle is 16 cm².

TRY IT OUT

Give the height and base of each right triangle. Then use the formula to find the area.

1.

   $h = $ ▦ units
   $b = $ ▦ units
   $A = $ ▦ square units

2.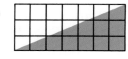

   $h = $ ▦ units
   $b = $ ▦ units
   $A = $ ▦ square units

3.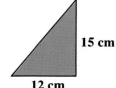

   $h = $ ▦ cm
   $b = $ ▦ cm
   $A = $ ▦ cm²

442

Give the height, base, and area of each right triangle.

□ = 1 square unit

1.

2.

3.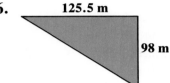

4.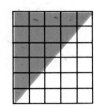

Find the area of each triangle.

5.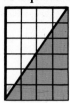

75 m

62 m

6. 125.5 m

98 m

7. 50 in.   50 in.

MATH REASONING

8. Does a right triangle with a base greater than the base of another right triangle always have the greater area? Give examples to support your reasoning.

PROBLEM SOLVING

9. What is the area of a triangular sail on a sailboat with height 42 m and base 2.4 m?

10. The city wants a park with an area of at least 1 km² but no more than 2 km². Which plan or plans could they use?

Plan 1

1.5 km

1.5 km

Plan 2

2.8 km

0.8 km

Plan 3

1.4 km   0.8 km

▶ **MENTAL MATH**

Study Julie's method for finding the area of a right triangle with height or base an even number. Use Julie's method to find the area of each figure.

Julie's Method

4 units

8 units

$\frac{1}{2}$ of 4 = 2

2 × 8 = 16

Area = 16 square units

11.

6 units

8 units

12.

7 units

4 units

13.

10 units

2 units

More About Area of Triangles

LEARN ABOUT IT

The faces of the Pyramids at Giza are triangular, but are not right triangles.

EXPLORE Make a Model

Use grid paper. Draw a rectangle of any size. Color a green triangle inside the rectangle as shown at the right. Cut out the rectangle and then the green triangle. Can you find a way to fit the 2 smaller white triangles exactly on top of the green triangle?

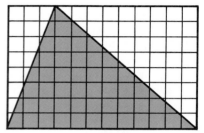

TALK ABOUT IT

1. What fractional part of the rectangle is the green triangle?
2. Is the area of any triangle the same as half the area of a rectangle with the same base and height? Why?

The area formula for a right triangle can be used to find the area of any triangle.

Area of a triangle $= \frac{1}{2} \times$ **base** $\times$ **height**

$A = \frac{1}{2} \times b \times h$

(area of a rectangle)

Example: Find the area of a triangle with base 8 cm and height 6 cm.

$A = \frac{1}{2} \times 8 \times 6$

$A = \frac{1}{2} \times 48 = 24$

The area of the triangle is 24 cm².

TRY IT OUT

Give the height and base of each triangle. Then use the formula to find the area for each.

1.

$h = $ ▦ units
$b = $ ▦ units
$A = $ ▦ square units

2.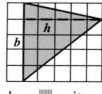

$h = $ ▦ units
$b = $ ▦ units
$A = $ ▦ square units

3.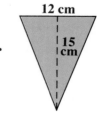

12 cm

15 cm

$h = $ ▦ cm
$b = $ ▦ cm
$A = $ ▦ cm²

444

Give the height, base, and area of each triangle.

1.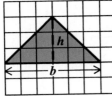

2.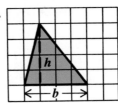

3.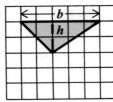

4.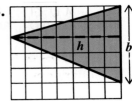

Find the area of each object.

5.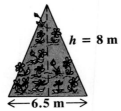
←6.5 m→

6.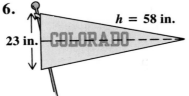
$h = 58$ in.
23 in.
COLORADO

7.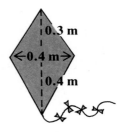
0.3 m
←0.4 m→
0.4 m

MATH REASONING

Give the height of a triangle with the same base as the triangle shown on the right but with

8. less area   **9.** more area

1.8 cm
←4.5 cm→

PROBLEM SOLVING

10. Janet made a model of a pyramid. The height, base, and area measurement of each triangular face was the same number. What is the number?

11. Fine Arts Data Bank   What is the area of each triangular face of the 2nd Pyramid at Giza? See page 479.

DATA BANK

▶ **ALGEBRA**

If the base and height of a triangle are whole number measurements, give two different values for b and h that make each equation true.

12. $A = 12$ cm², $b = $ ▥ cm, $h = $ ▥ cm   **13.** $A = 48$ m², $b = $ ▥ m, $h = $ ▥ m

Area of Parallelograms

A parallelogram has 2 pairs of sides the same length and 2 pairs of parallel sides.

EXPLORE Make a Model

Cut out a rectangle like the one shown at the right. Draw line segment *BE* on your rectangle. Cut along *BE.* Tape side *BC* to *AD* as shown.

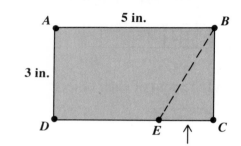

TALK ABOUT IT

1. What was the area of the original rectangle?

2. What type of figure results from cutting and taping the triangle?

3. What is the area of the new figure? How do you know?

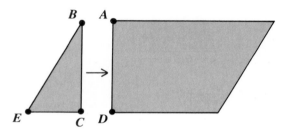

The activity above shows why the area formula for a parallelogram is related to the area formula for a rectangle.

Area of parallelogram = base × height

$A = b \times h$

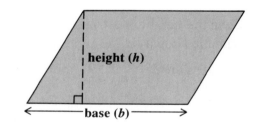

Find the area of each parallelogram.

1.
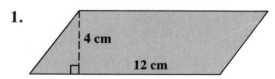
4 cm
12 cm

2. $b = 12.5$ m
   $h = 5.8$ m

3.
8 in.
10 in.

4. $b = 2\frac{1}{2}$ ft
   $h = 5\frac{1}{4}$ ft

446

Find the area of each parallelogram.

1.
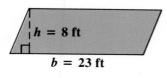
$h = 8$ ft
$b = 23$ ft

2.
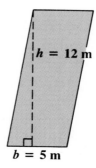
$h = 12$ m
$b = 5$ m

3.
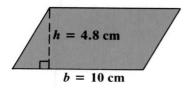
$h = 4.8$ cm
$b = 10$ cm

4.
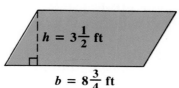
$h = 3\frac{1}{2}$ ft
$b = 8\frac{3}{4}$ ft

5. $h = 12$ m, $b = 15$ m   **6.** $h = 2.86$ cm, $b = 5.5$ cm   **7.** $h = 120$ yd, $b = 10$ yd

APPLY

MATH REASONING

8. Draw and label 3 different parallelograms, each with an area of 24 cm² and height and base an even number.

PROBLEM SOLVING

9. Suppose roofing material costs $1.95 per square foot. Estimate the cost of the material for the roof shown at the right. Remember to include both sides of the roof.

45 ft   24 ft

MIXED REVIEW

Write a percent for each fraction.

10. $\frac{3}{4}$ **11.** $\frac{4}{5}$ **12.** $\frac{6}{20}$ **13.** $\frac{1}{25}$ **14.** $\frac{8}{10}$ **15.** $\frac{8}{50}$

16. $\frac{19}{20}$ **17.** $\frac{16}{20}$ **18.** $\frac{2}{5}$ **19.** $\frac{20}{25}$ **20.** $\frac{1}{10}$ **21.** $\frac{15}{30}$

Find the perimeter of each rectangle.

22. 24 m × 12 m   **23.** 8 ft × 10 ft   **24.** 20 in. × 6 in.

More Practice, page 521, set E

Volume

EXPLORE Make a Model
Work in groups. How many different
rectangular prisms can you make with
24 cubes? with 25 cubes?

TALK ABOUT IT

1. Can you make the same number of rectangular prisms
   with 25 cubes as with 24 cubes? Explain.

2. How can you find the number of cubes in a prism
   without counting each one?

Volume is the number of cubic units an object can hold. We
can use a formula to find the volume of a rectangular prism.

Volume = length × width × height

$$V = \underbrace{l \times w}_{\text{number in a layer}} \times \underbrace{h}_{\text{number of layers}}$$

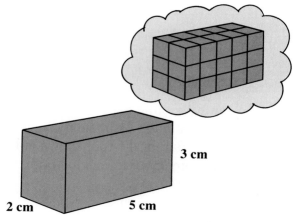

Example: $V = 5 \times 2 \times 3$
$V = 30$

The volume is 30 cm³ (cubic centimeters).

3 cm

2 cm   5 cm

TRY IT OUT

Give the length, width, and height of each rectangular
prism. Then use the formula to find each volume.

1.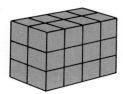

$h = $ ▦ units
$w = $ ▦ units
$l = $ ▦ units
$V = $ ▦ cubic units

2.

6 cm

2 cm   8 cm

$h = $ ▦ cm
$w = $ ▦ cm
$l = $ ▦ cm
$V = $ ▦ cm³

448

Give the length, width, height, and volume of each.

1.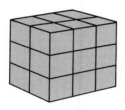

2.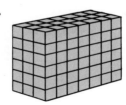

3.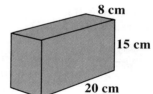
8 cm
15 cm
20 cm

Find the volume of each box made by the EZ Box Company.

	Box size	length	width	height	Volume
4.	A				
5.	B				
6.	C				
7.	D				

A
17 cm
18 cm   15 cm

B
12 cm
27 cm
11 cm

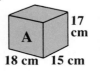
C
26 cm
18 cm   9 cm

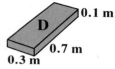
D
0.1 m
0.7 m
0.3 m

MATH REASONING

Give the height of each box.

8. $V = 30$ cm³

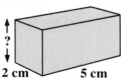
?
2 cm   5 cm

9. $V = 192$ cm³

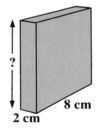
?
8 cm
2 cm

PROBLEM SOLVING

10. What would be the capacity (in milliliters) of a fish tank that is 40 cm long, 20 cm wide, and 30 cm high? Remember: 1 cm³ = 1 mL

11. Use Objects If cubes are used to build a rectangular prism that shows 4 cubes on each side, how many faces of the cubes do not form part of the surface of the prism?

▶ **USING CRITICAL THINKING   Use Visual Thinking**

12. Here are four views of the same cube. What figure is opposite the star?

Surface Area

EXPLORE Make a Model
When you fold a figure like this
into a box, do you think the faces
opposite each other will have the
same or different areas? To check,
trace and make the figure as shown.

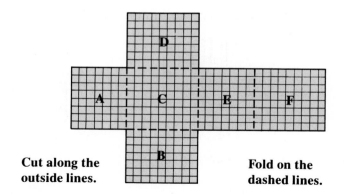

**Cut along the
outside lines.**

**Fold on the
dashed lines.**

TALK ABOUT IT

1. Give the area for each face in square units. Which faces
   are opposite? Do the opposite faces have the same area?

2. What is the total surface area of the box? How did you
   find your answer?

The formula for finding the area of a rectangle can be used
to help find the **surface area** of a rectangular prism.
Here is one method for finding the surface area of a
rectangular prism.

- Find the area of the top face, front face, and an end face.

- Multiply each area by 2 since the opposite faces have the
  same area.

- Find the sum of the three products.

Remember, for a
rectangle, $A = l \times w$.

TRY IT OUT

Find the surface area of each box. Use a calculator if available.

1.

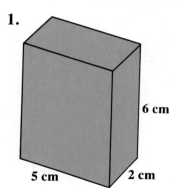

6 cm

5 cm   2 cm

2.

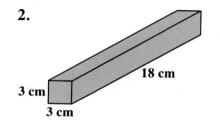

18 cm

3 cm

3 cm

3.

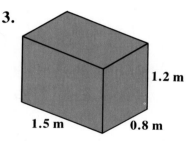

1.2 m

1.5 m   0.8 m

Find the surface area of each box. Use a calculator if possible.

1.
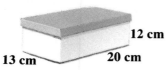
60 cm
90 cm
80 cm

2.

0.3 m
0.5 m
0.1 m

3.
2.2 m
0.8 m
1.1 m

Find the surface area of each object. Use a calculator if possible.

4. shoe box

12 cm
13 cm   20 cm

5. tool box

56 cm
95 cm   42 cm

6. suitcase
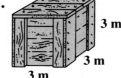
0.2 m
0.7 m   0.5 m

7. box for flowers
12 cm
15 cm   80 cm

MATH REASONING

Use **mental math** to find the surface area of these cubes.

8.
3 m
3 m
3 m

9.
5 cm
5 cm
5 cm

10.
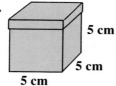
10 cm
10 cm
10 cm

PROBLEM SOLVING

11. If aluminum costs 8¢ a square meter, will a can company have to pay more than or less than 8¢ for enough aluminum to make this gasoline can?

GAS
0.5 m
0.4 m   0.2 m

12. Give the length, width, and height for two different boxes that have the same volume, but different surface areas.

▶ **COMMUNICATION   Write to Learn**

13. Write a paragraph to explain the difference between volume and surface area.

Data Collection and Analysis
Group Decision Making

UNDERSTAND
ANALYZE DATA
PLAN
ESTIMATE
SOLVE
EXAMINE

Doing a Simulation
Group Skill:
Disagree in an Agreeable Way

Every morning as you walk to school you have to cross three streets with stoplights. Each stop light has an equal chance of being either red or green. You usually wake up early enough to get to school on time, but this morning you slept a little longer than you should have. You need for all three stop lights to be green when you reach them. Do a simulation with your group to see what your chances are.

Collecting Data

1. Your group will need three coins to represent the three stop lights. Decide what each side of the coin will represent, a red light or a green light.

2. Toss all three coins at once. Were they all green lights? Keep a record of your tosses. Toss at least 100 times.

3 green lights	Not 3 green lights

Organizing Data

3. Count the number of times you got 3 green lights and the number of times you did not get 3 green lights. Make a bar graph to show your results.

Presenting Your Analysis

4. Write a paragraph to tell how you conducted your simulation and what your results were.

5. How many times out of 100 did you get all green lights and make it to school on time? Were you surprised? Explain.

Wrap Up

Picture This

Use the pictures to help you explain.

1. How are the areas of this triangle and rectangle related?

2. How do you find the perimeter and the area of this rectangle? What units do you use for each?

3. What do finding the area of an irregular shape and finding the surface area of a box have in common?

4. How do you find the volume of a box? What units do you use?

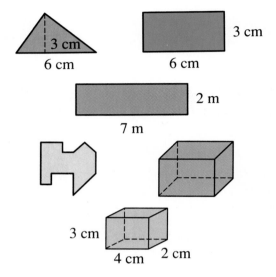

Sometimes, Always, Never

Complete each statement by writing **sometimes**, **always**, or **never**. Explain your choices.

5. You can __?__ use a formula to find perimeter.

6. Two rectangles with the same perimeter also __?__ have the same area.

7. The area of a rectangle is __?__ an even number.

8. The volume of a box is __?__ the number of cubic units it takes to "fill" it.

Project

Make or draw a three-dimensional figure that is made up of 20 centimeter cubes. Record the surface area and volume of your figure.

Make several other figures using the same 20 centimeter cubes. Record the surface area and volume of each. What changes? What remains the same?

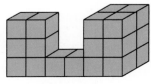

6 + 2 + 12 = 20 blocks

POWER PRACTICE/TEST

Part 1   Understanding

1. Draw and label two rectangles, both with a perimeter of 30 ft but with different areas.

2. Draw and label a rectangle with sides in whole units that has an area of 36 square units and the least possible perimeter.

What measures do you need to know in order to find the area or surface area?

3. square

4. triangle

5. parallelogram

6. rectangular prism

Part 2   Skills

Find the perimeter of each.

7. square with side of 3 cm

8. rectangle with length 6 cm, width 5 cm

9. square with side of 10 cm

10. rectangle with length 9 cm, width 8 cm

Find the area of each figure.

11. right triangle with base measuring 3.4 cm and height 2.7 cm.

12. parallelogram with base measuring 3.9 cm and height of 2.1 cm.

Find the volume of each rectangular prism.

13. 9 cm by 4 cm by 5 cm

14. 5 cm by 8 cm by 6 cm

Find the surface area of each rectangular prism.

15. 20 cm by 30 cm by 40 cm

16. 6 cm by 7 cm by 9 cm

Part 3   Applications

17. Joel has a box that measures 42 cm by 53 cm by 6 cm. He said that it would hold 133,560 cm^3. Estimate to decide whether his answer is reasonable.

18. **Challenge** What happens to the area if you enlarge a photo so that each side is double the length of the original? What happens to the area if you triple the length of each side?

455

ENRICHMENT
Estimating Area

1. Estimate the area covered by the hand. Tell what method you used. The area of each square is 1 square unit.

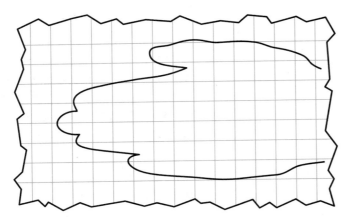

You can use averaging to estimate the area of any irregular shape such as a hand. Follow these steps to estimate the area of the hand.

- Count the full squares that are completely inside the outlines of the hand.

- Count all the squares used in covering the hand, those completely inside, and those only partly inside the hand.

- Find the average of those two numbers. (Add the two numbers and divide by 2.)

2. How does this estimate compare with your first estimate?

3. Trace the outline of your hand on graph paper. Use averaging to estimate its area.

4. Find 3 objects with irregular shapes. Trace them on graph paper. Use averaging to estimate their areas.

CUMULATIVE REVIEW

Use this grid for exercises 1 and 2.

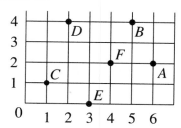

1. The coordinates for point E are

   A. (1,3)   **B.** (3,1)

   C. (0,3)   **D.** (3,0)

2. What point is at coordinate (4,2)?

   A. F **B.** D

   C. B **D.** C

3. Find the area of triangle ABC with a height of 8 cm and a base of 6 cm.

   A. 48 cm^2 **B.** 24 cm^2

   C. 30 cm^2 **D.** 40 cm^2

4. During the tennis season, Marcy won 15 out of 20 games, Kim won 18 out of 25 games, Lana won 37 out of 50 games, and Judy won 6 out of 10. Which player won the greatest percent of her games?

   A. Marcy   **B.** Kim

   C. Lana   **D.** Judy

5. Find the surface area of a box 12 in. long, 7 in. wide, and 2 in. high.

   A. 48 in.^{2} **B.** 366 in.^{2}

   C. 122 in.^{2} **D.** 244 in.^{2}

6. Find 88% of 25.

   A. 20   **B.** 21   **C.** 22   **D.** 23

Think of a number cube with 1, 2, 3, 4, 5, 6 on its faces for exercises 7–9.

7. If you were tossing this cube in a fair game, how many points should you give for tossing a number less than 3 if you give 4 points for tossing a number greater than 2?

   A. 2   **B.** 6   **C.** 4   **D.** 8

8. Find P (odd).

   A. $\frac{1}{6}$ **B.** $\frac{1}{2}$ **C.** $\frac{1}{3}$ **D.** $\frac{2}{3}$

9. If you toss the cube 100 times, how many times would you expect to get either 1 or 6?

   A. 60   **B.** 50   **C.** 33   **D.** 20

10. A printer's order form states that 1–10 copies cost 15¢ each, 11–25 copies cost 12¢ each, and more than 25 copies are 10¢ each. What would be the total cost of 20 copies?

   A. $3.00   **B.** $2.40

   C. $2.00   **D.** $2.70

11. If you have 2 red, 3 blue, 1 green, and 2 yellow chips in a bag, which colors are equally likely to be drawn?

   A. red, blue   **B.** red, green

   C. red, yellow   **D.** green, yellow

RESOURCE BANK AND APPENDIX

RESOURCE BANK

APPENDIX

Adding: Trading

There are two elementary schools in the Leland School district. Northeast has 349 students and Southwest has 276 students. What is the total number of elementary school students in the district?

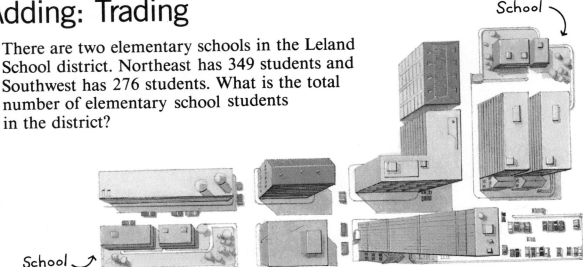

School

School

Since we want to find the total number of students, we add.

Add the ones. Trade if necessary.	Add the tens. Trade if necessary.	Add the hundreds.
$\overset{1}{349}$ $+\ 276$ $\overline{\hspace{20pt}5}$ (15 ones is 1 ten and 5 ones.)	$\overset{11}{349}$ $+\ 276$ $\overline{\hspace{15pt}25}$ (12 tens is 1 hundred and 2 tens.)	$\overset{11}{349}$ $+\ 276$ $\overline{\hspace{10pt}625}$

The total number of students in the school district is 625.

Other Examples

1.
$$\overset{11}{4{,}289}$$
$$+\ 2{,}186$$
$$\overline{6{,}475}$$

2.
$$\overset{\ 11}{3{,}094}$$
$$6{,}238$$
$$\overline{9{,}332}$$

3.
$$\overset{11\ 1}{47{,}570}$$
$$26{,}933$$
$$\overline{74{,}503}$$

4.
$$\overset{11\ 11}{66{,}495}$$
$$16{,}528$$
$$\overline{83{,}023}$$

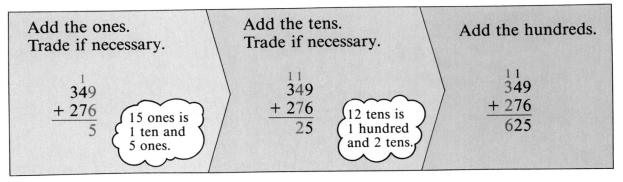

TRY IT OUT

Decide if you have to make a trade. Find the answer.

1. 684
   $+\ 29$

2. 996
   $+\ 428$

3. $9{,}732$
   $+\ 9{,}188$

4. $32{,}364$
   $+\ 18{,}707$

5. $63{,}988$
   $+\ 10{,}822$

Subtracting: Trading

Look at the chart on the right. How many more days does it take for Mars to orbit the sun than it does for Mercury?

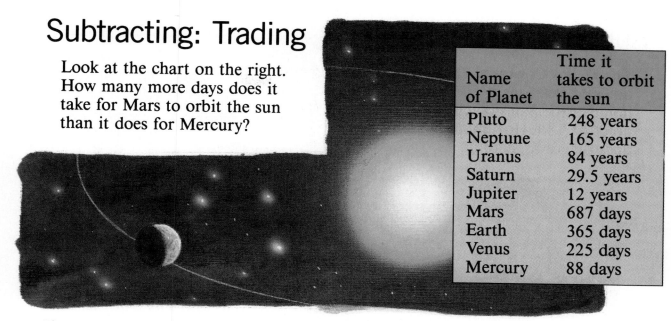

Name of Planet	Time it takes to orbit the sun
Pluto	248 years
Neptune	165 years
Uranus	84 years
Saturn	29.5 years
Jupiter	12 years
Mars	687 days
Earth	365 days
Venus	225 days
Mercury	88 days

Since we want to compare the numbers, we subtract.

Subtract the ones. Trade if necessary.	Subtract the tens. Trade if necessary.	Subtract the hundreds.
7 17 6 8 7 − 8 8 9	5 17 17 6 8 7 − 8 8 9 9	5 17 17 6 8 7 − 8 8 5 9 9

Mars takes 599 days longer to orbit the sun than Mercury.

Other Examples

| 13 17
1 4 7
−   7 9
6 8 | 7 13 11
8 4 1
− 7 9 5
4 6 | 8 14
8 9 4
−   8 6
8 0 8 | 1 15 16 12
2 6 7 2
− 1,8 9 4
7 7 8 | 4 16 12 14 17
5 7,3 5 7
− 1 9,5 9 8
3 7,7 5 9 |

TRY IT OUT

Subtract. Check by adding.

1. 211
−   98

2. 864
− 491

3. 474
−   89

4. 592
− 416

5. 2,161
− 1,988

461

Subtracting: With Zeros

The Dallas Cowboys' Texas Stadium holds 65,000 fans. Candlestick Park, home of the San Francisco 49ers, holds 61,185. How many more fans does the Texas stadium hold?

Since we want to compare the two numbers, we subtract.

Subtract the ones. Trade if necessary.	Subtract the tens. Trade if necessary.	Subtract the hundreds. Trade if necessary.	Subtract the thousands.
$$\begin{array}{r} {}^{4\ 9\ 9\ 10} \\ 6\,5,0\,0\,0 \\ -\ 6\,1,1\,8\,5 \\ \hline 5 \end{array}$$	$$\begin{array}{r} {}^{4\ 9\ 9\ 10} \\ 6\,5,0\,0\,0 \\ -\ 6\,1,1\,8\,5 \\ \hline 1\,5 \end{array}$$	$$\begin{array}{r} {}^{4\ 9\ 9\ 10} \\ 6\,5,0\,0\,0 \\ -\ 6\,1,1\,8\,5 \\ \hline 8\,1\,5 \end{array}$$	$$\begin{array}{r} {}^{4\ 9\ 9\ 10} \\ 6\,5,0\,0\,0 \\ -\ 6\,1,1\,8\,5 \\ \hline 3,8\,1\,5 \end{array}$$

The Dallas stadium holds 3,815 more fans than the San Francisco stadium.

Other Examples

$$\begin{array}{r} {}^{4\ 9\ 10} \\ 5\,0\,0 \\ -\ 2\,6\,6 \\ \hline 2\,3\,4 \end{array} \qquad \begin{array}{r} {}^{6\ 10} \\ 7\,0\,5 \\ -\ 5\,6\,1 \\ \hline 1\,4\,4 \end{array} \qquad \begin{array}{r} {}^{4\ 9\ 18\,12} \\ 5,0\,9\,2 \\ -\ 4,7\,9\,5 \\ \hline 2\,9\,7 \end{array} \qquad \begin{array}{r} {}^{4\ 9\ 9\ 12} \\ 5,0\,0\,2 \\ -\ 2,3\,7\,4 \\ \hline 2,6\,2\,8 \end{array} \qquad \begin{array}{r} {}^{7\ 9\ 9\ 9\ 10} \\ 8\,0,0\,0\,0 \\ -\ 2\,9,8\,6\,1 \\ \hline 5\,0,1\,3\,9 \end{array}$$

TRY IT OUT

Subtract. Check by adding.

1.	2.	3.	4.	5.
$\begin{array}{r} 600 \\ -\ 264 \end{array}$	$\begin{array}{r} 904 \\ -\ 642 \end{array}$	$\begin{array}{r} 8,071 \\ -\ 3,653 \end{array}$	$\begin{array}{r} 9,001 \\ -\ 4,543 \end{array}$	$\begin{array}{r} 60,000 \\ -\ 26,437 \end{array}$

Multiplying by a 1-Digit Factor

One golf ball has 336 dimples. What would be the total number of dimples on 5 golf balls?

Since we want to find the total for 5 equal amounts, we multiply.

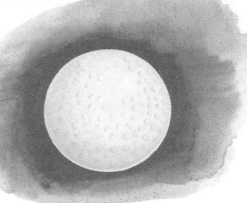

Multiply the ones. Trade if necessary.	Multiply the tens. Add any extra tens. Trade if necessary.	Multiply the hundreds. Add any extra hundreds.
$\overset{3}{3}36$ $\times\quad 5$ ——— 0	$\overset{1\,3}{3}36$ $\times\quad 5$ ——— 80	$\overset{1\,3}{3}36$ $\times\quad 5$ ——— $1{,}680$

There are 1,680 dimples on 5 golf balls.

Other Examples

$$\overset{2}{9}4 \times 6 = 564$$

$$\overset{6\,6}{1}89 \times 7 = 1{,}323$$

$$\overset{1}{8}03 \times 5 = 4{,}015$$

$$\overset{1\ \ 1}{8}{,}726 \times 2 = 17{,}452$$

TRY IT OUT

Multiply.

1. 28
    × 3

2. 146
    × 4

3. 407
    × 6

4. 537
    × 4

5. 75
    × 9

Multiplying by Multiples of 10 and 100

The loggers in Lake County are allowed to cut only 300 trees in each square mile. The area of the forest is 125 square miles. How many trees are the loggers allowed to cut down?

Since we want to find the total for a number of equal amounts, we multiply.

Multiply by the ones.	Multiply by the tens.	Multiply by the hundreds.
125 × 300 —— 0	125 × 300 —— 00	125 × 300 —— 37,500

The loggers are allowed to cut down 37,500 trees.

Other Examples

$$\begin{array}{r} {}^{1}\ \\ 85 \\ \times\ 30 \\ \hline 2{,}550 \end{array}$$

$$\begin{array}{r} {}^{1\ 3}\ \\ 125 \\ \times\ \ 60 \\ \hline 7{,}500 \end{array}$$

$$\begin{array}{r} {}^{1}\ \\ 507 \\ \times\ 200 \\ \hline 101{,}400 \end{array}$$

$$\begin{array}{r} {}^{2}\ \\ 780 \\ \times\ 300 \\ \hline 234{,}000 \end{array}$$

$$\begin{array}{r} 61 \\ \times\ 700 \\ \hline 42{,}700 \end{array}$$

TRY IT OUT

Multiply.

1. 46
× 60

2. 143
× 50

3. 380
× 600

4. 970
× 700

5. 497
× 300

6. 35
× 40

7. 207
× 60

8. 170
× 500

9. 420
× 400

10. 760
× 800

Multiplying by a 2-Digit Factor

The fifth grade class figures it will take about 47 pieces of tile for each square foot of the mosaic they plan to make. A mosaic that measures 16 square feet will take how many pieces?

Since we want to find the total of a number of equal amounts, we multiply.

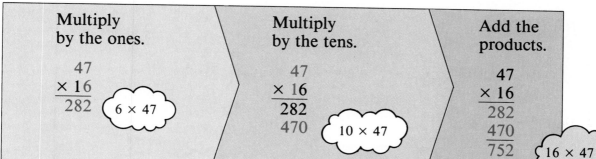

Multiply by the ones.	Multiply by the tens.	Add the products.
47 × 16 282 (6 × 47)	47 × 16 282 470 (10 × 47)	47 × 16 282 470 752 (16 × 47)

The students will need about 752 pieces of tile to complete their mosaic.

Other Examples

```
    24          309          468
  × 53        ×  68        ×  23
    72         2472         1404
  1200        18540         9360
 1,272       21,012       10,764
```

TRY IT OUT

Multiply.

1. 69
   × 28

2. 92
   × 45

3. 67
   × 74

4. 26
   × 89

5. 67
   × 29

Multiplying by a 3-Digit Factor

An average of 286 tourists visit Stonehenge in Wiltshire, England, each day. How many visit in a year? (Use 365 days in a year.)

To find the total for a number of equal amounts, we multiply.

Multiply by the ones.	Multiply by the tens.	Multiply by the hundreds.	Add the products.
286 × 365 1430	286 × 365 1430 17160	286 × 365 1430 17160 85800	286 × 365 1430 17160 85800 104,390
5 × 286	60 × 286	300 × 286	365 × 286

104,390 tourists visit Stonehenge in a year.

Other Examples

```
   429          327          258          628
 × 261        × 650        × 600        × 543
   429        16350      154,800        1884
 25740       196200                    25120
 85800       212,550                  314000
111,969                              341,004
```

Multiply.

1. 214 × 326 **2.** 138 × 248 **3.** 708 × 239 **4.** 285 × 500 **5.** 926 × 362

Money: Making Change

Lisa works in the rental room of a roller skating rink. A customer rented skates for $3.09 and gave her a $5 bill. What change did Lisa give the customer?

Lisa starts with the cost of the skates and counts out enough coins and bills to bring the total to $5.00.

Count these coins and bills to see that the total amount of change given was $1.91. Then check by subtracting $3.09 from $5.00.

$$\begin{array}{r} {\scriptstyle 4\ 9\ 10} \\ \$5.00 \\ +\ \ 3.09 \\ \hline \$1.91 \end{array}$$

Lisa says:	She gives the customer:	
"$3.09"		
"$3.10"	penny	
"$3.15"	nickel	
"$3.25"	dime	
"$3.50"	quarter	
"$4.00"	half dollar	
"$5.00"	dollar bill	

TRY IT OUT

List in order each coin or bill you would count out as change. Use the fewest possible coins and bills.

Example: Cost $2.60. Customer paid with $5.00.
Answer: 5¢, 10¢, 25¢, $1, $1

1. Cost $0.77. Customer paid with $1.00.
2. Cost $0.49. Customer paid with $1.00.
3. Cost $3.24. Customer paid with $5.00.
4. Cost $4.45. Customer paid with $10.00.

Math and Language Arts Data Bank

Dewey Decimal Number Groups

000–099	Encyclopedias, periodicals, journalism
100–199	Philosophy, psychology, logic
200–299	Religion
300–399	Social sciences
400–499	Language, grammar, dictionaries
500–599	Physical and life sciences, mathematics
600–699	Medicine, engineering, business, media
700–799	The arts
800–899	Novels, poetry, plays
900–999	Geography, history, biography

Egyptian Hieroglyphic Numerals

The Egyptians of long ago used pictures called hieroglyphics to represent numbers. They did not use place value, but simply added the value of each symbol to get the number. For example, ∩∩ ||| = 23.

Stroke	Arch	Coiled Rope	Lotus Flower	Pointed Finger	Tadpole	Surprised Person
1	10	100	1,000	10,000	100,000	1,000,000

Braille Alphabet and Numerals

a b c d e f g h i j k l m

n o p q r s t u v w x y z

1 2 3 4 5 6 7 8 9 0

Math and Language Arts Data Bank

A Treasury of Great Poems
(Recorded Readings)

	Listening Time
(Side 1)	
1. An Introduction: What is Poetry?	$3\frac{1}{4}$ min
2. Paul Revere's Ride (Longfellow)	$6\frac{1}{4}$ min
3. Gunga Din (Kipling)	$4\frac{1}{2}$ min
4. The Highwayman (Noyes)	7 min
(Side 2)	
1. Lord Randal (Anon.)	$1\frac{1}{2}$ min
2. Little Breeches (Hay)	$2\frac{1}{2}$ min
3. Annabelle Lee (Poe)	3 min
4. I Never Saw a Moor (Dickinson)	1 min
5. The Eagle (Tennyson)	$1\frac{1}{4}$ min
6. I Hear America Singing (Whitman)	1 min
7. Get Up and Bar the Door (Anon.)	3 min
8. The Fox and the Grapes (Untermeyer)	$1\frac{1}{4}$ min
9. The Owl and the Pussycat (Lear)	$1\frac{3}{4}$ min
10. The Last Leaf (Holmes)	$2\frac{1}{4}$ min
11. Great Lines from Great Poems	$2\frac{1}{2}$ min

Comparison of Two Reading Series
Types of Writing as Fractions of Total Content

Reading Series A

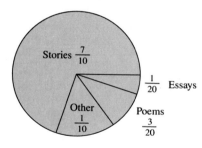

Reading Series B

Math and Science Data Bank

Household Electricity Use

Appliance	Cost per Hour
Clothes dryer	$0.37
Clothes washer	0.03
Color television	0.04
Hair dryer	0.12
Iron	0.09
Oven	0.11
Portable heater	0.13
Refrigerator	0.02
Toaster	0.10

(based on average wattages and temperatures)

Power Generated by Windmills

Model	Wattage*
Elektro W50	50 watts
Wind Wizard	600 watts
Wind Titan (10 ft)	500 watts
Kedco 1205	1,900 watts
Dunlite 2000W	2,000 watts
Eagle III	3,000 watts
Merkham Machine (40 ft)	45,000 watts

*at optimum wind speed

Math and Science Data Bank

Circulatory System Facts

In a drop of blood there are about

- 5,400,000 red blood cells.
- 5,000 white blood cells.
- 340,000 platelets.

The average heartbeat is 72 beats per minute. At rest, the heart pumps about 4.7 L of blood per minute.

Respiratory System Facts

The average person takes about 14 breaths per minute. Each breath takes in about 500 mL of air. After hard exercise, a person might take in as much as 118 L of air per minute.

Math and Science Data Bank

Does the Sand on a Beach Stand Still?

The action of the waves actually makes sand travel. Waves often strike a beach at an angle and create a longshore current. This current moves sand slowly along the shoreline. Each wave might move the grains of sand about ¼ inch. Scientists studying one beach found that on an average day, 14,000 waves struck the shore.

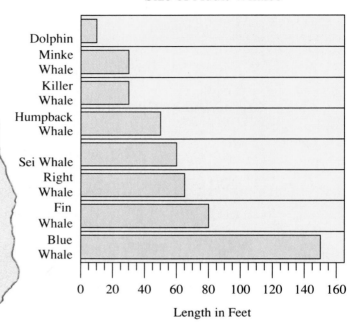

Size of Adult Whales

Length in Feet

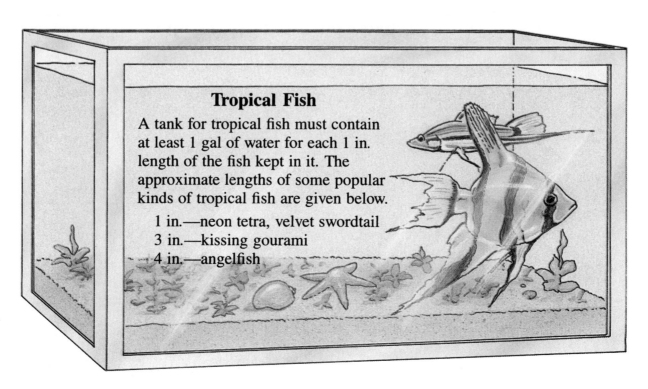

Tropical Fish

A tank for tropical fish must contain at least 1 gal of water for each 1 in. length of the fish kept in it. The approximate lengths of some popular kinds of tropical fish are given below.

1 in.—neon tetra, velvet swordtail
3 in.—kissing gourami
4 in.—angelfish

Math and Science Data Bank

AMAZING CHANGES IN TEMPERATURE

December 24, 1924, Fairfield, Montana

The temperature fell 84° F in only 12 hours, from 63° F at noon to −21° F at midnight.

January 22, 1943, Spearfish, South Dakota

The temperature rose 49° F in only 2 minutes, from −4° F at 7:30 a.m. to 45° F at 7:32 a.m.

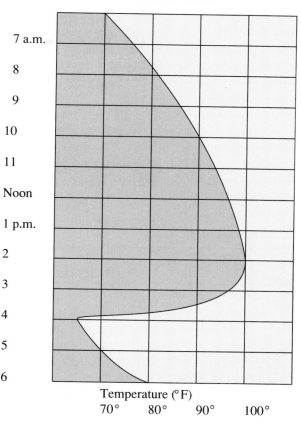

Temperatures on the Day of a Summer Storm

Time (7 a.m., 8, 9, 10, 11, Noon, 1 p.m., 2, 3, 4, 5, 6)

Temperature (°F): 70° 80° 90° 100°

Days of Rain or Snow per Year

City	Days having rain or snow	Percent of days with rain or snow
Los Angeles, CA	36	10%
San Antonio, TX	81	22%
Tampa, FL	107	29%
Chicago, IL	127	35%
Buffalo, NY	169	46%
Juneau, AK	220	60%

Air Temperatures at High Altitudes

Air grows colder as the distance from sea level increases. For every 1,000 ft of altitude above sea level, the air temperature drops by 3° F. This is generally true for altitudes up to 40,000 feet.

Math and Health and Fitness Data Bank

Hours of Sleep per Day Needed by Average Humans		
Age	Minimum hours	Maximum hours
newborn infant	20	22
4 years	10	14
10 years	9	12
20–60 years	7	9
over 60	5	7

Nutritional Values of Common Foods						Vitamins		
Food	Portion	Calories	Protein (g)	Calcium (mg)	Iron (mg)	A (I.U.)	C (mg)	D (I.U.)
Apple, raw	1 large	117	0.6	12	0.6	180	9	0
Banana, raw	1 large	176	2.4	16	1.2	860	20	0
Beans, green, cooked	1 cup	27	1.8	45	0.9	830	18	0
Beef, round, cooked	1 serving	214	24.7	10	3.1	0	0	0
Broccoli, cooked	⅔ cup	29	3.3	130	1.3	3,400	74	0
Butter	1 tablespoon	100	0.1	33	0.0	460	0	5
Cabbage, cooked	½ cup	20	1.2	39	0.4	75	27	0
Carrots, raw	1 cup, shredded	42	1.2	39	0.8	12,000	6	0
Chicken, fried	½ breast	232	26.8	19	1.3	460	0	0
Egg, boiled	1 medium	77	6.1	26	1.3	550	0	27
Margarine, fortified	1 tablespoon	101	0.1	3	0.0	460	0	0
Milk, whole, cow's	1 glass	124	6.4	216	0.2	293	2	4
Orange, whole	1 medium	68	1.4	50	0.6	285	74	0
Pork, shoulder, roasted	2 slices	320	19.2	9	2.0	0	0	0
Tomatoes, raw	1 large	40	2.0	22	1.2	2,200	46	0
Potatoes, white, baked	1 medium	98	2.4	13	0.8	20	17	0
Rice, white, cooked	1 cup	201	4.2	13	0.5	0	0	0

g = grams; mg = milligrams; mcg = micrograms; I.U. = International Units; tr. = trace.

Math and Health and Fitness Data Bank

Olympic Gold Medal Winners Women's 800-Meter Run		
1928	Lina Radke, Germany	2 min 16.8 s
1960	Ljudmila Shevcova, USSR	2 min 4.3 s
1964	Ann Packer, Great Britain	2 min 1.1 s
1968	Madeline Manning, United States	2 min 0.9 s
1972	Hildegard Falck, West Germany	1 min 58.6 s
1976	Tatiana Kazankina, USSR	1 min 54.94 s
1980	Nadezhda Olizarenko, USSR	1 min 53.5 s
1984	Doina Melinte, Romania	1 min 57.60 s
1988	Sigrun Wodars, East Germany	1 min 56.10 s

Olympic Men's Pole Vault			
	Gold	Silver	Bronze
1972	Wolfgang Nordwig (GDR) 5.50m	Robert L. Seagren (USA) 5.40m	Jan E. Johnson (USA) 5.35m
1976	Tadeusz Slusarski (POL) 5.50m	Antti Kalliomaki (FIN) 5.50m	David Roberts (USA) 5.50m
1980	Wladyslaw Kozakiewicz (POL) 5.78m	Konstantin Volkov (URS) 5.65m	Tadeusz Slusarski (POL) 5.65m
1984	Pierre Quinon (FRA) 5.75m	Mike Tully (USA) 5.65m	Earl Bell (USA) 5.60m Thierry Vigneron (FRA) 5.60m
1988	Sergey Bubka (USSR) 5.90m	Radion Gataoulline (USSR) 5.85m	Grigory Egorov (USSR) 5.80m

Math and Health and Fitness Data Bank

Dimensions of Sports Playing Areas

Sport	Length	Width
Table tennis surface	9 ft	5 ft
Boxing ring	20 ft	20 ft
Karate area	26 ft	26 ft
Tennis court (doubles)	26 yd	12 yd
Ice hockey rink	200 ft	100 ft
U.S. football field	120 yd	160 ft
Soccer field	110 yd	80 yd

Baseball Field Dimensions

All baseball fields have square areas called "diamonds" measuring 90 ft by 90 ft. The dimensions shown here are distances from home plate to outfield walls.

Stadium	Left	Left-center	Center	Right-center	Right
Astrodome (Houston)	330	375	400	375	330
Candlestick (San Francisco)	335	365	410	375	335
Fenway (Boston)	305	388	423	380	302
Fulton Co. (Atlanta)	330	375	400	375	330
Jack Murphy (San Diego)	380	370	420	370	380
Memorial (Baltimore)	309	378	405	378	309
Royals (Kansas City, MO)	330	385	410	385	330

Outline of a Basketball Court

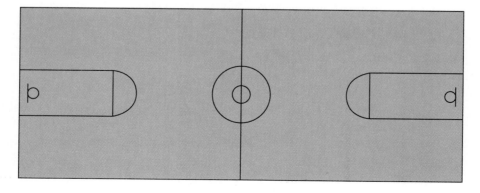

Math and Fine Arts Data Bank

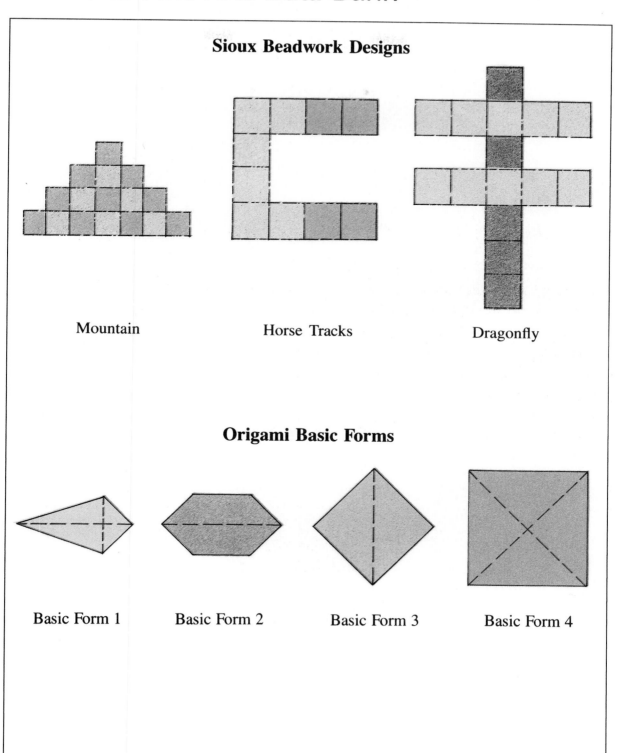

Sioux Beadwork Designs

Mountain

Horse Tracks

Dragonfly

Origami Basic Forms

Basic Form 1

Basic Form 2

Basic Form 3

Basic Form 4

Math and Fine Arts Data Bank

Seating Plan for a Typical Orchestra

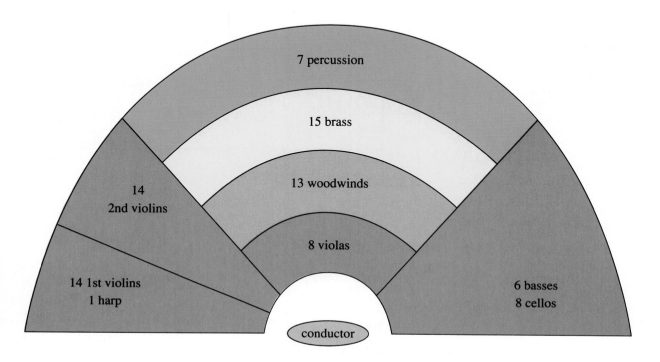

7 percussion

15 brass

13 woodwinds

14
2nd violins

8 violas

14 1st violins
1 harp

6 basses
8 cellos

conductor

Total instruments: 86

Instrument Families

Strings

Woodwinds

Brass

Percussion

Math and Fine Arts Data Bank

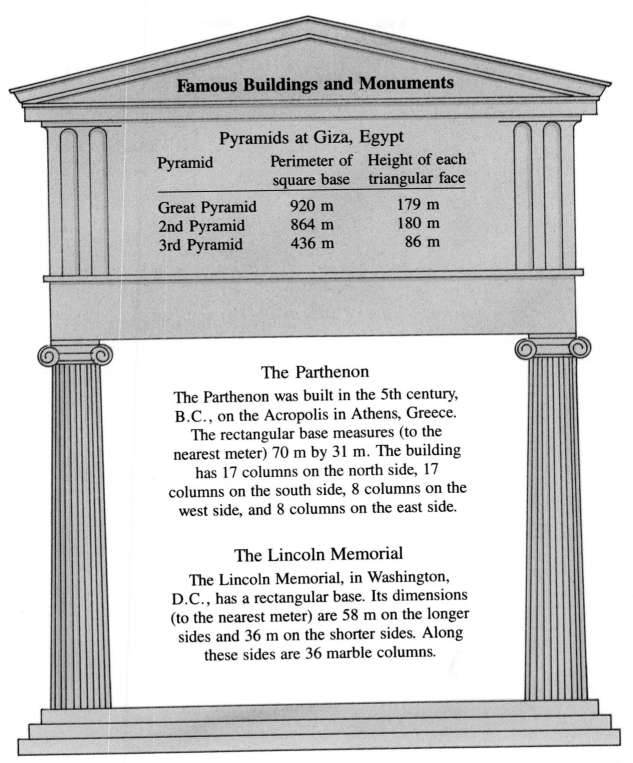

Famous Buildings and Monuments

Pyramids at Giza, Egypt

Pyramid	Perimeter of square base	Height of each triangular face
Great Pyramid	920 m	179 m
2nd Pyramid	864 m	180 m
3rd Pyramid	436 m	86 m

The Parthenon

The Parthenon was built in the 5th century, B.C., on the Acropolis in Athens, Greece. The rectangular base measures (to the nearest meter) 70 m by 31 m. The building has 17 columns on the north side, 17 columns on the south side, 8 columns on the west side, and 8 columns on the east side.

The Lincoln Memorial

The Lincoln Memorial, in Washington, D.C., has a rectangular base. Its dimensions (to the nearest meter) are 58 m on the longer sides and 36 m on the shorter sides. Along these sides are 36 marble columns.

Math and Social Studies Data Bank

Facts About the Original 13 States

Original 13 States	Date of Entry into Union	Population 1780	Population 1980	Area in Square Miles (mi^2)	Population per Square Mile (1980)
Connecticut	Jan. 1788	207,000	3,153,000	5,009	629.47
Delaware	Dec. 1787	45,000	602,000	2,057	292.66
Georgia	Jan. 1788	56,000	5,639,000	58,876	95.78
Maryland	Apr. 1788	246,000	4,265,000	10,577	403.23
Massachusetts	Feb. 1788	269,000	5,781,000	8,257	700.13
New Hampshire	June 1788	88,000	951,000	9,304	102.21
New Jersey	Dec. 1787	140,000	7,438,000	7,836	949.21
New York	July 1788	211,000	17,659,000	49,576	356.20
North Carolina	Nov. 1789	270,000	6,019,000	52,586	114.46
Pennsylvania	Dec. 1787	327,000	11,865,000	45,333	261.73
Rhode Island	May 1790	53,000	958,000	1,214	789.13
South Carolina	May 1788	180,000	2,203,000	31,055	70.94
Virginia	June 1788	538,000	5,491,000	40,817	134.53

Centuries and Decades

There are 100 years in a century.

16th Century	17th Century	18th Century	19th Century	20th Century
1501–1600	1601–1700	1701–1800	1801–1900	1901–2000

There are 10 decades in a century.

20th Century

1900s	1910s	1920s	1930s	1940s	1950s	1960s	1970s	1980s	1990s

There are 10 years in a decade.

1990s

1991	1992	1993	1994	1995	1996	1997	1998	1999	2000

Math and Social Studies Data Bank

Inventions Timeline

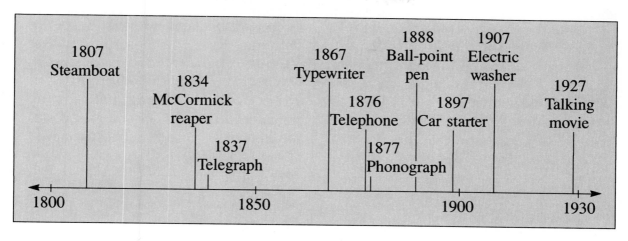

1807 Steamboat
1834 McCormick reaper
1837 Telegraph
1867 Typewriter
1876 Telephone
1877 Phonograph
1888 Ball-point pen
1897 Car starter
1907 Electric washer
1927 Talking movie

1800 · 1850 · 1900 · 1930

Patents on Inventions, 1836–1840

Year	Number of Patents Requested	Number of Patents Given
1840	765	458
1839	800	404
1838	900	514
1837	650	426
1836	400	103

Presidents of the U.S.

Name	Year Inaugurated	Age When Inaugurated
George Washington	1789	57
John Adams	1797	61
Thomas Jefferson	1801	57
James Madison	1809	57
James Monroe	1817	58
John Quincy Adams	1825	57
Andrew Jackson	1829	61
Martin Van Buren	1837	54
William Henry Harrison	1841	68

Math and Social Studies Data Bank

The National Road

One of the first good roads built in the United States was the National Road. It was made of stones broken into small pieces. The road was made highest in the middle so that water would run off to the sides. At the sides were gutters made of larger stones. The National Road was 130 miles long. It went from Cumberland, Maryland, on the Potomac River, to Wheeling, West Virginia, on the Ohio River. The work was begun in 1811 and was finished in 1818. Workers cleared a path for the road 66 feet wide. The road itself was 20 feet wide. Building the road cost about $13,000 per mile.

Railroad and Highway Travel Speeds

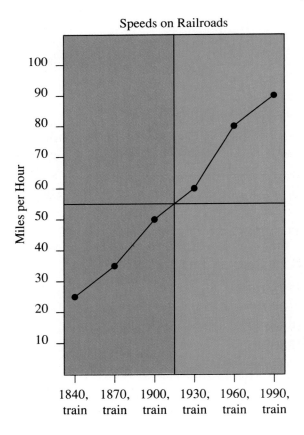

Speeds on Railroads

Miles per Hour

1840, train | 1870, train | 1900, train | 1930, train | 1960, train | 1990, train

Year, Vehicle

Speeds on Roads/Highways

Miles per Hour

1840, stagecoach | 1870, stagecoach | 1900, car | 1930, car | 1960, car | 1990, car

Year, Vehicle

Math and Social Studies Data Bank

Games Played by American Indians

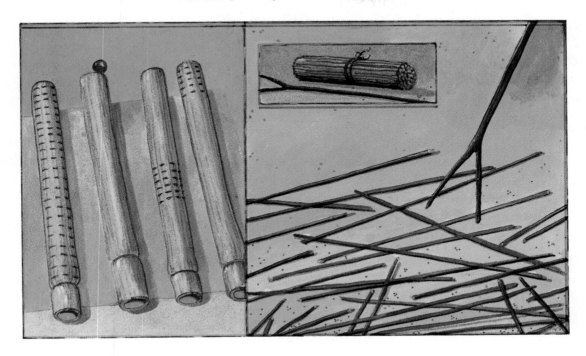

Hidden-Bean Game (Papagos)

Use 4 hollow reeds. Hide a bean in one of them. The other players try to guess which reed the bean is hidden in.

Which Hand?

About 100 different tribes played this game. Use two objects made of wood or bone. One of them is decorated. A player hides the objects, one in each hand. The other players try to guess which hand the decorated object is in.

Stick Game 1 (Hurons)

Have an odd number of sticks in a pile. One player uses a dividing pole to separate out a group of sticks, which he keeps. The other player keeps the other sticks. They count the sticks. The player with the odd number of sticks wins.

Stick Game 2 (Havasupais)

Play with 3 flat sticks. Each stick has a white side and a red side. Toss the sticks in the air and see how they land. Score like this:

Outcome	Score
3 white	10 points
2 white, 1 red	2 points
2 red, 1 white	3 points
3 red	5 points

Basic Operations

To do arithmetic operations on your calculator, enter the key code just the way you say the problem. If you make an error, press CE/C to clear the last entry. Pressing CE/C CE/C clears the display and operation. Pressing ON/AC clears the memory as well as the display and the operation.

Problem	Enter	Display
Seventy and one tenth minus thirteen	70.1 − 13 =	57.1
Eight thousand two times fifteen	8002 × 15 =	120030
Twelve million divided by four tenths	12000000 ÷ .4 =	30000000
Two ten-thousandths divided by fifty thousand	.002 ÷ 50000 =	Error U
Nine hundred and four tenths divided by zero	900.4 ÷ 0 =	Error A

The last two problems create **Error** displays. When a number is too small, many calculators will show an **Underflow Error.** Division by zero is not allowed. It gives a **Logic,** or **Arithmetic, Error.**

The largest number most calculators can display is 99999999. What happens when you add one to this number? Enter 99999999 + 1 =. If the number is too large, many calculators show an **Overflow Error.**

With most calculators, the result of dividing 82 by 5 is 16.4. On the Math Explorer calculator, you can use the INT÷ key to find the quotient and remainder.

Enter	Display	
82 INT÷ 5 =	16	2
	Q	R

Activity

Find two numbers in the box with:

1. a sum of 892.04
2. a difference of 0.0488
3. a quotient of 17 R 450
4. a quotient too small for the display
5. a product too large for the display

0.8	9800	550
70000	0.0012	
342.04	0.05	

Counting and Counting Patterns

Make your calculator count by threes. Try these key codes.

[ON/AC] [+] 3 [Cons] [Cons] [Cons] [Cons] [Cons] ...
[ON/AC] [+] 3 [=] [=] [=] [=] [=] ...

Entering [+] 3 [Cons] or [+] 3 sets up a **constant,** a number that stays the same. Each time you press [Cons] or [=], the calculator adds 3 to the number in the display.

Use your calculator to count by 1.5. Start at 20. Your display should show 21.5, 23, 24.5, 26, 27.5, and so on.

Now **count backward** by 1.5, starting from 30. Your display should show 28.5, 27, 25.5, 24, and so on.

Use the **multiplication constant** to multiply 4, 5.5, and 9 by 5.

Enter [ON/AC] [×] 5 [Cons] 4 [Cons] 5.5 [Cons] 9 [Cons]
or   [ON/AC] 4 [×] 5 [=] 5.5 [=] 9 [=]

Your display should show 20, 27.5, and 45.

Use the **division constant** to divide 16, 64, and 88.8 by 8.

Enter [ON/AC] [÷] 8 [Cons] 16 [Cons] 64 [Cons] 88.8 [Cons]
or   [ON/AC] 16 [÷] 8 [=] 64 [=] 88.8 [=]

Your display should show 2, 8, and 11.1.

Activity

Use your calculator to find the first 5 numbers in each pattern. Find the next two numbers mentally. Check with your calculator.

1. Start at 11011.
Count by 1001.

2. Start at 88888
Count back by 1001.

3. 234 × 1001
345 × 1001
456 × 1001
567 × 1001
678 × 1001
789 × 1001
890 × 1001

4. 20000 ÷ 1001
30000 ÷ 1001
40000 ÷ 1001
50000 ÷ 1001
60000 ÷ 1001
70000 ÷ 1001
80000 ÷ 1001

Order of Operations: Memory Keys

To solve a problem involving more than one operation, perform operations within parentheses first. Next multiply and divide from left to right. Then add and subtract from left to right.

For $75 \div 15 + 3 \times 21$, first find $75 \div 15$, then 3×21. Then add.

ON/AC 75 ÷ 15 =	5
ON/AC 3 × 21 =	63
ON/AC 5 + 63 =	68

You can use the **memory keys** on your calculator to make the calculator remember the result of one calculation while it does another calculation.

M+	Adds the display to the calculator's memory
M−	Subtracts the display from the calculator's memory
MR	Recalls the total in memory

Find $5 \times (12 - 6) - 3 \times 8$.

	Enter	Display
ON/AC 12 − 6 = × 5 = M+		30
3 × 8 = M−		24
MR		6

The Math Explorer calculator follows order of operations. You can enter the problem just as it is written. To do the problem above, enter:

ON/AC 5 × ((12 − 6)) − 3 × 8 =

Activity

Arrange the numbers and signs to make a true equation.

1. 4, 7, 9, 67, +, ×, =

2. 1, 4, 9, 45, −, ÷, =

3. 2, 3, 6, 10, 12, +, ×, ÷, ( ), =

4. 5, 6, 9, 10, 12, −, ×, ÷, ( ), =

Fractions and Decimals

To find the decimal equivalent of a fraction, you can use your calculator to divide the numerator by the denominator. To find the decimal for $\frac{2}{5}$ enter $\boxed{\text{ON/AC}}$ 2 $\boxed{\div}$ 5 $\boxed{=}$. The display shows 0.4.

Find the decimal for $\frac{5}{8}$, $\frac{9}{4}$, and $\frac{2}{3}$.

The $\boxed{\text{F}\rightleftarrows\text{D}}$ key on the Math Explorer calculator changes a fraction to a decimal or a decimal to a fraction (if the decimal has 3 or fewer places). To change $\frac{19}{20}$ to the decimal 0.95, enter $\boxed{\text{ON/AC}}$ 19 $\boxed{/}$ 20 $\boxed{\text{F}\rightleftarrows\text{D}}$.

Find the decimal for $\frac{7}{8}$, $\frac{13}{5}$, and $\frac{1}{6}$ using the $\boxed{\text{F}\rightleftarrows\text{D}}$ and $\boxed{/}$ keys. (0.875, 2.6, and 0.1666667)

Now find the decimal for $\frac{12}{25}$.

Enter	Display
$\boxed{\text{ON/AC}}$ 12 $\boxed{/}$ 25 $\boxed{\text{F}\rightleftarrows\text{D}}$	0.48
Press $\boxed{\text{F}\rightleftarrows\text{D}}$ again.	48/100

Pressing $\boxed{\text{F}\rightleftarrows\text{D}}$ the second time changes the decimal 0.48 back to a fraction. The N/D → n/d in the display means that the fraction is not in simplest form (lowest terms). To simplify the fraction, enter $\boxed{\text{Simp}}$ $\boxed{=}$ until N/D → n/d disappears from the display.

$\boxed{\text{Simp}}$ $\boxed{=}$	24/50
$\boxed{\text{Simp}}$ $\boxed{=}$	12/25

Find the simplest fraction for 1.45.

Enter	Display
1.45 $\boxed{\text{F}\rightleftarrows\text{D}}$	1 u 45/100
$\boxed{\text{Simp}}$ 5 $\boxed{=}$	1 u 9/20

1 is the whole number or **unit** part of the mixed number.

Activity

Write as many different fractions as you can from the numbers 12, 7, 5, and 1. Give the decimal equivalent of each fraction.

Adding and Subtracting Fractions

To add or subtract fractions using a calculator, change them to decimals. Write down the decimal for each fraction or use memory keys.

Add $\frac{4}{5} + \frac{3}{4}$.

	Enter	Display
	ON/AC 4 ÷ 5 =	0.8
	ON/AC 3 ÷ 4 =	0.75
	ON/AC .8 + .75 =	1.55

To add or subtract mixed numbers, first change the mixed number to an improper fraction. For example, $2\frac{1}{4} - 1\frac{5}{8} = \frac{9}{4} - \frac{13}{8}$.

Enter	Display
ON/AC 9 ÷ 4 = M+ 13 ÷ 8 = M− MR	0.625

To add or subtract fractions on the Math Explorer, enter the key code just the way you write the problem. Use the Unit key to enter the whole number part of a mixed number.

Problem	Key Code	Display
$\frac{11}{10} - \frac{1}{2}$	11 / 10 − 1 / 2 = Simp =	6/10 3/5
$2\frac{1}{2} + 1\frac{3}{8}$	2 Unit 1 / 2 + 1 Unit 3 / 8 =	3 u 7/8
$\frac{7}{9} + \frac{2}{3}$	7 / 9 + 2 / 3 = Ab/c	13/9 1 u 4/9
$2\frac{3}{4} + \frac{1}{2}$	2 Unit 3 / 4 + 1 / 2 = Ab/c	2 u 5/4 3 u 1/4

Note that the Ab/c key changes improper fractions to mixed numbers.

Activity

Use these numbers: 1, 2, 3, 4, 5, 8, and 9. Make true equations.

1. $\frac{|||||}{|||||} + \frac{|||||}{|||||} = \frac{8}{9}$

2. $|||||\frac{|||||}{|||||} + |||||\frac{|||||}{|||||} = 6\frac{3}{10}$

3. $\frac{|||||}{|||||} - \frac{|||||}{|||||} = \frac{1}{8}$

4. $|||||\frac{|||||}{|||||} - |||||\frac{|||||}{|||||} = 2\frac{1}{8}$

Multiplying and Dividing Fractions

You can multiply or divide fractions by multiplying or dividing their decimal equivalents. Multiply $\frac{5}{8} \times \frac{3}{4}$.

	Display
Enter [ON/AC] 5 [÷] 8 [×] 3 [÷] 4 [=]	0.46875
or [ON/AC] 5 [÷] 8 [=] [M+] 3 [÷] 4 [×] [MR] [=]	0.46875

Divide $\frac{15}{16}$ by $\frac{3}{4}$. Find the decimal for the divisor first.

[ON/AC] 3 [÷] 4 [=] [M+]	0.75
15 [÷] 16 [=]	0.9375
[÷] [MR] [=]	1.25

To multiply or divide mixed numbers, first change the mixed number to an improper fraction. For instance, $2\frac{1}{2} \times 3\frac{1}{4}$, $= \frac{5}{2} \times \frac{13}{4}$.

[ON/AC] 5 [÷] 2 [=] [M+] 13 [÷] 4 [×] [MR] [=]	8.125

With the Math Explorer calculator, you can enter multiplication and division problems just the way they are written. Try these.

Problem	Key Code	Display
$\frac{7}{9} \times \frac{3}{5}$	7 [/] 9 [×] 3 [/] 5 [=] [Simp] [=]	7/15
$1\frac{5}{6} \times 3\frac{2}{3}$	1 [Unit] 5 [/] 6 [×] 3 [Unit] 2 [/] 3 [=] [Ab/c]	121/18 6 u 13/18
$\frac{3}{4} \div \frac{3}{10}$	3 [/] 4 [÷] 3 [/] 10 [=] [Ab/c]	30/12 2 u 6/12
	[Simp] 6 [=]	2 u 1/2

Activity

Put these numbers in the boxes to make a true equation: 2, 3, 4, 5, 6, 8, 9, and 10.

$$\frac{\boxed{}}{\boxed{}} \times \frac{\boxed{}}{\boxed{}} = \frac{\boxed{}}{\boxed{}} \div \frac{\boxed{}}{\boxed{}}$$

Percent

The percent key $\boxed{\%}$ converts the number in the display to a decimal by dividing it by 100 (or by multiplying it by 0.01).

> Enter $\boxed{\text{ON/AC}}$ 63 $\boxed{\%}$. The display will show 0.63.

Find the decimal for each percent: 83%, 99%, 1%, and 192%. Your calculator should display 0.83, 0.99, 0.01, and 1.92.

On the Math Explorer calculator, you can find the fraction for a percent. Try this.

	Display
$\boxed{\text{ON/AC}}$ 85 $\boxed{\%}$ $\boxed{\text{F⇄D}}$	85/100
$\boxed{\text{Simp}}$ $\boxed{=}$	17/20

Find the fractions for 20%, 5%, 150%, and .5%. Your calculator should display 1/5, 1/20, 1 u 1/2, and 1/200.

Multiply to find the percent of a number. For example, to find 15% of 175:

> $\boxed{\text{ON/AC}}$ 175 $\boxed{\times}$ 15 $\boxed{\%}$ $\boxed{=}$ 26.25

Find 190% of 310. Your display should show 589.

Find 6% of $12.90. Your display should show 0.774.

Activity

This circle graph shows the computer use at Brown's Feed Company.

If the graph is based on a study of 3,600 hours of computer use, how many hours is the computer used for each job?

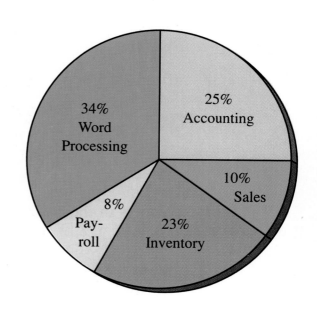

Squares and Square Roots

To square a number, that is, to multiply a number by itself, use the $\boxed{\times^2}$ key on your calculator. To find the area of a square 7 units on each side, find 7^2.

	Display
$\boxed{\text{ON/AC}}$ 7 $\boxed{\times}$ 7 $\boxed{=}$	49
or $\boxed{\text{ON/AC}}$ 7 $\boxed{\times^2}$	49

Find 8^2, 120^2, and 2.2^2. Your display should show 64, 14400, and 4.84.

Use the $\boxed{\sqrt{}}$ key on your calculator to find the square root of a number. The square root is a number that can be multiplied by itself to equal the number in the display. The $\boxed{\sqrt{}}$ key "undoes" the work of the $\boxed{\times^2}$ key. To find the length of the side of a square if its area is 49, find the square root of 49, which is written $\sqrt{49}$.

	Display
$\boxed{\text{ON/AC}}$ 49 $\boxed{\sqrt{}}$	7

Find the square root of 81, 14400, and 4.84. Your display should show 9, 120, and 2.2.

Activity

Find the missing length or area in each figure below.

1.
$l = 10$ A = ?

2.
$l = ?$ A = 169

3.
$l = 5.5$ A = ?

4.
$l = ?$ A = 22,500

5.
$l = 72$ A = ?

6.
$l = ?$ A = 6,561

Front-End Estimation

Vicki kept a record of how many miles she rode her bicycle each week. She wanted to estimate the total distance she had ridden in 6 weeks. She decided to use front-end estimation to get a good estimate of the sum.

Bicycle Distances

Week	Distance
Week 1	59
Week 2	83
Week 3	91
Week 4	87
Week 5	88
Week 6	55

How far do you think she rode?

The computer program below will give you practice in estimating sums using the front-end method. You can often make a better estimate with this method than you can by rounding the numbers.

```
10   PRINT"FRONT-END ESTIMATION":GOSUB 200
20   PRINT:INPUT"HOW MANY NUMBERS TO ADD?";N: DIM X(N)
30   S = 0:FOR I = 1 TO N:X(I) = INT (90*RND(1) + 10)
40   S = S+ X(I):NEXT I
50   PRINT"HERE IS YOUR ADDITION PROBLEM.":PRINT
60   FOR I = 1 TO N − 1
70   PRINT TAB(2)X(I):PRINT:NEXT I
80   PRINT"+";X(N)
90   PRINT"____"
100 PRINT:PRINT "WHAT IS THE ESTIMATED SUM OF THE TENS":INPUT
        "DIGITS?";T
110 PRINT"ABOUT HOW MANY MORE TENS DO YOU":INPUT"ESTIMATE FROM
        THE ONES SUM?";O
120 PRINT:PRINT"YOUR ESTIMATE IS";10*(T + O)
130 PRINT"THE EXACT SUM IS";S
140 PRINT:INPUT"WANT TO TRY ANOTHER PROBLEM?";Y$
150 IF LEFT$(Y$,1) = "Y" THEN GOTO 30
160 END
200 PRINT"USE THE FRONT-END METHOD TO ESTIMATE":PRINT "THE
        FOLLOWING SUMS. YOU CAN OFTEN MAKE"
210 PRINT"A BETTER ESTIMATE WITH THIS METHOD THAN":PRINT"YOU CAN
        BY ROUNDING THE NUMBERS."
220 RETURN
```

Estimating Products

Manny wants to plant a small patch
of tomatoes. He has space for 23
rows and plans to put 38 plants in
each row. How many tomato plants
will he need?

Since there will be the same number of plants in
each row, you can find the total by multiplying.
First, try to estimate the number of plants. Then
find the exact number.

The computer program below will give you practice
in estimation skills in multiplication. It will also tell
you how close your estimate is to the exact product.

```
10   PRINT:PRINT:PRINT"ESTIMATING PRODUCTS"
20   F1 = INT (90*RND(1) + 1):F2 = INT (90* RND (1) + 1)
30   P = F1*F2
40   PRINT"ESTIMATE THIS PRODUCT."
50   PRINT:PRINT TAB(15 - LEN(STR$(F1)))F1:PRINT
60   PRINT TAB(12)"x";TAB(15 - LEN(STR$(F2)))F2
70   PRINT TAB(12)"____"
80   PRINT:INPUT"ESTIMATE =";P1
90   PRINT:PRINT"THE EXACT PRODUCT IS ";P
100 D = ABS (P - P1): IF D < 10 THEN GOTO 120
110 PRINT"YOUR ESTIMATE IS OFF BY";D:GOTO 130
120 PRINT P1;"IS A VERY GOOD ESTIMATE."
130 PRINT:INPUT"DO YOU WANT TO TRY ANOTHER PROBLEM?";Y$
140 IF LEFT$(Y$,1) = "Y" THEN GOTO 10
150 END
```

Perimeter Problems

Mr. Johnson had 32 m of fencing. He wanted to use all of it to put a fence around a rectangular garden. He decided to make the length of the garden 3 times as long as the width.

Can you help Mr. Johnson find out how long and how wide his garden must be?

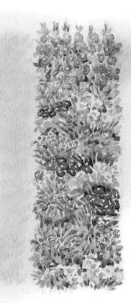

What strategies would you use to try to solve the problem above? Would you Draw a Picture? Would you use Guess and Check? The computer program below will help you develop your problem solving skills.

```
10   PRINT:PRINT:PRINT"PERIMETER PROBLEMS"
20   W = INT (10*RND(1) + 1):T = INT (5*RND (1) + 1):L = T*W
30   P = 2*(L + W)
40   PRINT"THE PERIMETER OF A RECTANGLE IS";P
50   PRINT"UNITS. THE LENGTH IS ";T;" TIMES THE":PRINT"WIDTH."
60   PRINT:INPUT "WHAT IS THE LENGTH?";L1
70   INPUT "WHAT IS THE WIDTH?";W1:PRINT
80   PRINT "THE PERIMETER IS 2 X";L1;" + 2X";W1;" = ";2*(L1 + W1);".":PRINT
       T;" TIMES THE WIDTH GIVES A LENGTH OF";T*W1;"."
90   IF L1 = T*W1 AND 2*(L1 + W1) = P THEN PRINT "CORRECT.":GOTO 130
100  PRINT "NOT CORRECT"
110  PRINT:INPUT"DO YOU WANT TO TRY AGAIN?";Y$
120  IF LEFT$(Y$,1) = "Y" THEN PRINT:GOTO 40
130  INPUT"DO YOU WANT TO TRY ANOTHER PROBLEM?";Y$
140  IF LEFT$(Y$,1) = "Y" THEN GOTO 10
150  END
```

Finding Total Amounts

Kwang had $10 to spend at the electronics store. He wanted to buy as much as he could. There was a sales tax of 6 cents on each dollar to be added on. How close can Kwang come to spending his $10 if he chooses from the items shown here? Is $10 enough to buy all of the items?

Videotape	$3.39
Audiotape	1.89
Electrical outlet	4.25
AAA batteries	0.89

Use the computer program below to help develop your addition estimation skills.

```
10  PRINT:PRINT:PRINT"FINDING TOTAL AMOUNTS":T = 0:1 = 0
20  A = INT(1000*RND(1) + 1)/100:B = INT(1000* RND(1) + 1)/100:IF ((A > = 1)
    AND (LEN(STR$(A)) < 4)) OR ((B > = 1) AND (LEN(STR$(B)) < 4)) THEN
    GOTO 20
30  C = INT(1000*RND(1) + 1)/100:D = INT(1000*RND(1)+ 1)/100:IF((C > = 1)
    AND (LEN(STR$(C)) < 4)) OR ((D > = 1) AND (LEN(STR$(D)) < 4)) THEN
    GOTO 30
40  PRINT"CHOOSE AS MANY OF THE FOLLOWING":PRINT"AMOUNTS AS YOU
    CAN TO FIND A TOTAL"
50  PRINT"UNDER $10.A 6% SALES TAX IS ADDED."
60  PRINT:PRINT"$"; TAB(6 - LEN(STR$(A)))A:PRINT"$"; TAB(6 -
    LEN(STR$(B)))B:PRINT"$"; TAB(6 - LEN(STR$(C)))C:PRINT"$";TAB(6 -
    LEN(STR$(D)))D
70  I = I + 1
80  PRINT:PRINT"TYPE AN AMOUNT WITHOUT THE DOLLAR":INPUT"SIGN.";X(I)
90  T = T + X(I)
100 PRINT:INPUT"WANT ANOTHER CHOICE?TYPE Y OR N.";Y$
110 IF LEFT$(Y$,1) = "Y" THEN GOTO 70
120 PRINT:Z = INT(100*T*.06)/100
130 FOR N = 1 TO I:PRINT TAB(15)"$";TAB(20 - LEN(STR$(X(N))))X(N):PRINT:
    NEXT N
140 PRINT TAB(10)"TAX +";TAB(20 - LEN(STR$(Z)))Z:PRINT TAB(14)"____":PRINT
150 IF T + Z = 10 THEN PRINT TAB(8)"TOTAL $10.00":PRINT:PRINT"YOU HAVE
    ENOUGH MONEY.":GOTO 180
160 IF T + Z > 10 THEN PRINT TAB(8)"TOTAL $"T + Z:PRINT;PRINT "YOU DO
    NOT HAVE ENOUGH MONEY.":GOTO 180
170 PRINT TAB(8)"TOTAL $";TAB(20 - LEN(STR$(T + Z)))T + Z:PRINT:PRINT"YOU
    HAVE ENOUGH MONEY."
180 INPUT"DO YOU WANT ANOTHER PROBLEM?";Y$
190 IF LEFT$(Y$,1) = "Y" THEN GOTO 10
200 END
```

Guess and Check

Milly thought of two numbers. She told Lalo the sum of the two numbers was 30 and the difference of the two numbers was 6. Lalo tried to use the strategy of Guess and Check to find the two numbers.

He thought: $20 + 10 = 30$, but $20 - 10 = 10$, so 20 and 10 did not check. The sum was correct but the difference was too large. Lalo thought he must be close to the two numbers so he must guess again and then check his guess.

What do you think Milly's two numbers were?

You can use the computer program below to practice using the Guess and Check strategy.

```
10   PRINT:PRINT:PRINT"GUESS AND CHECK STRATEGY"
20   A = INT(20*RND(1) + 1):B = INT(20* RND(1) +)
30   IF A < = B THEN GOTO 20
40   PRINT"THE SUM OF TWO NUMBERS IS "A + B". THE"
50   PRINT"DIFFERENCE OF THE TWO NUMBERS IS "A - B"."
60   PRINT"GUESS THE TWO NUMBERS.LIST THE":PRINT"LARGEST ONE
        FIRST."
70   PRINT:INPUT"FIRST NUMBER = ";F:INPUT"SECOND NUMBER = ";S
80   PRINT:PRINT"SUM = ";F + S,"DIFFERENCE = ";F - S
90   IF A = F AND B = S THEN GOTO 120
100  PRINT:PRINT"NOT CORRECT":INPUT"DO YOU WANT TO TRY AGAIN?";Y$:IF
        LEFT$(Y$,1) = "Y" THEN PRINT:PRINT:GOTO 40
110  GOTO 130
120  PRINT:PRINT"YOU HAVE FOUND THE TWO NUMBERS."
130  INPUT"DO YOU WANT ANOTHER PROBLEM?";Y$
140  IF LEFT$(Y$,1) = "Y" THEN GOTO 10
150  END
```

Probability Experiment

Joseph and Tami were tossing a
number cube with faces numbered
1 through 6. Joseph thought if they
tossed the cube 1,000 times, one of
the faces would come up many more
times than another. Tami thought
each face would come up about the
same number of times.

What do you think will happen in
1,000 tosses of the number cube?

Computers can be programmed to simulate
probability problems. The program below can be
used to simulate a spinner with any number of equal
sectors. It can simulate the number cube by choosing
the outcome for a spinner with 6 equal-size sectors.
To simulate a coin toss, choose a spinner with
2 same-size sectors. You can choose any number of
trials for the spinner.

```
10  PRINT"PROBABILITY SPINNER":PRINT"THIS IS AN EXPERIMENT IN
        PROBABILITY.":PRINT"CHOOSE A SPINNER WITH ANY NUMBER
        OF":PRINT"EQUAL PARTS. CHOOSE ANY NUMBER OF":PRINT"SPINS.
        THE COMPUTER WILL QUICKLY GIVE":PRINT"THE OUTCOME."
20  PRINT:INPUT"HOW MANY SECTORS OF EQUAL SIZE?";X
30  DIM D(X)
40  FOR N = 1 TO X:D(N) = 0:NEXT N
50  INPUT"HOW MANY SPINS DO YOU WANT?";Y:PRINT
60  FOR I = 1 TO Y:R = INT (X*RND (1)) + 1
70  LET D(R) = D(R) +1: NEXT I
80  PRINT:"NUMBER","FREQUENCY"
90  FOR N = 1 TO X:PRINT N,D(N):NEXT N
100 END
```

Computer Graphs

Lisa wanted to make a simple pictograph of the data in the table. She decided to use stars, (*), to represent the meters in the table. She had to decide how many meters each star would represent in the graph. At first she was going to use 1 star for every 4 m, but she found that this would take too many stars.

Highest Points (meters)	
Illinois	376
Indiana	383
Michigan	804
Minnesota	701
Ohio	472
Wisconsin	595

She decided to use 1 star for every 15 m. How many stars would she need for each state?

You can use the computer program below to make a pictograph of the data. You must decide how much each symbol represents. Try the program with some data from the Data Bank (pages 468–483).

```
10   PRINT:PRINT:PRINT"COMPUTER GRAPHING":PRINT"ENTER THE
         FOLLOWING INFORMATION AND THE":PRINT"COMPUTER WILL CREATE A
         GRAPH."
20   PRINT:INPUT"HOW MANY NUMBERS FOR THE GRAPH?";N
30   DIM N$(N):DIM X(N)
40   PRINT"FOR EACH ITEM, TYPE THE NAME AND THE":PRINT"NUMBER
         SEPARATED BY A COMMA."
50   FOR I = 1 TO N:INPUT N$(I),X(I):NEXT I
60   S = 1:FOR Q = 1 TO N:S1 = INT (X(Q)/23 + 1):IF S1 > S THEN S =S1
70   NEXT Q:INPUT "TYPE THE NAME OF THE GRAPH.";G$
80   PRINT:PRINT TAB(20)G$
90   PRINT"_____"
100 FOR I = 1 TO N:PRINT N$(I),
110 FOR J = 1 TO INT (X(I)/S + .5):PRINT"*";:NEXT J
120 PRINT:NEXT I
130 PRINT"_____":PRINT
140 PRINT:"EACH*=";S
150 END
```

Estimating Length

Estimate the length of your desk top or table in centimeters. Then estimate the width of your desk top or table. Use a centimeter ruler to check your estimates. Were they within 5 to 10 cm of the actual measures?

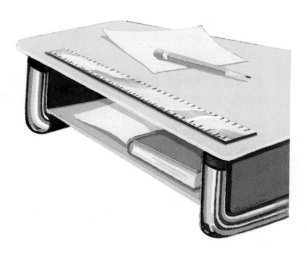

It is important to develop good estimation skills. In the computer program below you can practice estimating the lengths of objects using different units.

```
10   U = INT (6*RND (1) +3)
20   S = INT (78*RND (1) +1)
30   IF S < U THEN 10
40   L = INT (S/U*10)/10
50   PRINT:PRINT:FOR N = 1 TO U:PRINT"-";:NEXT N:PRINT"1
        UNIT":PRINT:PRINT:FOR N = 1 TO S:PRINT"-";:NEXT N
60   PRINT"?UNITS":PRINT:PRINT:GOSUB 150:PRINT:INPUT"WHAT IS YOUR
        ESTIMATE?";E
70   PRINT"LENGTH","EST.","DIFF."
80   PRINT L,E,ABS (L-E)
90   INPUT"TRY AGAIN? (Y/N)";Y$
100 IF LEFT$(Y$,1) = "Y"THEN 10
120 END
130 PRINT"ESTIMATING LENGTH":PRINT"USE THE UNIT SEGMENT SHOWN TO
        ESTIMATE":PRINT"THE LENGTH OF THE GIVEN SEGMENT TO
        THE":PRINT"NEAREST UNIT."
140 RETURN
```

Set A For use after page 5.
Write each numerical expression using symbols.

1. nine divided by three

2. six more than one

3. eleven less two

4. the sum of five and two

5. twelve minus seven

6. two times ten

Choose the correct symbols for the math words.
More than one choice may be correct.

7. fifteen multiplied by eight
   A. $\frac{15}{8}$ **B.** 8×15 **C.** $15 + 8$

8. twelve less three
   A. $12 < 3$ **B.** $3 - 12$ **C.** $12 - 3$

9. eleven more than seven
   A. $11 + 7$ **B.** $11 > 7$ **C.** $7 + 11$

10. sixteen divided by four
    A. $16 \div 4$ **B.** $\frac{16}{4}$ **C.** $\frac{4}{16}$

Set B For use after page 7.
Find the value of each expression.

1. $(35 \div 5) + 4$

2. $(3 + 5) + 8$

3. $14 - (3 \times 3)$

4. $(11 - 8) \times 5$

5. $4 + (5 + 4)$

6. $15 - (27 \div 3)$

7. $(14 \div 2) + 5$

8. $9 - (3 + 6)$

9. $8 \times (4 + 1)$

Set C For use after page 9.
Show how you would change the order and grouping.
Then solve using mental math.

1. $25 + 18 + 75$

2. $5 \times 13 \times 20$

3. $120 + 98 + 80 + 2$

4. $4 \times 35 \times 25$

5. $525 + 19 + 75$

6. $50 \times 17 \times 2$

7. $95 + 137 + 5$

8. $25 \times 19 \times 4$

9. $75 + 97 + 25 + 3$

Set D For use after page 29.
Use place value to tell what each red digit means.

1. 3,574

2. 6,384

3. 3,596

4. 23,329

5. 45,520

6. 72,521

7. 425

8. 197,600

9. 165,372

10. 24,819

11. 361,472

12. 910,345

MORE PRACTICE BANK

Set A   For use after page 31.

Use place value to tell what each red digit means.

1. 59,876,476   **2.** 864,327,413   **3.** 362,470,198

4. 5,468,294,300   **5.** 42,385,297   **6.** 3,576,284

Set B   For use after page 33.

Write > (greater than) or < (less than) for each ∭.

1. 251 ∭ 261   **2.** 6,900 ∭ 6,799   **3.** 5,055 ∭ 5,505

Order from least to greatest.

4. 3,191; 3,011; 3,121; 3,111   **5.** 28,303; 29,003; 28,330; 28,033

Set C   For use after page 35.

Round to the nearest ten. Then round to the nearest hundred.

1. 841   **2.** 513   **3.** 1,458   **4.** 8,325   **5.** 5,899

Round to the nearest thousand. Then round to the nearest ten thousand.

6. 16,450   **7.** 8,674   **8.** 34,489   **9.** 27,510   **10.** 64,399

Set D   For use after page 41.

Write the word name for each decimal.

1. 16.1   **2.** 0.49

3. 12.15   **4.** 8.08

Write the decimal.

5. thirty-two hundredths   **6.** five and two tenths   **7.** seven hundredths

Set E   For use after page 43.

Write in standard form.

1. five hundredths   **2.** one and two tenths   **3.** forty-two thousandths

Write the word name for each decimal.

4. 0.323   **5.** 0.41   **6.** 1.21   **7.** 1.210   **8.** 8.62

Set A   For use after page 45.

Write >, <, or = for each ▦.

1. 0.9 ▦ 0.09   **2.** 3.2 ▦ 3.32   **3.** 68.1 ▦ 68.11   **4.** 0.303 ▦ 0.033

Order the numbers from least to greatest.

5. 0.0312; 0.039; 0.0041; 0.0301; 0.0049

6. 0.1043; 0.0976; 0.0909; 0.1100; 0.1009

Set B   For use after page 47.

Round to the nearest tenth, then to the nearest hundredth.

1. 1.983   **2.** 6.0451   **3.** 0.057   **4.** 1.1192   **5.** 20.022

Round to the nearest whole number.

6. 8.5   **7.** 3.27   **8.** 16.0003   **9.** 54.587   **10.** 0.54

Set C   For use after page 59.

Estimate by rounding to the nearest thousand.

1.	**2.**	**3.**	**4.**	**5.**
11,873	3,866	23,788	5,870	18,625
− 9,260	+ 2,149	− 14,022	+ 4,366	− 10,440

Estimate by rounding to the nearest dollar.

6.	**7.**	**8.**	**9.**	**10.**
$6.50	$19.52	$13.60	$6.49	$20.89
+ 3.25	− 12.80	+ 5.80	+ 3.71	+ 3.90

Set D   For use after page 61.

Add or subtract.

1.	**2.**	**3.**	**4.**	**5.**
239	521	1,297	35,008	$40.00
87	893	793	− 14,397	− 23.12
+ 125	+ 326	+ 3,442		

Set E   For use after page 63.

Estimate. Use the front-end method.

1.	**2.**	**3.**	**4.**	**5.**
317	442	224	$6.31	$10.68
+ 985	+ 365	+ 977	+ 4.72	+ 5.35

MORE PRACTICE BANK

Set A   For use after page 69.
Add.

1.	4.7	2.	0.55	3.	47.5	4.	6.472	5.	0.082
	+ 8.6		+ 0.78		+ 26.4		+ 1.131		+ 0.69

6.	622.8	7.	0.045	8.	61.0	9.	172.61	10.	3.472
	+ 67.3		+ 0.264		+ 9.71		+ 148.94		+ 2.5188

11.	5.98	12.	12.64	13.	9.459	14.	$37.68	15.	$ 5.26
	+ 27.15		+ 9.77		+ 0.571		+ 82.43		+ 94.99

16. 15.6 + 3.54 + 12.75 **17.** 9.08 + 1.743 + 8.5 **18.** $78.95 + $183.69

Set B   For use after page 77.
Subtract.

1.	9.2	2.	0.61	3.	4.63	4.	0.518	5.	7.546
	− 2.6		− 0.17		− 3.55		− 0.245		− 2.485

6.	0.73	7.	2.585	8.	0.7655	9.	1.42	10.	4.7642
	− 0.42		− 2.499		− 0.4645		− 1.265		− 1.5887

11.	7.83	12.	$56.70	13.	$80.35	14.	3.54	15.	6.0102
	− 6.09		− 16.80		− 37.28		− 1.467		− 4.8213

16. 10.07 − 8.8   **17.** 0.9452 − 0.7643   **18.** $95.39 − $29.49

Set C   For use after page 79.
Use compensation to find the sums and differences
mentally.

1. 152 + 97   **2.** 202 + 349   **3.** 197 + 468   **4.** 584 + 196

5. 253 − 98   **6.** 312 − 202   **7.** 896 − 497   **8.** 388 − 198

Set D   For use after page 103.
Find the range, mean, median, and mode for each
set of numbers.

1. 43, 29, 38, 26, 19   **2.** 17, 24, 34, 27, 18, 24

3. 20, 15, 24, 28, 31, 20, 30

MORE PRACTICE BANK

Set A   For use after page 109.
Substitute compatible numbers to estimate each sum
or difference.

1. 198 − 96

2. $81 + $201 + $19

3. 576 − 174

4. 592 + 24 + 78

5. $76 + $5 + $194 + $123

6. $1.19 + $4.98 + $0.78 + $15.04

Set B   For use after page 121.
Find the products using mental math.

1. 10 × 10   **2.** 100 × 10   **3.** 10 × 1,000   **4.** 100 × 100

5. 90 × 40   **6.** 30 × 70   **7.** 60 × 30   **8.** 80 × 60

9. 20 × 90   **10.** 30 × 500   **11.** 200 × 400   **12.** 10 × 500 × 20

Set C   For use after page 123.
Estimate these products by rounding 2-digit numbers
to the nearest ten and 3-digit numbers to the nearest
hundred.

1. 6 × 72   **2.** 4 × 98   **3.** 8 × 53   **4.** 5 × 894   **5.** 3 × 456

6. 7 × 634   **7.** 2 × 279   **8.** 9 × 852   **9.** 29 × 74   **10.** 38 × 43

Set D   For use after page 125.
Multiply.

1. 42 × 2   **2.** 91 × 3   **3.** 27 × 7   **4.** 29 × 19   **5.** 35 × 27

6. 61 × 23   **7.** 469 × 39   **8.** 625 × 30   **9.** 289 × 78   **10.** 456 × 37

Set E   For use after page 130.
Use the distributive property to find the products
mentally.

1. 3 × 15   **2.** 2 × 18   **3.** 4 × 17   **4.** 17 × 3

5. 6 × 12   **6.** 3 × 52   **7.** 4 × 33   **8.** 2 × 26

MORE PRACTICE BANK

Set A   For use after page 135.

Multiply. Use models if necessary.

1. 3.4 $\times\ 0.6$	2. 2.8 $\times\ 5.9$	3. 0.35 $\times\ \ \ 6$	4. 4.28 $\times\ \ \ \ 9$	5. 26.5 $\times\ 0.46$
6. 1.765 $\times\ \ \ \ \ 8$	7. 3.46 $\times\ 2.9$	8. 2.78 $\times\ 4.6$	9. ~~437.9~~ $\times\ $ ~~26.4~~	10. 7.23 $\times\ \ \ 4.5$
11. 4.5 $\times\ 2.8$	12. 7.9 $\times\ 8.4$	13. 0.23 $\times\ \ \ 5$	14. 3.79 $\times\ \ \ 4$	15. 1.29 $\times\ 0.27$

Set B   For use after page 137.

Estimate the products by rounding so that you can
use a basic fact.

1. 4.8 $\times\ 3.2$	2. 5.34 $\times\ \ \ 3$	3. 9.26 $\times\ 3.44$	4. $6.67 $\times\ \ \ 4.9$	5. $214.85 $\times\ \ \ \ \ \ 8.7$

Estimate each sum. Use clustering.

6. 411 + 395 + 407 + 394   **7.** 6,989 + 6,978 + 7,031 + 7,019

8. 0.96 + 1.1 + 0.98 + 0.9 + 1.11   **9.** $8.04 + $7.89 + $7.93 + $8.08

Set C   For use after page 139.

Multiply.

1. 0.2 $\times\ 0.9$	2. 0.05 $\times\ 0.03$	3. 6.8 $\times\ 0.7$	4. 3.08 $\times\ 0.07$	5. 12.26 $\times\ 0.005$
6. 25.03 $\times\ \ \ 0.2$	7. 5.79 $\times\ 0.06$	8. 89.22 $\times\ \ 0.13$	9. 0.062 $\times\ \ \ 0.07$	10. 124.3 $\times\ 0.006$
11. 3.07 $\times\ 0.08$	12. 0.90 $\times\ 0.11$	13. 0.05 $\times\ 0.02$	14. 1.009 $\times\ \ \ 0.04$	15. 2.3 $\times\ 0.008$

Set D   For use after page 143.

Multiply. Write only the answers.

1. 8.51 × 10   **2.** 0.03 × 100   **3.** 10 × 5.921   **4.** 3.245 × 1,000

5. 100 × 0.45   **6.** 7.68 × 10   **7.** 1,000 × 0.399   **8.** 100 × 4.6

MORE PRACTICE BANK

Set A   For use after page 153.

Choose the measure that is most reasonable.

1. length of a pencil
   19 mm   19 cm   19 dm

2. length of a housefly
   8 mm   8 cm   8 m

Which unit (m, cm, or mm) would you use to measure

3. the width of your book?

4. the length of a soccer field?

5. the thickness of a book cover?

6. the height of a flagpole?

Set B   For use after page 155.

Give the number for each ▦.

1. 3.64 m = ▦ cm

2. 9.68 m = ▦ cm

3. 0.86 m = ▦ cm

4. ▦ cm = 0.9 m

5. 79 cm = ▦ m

6. 3.4 m = ▦ cm

7. 1,000 cm = ▦ m

8. ▦ cm = 1.75 m

9. ▦ m = 550 cm

Set C   For use after page 157.

Give the number for each ▦.

1. 1 cm = ▦ mm

2. 1 mm = ▦ cm

3. 8.4 cm = ▦ mm

4. ▦ cm = 500 mm

5. 4.9 cm = ▦ mm

6. 150 mm = ▦ cm

Set D   For use after page 159.

Find the area of each rectangular region.

1. Kitchen floor
   $l = 6.4$ m
   $w = 4.5$ m

2. Lot for a house
   $l = 45$ m
   $w = 36$ m

3. Kitchen wall
   $l = 4.8$ m
   $w = 2.5$ m

4. Calendar
   $l = 29$ cm
   $w = 26.5$ cm

5. Envelope
   $l = 24$ cm
   $w = 10.3$ cm

6. Postage stamp
   $l = 38$ mm
   $w = 25$ mm

Set E   For use after page 160.

Give the number for each ▦.

1. 5.876 km = ▦ m

2. 7.8 km = ▦ m

3. 867 m = ▦ km

4. 98 m = ▦ km

5. 1,264 m = ▦ km

6. 2,876 m = ▦ km

Set A   For use after page 163.

Choose the best estimate for the capacity of each container.

1. goldfish tank
   40 mL   40 L

2. fruit juice glass
   200 mL   200 L

3. gas tank of a car
   65 mL   65 L

Give the number for each ▦.

4. 7 L = ▦ mL

5. 375 mL = ▦ L

6. ▦ L = 5,000 mL

7. 25 mL = ▦ L

8. 3.4 L = ▦ mL

9. ▦ L = 2,750 mL

Set B   For use after page 165.

Give the number for each ▦.

1. 5 kg = ▦ g

2. 0.250 kg = ▦ g

3. 8,346 g = ▦ kg

4. 750 g = ▦ kg

5. 5,243 g = ▦ kg

6. 0.41 kg = ▦ g

Set C   For use after page 169.

Give the number for each ▦.

1. 3 h = ▦ min   **2.** 120 s = ▦ min **3.** 240 min = ▦ h **4.** 2 min 30 s = ▦ s

5. 7 d = ▦ h   **6.** 120 h = ▦ d   **7.** ▦ h = 2 d 12 h **8.** ▦ s = 8 min

Set D   For use after page 181.

Find the quotients. Use pencils for answers only

1. 210 ÷ 7

2. 180 ÷ 3

3. 560 ÷ 7

4. 2,700 ÷ 9

5. 4,800 ÷ 8

6. 45,000 ÷ 5

7. 4,000 ÷ 8

8. 8,100 ÷ 9

9. 1,800 ÷ 9

10. 2,100 ÷ 7

11. 720 ÷ 8

12. 30,000 ÷ 6

13. 630 ÷ 7

14. 54,000 ÷ 6

15. 28,000 ÷ 4

16. 32,000 ÷ 8

Set E   For use after page 183.

Estimate these quotients. Choose compatible numbers so that you can use a basic fact.

1. 284 ÷ 7

2. 555 ÷ 8

3. 535 ÷ 6

4. 398 ÷ 8

5. 268 ÷ 3

6. 295 ÷ 5

7. 475 ÷ 6

8. 809 ÷ 9

Set A   For use after page 187.
Divide and check.

1. $2\overline{)28}$ 2. $6\overline{)84}$ 3. $3\overline{)86}$ 4. $5\overline{)59}$ 5. $9\overline{)198}$ 6. $7\overline{)164}$

7. $3\overline{)175}$ 8. $8\overline{)576}$ 9. $4\overline{)332}$ 10. $3\overline{)139}$ 11. $8\overline{)216}$ 12. $7\overline{)96}$

13. $3\overline{)547}$ 14. $6\overline{)278}$ 15. $7\overline{)963}$ 16. $2\overline{)587}$ 17. $4\overline{)689}$

Use mental math to find each quotient.

18. $5\overline{)450}$ 19. $8\overline{)640}$ 20. $6\overline{)1,800}$ 21. $9\overline{)540}$ 22. $7\overline{)5,600}$

Set B   For use after page 189.
Divide and check.

1. $2\overline{)187}$ 2. $4\overline{)283}$ 3. $7\overline{)476}$ 4. $5\overline{)207}$ 5. $9\overline{)499}$

6. $8\overline{)987}$ 7. $6\overline{)273}$ 8. $2\overline{)197}$ 9. $4\overline{)255}$ 10. $3\overline{)907}$

11. $5\overline{)385}$ 12. $9\overline{)972}$ 13. $7\overline{)678}$ 14. $6\overline{)726}$ 15. $8\overline{)954}$

Use mental math to find each quotient.

16. $3\overline{)210}$ 17. $5\overline{)305}$ 18. $8\overline{)824}$ 19. $4\overline{)364}$ 20. $6\overline{)618}$

Set C   For use after page 191.
Divide.

1. $7\overline{)1,431}$ 2. $4\overline{)2,121}$ 3. $8\overline{)1,650}$ 4. $6\overline{)2,450}$ 5. $9\overline{)4,563}$

6. $5\overline{)4,511}$ 7. $7\overline{)5,666}$ 8. $6\overline{)3,047}$ 9. $8\overline{)3,846}$ 10. $4\overline{)3,630}$

11. $3\overline{)2,573}$ 12. $9\overline{)3,762}$ 13. $2\overline{)1,356}$ 14. $5\overline{)4,217}$ 15. $6\overline{)2,965}$

Set D   For use after page 192.
Find the average of these sets of numbers.

1. 76, 84, 96, 80   2. 98, 91, 86, 93   3. 99, 89, 82   4. 58, 70, 63, 49

5. 67, 74, 86, 92, 96   6. 71, 75, 86, 94, 82, 72   7. 84, 98, 79, 83, 76

8. 389, 373, 401, 361, 396   9. 2,105; 2,314; 1,921; 2,142; 1,973

MORE PRACTICE BANK

Set A For use after page 201.
Divide.

1. $2\overline{)7.24}$
2. $4\overline{)31.76}$
3. $3\overline{)17.52}$
4. $5\overline{)30.15}$
5. $7\overline{)63.84}$

6. $6\overline{)2.898}$
7. $8\overline{)8.344}$
8. $9\overline{)0.5733}$
9. $4\overline{)93.04}$
10. $3\overline{)168.6}$

11. $7\overline{)5.81}$
12. $5\overline{)13.30}$
13. $9\overline{)27.45}$
14. $4\overline{)121.6}$
15. $7\overline{)36.61}$

Use mental math to find the quotients.

16. $6\overline{)48.06}$
17. $8\overline{)16.16}$
18. $3\overline{)21.6}$
19. $5\overline{)45.5}$
20. $9\overline{)8.19}$

Set B For use after page 213.
Find the quotients. Use pencils for answers only.

1. $420 \div 70$
2. $540 \div 60$
3. $3,600 \div 40$
4. $6,300 \div 90$

5. $18,000 \div 60$
6. $27,000 \div 30$
7. $210 \div 70$
8. $2,800 \div 40$

9. $180 \div 90$
10. $1,600 \div 20$
11. $3,500 \div 70$
12. $560 \div 80$

13. $7,200 \div 90$
14. $20,000 \div 50$
15. $36,000 \div 90$
16. $1,600 \div 40$

Set C For use after page 215.
Estimate the quotients. Multiply to check.

1. $30\overline{)125}$
2. $60\overline{)427}$
3. $20\overline{)163}$
4. $50\overline{)306}$
5. $70\overline{)362}$

6. $80\overline{)337}$
7. $90\overline{)456}$
8. $50\overline{)462}$
9. $60\overline{)274}$
10. $70\overline{)508}$

11. $40\overline{)331}$
12. $20\overline{)172}$
13. $50\overline{)363}$
14. $80\overline{)652}$
15. $70\overline{)641}$

16. $90\overline{)550}$
17. $60\overline{)435}$
18. $30\overline{)254}$
19. $40\overline{)293}$
20. $80\overline{)582}$

Set D For use after page 217.
Divide and check.

1. $42\overline{)381}$
2. $62\overline{)546}$
3. $23\overline{)218}$
4. $45\overline{)360}$
5. $72\overline{)655}$

6. $95\overline{)760}$
7. $59\overline{)413}$
8. $61\overline{)317}$
9. $75\overline{)450}$
10. $99\overline{)912}$

11. $54\overline{)417}$
12. $32\overline{)256}$
13. $43\overline{)303}$
14. $86\overline{)434}$
15. $65\overline{)392}$

16. $94\overline{)382}$
17. $29\overline{)261}$
18. $76\overline{)535}$
19. $63\overline{)504}$
20. $84\overline{)760}$

MORE PRACTICE BANK

Set A   For use after page 219.
Divide. Watch for estimates that need to be changed.

1. $52\overline{)315}$ 2. $58\overline{)563}$ 3. $26\overline{)210}$ 4. $53\overline{)368}$ 5. $84\overline{)589}$

6. $36\overline{)183}$ 7. $68\overline{)333}$ 8. $43\overline{)426}$ 9. $73\overline{)442}$ 10. $56\overline{)506}$

Set B   For use after page 221.
Divide and check.

1. $23\overline{)1,035}$ 2. $56\overline{)952}$ 3. $61\overline{)1,586}$ 4. $39\overline{)1,992}$ 5. $54\overline{)1,404}$

6. $57\overline{)3,881}$ 7. $35\overline{)4,486}$ 8. $53\overline{)2,188}$ 9. $86\overline{)3,637}$ 10. $87\overline{)4,824}$

11. $64\overline{)5,196}$ 12. $75\overline{)3,855}$ 13. $19\overline{)2,784}$ 14. $37\overline{)8,895}$ 15. $93\overline{)2,604}$

Set C   For use after page 222.
Choose a calculation method and solve.

1. $360 \div 20$ 2. $104 \div 8$ 3. $552 \div 4$ 4. $525 \div 5$

5. $2,580 \div 15$ 6. 57×8 7. $1,600 \div 8$ 8. $660 \div 55$

9. $416 \div 2$ 10. 5×198 11. $498 \div 6$ 12. 60×102

Set D   For use after page 225.
Divide.

1. $43\overline{)2,580}$ 2. $67\overline{)6,045}$ 3. $53\overline{)3,551}$ 4. $32\overline{)6,562}$

5. $89\overline{)9,970}$ 6. $74\overline{)7,548}$ 7. $26\overline{)6,240}$ 8. $20\overline{)1,030}$

9. $38\overline{)9,984}$ 10. $22\overline{)8,866}$ 11. $43\overline{)21,844}$ 12. $67\overline{)13,738}$

Set E   For use after page 229.
Divide. Write only the answers.

1. $3.7 \div 10$ 2. $12.19 \div 10$ 3. $7.05 \div 10$ 4. $61.9 \div 100$

5. $0.7 \div 100$ 6. $652.3 \div 100$ 7. $3.9 \div 1,000$ 8. $4.22 \div 10$

Use mental math to find the missing numbers.

9. $43.75 \div 100 = a$ 10. $11.17 \div 10 = b$ 11. $56.3 \div 1,000 = c$

Set A   For use after page 241.

Write the fraction.

1. two fifths   **2.** four sixths   **3.** one third

4. seven twelfths   **5.** five sevenths   **6.** three tenths

Write the word name for each fraction.

7. $\frac{2}{3}$ **8.** $\frac{1}{10}$ **9.** $\frac{3}{4}$ **10.** $\frac{5}{8}$ **11.** $\frac{5}{6}$ **12.** $\frac{4}{5}$

Set B   For use after page 245.

Find equivalent fractions by multiplying the numerator and denominator by 2.

1. $\frac{1}{2} = \frac{|||||}{|||||}$ **2.** $\frac{3}{5} = \frac{|||||}{|||||}$ **3.** $\frac{3}{8} = \frac{|||||}{|||||}$ **4.** $\frac{2}{3} = \frac{|||||}{|||||}$

Find equivalent fractions by multiplying the numerator and denominator by 3.

5. $\frac{1}{3} = \frac{|||||}{|||||}$ **6.** $\frac{5}{6} = \frac{|||||}{|||||}$ **7.** $\frac{3}{10} = \frac{|||||}{|||||}$ **8.** $\frac{1}{4} = \frac{|||||}{|||||}$

Tell what number the numerator and denominator of the first fraction were multiplied or divided by to get the equivalent fraction.

9. $\frac{3}{5} = \frac{9}{15}$ **10.** $\frac{8}{12} = \frac{2}{3}$ **11.** $\frac{6}{8} = \frac{3}{4}$ **12.** $\frac{3}{8} = \frac{15}{40}$

Give the next three equivalent fractions.

13. $\frac{1}{5} = \frac{|||||}{|||||}, \frac{|||||}{|||||}, \frac{|||||}{|||||}$ **14.** $\frac{1}{8} \frac{|||||}{|||||}, \frac{|||||}{|||||}, \frac{|||||}{|||||}$ **15.** $\frac{3}{4} \frac{|||||}{|||||}, \frac{|||||}{|||||}, \frac{|||||}{|||||}$ **16.** $\frac{5}{6} = \frac{|||||}{|||||}, \frac{|||||}{|||||}, \frac{|||||}{|||||}$

Set C   For use after page 247.

Find the greatest common factor for each pair of numbers.

1. $\frac{8}{20}$ **2.** $\frac{6}{26}$ **3.** $\frac{20}{16}$ **4.** $\frac{35}{50}$ **5.** $\frac{16}{48}$ **6.** $\frac{7}{15}$

7. $\frac{21}{28}$ **8.** $\frac{6}{32}$ **9.** $\frac{8}{52}$ **10.** $\frac{21}{56}$ **11.** $\frac{24}{60}$ **12.** $\frac{18}{54}$

Set D   For use after page 249.

Write each fraction in lowest terms.

1. $\frac{6}{21}$ **2.** $\frac{9}{30}$ **3.** $\frac{8}{28}$ **4.** $\frac{25}{40}$ **5.** $\frac{15}{35}$ **6.** $\frac{14}{42}$

7. $\frac{12}{32}$ **8.** $\frac{18}{45}$ **9.** $\frac{20}{42}$ **10.** $\frac{36}{60}$ **11.** $\frac{16}{20}$ **12.** $\frac{24}{30}$

MORE PRACTICE BANK

Set A   For use after page 255.

Compare the fractions two at a time. Then list them in order from least to greatest.

1. $\frac{3}{10}, \frac{2}{7}, \frac{2}{5}$ 2. $\frac{4}{7}, \frac{1}{3}, \frac{9}{14}$ 3. $\frac{2}{3}, \frac{5}{9}, \frac{4}{7}$ 4. $\frac{1}{7}, \frac{7}{8}, \frac{1}{4}$

Set B   For use after page 257.

Write each improper fraction as a mixed number or whole number.

1. $\frac{10}{3}$ 2. $\frac{22}{5}$ 3. $\frac{22}{6}$ 4. $\frac{33}{2}$ 5. $\frac{56}{8}$ 6. $\frac{67}{10}$

Write each mixed number as an improper fraction.

7. $2\frac{4}{5}$ 8. $1\frac{7}{10}$ 9. $5\frac{2}{9}$ 10. $3\frac{4}{7}$ 11. $5\frac{3}{8}$ 12. $4\frac{1}{10}$

Set C   For use after page 259.

Write each improper fraction as a mixed number or whole number.

1. $\frac{37}{15}$ 2. $\frac{29}{4}$ 3. $\frac{28}{13}$ 4. $\frac{44}{9}$ 5. $\frac{95}{5}$ 6. $\frac{49}{6}$

Write each mixed number as an improper fraction.

7. $9\frac{5}{8}$ 8. $2\frac{7}{11}$ 9. $7\frac{3}{5}$ 10. $6\frac{5}{9}$ 11. $7\frac{2}{3}$ 12. $10\frac{1}{5}$

Set D   For use after page 271.

Add or subtract.

1. $\begin{array}{r} \frac{5}{6} \\ + \frac{1}{6} \\ \hline \end{array}$ 2. $\begin{array}{r} \frac{3}{11} \\ + \frac{2}{11} \\ \hline \end{array}$ 3. $\begin{array}{r} \frac{4}{5} \\ + \frac{3}{5} \\ \hline \end{array}$ 4. $\begin{array}{r} \frac{9}{10} \\ - \frac{3}{10} \\ \hline \end{array}$ 5. $\begin{array}{r} 10\frac{4}{5} \\ - 3\frac{1}{5} \\ \hline \end{array}$

6. $\begin{array}{r} \frac{7}{8} \\ - \frac{2}{8} \\ \hline \end{array}$ 7. $\begin{array}{r} \frac{3}{5} \\ + \frac{2}{5} \\ \hline \end{array}$ 8. $\begin{array}{r} \frac{11}{12} \\ - \frac{5}{12} \\ \hline \end{array}$ 9. $\begin{array}{r} \frac{5}{6} \\ - \frac{4}{6} \\ \hline \end{array}$ 10. $\begin{array}{r} \frac{7}{10} \\ + \frac{4}{10} \\ \hline \end{array}$

Set E   For use after page 273.

Find the least common denominator of these fractions.

1. $\frac{3}{8}, \frac{1}{16}$ 2. $\frac{5}{12}, \frac{1}{3}$ 3. $\frac{3}{4}, \frac{2}{7}$ 4. $\frac{1}{2}, \frac{3}{5}$ 5. $\frac{5}{8}, \frac{1}{6}, \frac{2}{3}$

6. $\frac{3}{10}, \frac{3}{4}$ 7. $\frac{1}{2}, \frac{3}{20}$ 8. $\frac{5}{24}, \frac{7}{8}$ 9. $\frac{4}{5}, \frac{3}{7}$ 10. $\frac{2}{3}, \frac{7}{12}, \frac{4}{5}$

MORE PRACTICE BANK

Set A   For use after page 277.

Add or subtract.

1. $\frac{3}{10}$
   $+ \frac{2}{5}$

2. $\frac{4}{5}$
   $+ \frac{1}{2}$

3. $\frac{2}{3}$
   $+ \frac{1}{2}$

4. $\frac{3}{2}$
   $- \frac{1}{4}$

5. $\frac{3}{4}$
   $- \frac{3}{8}$

6. $\frac{2}{3}$
   $- \frac{1}{4}$

7. $\frac{1}{8}$
   $+ \frac{3}{4}$

8. $\frac{2}{3}$
   $+ \frac{1}{6}$

9. $\frac{1}{10}$
   $+ \frac{2}{5}$

10. $\frac{3}{4}$
    $- \frac{7}{16}$

11. $\frac{4}{5}$
    $- \frac{3}{4}$

12. $\frac{5}{6}$
    $- \frac{5}{18}$

13. $\frac{5}{8}$
    $- \frac{1}{4}$

14. $\frac{7}{10}$
    $+ \frac{1}{5}$

15. $\frac{5}{6}$
    $- \frac{5}{12}$

16. $\frac{3}{4}$
    $+ \frac{7}{8}$

17. $\frac{2}{3}$
    $- \frac{2}{9}$

18. $\frac{1}{2}$
    $- \frac{3}{8}$

Set B   For use after page 285.

Find the sums.

1. $2\frac{3}{8}$
   $+ 4\frac{3}{4}$

2. $3\frac{3}{4}$
   $+ 5\frac{1}{2}$

3. $7\frac{1}{4}$
   $+ 2\frac{1}{6}$

4. $14\frac{4}{5}$
   $+ 6$

5. $13\frac{2}{3}$
   $+ 4\frac{2}{5}$

6. $3\frac{1}{2}$
   $+ 2\frac{3}{8}$

7. $10\frac{1}{6}$
   $+ 3\frac{1}{12}$

8. $1\frac{4}{5}$
   $+ 3\frac{2}{15}$

9. $15\frac{1}{3}$
   $41\frac{5}{6}$
   $+ 29\frac{1}{6}$

10. $68\frac{2}{3}$
    $9\frac{1}{4}$
    $+ 10\frac{5}{12}$

Set C   For use after page 287.

Subtract.

1. $20\frac{11}{12}$
   $- 15\frac{3}{4}$

2. $16\frac{4}{9}$
   $- 7\frac{1}{6}$

3. $12\frac{4}{5}$
   $- 12\frac{2}{3}$

4. $8\frac{3}{4}$
   $- 3\frac{2}{5}$

5. $9\frac{5}{6}$
   $- 7\frac{3}{4}$

6. $47\frac{5}{8}$
   $- 11\frac{1}{4}$

7. $41\frac{1}{2}$
   $- 27\frac{1}{10}$

8. $86\frac{1}{3}$
   $- 38\frac{3}{4}$

9. $60\frac{1}{6}$
   $- 7\frac{4}{5}$

10. $52\frac{3}{8}$
    $- 27\frac{4}{5}$

MORE PRACTICE BANK

Set A   For use after page 289.

Add or subtract. Give answers in lowest terms.

1. $\frac{5}{6}$ $+\frac{1}{4}$ **2.** $\frac{5}{16}$ $+\frac{7}{8}$ **3.** $\frac{2}{3}$ $-\frac{1}{4}$ **4.** $\frac{1}{4}$ $-\frac{1}{5}$ **5.** $2\frac{1}{4}$ $+5\frac{1}{4}$ **6.** $7\frac{3}{8}$ -5

7. $3\frac{4}{5}$ $+5\frac{1}{5}$ **8.** $4\frac{1}{2}$ $+6$ **9.** $13\frac{5}{6}$ $-8\frac{3}{4}$ **10.** $9\frac{1}{8}$ $+7\frac{3}{4}$ **11.** $15\frac{1}{2}$ $-6\frac{1}{3}$ **12.** $12\frac{1}{4}$ $-5\frac{3}{4}$

13. 5 $-4\frac{1}{3}$ **14.** $3\frac{1}{2}$ $+4\frac{2}{3}$ **15.** $4\frac{1}{4}$ $-2\frac{3}{8}$ **16.** $13\frac{5}{6}$ $+5\frac{1}{3}$ **17.** 12 $-2\frac{5}{6}$ **18.** $7\frac{3}{4}$ $+2\frac{5}{8}$

Set B   For use after page 291.

Solve. Use mental math when you can.

1. $1\frac{3}{4}$ $+2\frac{1}{4}$ **2.** 9 $+2\frac{5}{8}$ **3.** $6\frac{3}{8}$ $-4\frac{1}{8}$ **4.** $8\frac{1}{2}$ $-3\frac{5}{8}$ **5.** $12\frac{1}{2}$ $+8\frac{1}{2}$ **6.** $4\frac{5}{6}$ $-2\frac{1}{3}$

7. 3 $-1\frac{1}{4}$ **8.** $4\frac{3}{8}$ $+2\frac{1}{8}$ **9.** $6\frac{1}{4}$ $-3\frac{3}{4}$ **10.** $2\frac{3}{8}$ $+7\frac{5}{8}$ **11.** $7\frac{1}{2}$ $-4\frac{2}{3}$ **12.** $5\frac{2}{3}$ $+2\frac{1}{6}$

Set C   For use after page 301.

Give the number for each ▓.

1. 4 ft = ▓ in.   **2.** 24 in. = ▓ ft   **3.** $2\frac{1}{2}$ ft = ▓ in.

4. 3 ft = ▓ in.   **5.** 5 ft 4 in. = ▓ in.   **6.** 72 in. = ▓ ft

Set D   For use after page 303.

Measure each segment to the nearest $\frac{1}{2}$ in.

1. _____   **2.** _____

Measure each segment to the nearest $\frac{1}{4}$ in.

3. _____   **4.** _____

Set A For use after page 305.

Give the unit (**in., ft, yd, mi**) that would be most reasonable to use to measure each.

1. length of a ballpoint pen

2. length of a football field

3. length of a carrot

4. distance between two cities

5. width of a classroom

6. length of a river

Set B For use after page 308.

Give the temperature in Fahrenheit degrees (F°) to the nearest tenth of a degree.

1.

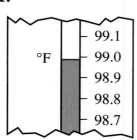

2.

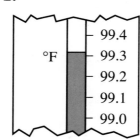

3.

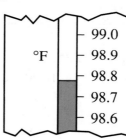

4.

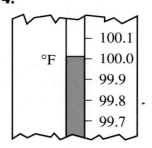

Set C For use after page 311.

Give the number for each ▦.

1. 2 oz = ▦ tablespoons

2. 2 c = ▦ oz

3. 3 pt = ▦ c

4. 2 gal = ▦ qt

5. 1 gal = ▦ pt

6. 1 gal = ▦ c

Set D For use after page 313.

Give the number for each ▦.

1. 1 lb = ▦ oz

2. 1 T = ▦ lb

3. 4 T = ▦ lb

4. $\frac{3}{4}$ lb = ▦ oz

5. 32 oz = ▦ lb

6. 10,000 lb = ▦ T

Set E For use after page 325.

Multiply.

1. $\frac{1}{2} \times 20$

2. $\frac{3}{4} \times 36$

3. $\frac{1}{3} \times 12$

4. $\frac{1}{8} \times 32$

5. $\frac{3}{8} \times 32$

6. $\frac{1}{10} \times 40$

7. $\frac{3}{10} \times 60$

8. $\frac{1}{7} \times 28$

MORE PRACTICE BANK

Set A For use after page 327.

Substitute compatible numbers to estimate each of the following.

1. $\frac{1}{8} \times 23$
2. $\frac{1}{4} \times 35$
3. $\frac{1}{5} \times 97$
4. $\frac{5}{8} \times 42$

5. $\frac{2}{3} \times 11$
6. $\frac{5}{6} \times 19$
7. $\frac{1}{6} \times 32$
8. $\frac{9}{10} \times 48$

9. $\frac{1}{5} \times 26$
10. $\frac{3}{8} \times 15$
11. $\frac{7}{10} \times 29$
12. $\frac{1}{4} \times 27$

13. $\frac{5}{6} \times 11$
14. $\frac{1}{8} \times 65$
15. $\frac{3}{5} \times 31$
16. $\frac{2}{3} \times 28$

Set B For use after page 331.

Give the product in lowest terms.

1. $\frac{2}{5} \times \frac{1}{3}$
2. $\frac{1}{2} \times \frac{1}{4}$
3. $\frac{3}{4} \times \frac{7}{8}$
4. $\frac{5}{6} \times \frac{2}{3}$

5. $\frac{2}{3} \times \frac{3}{5}$
6. $\frac{7}{4} \times \frac{3}{2}$
7. $\frac{4}{5} \times \frac{5}{4}$
8. $\frac{3}{4} \times \frac{1}{3}$

9. $\frac{1}{6} \times \frac{6}{7}$
10. $\frac{1}{10} \times \frac{9}{10}$
11. $\frac{7}{3} \times \frac{1}{2}$
12. $\frac{4}{3} \times \frac{5}{2}$

13. $\frac{3}{8} \times \frac{8}{3}$
14. $\frac{5}{6} \times \frac{3}{4}$
15. $\frac{5}{8} \times \frac{2}{3}$
16. $\frac{2}{5} \times \frac{3}{4}$

17. $\frac{2}{5} \times \frac{9}{3}$
18. $\frac{3}{10} \times 20$
19. $\frac{5}{6} \times \frac{3}{5}$
20. $15 \times \frac{2}{3}$

21. $\frac{3}{8} \times \frac{2}{3}$
22. $\frac{4}{5} \times \frac{5}{8}$
23. $16 \times \frac{3}{4}$
24. $\frac{3}{5} \times 30$

Set C For use after page 337.

Give the product in lowest terms.

1. $1\frac{1}{3} \times 4\frac{1}{2}$
2. $1\frac{3}{8} \times 1\frac{3}{5}$
3. $2\frac{2}{3} \times 3$
4. $1\frac{5}{9} \times 3\frac{6}{7}$

5. $12 \times 1\frac{5}{6}$
6. $3\frac{1}{3} \times 1\frac{3}{5}$
7. $3\frac{3}{7} \times 3\frac{1}{2}$
8. $2\frac{1}{3} \times 1\frac{5}{28}$

9. $3\frac{4}{5} \times 2\frac{3}{8}$
10. $2\frac{1}{6} \times 1\frac{5}{8}$
11. $3\frac{2}{3} \times 2\frac{4}{5}$
12. $1\frac{5}{6} \times 3\frac{7}{8}$

13. $4\frac{1}{2} \times 7\frac{2}{3}$
14. $2\frac{1}{8} \times 1\frac{1}{6}$
15. $3\frac{1}{3} \times 2\frac{3}{4}$
16. $5\frac{1}{3} \times 1\frac{1}{8}$

MORE PRACTICE BANK

Set A   For use after page 341.

Use fraction pieces or draw pictures to answer the questions.

1. How many halves are in 3?

2. How many fourths are in $\frac{5}{2}$?

3. How many sixths are in $\frac{2}{3}$?

4. How many fourths are in $2\frac{1}{4}$?

5. How many thirds are in 3?

6. How many eighths are in $\frac{3}{4}$?

Set B   For use after page 351.

Name the following solid figures.

1.   **2.**   **3.**   **4.**   **5.**

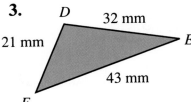

Set C   For use after page 353.

Tell whether the triangle is **scalene, isosceles,** or **equilateral.**

1.

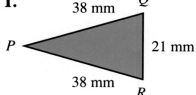

38 mm Q
P 21 mm
38 mm R

2.

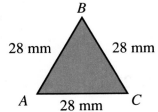

B
28 mm   28 mm
A 28 mm C

3.

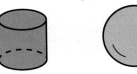

D 32 mm
21 mm E
43 mm
F

Set D   For use after page 355.

Tell whether each triangle is **acute, right,** or **obtuse.**

1.   **2.**   **3.**

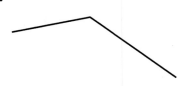   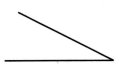   

Draw angles (without using a protractor) which you estimate to have the measures given below. Then measure each angle to check your estimate.

4. 45°   **5.** 60°   **6.** 95°   **7.** 120°   **8.** 145°   **9.** 175°

MORE PRACTICE BANK

Set A   For use after page 357.
Name the following quadrilaterals.

1.   2.    3.    4.    5.

Set B   For use after page 359.
Draw the following shapes. Then give the number of lines of symmetry for each shape.

1. parallelogram   **2.** rhombus   **3.** kite

Set C   For use after page 363.
Is figure **A** congruent to figure **B**? Write **yes** or **no**.

1. A B   2. A B   3. A B

Set D   For use after page 367.
Name each of these polygons.

1.   2.   3.   4.

Set E   For use after page 369.
Give the missing length.

1. Radius: 4 cm   **2.** Radius: 3.5 m   **3.** Diameter: 12 cm   **4.** Diameter: 4.6 mm

4 cm

3.5 m

12 cm

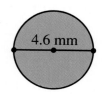
4.6 mm

Diameter: ▦   Diameter: ▦   Radius: ▦   Radius: ▦

Set F   For use after page 371.
Find the circumference for a circle with the given diameter or radius. Use 3.14 for π.

1. $d = 2.5$ cm   **2.** $r = 6$ mm   **3.** $d = 5.2$ cm   **4.** $r = 3.1$ m

518

MORE PRACTICE BANK

Set A   For use after page 373.

On a piece of graph paper, graph the following
figures. Give the coordinates of the vertices.

1. triangle   **2.** pentagon   **3.** rectangle   **4.** trapezoid

Graph and connect each point.

5. (1,1), (3,6), (6,3), (1,1)   **6.** (2,2), (2,6), (8,6), (8,2), (2,2)

Name the figure formed by graphing and connecting the points.

7. (1,1), (3,6), (6,3), (1,1)   **8.** (2,2), (2,6), (8,6), (8,2), (2,2)

9. (0,1), (2,3), (4,3), (6,1), (0,1)   **10.** (3,1), (1,4), (3,6), (5,4), (3,1)

Set B   For use after page 383.

Write each ratio in 2 other ways.

1. Bike flags: 2 for $5. What is the
ratio of flags to dollars?

2. Arturo rode 47 km in 2 h. What is
the ratio of kilometers to hours?

3. 4 to 5

4. 7:10

5. 3 out of 7

6. 3 for every 2

Set C   For use after page 385.

Copy and complete each ratio table.

1.

1	2	3	4	5
2				

2.
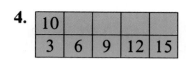

3				
4	8	12	16	20

3.
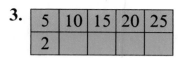

5	10	15	20	25
2				

4.

10				
3	6	9	12	15

Set D   For use after page 387.

Solve the proportions.

1. $\frac{1}{4} = \frac{n}{48}$ **2.** $\frac{4}{5} = \frac{n}{60}$ **3.** $\frac{3}{8} = \frac{n}{96}$ **4.** $\frac{2}{3} = \frac{n}{45}$ **5.** $\frac{4}{7} = \frac{n}{28}$

6. $\frac{3}{4} = \frac{n}{24}$ **7.** $\frac{1}{3} = \frac{n}{48}$ **8.** $\frac{3}{10} = \frac{n}{100}$ **9.** $\frac{5}{6} = \frac{n}{90}$ **10.** $\frac{6}{5} = \frac{n}{60}$

MORE PRACTICE BANK

Set A   For use after page 391.
   Write each ratio as a percent.

1. 24 to 100   **2.** 50 to 100   **3.** 10 to 100   **4.** 8 to 100   **5.** 1 to 100

Write each percent as a fraction.

6. 25%   **7.** 35%   **8.** 40%   **9.** 17%   **10.** 110%

Set B   For use after page 393.
   Write each decimal or fraction as a percent.

1. 0.25   **2.** 0.67   **3.** $\frac{40}{100}$ **4.** 0.12   **5.** 0.10   **6.** $\frac{9}{100}$

Write each percent as a decimal.

7. 43%   **8.** 26%   **9.** 17%   **10.** 8%   **11.** 40%   **12.** 2%

Set C   For use after page 394.
   Write a lowest-terms fraction for each percent.

1. 25%   **2.** 30%   **3.** 14%   **4.** 43%   **5.** 32%

6. 85%   **7.** 6%   **8.** 48%   **9.** 115%   **10.** 35%

Set D   For use after page 397.
   Find the percent of each number using mental math.

1. 75% of 20   **2.** 21% of 200   **3.** $12\frac{1}{2}$% of 400   **4.** 15% of 300

5. 25% of 800   **6.** $33\frac{1}{3}$% of 60   **7.** 90% of 200   **8.** 40% of 300

Estimate the percent of the number.

9. 24% of 80   **10.** 34% of 300   **11.** 9% of 70   **12.** 19% of 50

13. 35% of 90   **14.** 32% of 150   **15.** 26% of 32   **16.** 76% of 400

Set E   For use after page 399.
   Find the percent of each number or amount.

1. 19% of 26   **2.** 43% of 85   **3.** 76% of 95   **4.** 15% of 72

5. 31% of 90   **6.** 78% of 100   **7.** 25% of 240   **8.** 12% of 150

9. 20% of $180   **10.** 50% of $12.98   **11.** 30% of $115   **12.** 8% of $29.50

MORE PRACTICE BANK

Set A   For use after page 415.
Give the probability of each outcome.

1. Toss a coin.
P (Heads) = ▦

2. Toss a number cube (1–6).
P (Odd number) = ▦

3. Toss a number cube (1–6).
P (4) = ▦

Set B   For use after page 435.
Find the perimeter of each figure.

1.
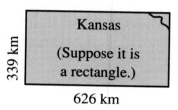
339 km
Kansas
(Suppose it is a rectangle.)
626 km

2.

Pentagon Building Washington, D.C.
276.3 m

3.
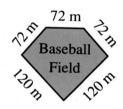
72 m
72 m
72 m
Baseball Field
120 m
120 m

Set C   For use after page 439.
Find the area of each figure.

1.
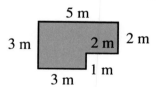
5 m
3 m
2 m
2 m
1 m
3 m

2.
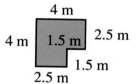
4 m
4 m
1.5 m
2.5 m
1.5 m
2.5 m

3.
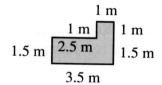
1 m
1 m
1 m
1.5 m
2.5 m
1.5 m
3.5 m

Set D   For use after page 445.
Find the area of each figure.

1.

95 m
70 m

2.

25 cm
25 cm
25 cm

3.

60 m
47 m

Set E   For use after page 447.
Find the volume of each box.

1. $l = 15$ cm
$w = 3.5$ cm
$h = 10$ cm

2. $l = 4$ m
$w = 1.5$ m
$h = 2$ m

3. $l = 10.8$ cm
$w = 7.0$ cm
$h = 5.5$ cm

MORE PRACTICE BANK

Set A   For use after page 449.

Find the surface area of each box.

1.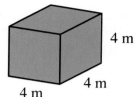

4 m

4 m

4 m

2.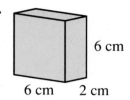

6 cm

6 cm   2 cm

3.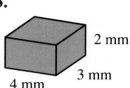

2 mm

3 mm

4 mm

Set B   For use after page 17.

Solve. Use the 6-Point Checklist.

1. Eddie went on 6 rides an hour for 5 hours. How many rides did he take?

2. Jenny rode 14 rides in the first 3 hours. Nan rode 6 less than this. How many rides did Nan take?

Set C   For use after page 19.

Decide whether to estimate or find an exact answer.

1. Someone asks you how far it is from your town to Montreal, Canada.

2. You receive 20 cents for every mile between your town and Montreal, Canada.

Set D   For use after page 37.

Solve by drawing a picture.

1. Five girls ran in a 100-m dash. Debbie finished ahead of Carmen, and Carmen was not last. Betty finished far ahead of Carmen, and Evelyn finished just behind Betty. If Darlene finished last, which girl finished next to last?

2. Derek has a ribbon 180 cm long. He wants to cut the ribbon into pieces 20 cm long. How many cuts will he have to make?

Set E   For use after page 65.

Solve by using the guess and check strategy.

1. A test had 10 questions worth 3 points and 10 worth 5 points. Scott had 15 correct answers and a total score of 57 points. How many questions of each kind did he answer correctly?

2. Paula is 6 years old. Her Uncle Steve is 4 times as old. How old will Paula be when she is half as old as her uncle?

522

Set A   For use after page 73.

Choose a calculation method. Then solve.

1. The total cost of having a magazine sent to you each week for 52 weeks is $51.75. Is this cost per copy more than or less than the newsstand cost of $1.25 per copy?

2. Which charge for developing 35-mm film is cheaper, 36 pictures for $7.56 or 24 pictures for $3.12?

Set B   For use after page 111.

Solve.

1. The cost of a fully equipped motorcycle is $1,050 more than the cost of a basic cycle for each of four models. The basic models cost $2,058, $2,575, $2,955, and $3,324. What is the cost of the least expensive fully equipped model you could buy?

2. A basic model of an electronic keyboard costs $153 less than each of three deluxe models. The deluxe models cost $710, $953, and $1,125. What is the cost of the least expensive basic model?

Set C   For use after page 127.

Solve.

1. A person's heart pumps about 5 L of blood every minute. How many liters is this per day?

2. The eyes of an average person blink 25 times per minute. How many blinks is this per day? per year?

Set D   For use after page 141.

Solve.

1. For their hiking trip Duffy's family needed to buy 4 backpacks, 4 sleeping bags, and a first aid kit. The backpacks cost $18 each, the sleeping bags cost $47 each, and the first aid kit cost $9. What was the total cost?

2. In June a ranger took 23 groups of visitors on hikes. There were 18 in each group. In July she took 38 groups on hikes, with 14 in each group. How many more did she take in one month than in the other?

Set A   For use after page 167.

Solve by making an organized list.

1. Shelly has white, tan, and gray shorts. She has brown, red, blue, and green shirts. How many different outfits can she wear?

2. How many different playing orders are possible for 4 players on a tennis team? (One possible order would be 1, 2, 3, 4.)

Set B   For use after page 171.

Solve.

1. At noon the temperature was 13°C. At midnight the temperature was 5°C lower. What was the temperature at midnight?

2. One day the hottest temperature was 8°C higher than the coldest. If the coldest was 12°C, what was the hottest?

Set C   For use after page 195.

Solve. Think carefully about the remainder.

1. The cook had 38 eggs. He needed 4 eggs for each cake. He made as many cakes as he could. How many cakes did he make?

2. The cook needed 430 rolls. Each package held 8 rolls. How many packages did the cook need to buy?

Set D   For use after page 197.

Solve by working backward.

1. Chuck bought some picture post cards for $0.29 and a ball point pen that cost 3 times as much as the cards. He has $3.18 left. How much did he have at the start?

2. Kate spent $6.75 of her paycheck on a tape. She spent twice that amount for a book. Then she had $9.75 left. What was the amount of her paycheck?

Set E   For use after page 203.

For each problem, tell whether the answer is reasonable. If it is not reasonable, tell why not.

1. Sean had $20 to use for party snacks. He spent $3.98 for fruit, $4.03 for crackers, and $9.89 for mix for punch. How much money did he have left? **Answer: $4.79**

2. Marian bought 6 new stamps for her stamp collection. The total cost was $19.08. What was the average cost for each stamp? **Answer: $3.18**

MORE PRACTICE BANK

Set A For use after page 227.
Solve by finding a pattern.

1. What is the greatest number of roads that can go through 8 cities if each road goes through exactly two of the cities?

2. If a job paid $1 the first day, $2 the second day, $3 the third day, and so on, how much would a worker earn for 14 days' work?

Set B For use after page 231.
Before solving each problem, estimate the answer. Then solve.

1. Each shelf can hold 9 softball bats. How many shelves are needed for 108 bats?

2. A school paid $343 for 7 pairs of football shoes. What was the average cost of each pair?

Set C For use after page 253.
Solve by using logical reasoning.

1. Nan, Fran, Dan, and Jan are two sets of twins. One is a doctor, one a lawyer, one a teacher, and one an engineer. The teacher is not female. Nan and Fran have lunch every week with the lawyer. Fran's sister is her doctor. Give the profession of each person.

2. Anna, Bob, Cathy, and Don have different favorite weekend activities. One likes hiking, one swimming, one bicycling, and one softball. Cathy and Don do not like bicycling. Bob thinks hiking is great fun. Don does not swim. What is each person's favorite weekend activity?

Set D For use after page 261.
Solve.

1. The longest ski run at Blue Valley is 4.8 miles. The longest run at Rocky Mount is just 0.8 times that long. How long is the run at Rocky Mount?

2. One of the chair lifts at Snowy Heights rises 1,128 ft in 6 minutes. What is the average number of feet the lift rises in 1 minute?

3. At Blue Valley, $\frac{7}{10}$ of the students in the beginners class were children. At Rocky Mount $\frac{3}{5}$ of the students were children. Which place had the greater fraction of students who were children?

4. Carlo spent 5 h 15 min skiing at Rocky Mount. Angela spent 345 min skiing. Who spent more time skiing? How much more time was that?

MORE PRACTICE BANK

Set A   For use after page 291.

Solve.

1. Bus 26 travels $5\frac{3}{4}$ miles on its morning route and $8\frac{3}{4}$ miles on its afternoon route. What is the total distance Bus 26 travels?

2. Bus 17 has an oil leak. On Monday the bus needed $2\frac{1}{4}$ quarts of oil. On Tuesday it needed $3\frac{3}{4}$ quarts of oil. What was the total amount of oil Bus 17 needed on those two days?

Set B   For use after page 307.

Solve. Be sure to check for more than one answer.

1. Tom had 8 cans of juice that he wanted to share with three of his friends. How many cans could each person get?

2. How many coins does it take to make 10 cents?

Set C   For use after page 315.

In which situation would you estimate? In which would you find an exact answer?

1. You are deciding how many quarts of soft drinks to buy for a party.

2. You are deciding how much to charge a customer who buys a $200 suit at 20% off.

Set D   For use after page 339.

Solve.

1. Art's T-Shirt Shop sells $\frac{1}{2}$ as many extra large shirts as large shirts. The shop sells $\frac{1}{2}$ as many large shirts as medium shirts. If the shop sells 88 medium shirts, how many extra large shirts does it sell?

2. Marlene worked $12\frac{1}{2}$ h last week. This week she worked $1\frac{1}{2}$ times as that. How many hours in all did Marlene work in the last two weeks?

3. A recipe for making tortillas for ten people calls for $1\frac{1}{4}$ cups of corn flour. Julio needs to make tortillas for 40 people. How much corn flour does he need to use?

4. Rusty is making a spicy sauce that calls for using $1\frac{1}{2}$ teaspoons of curry powder. It also calls for $\frac{2}{3}$ as much salt as curry powder and $\frac{1}{2}$ as much paprika as salt. How much paprika does she need to use?

526

Set A   For use after page 365.
Solve.

1. One of the angles of a ship's triangular sail has a measure of 35°. Another angle of the sail has a measure of 90°. What is the measure of the third angle?

2. A ship's triangular sail has a base that measures 30 ft. Its height is 44 ft. What is the area of the sail?

Set B   For use after page 401.
Solve.

1. Marcus deposited $50 in a savings account. The rate of interest was 8% per year. How much interest did he receive at the end of a year?

2. The bank paid Joan 10% interest on $280 she deposited in a savings account. How much money did the bank pay Joan for using her money for 1 year?

Set C   For use after page 421.
Solve.

1. One hiker weighed 56 kg. Her backpack weighed $\frac{1}{4}$ as much as she did. What was the total weight of the hiker and the backpack?

2. Yellowstone National Park has $\frac{3}{4}$ million hectares of land. Forest covers $\frac{4}{5}$ of this land. How many million hectares is covered by forest?

Set D   For use after page 437.
Draw a picture in order to solve the problems.

1. The width of a garden is 8.4 m. Its length is 16.8 m. What is the perimeter of the garden?

2. The width of a soccer field is 46 m. The length is 45 m greater than the width. What is the perimeter of the field?

First estimate the answer. Then solve the problem and check to be sure that your answer is reasonable.

3. The length of each side of a pentagon is 4.9 cm. The length of each side of an octagon is 3.9 cm. Which figure has the greater perimeter? How much greater is that?

4. A farmer has $10\frac{3}{4}$ acres planted with barley, $9\frac{1}{4}$ acres with oats, $11\frac{1}{2}$ acres with corn, and $5\frac{1}{2}$ acres with rye. How many acres does he have planted in all?

527

TABLE OF MEASURES

Metric System Customary System

Length

1 centimeter (cm)	10 millimeters (mm)	1 foot (ft)	12 inches (in.)
1 decimeter (dm)	100 millimeters (mm) 10 centimeters (cm)	1 yard (yd)	36 inches (in.) 3 feet (ft)
1 meter (m)	1,000 millimeters (mm) 100 centimeters (cm) 10 decimeters (dm)	1 mile (mi)	5,280 feet (ft) 1,760 yards (yd)
1 kilometer (km)	1,000 meters (m)		

Area

1 square meter (m²)	100 square decimeters (dm²) 10,000 square centimeters (cm²)	1 square foot (ft²)	144 square inches (in.²)

Volume

1 cubic decimeter (dm³)	1,000 cubic centimeters (cm³) 1 liter (L)	1 cubic foot (ft³)	1,728 cubic inches (in.³)

Capacity

1 teaspoon	5 milliliters (mL)	1 cup (c)	8 fluid ounces (fl oz)
1 tablespoon	12.5 milliliters (mL)	1 pint (pt)	16 fluid ounces (fl oz) 2 cups (c)
1 liter (L)	1,000 milliliters (mL) 1,000 cubic centimeters (cm³) 1 cubic decimeter (dm³) 4 metric cups	1 quart (qt)	32 fluid ounces (fl oz) 4 cups (c) 2 pints (pt)
		1 gallon (gal)	128 fluid ounces (fl oz) 16 cups (c) 8 pints (pt) 4 quarts (qt)

Mass Weight

1 gram (g)	1,000 milligrams (mg)	1 pound (lb)	16 ounces (oz)
1 kilogram (kg)	1,000 grams (g)	1 ton (T)	2,000 pounds (lb)

Time

1 minute (min)	60 seconds (s)	1 year (yr)	365 days 52 weeks 12 months
1 hour (h)	60 minutes (min)		
1 day (d)	24 hours (h)		
1 week (w)	7 days (d)	1 decade	10 years
1 month (mo)	about 4 weeks	1 century	100 years

PERFORMANCE ASSESSMENT

Chapter 1 Numbers and Operations

Figure out what all but one of these numerical expressions
have in common.

29 + 39 - 49 + 59 - 69   88 ÷ 2 ÷ 2 ÷ 2 - 2

2 + 4 + 6 + 8 + 1 0 + 12 + 14 + 16 + 18 - 1 - 3 - 5 - 7 - 9 - 11 - 13 - 15 - 17

9,999 ÷ 1,111   (1 × (2 + 3) + 4 × (5 + 6)) ÷ 7

What is the common property of four of these five
expressions?

Make five more numerical expressions that have the same
property as all but one of the expressions above.

Chapter 2 Place Value: Whole Numbers and Decimals

Draw a number line with the numbers 0,
1, and 0.1 on it. Draw it as accurately as
you can.

Now draw a number line the same length
as the one above, but with the numbers 0,
0.1, and 0.01 on it. Again, draw it as
accurately as you can.

Now draw a number line the same
length as before but with the numbers
0, 0.01, and 0.001 on it.

Think about doing this over and over
again. What is the smallest number
that is larger than 0 that you could
picture this way?

Do you agree with this statement:
"For any number that you name that is
close to 0, but not 0, I can name a
number that is even closer."

Chapter 3 Addition and Subtraction: Whole Numbers and Decimals

Work the following subtraction problems using pencil and paper.

3200	320	32	3.2	0.32	0.032
- 1540	- 154	- 15.4	- 1.54	- 0.154	-0.0154

Describe in writing any patterns you see. Tell why working one problem can help you to work the others more easily.

Chapter 4 Data and Graphs

The following article appeared in the business section of the Daily Times.

> BigTime Video Company's latest report states that video rentals for the first six months were in flux. Over 1,000 were rented in January, and 100 more than that rented in February. In March, there was a decline of 150 from February. In April, BigTime rented only 700 videos. May and June were the same at about 50 videos fewer than in April. Meanwhile, video sales were fairly steady at about 300 per month during the same six month period.

Make a multiple-line graph and a double-bar graph of the data.

Which seems to be a better way to display the data: words, a bar graph, or a line graph? Consider possible uses of the data. Explain your reasoning.

Chapter 5 Multiplication: Whole Numbers and Decimals

GOOD MORNING CAFE MENU			
Breakfast All Day Long			
2 eggs, any style	2.25	grits	1.15
steak & eggs	4.75	hash browns	1.25
ham & eggs	4.40	melon slice	2.00
toast included with the above		toast and butter	.75
waffles	3.35	orange juice	1.00
French toast	2.95	milk	1.15
oatmeal	1.15	coffee or tea	.90

You and two friends stop for breakfast at the Good Morning Cafe. Each of you picks out a different, good tasting, well-balanced meal. What is the total cost? Would you get change back from a $10 bill and a $20 bill? Don't forget to include a tip of about fifteen cents for every dollar. Make an organized list to show your calculations.

Chapter 6 Metric Measurement

Think about this. The metric system of measurement is based upon the number 10, and powers of 10. Look at the table on page 148. It shows powers of 10. However, units of time are not related to each other the same way metric system measures are. Look at page 528 for time measures.

How might you change units of time so that time was metric, too? Write down your ideas, and tell about any problems there might be.

Chapter 7 Division: Whole Numbers and Decimals

Make up ten different division problems that have 1-digit divisors and 3-digit dividends. They must also satisfy the following conditions:

The first problem must have a remainder of 0.

The second problem must have a remainder between 5 and 10.

The third, fourth, fifth, and sixth problems must have different divisors and the remainder 5.

The seventh, eighth, ninth, and tenth problems must have the divisor 7 and the remainder 3, but all have different quotients.

Pick two of your examples and explain how you came up with them.

Chapter 8 More Division: Whole Numbers and Decimals

Mike is planning a bike trip from Palo Alto to Pescadero Beach, a distance of 54.8 km. The trip involves crossing a small mountain range (about 600 km high), so Mike thinks he will be able to travel at about 19 km/h to the beach and 16 km/h from the beach. He plans to stay at the beach about 1 hour. He wants to get back to Palo Alto by 5 p.m.

Suggest a good time for Mike to start the trip, and explain your reasoning. Drawing a picture may help.

Chapter 9 Understanding Fractions and Mixed Numbers

Here is a 4-by-4 square.

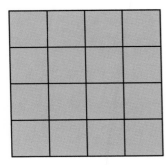

Can you show $\frac{1}{8}$ of the square in more ways than you can show $\frac{1}{4}$ of the square? To show $\frac{1}{8}$ or $\frac{1}{4}$ of the square you must have one side of one square touching another. Explain and picture your answer.

Suppose you do not have to have sides touching when you show $\frac{1}{4}$. Does that change your answer? Why or why not?

Chapter 10 Addition and Subtraction: Fractions and Mixed Numbers

$\frac{1}{2}$ of the students in the class like cats. $\frac{1}{2}$ of the students in the class like dogs. How many students like both dogs and cats? Explain your answer.

What if you knew that $\frac{1}{4}$ of the students do not like dogs or cats. How many students now like both dogs and cats? Explain your answer.

PERFORMANCE ASSESSMENT

Chapter 11   Customary Measurement

A monsterasaurus weighs between 2 lb and 6 lb at birth. It is usually 3 ft to 5 ft long. During the first year of its life, both its weight and length double every month.

What size would the monsterasaurus be at its first birthday party? What shape do you think it might have?

Chapter 12   Multiplication and Division of Fractions

You are going to build a dog house approximately $3\frac{1}{2}$ ft long, $2\frac{1}{2}$ ft wide, $2\frac{1}{2}$ ft high in front, and 2 ft high in back. You have a supply of boards that are 1 in. thick, 6 in. wide and 6 ft long.

Tell how many boards you would expect to use and why.

PERFORMANCE ASSESSMENT

Chapter 13 Geometry

A machinist can make hexagonal rods from round rods. The size of the hexagonal rod is normally described in technical drawings by distance from flat side to opposing flat side (shown by the arrow). However, a round rod is described by its diameter.

The machinist is asked to make a 2-inch hexagonal rod. Decide approximately what minimum size round rod is needed, to the nearest 0.01 or $\frac{1}{16}$ inch. Then, if you can, come up with a rule for finding the size of the round rod needed to make any-sized hexagonal rod.

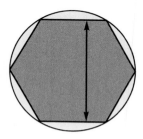

Chapter 14 Ratio and Percent

The city has decided to build a playground in a 100 yard by 100 yard lot. Each of the following activity areas must use **at least** the following percentage of the land.

Playing fields	35%
Basketball courts	20%
Climbing equipment	10%
Swings	5%
Sand areas	5%

Use grid paper to make a map for your playground. Label all areas. Tell why you made the playground the way you did.

PERFORMANCE ASSESSMENT

Chapter 15 Probability

This square is a dart board. What do you think is the probability that a dart thrown at the target will hit a region with an odd number in it?

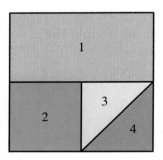

Art Smith threw darts 40 times at the dart board. Art got these results:

Region	Hits
1	18
2	9
3	4
4	9

After seeing these results, now what do you think the probability is that a dart thrown at the target will hit a region with an odd number in it?

Chapter 16 Perimeter, Area, and Volume

In your job at the No Drop Shipping Company, you must decide how to send orders to customers. You operate a machine that puts 1-in. packages into boxes that are either a 1-ft cube or a 2-ft cube. It costs $4 to pack and ship the 1-ft cube. It costs $24 to pack and ship the 2-ft cube.

You have an order for 20,000 1-in. packages and 40,000 1-in. packages. How would you ship each and why?

a.m.   A way to indicate time from 12:00 midnight to 12:00 noon. See also **p.m.**

acute angle   An angle that has a measure less than 90°.

addend   One of the numbers to be added.

Example: addends

$$\begin{array}{r} 3 \\ + 5 \\ \hline 8 \end{array}$$

addition   An operation that gives the total number when you put together two or more numbers.

algebraic expression   An expression that contains at least one variable; for example, $n + 5$.

angle   Two rays from a single point.

area   The measure of a region, in square units.

associative (grouping) property   The sum (or product) of three or more numbers is the same regardless of grouping.

Examples: $2 + (8 + 6) = (2 + 8) + 6$
$3 \times (4 \times 2) = (3 \times 4) \times 2$

average   The quotient when the sum of a set of numbers is divided by the number of addends.

bar graph   A diagram that uses vertical or horizontal bars to show information.

benchmark   An object of known measure used to estimate the measure of another object.

breaking apart   Breaking a number into addends or factors in order to make mental calculations easy.

Example: $7\frac{5}{8} - 3\frac{2}{8} = 7 - 3$ plus $\frac{5}{8} - \frac{2}{8}$

capacity   The volume of a space figure given in terms of liquid measurement.

center   The point from which all points on a circle are equally distant.

chances   The probability that a particular event will occur.

chord   A straight line with both endpoints on a circle.

circle   A plane figure in which all the points are the same distance from a point called the center.

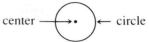

circle graph   A graph in the form of a circle that is divided into sectors showing how the whole is broken into parts.

circumference   The distance around a circle.

clustering   Finding addends or factors that are nearly alike in order to make estimating easy.

Example:
$28 + 31 + 29 + 32 \longrightarrow 4 \times 30 = 120$

common factor   A number that is a factor of two different numbers is a common factor of those two numbers.

common multiple   A number that is a multiple of two different numbers is a common multiple of those two numbers.

commutative (order) property   The sum (or product) of any two numbers is the same regardless of the order in which they are added (or multiplied).

Examples: $17 + 13 = 13 + 17$
$5 \times 24 = 24 \times 5$

compass   An instrument used to make circles.

compatible numbers   Combinations of numbers that are easy to compute with mentally.

Examples: $25 + 175, 5 \times 20, 360 \div 9$

composite number   Any whole number greater than 1 that has more than two different factors.

cone   A space figure with one circular face and one vertex.

congruent figures   Figures that have the same size and shape.

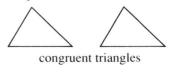

congruent triangles

529

GLOSSARY

constant A key on a calculator that allows you to use the same number over and over. For example, you can use the constant key to multiply different numbers by the same factor or to divide different numbers by the same divisor.

coordinates Number pair used in graphing.

cross products Products obtained by multiplying the numerator of one fraction by the denominator of a second fraction, and the denominator of the first fraction by the numerator of the second fraction.

cube A space figure whose faces are all squares.

customary units of measure See Table of Measures, page 528.

cylinder A space figure with two congruent circular faces.

data bank A place where information is stored.

decimal Any base-ten numeral written using a decimal point.

3.2 ← decimal
↑— decimal point

degree A unit of measure for angles.

degree Celsius (°C) A unit for measuring temperature in the metric system.

degree Fahrenheit (°F) A unit for measuring temperature in the customary system.

denominator The number below the line in a fraction.

$\frac{3}{4}$ ← denominator

diagonal A segment, other than a side, connecting two vertices of a polygon.

diagonal — vertex

vertex

diameter A segment containing two points of a circle and the center.

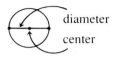
diameter
center

difference The number obtained by subtracting one number from another.

Example:
$$\begin{array}{r} 9 \\ -\ 4 \\ \hline 5 \end{array}$$ ← difference

digits The symbols used to write numerals: 0, 1, 2, 3, 4, 5, 6, 7, 8, and 9.

distributive property Multiplying a sum by a number is the same as multiplying each addend by the number and then adding the products.

Example: $3 \times (2 + 4) = 18$
$(3 \times 2) + (3 \times 4) = 18$

dividend A number to be divided.

$7\overline{)28}$ ← dividend

division An operation that tells how many sets or how many in each set.

divisor The number by which a dividend is divided.

divisor → $7\overline{)28}$

double bar graph A bar graph that uses pairs of bars to compare information.

edge One of the segments making up any of the faces of a space figure.

 ← edge

END An instruction in a computer program that tells the computer to stop.

equality (equals, or =) A mathematical relation of being exactly the same.

equally likely outcomes Outcomes that have the same chance of occurring.

equal ratios Ratios that give the same comparison. $\frac{9}{27}$ and $\frac{1}{3}$ are equal ratios.

equation   A number sentence that uses the equality symbol to show that two expressions have the same value.

Example: $9 + 2 = 11$

equilateral triangle   A triangle with all 3 sides the same length and all angles the same measure.

equivalent fractions   Fractions that name the same amount.

Example: $\frac{1}{2}$ and $\frac{2}{4}$

estimate   To find an answer that is close to the exact answer.

evaluate   To find the number that an algebraic expression names.

even number   A whole number that has 0, 2, 4, 6, or 8 in the ones place.

expanded form   A way to write numbers that shows the place value of each digit.

Example: $9,000 + 300 + 20 + 5$

experimental probability   Probability based on the results of an experiment.

exponent   A number that tells how many times another number is to be used as a factor.

$5 \times 5 \times 5 = 5^3$ ← Exponent
← Base

face   One of the plane figures (surfaces) making up a space figure.

face

factors   Numbers that are combined in the multiplication operation to give a number called the product.

factors → $6 \times 7 = 42$

factor tree   A diagram used to find the prime factors of a number.

Example:
42
6 x 7
3 x 2 x 7

fair game   A game in which each player has the same chance of winning.

flip   To turn a figure to its reverse side. A flip and a slide result in a reflection image.

flowchart   A chart that shows a step-by-step way of doing something.

formula   A general rule expressed by symbols. For example, the area (A) of any parallelogram with base b and height h is given by the formula $A = bh$.

fraction   A number that expresses parts of a whole or a set.

Example: $\frac{3}{4}$

front-end estimation   A method of estimating by adding or subtracting the digits with the greatest place value. Often the other digits are used to adjust the estimate.

GOTO   An instruction in a computer program that causes the computer to skip to a specified line in the program.

graph   A picture that shows information in an organized way.

greater than ($>$)   The relationship of one number being larger than another number.

Example: $6 > 5$, read "6 is greater than 5."

greatest common factor (GCF)   The greatest number that is a factor of each of two numbers.

grouping property   See *associative property*.

hexagon   A polygon with six sides.

improper fraction   A fraction whose numerator is greater than or equal to the denominator.

INPUT   An instruction in a computer program that causes the computer to stop and request data while running a program.

integers   The whole numbers together with their opposites.

Examples: $^-5$, 0, 23

interval   The number of units between spaces on a graph's scale.

isosceles triangle   A triangle with at least 2 sides the same length and at least 2 angles the same measure.

least common denominator (LCD)   The least common multiple of two denominators.

least common multiple (LCM)   The smallest nonzero number that is a multiple of each of two given numbers.

less than (<)   The relationship of one number being smaller than another number.

Example: 5 < 6, read "5 is less than 6."

line   A straight path that is endless in both directions.

line graph   A diagram that uses a rising or falling line to show increases or decreases over a period of time.

line of symmetry   A line on which a figure can be folded so that the two parts fit exactly.

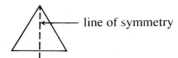

line of symmetry

line segment   Part of a line that extends from one point to another point.

LIST   A copy of a set of instructions that tells a computer what to do.

Logo   A computer language that can be used for computer graphics.

lowest terms   A fraction is in the lowest terms if the numerator and denominator have no common factor greater than 1.

Examples: $\frac{3}{8}, \frac{5}{6}, \frac{2}{3}$

mass   The amount of matter that something contains.

mathematical probability   The probability of a certain outcome if the number of trials is extended indefinitely.

mean   The average of a set of numbers; found by dividing the sum of the numbers by the number of addends.

median   The middle number when numbers are arranged in order. If there is no one middle number, then the median is the average of the two middle numbers.

memory key   A key on a calculator that allows the calculator to store in its memory the result of one calculation while it performs another calculation.

mental math   Performing calculations in your mind, without using pencil and paper or a calculator.

metric units of measure   See Table of Measures, page 528.

mixed number   A number that has a whole number part and a fraction part, such as $2\frac{3}{4}$.

mode   The number or numbers that occur most often in a set of numbers.

multiple   A number that is the product of a given number and a whole number.

multiplication   An operation that combines two numbers, called factors, to give one number, called the product.

negative number   A number that is less than zero.

number line   A line that shows numbers in order.

7   8   9   10

number pair   Two numbers that are used to give the location of a point on a graph.

Example: (3,2)

number properties   Number properties include the associative (grouping) property, the commutative (order) property, the distributive property, the one property of multiplication, the zero property of addition, and the zero property of multiplication.

numeral   A symbol for a number.

numerator   The number above the line in a fraction.

$\frac{3}{4}$ ← numerator

numerical expression   An expression (name for a number) that contains two or more numbers. Example: 4 + 5

obtuse angle   An angle with a measure greater than 90° and less than 180°.

odd number   A whole number that has 1, 3, 5, 7, or 9 in the ones place.

one property   In multiplication, when either factor is 1, the product is the other factor.

order property   See *commutative property*.

ordered pairs   See *coordinates*.

ordinal number   A number used to tell order.

Examples: first, fifth

outcome   A possible result in a probability experiment.

p.m.   A way to indicate time from 12:00 noon to 12:00 midnight. See also **a.m.**

parallel lines   Two lines that lie in the same plane and do not intersect.

parallelogram   A quadrilateral with two pairs of parallel sides.

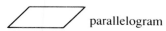
parallelogram

pentagon   A polygon with five sides.

percent   Per 100; a way to compare a number with 100.

perimeter   The distance around a figure.

period   In large numbers, a group of three digits separated from other groups by commas.

perpendicular lines   Two lines that intersect at right angles.

pi (π)   The ratio of the circumference of a circle to its diameter. The decimal for π is 3.141592... As approximations for π, we often use 3.14 or $3\frac{1}{7}$.

pictograph   A kind of graph that uses pictures or symbols to represent numbers.

place value   The value given to the place a digit occupies in a number.

Example: 3 5 6

hundreds place ⌐
tens place ⌐
ones place ⌐

plane figure   A figure that lies on a flat surface.

Examples:

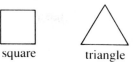

square   triangle   circle

point   A single, exact location, often represented by a dot.

polygon   A closed figure formed by line segments.

prediction   An educated guess about what will happen.

prime factorization   Expressing a composite number as a product of prime factors.

prime number   A number that has exactly 2 factors (the number itself and 1).

PRINT   An instruction in a computer program that tells a computer to type something.

prism   A space figure whose bases are congruent polygons in parallel planes and whose faces are parallelograms.

probability   The probability that an event will occur in a set of equally likely outcomes is the number of ways the event can occur divided by the total number of possible outcomes.

product   The result of the multiplication operation.

Example: $6 \times 7 = 42$
                    ↑
                product

program   A set of instructions that tells a computer what to do.

proportion   An equation showing that two ratios are equal.

Example: $\frac{6}{8} = \frac{3}{4}$

protractor   An instrument used for measuring angles.

pyramid   A space figure whose base is a polygon and whose faces are triangles with a common vertex.

quadrilateral   A polygon with four sides.

quotient   The number (other than the remainder) that is the result of the division operation.

Examples:

$$45 \div 9 = \underset{\uparrow}{5} \qquad 7\overline{)45}$$

quotient

radius   A segment from the center of a circle to a point on the circle.

range   The difference between the highest and the lowest numbers in a set of numbers.

ratio   A pair of numbers used in making certain comparisons. The ratio of 3 to 4 can be written 3 to 4, 3:4, or $\frac{3}{4}$.

ratio table   A chart or table that displays a set of equal ratios.

ray   A part of a line, having only one end point.

ray

rectangle   A quadrilateral that has four right angles.

rectangle

reflection image   The new figure obtained by sliding and flipping a figure.

regular polygon   A polygon with all sides the same length and all angles the same measure.

remainder   The number less than the divisor that remains after the division process is completed.

$$\text{Example: } 7\overline{)47}$$
$$\underline{42}$$
$$5 \leftarrow \text{remainder}$$

rhombus   A quadrilateral with all sides the same length.

rhombus

right angle   An angle that has a measure of 90 degrees.

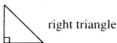

right angle

right triangle   A triangle that has one right angle.

right triangle

Roman numerals   Numerals used by the Romans.

Examples: I = 1
V = 5
VI = 6

rotation image   The new figure obtained by sliding and turning a figure.

rounding   Replacing specific numbers with numbers expressed in even units, such as tens, hundreds, or thousands.

Example: 23 rounded to the nearest 10 is 20.

RUN   A command that tells the computer to execute a program.

sample   A representative part of a larger group.

scale   Numbers along the side or bottom of a graph. Also, a ratio that shows the relationship between a scale drawing and the actual object or between distances on a map and actual distances.

scalene triangle   A triangle with no sides the same length and no angles the same measure.

segment   A straight path from one point to another.

sequence   A set of numbers in a particular pattern or order.

similar figures   Two figures that have the same shape.

similar figures

simulation   A way of acting out or creating a situation like one in the real world to see what is likely to happen in the real world.

GLOSSARY

skip counting Counting by a number other than 1.

> Example: 0, 5, 10, 15
> skip counting by fives

slide To obtain another figure by moving a figure without flipping or turning it. A slide results in a translation image.

space figure A figure that has volume.

> Examples:

> cube cylinder

sphere A space figure in which all the points are the same distance from a center point.

> sphere

square A quadrilateral with four right angles and all sides the same length.

> square

square of a number The product of a number and itself

subtraction An operation that tells the difference between two numbers, or how many are left when some are taken away.

sum The number obtained by adding numbers.

> Example:
> ```
>    3
>  + 2
>  ___
>    5  ← sum
> ```

surface area The sum of the areas of all the faces of a space figure.

symmetric figure A plane figure that can be folded in half so that the two halves match.

tally A mark used to keep track of items when counting. Tally marks are in groups of five, with the fifth in the group recorded as a slash.

> Example:

trading To make a group of ten from one of the next highest place value, or one from ten of the next lowest place value. Examples: one hundred can be traded for ten tens; ten ones can be traded for one ten.

translation image The new figure obtained by sliding a figure without flipping or turning it.

trapezoid A quadrilateral with only one pair of parallel sides.

> trapezoid

triangle A polygon with three sides.

turn To obtain a new figure by rotating a figure into a different position. The result of a turn is a rotation image.

unit One of something. An amount or quantity used as a standard of measurement. Set Table of Measures, page 528.

unitizing Estimating size by visually dividing an object into smaller parts and using the estimated size of one part to estimate the total size.

variable A symbol, usually a letter, used to represent a number or a range of numbers.

vertex (plural, **vertices**) The point that the two rays of an angle have in common.

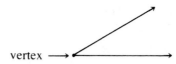

> vertex →

volume the number of cubic units of space that a space figure holds.

zero property In addition, 0 added to any number does not change that number. In subtraction, 0 subtracted from any number gives the original number. In multiplication, the product of any number multiplied by 0 is 0.

INDEX

ACKNOWLEDGMENTS

Illustration Acknowledgments

Alex Bloch p. 404, 465, 467

Barbara Counsellar p. 58, 73, 132, 397, 442

Tony Crnkovich p. 376

David Cunningham p. 24a

Marie DeJohn p. 152, 153, 312, 313

Simon Galkin p. 114, 208, 430, 462

Betty Gee p. 468b, 469b, 471a, 472c

Bill Gerhold p. 84, 467

Jeff Hukill p. 70, 76, 472a, 472b, 477a, 479a, 481a

Susan Jaekel p. 63, 122, 123, 134

Tom Leonard p. 29

Susan Lexa p. 162, 163, 164, 165, 270, 304 b & c

Rich Lo p. 54

Laurie Marks p. 244

Tim McWilliams p. 266

Judy Nostrant p. 14, 32, 33, 34, 41, 46, 106, 197, 226, 258, 288, 308, 383

Tim O'Toole p. 148, 464, 494

Rodney Pate p. 12, 36, 37

Alison Perreault p, 346a, 463, 499

Walter Porter p. 72, 100, 105, 109, 124, 129, 130, 180, 182b, 183, 186, 187, 214, 215, 272, 335, 350, 351, 361, 364, 365, 369, 382, 388, 389, 395, 398, 446, 448, 451

Rick Sams p. 470a, 470b, 483a

Margaret Sanfilippo p. 30, 196, 259, 261, 304a, 334, 340, 410, 412, 416

Seventeenth Street Studios, Valerie Winemiller p. 280, 371

Joel Snyder p. 140, 141, 192

Rosalind Solomon p. 468a, 469a, 473a

Andrea Tachiera p. 69, 108, 260, 286, 287

Karen Tafoya p. 198a & c, 273

Dave Taylor p. 421f, 461

Pat Traub p. 59, 302, 303, 306

Laslo Vespremi p. 58, 157, 171, 182a, 217, 227, 330

Nancy Lee Walters p. 236

Photo Acknowledgments

Table of Contents: iii Ken Karp*; iv Ken Karp*; v Lawrence Migdale*; vi Janice Sheldon*; vii Stephen Frisch*; viii Ken Karp*; ix Ken Karp*; x Janice Sheldon*; xi Ken Karp*; xii Ken Karp*.

Chapter 1: 2-3 Robert Caputo/Stock, Boston; 4 Janice Sheldon*; 6 Ken Karp*; 7 Ken Karp*; 8 Jeffry W. Myers/The Stock Market; 11 Ken Karp*; 16 Douglas L. Peck*; 17 Barbara Von Hoffmann/Tom Stack & Associates; 18 Ken Karp*; 20-21 Douglas L. Peck*.

Chapter 2: 26-27 Leif Skoogfors/Woodfin Camp & Associates; 28 Janice Sheldon*; 38 Janice Sheldon*; 44 Christiana Dittman/ Rainbow; 48 James W. Kay/Bruce Coleman Inc.; 50-51 Erwin & Peggy Bauer/Bruce Coleman Inc.; 54 Janice Sheldon*.

Chapter 3: 56-57 Bob Daemmrich/Stock, Boston; 60 John Elk III/Stock, Boston; 61 Matt Bradley/Bruce Coleman Inc.; 62 Janice Sheldon*; 64 Janice Sheldon*; 66 Janice Sheldon*; 78 Douglas L. Peck*; 79 Douglas L. Peck*; 80 John Cancalosi/Tom Stack & Associates; 81 Ken Straiton/The Stock Market; 82-83 John Elk III/Stock, Boston; 86 Janice Sheldon*.

Chapter 4: 88-89 Eric Lars Bakke; 96 Jeff Persons/Stock, Boston; 98 Janice Sheldon*; 99 Hank Morgan/Rainbow; 102 Jon Feingersh/Stock, Boston; 103 Harry S Truman Library; 104 Janice Sheldon*; 110 Tim Davis; 111 M.A. Chappell/Animals, Animals; 112-113 Nick Pavloff*.

Chapter 5: 118-119 Robert Rathe/Stock, Boston; 120 Thomas Braise/The Stock Market; 121 David Madison/Bruce Coleman Inc.; 126 Lawrence Migdale*; 127 Janice Sheldon*; 138 Janice Sheldon*; 143 Ken Karp*; 144-145 Wayland Lee*/Addison-Wesley Publishing Company.

Chapter 6: 150-151 Bill Ross/West Light; 154 Wally McNamee/ Woodfin Camp & Associates; 166 Norman Tomalin/Bruce Coleman Inc.; 167 David Madison; 168-169 Gerry Cranham/Photo Researchers; 172-173 Tim Davis*.

Chapter 7: 178-179 Michael Tamborrino/The Stock Market; 184 Janice Sheldon*; 188 Jeffry W. Myers/Stock, Boston; 190 Bob Daemmrich/Stock, Boston; 191 Wayland Lee*/Addison-Wesley Publishing Company; 194 Doug Greene/The Stock Market; 195 David Stoecklein/The Stock Market; 198 Janice Sheldon*; 202 Wayland Lee*/Addison-Wesley Publishing Company; 203 Larry Lefever/Grant Heilman; 204-205 Tim Davis*; 208 Lawrence Migdale*.

Chapter 8: 210-211 Gerd Ludwig/Woodfin Camp & Associates; 216 Barbara Kirk/The Stock Market; 217 Wayland Lee*/ Addison-Wesley Publishing Company; 218 Ken Karp*; 222 Douglas L. Peck*; 224 David Madison; 231 Charles Feil/Stock, Boston; 232-233 Tim Davis*; 234 Janice Sheldon*.

Chapter 9: 238-239 Janice Sheldon*; 240 Dagmar Fabricius/ Stock, Boston; 246 Ken Karp*; 248 Ken Karp*; 252 Vince Streano/The Stock Market; 256 Ken Karp*; 257 Ken Karp*; 262 Stephen Frisch*; 263A Stephen Frisch*; 263B Charles Thatcher/ Tony Stone Worldwide; 263C NASA.

Chapter 10: 268-269 Stephen Frisch*; 274 Janice Sheldon*; 276 Wayland Lee*/Addison-Wesley Publishing Company; 278 Tim Davis*; 279 Tim Davis*; 282 Janice Sheldon*; 284 Tim Davis*; 290 Tim Davis*; 292-293 Tim Davis*.

Chapter 11: 298-299 Paul Chesley/All Stock; 300 Tim Davis*; 305 Janice Sheldon*; 310 Mark Tuschman; 314 Ken Karp*; 315 Ken Karp*; 317 Nick Pavloff*; 320 Janice Sheldon*.

545

ACKNOWLEDGMENTS

Chapter 12: 322-323 Richard Pasley/Stock, Boston; 324 Nick Pavloff*; 325 Joe McDonald/Bruce Coleman Inc.; 326 Menschenfreund/The Stock Market; 328 Janice Sheldon*; 332 Janice Sheldon*; 336 Janice Sheldon*; 337 Thomas Kitchin/Tom Stack & Associates; 338 Lawrence Migdale; 339 Ken Karp*; 342-343 Ken Karp*.

Chapter 13: 348-349 Warren Morgan/West Light; 358 Focus On Sports; 362 David Madison; 366 Janice Sheldon*; 368 David Barnes/The Stock Market; 370 Janice Sheldon*; 374-375 Elliott Smith*.

Chapter 14: 380-381 Janice Sheldon*; 384 Tim Davis*; 386 Gary Milburn/Tom Stack & Associates; 387 Sandy Roessler/The Stock Market; 394 Kasz Maciag/The Stock Market; 399 Ken Karp*; 402-403 Wayland Lee*/Addison-Wesley Publishing Company; 406 Ken Karp*.

Chapter 15: 408-409 Lawrence Migdale; 410 Janice Sheldon*; 418 David C. Bitters; 420 E.R. Degginger/Bruce Coleman Inc.; 421B David Madison; 421T Terry Eiler/Stock, Boston; 423 David Madison; 426 Vatican, Museo Missionario Etnografico/Art Resource, New York; 427A Smithsonian Institution, Museum of African Art/Art Resource, New York; 427B New York, Museum of Primitive Art/Giraudon/Art Resource, New York.

Chapter 16: 432-433 David Hurn/Magnum Photos; 434 Brent Peters/The Stock Market; 444 Bill Gallery/Stock, Boston; 453 Janice Sheldon*.

*Photographed expressly for Addison-Wesley Publishing Company, Inc.

Special thanks to Shell Self-Serve Gas Station, The Alamada, Berkeley, California; Department of Geology, University of California, Berkeley, California; Black American West Museum, Denver, Colorado; Anshen & Allen, San Francisco, California; Berkeley Cycle, Berkeley, California; Desktop Products, Inc., Emeryville, California; Murray's Cheese Shop, New York, New York; Davidson Middle School, San Rafael, California; Rodney's Video Warehouse, White Plains, New York.